Behind Bars

Also by Suzanne Oboler

Ethnic Labels, Latino Lives: Identity and the Politics of (Re)Presentation in the United States, 1995.

Neither Enemies nor Friends: Latinos, Blacks, Afro-Latinos (with Anani Dzidzienyo), 2005.

The Oxford Encyclopedia of Latinos and Latinas in the United States, 4 Volumes (with Deena J. González), 2005.

Latinos and Citizenship: The Dilemma of Belonging, 2006.

The Oxford Encyclopedia of Latino/as, Politics and the Law, 2 Volumes (with Deena J. González), forthcoming, 2011

Behind Bars

Latino/as and Prison in the United States

Edited by Suzanne Oboler

BEHIND BARS
Copyright © Suzanne Oboler, 2009.

All rights reserved.

Cover drawing by Elizabeth Oboler

First published in 2009 by PALGRAVE MACMILLAN® in the United States—a division of St. Martin's Press LLC, 175 Fifth Avenue, New York, NY 10010.

Where this book is distributed in the UK, Europe, and the rest of the world, this is by Palgrave Macmillan, a division of Macmillan Publishers Limited, registered in England, company number 785998, of Houndmills, Basingstoke, Hampshire RG21 6XS.

Palgrave Macmillan is the global academic imprint of the above companies and has companies and representatives throughout the world.

Palgrave® and Macmillan® are registered trademarks in the United States, the United Kingdom, Europe and other countries.

Rafael Cancel Miranda. *La alegría de tener vergüenza*. From *Pólvora y Palomas*. Mayagüez, Puerto Rico: private edition. September, 1995, p. 90.

Raúl Salinas. Peltier 1 and Peltier 2. From *Indio Trails: A Xicano Odyssey Through Indian Country*. Wings Press, 2006. pp 32 & 34

ISBN: 978-0-230-61949-4 (paperback)
ISBN: 978-0-230-61924-1 (hardcover)

Behind bars : Latino/as and prison in the United States / edited by Suzanne Oboler.
    p. cm.
    Includes bibliographical references and index.
    ISBN 0-230-61949-5 (alk. paper)—ISBN 0-230-61924-X
    1. Hispanic American prisoners—United States. 2. Discrimination in criminal justice administration—United States. I. Oboler, Suzanne.
    HV9471.B394 2009
    365'.608968073—dc22   2009021747

A catalogue record of the book is available from the British Library.

Design by Scribe Inc.

First edition: December 2009

10 9 8 7 6 5 4 3 2 1

Printed in the United States of America.

En homenaje . . .
raúlrsalinas
elder, teacher, grandfather, father, chicanindio, poeta revolutionario

Photograph by Janna Birchum
March 17, 1934–February 13, 2008

Contents

Introduction: *"Viviendo en el olvido . . ."*: Behind Bars—Latino/as and
Prison in the United States   1
Suzanne Oboler

Part I: The Issues   **15**

1   Latino/as and U.S. Prisons: Trends and Challenges   17
José Luis Morín

2   Pursuant to Deportation: Latinos and Immigrant Detention   39
David Manuel Hernández

3   *"Nuestras vidas corren casi paralelas"*: Chicanos, *Independentistas,*
and the Prison Rebellions in Leavenworth, 1969–72   67
Alan Eladio Gómez

4   The Racial Politics of Youth Crime   97
Victor M. Rios

5   Caught in the Net: Language and Cultural Resistance among Latina
Adolescents in Juvenile Detention   113
Laurie Schaffner

6   Lost Votes, Lost Bodies, Lost Jobs: The Effects of Mass Incarceration
on Latino Civic Engagement   133
Juan Cartagena

Part II: The Lived Experience   **149**

7   Checkpoint in Montebello: Inciting Riots, Up Against the Wall, and
Earning the Right to be on the Street with Signs that Say *"Retén"*   151
Mercedes Victoria Castillo

8   The Interpreter as a Bridge: Language Issues in Chicago's Cook
County Jail   155
Laura E. Garcia

9   Interpreting After the Largest ICE Raid in U.S. History: A Personal
Account   159
Erik Camayd-Freixas

10 Waste Is a Terrible Thing to Mind   175
    Dicxon Valderruten

11 Closing The Gap: Mentoring Latina Students to Reach Out to
    Incarcerated Latinas   181
    Marcia Esparza

Part III: The Art of Resistance   **187**

12 Latino Visual Culture Behind Bars: Artistic Inspiration and
    Redemption Within the Bowels of Despair   189
    Víctor Alejandro Sorell

13 "Troubadour of Justice": An Interview With raúlrsalinas   213
    Alan Eladio Gómez

14 Peltier 1 / Peltier 2   223
    raúlrsalinas

15 *"Estoy como cuero de jicotea, que ni las balas me pasan"*: An Interview
    with Rafael Cancel Miranda   227
    Gabriel Torres-Rivera

16 *La alegría de tener vergüenza*   235
    Rafael Cancel Miranda

Part IV: The Way Forward   **237**

17 Chicana(o)/Latina(o) Prisoners: Ethical and Methodological
    Considerations, Collaborative Research Methods, and Case Studies   239
    Juanita Díaz-Cotto

18 Toward a Pinta/o Human Rights? New and Old Strategies for
    Chicana/o Prisoner Research and Activism   261
    B. V. Olguín

Contributors   281

Index   285

Introduction

"*Viviendo en el olvido . . .*"

Behind Bars—Latino/as and Prison in the United States

Suzanne Oboler

Before I built a wall I'd ask to know,
What I was walling in or walling out.

—Robert Frost, "*Mending Wall*"

The worst thing about being in prison isn't even the loss of my freedom. *Es saber que estoy viviendo en el olvido.* [It is knowing that I am alive, but forgotten.]

—Carlos, prisoner, upstate New York

These are the words of an incarcerated Latino currently in a prison in upstate New York: words that echo throughout the penal system of the United States, whether from the jails, the state and federal prisons, the immigrant detention centers, the high-security facilities, the private incarceration buildings, the military prison in Guantanamo Bay. This anthology is a direct response to those words—an effort to say to that incarcerated Latino and to all the men and women in the U.S. criminal justice system, "No! You are not living '*en el olvido*.' You, your lives, your presence as part of both our community and our society—whether behind walls or barbed-wire fences—*are* important to those of us on the outside. You have not been forgotten!"

As Supreme Court Justice William Brennan wrote, "Prisoners are persons whom most of us would rather not think about. Banished from everyday sight, they exist in a shadow world that only dimly enters our awareness. . . . Nothing can change the fact, however, that the society that these prisoners inhabit is our own. Prisons may exist on the margins of that society, but no act of will can sever them them from the body politic" (quoted in Elsner 2006, 16).

The struggle of incarcerated Latino/as—indeed, of all incarcerated people in the United States—for their dignity and their humanity is the struggle that Latino/as and this society as a whole must engage today—now. There must be a firm societal response to the government's insistence on using imprisonment as both a means for dealing with the nation's minorities and poor populations and as a source of jobs—as well as free prison labor—in the small rural towns in regions now depleted of previous sources of economic well-being.

What is being "walled in"—to use the words penned by Robert Frost—in these prisons? What histories, what life stories, what justifications, what violations and abuses, what secret methods of breaking the human spirit? And, similarly, what part of our society's role in ensuring justice, equality, respect, and human dignity for all—indeed, what part of our humanity—is being "walled out"?

The Issues

The authors of the articles and essays in this anthology address these questions in various ways. Undoubtedly, the fact that Latinos are, as José Luis Morín observes in his chapter, the fastest growing group in the U.S. prison system—accounting, by the end of 2004, for 19.2 percent of the total population in U.S. state and federal jurisdictions—is also an underlying cause for the urgency of this book.[1] Providing an overview of the U.S. criminal justice system and its implications for U.S. society, Morín explains that although "differences between Latino/as and African Americans also exist, most notably that Latino/as are subject to myths linking criminality to immigrant status," there are several reasons why Latinos, like African Americans, are increasingly "trapped" by the phenomenon of "mass imprisonment."[2] Thus, he retells key moments in the history and experiences of Latino/as in the United States, providing an overview of various prominent trends that feed into this society's penal system, including the racialization of crime, the manner in which criminal justice policy is formulated and justified around the fear of crime, how the courts and the criminal justice system operate, and the role of the media in promoting negative images of Latino/as.

Indeed, the current increase in the incarceration rates of Latino/as, whether in state or federal prisons or in immigrant detention facilities, and the rush to control the borders, to conduct raids, to build fences, to demand national identity cards—like the current inhumanity of mainstream politicians and the media toward immigrants—demeans us all. These actions are also reducing citizenship rights and the freedom of movement and human creativity that the ideals of this society's democratic traditions guarantee to all who live in this country. In their place, what seems to be emerging is an impermeable barrier of complacency and indifference grounded in social insecurity, fear, and even terror of one another (Glassner 1999). Public anxieties are creating new policies and methods of addressing these fears that are challenging the basic premises and traditional practice of the nation's constitutional history and laws, including the very requirements of criminal law curricula in the law schools of the United States. As one prominent law professor recently wrote:

I am a criminal law professor. I know about penal codes, police practices, sentencing, and the use of incarceration to punish criminals. Like most criminal law professors, I know precious little about American immigration law. I have always considered it to be a different part of the law school curriculum, and one that had little, if anything, to do with criminal law. Even in my federal criminal law course, immigration law played no part in the curriculum. Lately, however, it has become evident that things have changed. In today's world, immigration enforcement and criminal law enforcement activities are two sides of the same coin, at least for non-citizens. What criminal law professors and practitioners alike are discovering is that immigration law—including the practices of detention and deportation, as well as prosecution for reentry and document fraud—has emerged as a key missing chapter in American criminal law. (Guerra-Thompson 2007)

Guerra-Thompson's observation was confirmed in a recent *New York Times* article reporting on the Pew Hispanic Foundation study on Latino/as and incarceration (Lopez and Light, 2009). Noting that they currently make up 13 percent of the U.S. population, the study found that, in 2007, Latino/as became "the largest ethnic group in the federal prison system, accounting for 40 percent [or one third] of those convicted for federal crimes," almost half of whom (48 percent) were behind bars for immigration crimes. Quoting Lucas Guttentag, a lawyer for the American Civil Liberties Union, the article goes on to affirm that, "the immigration system has essentially become criminalized at a huge cost to the criminal justice system, to courts, to judges, to prisons and prosecutors. And the government has diverted the resources of the criminal justice system from violent crimes, financial skullduggery and other areas that have been the traditional area of the Justice Department" (Moore 2009). The growing connection and increasing convergence between immigration and criminal law, now referred to as "crimmigration law," has become, in the words of one scholar, "the most important development in immigration law today" (Stumpf, 2006).

It is almost a cliché today to state that immigration has traditionally been one of the key foundational pillars of this nation's self-image and development. A renewed concern and, indeed, widespread hysteria about the presence of immigrants, particularly Latino/as, permeates the society, and heinous hate crimes against people of Latin American descent are increasingly reported across the country. Equally widespread is the unfounded perception of the threat (curiously detached from the nation's political economy) that Latino/as supposedly pose to the United States (Chavez, 2008). In short, US society is being treated today to an unrelenting racialization and demonization of immigrants, again, most specifically of Latin American immigrants, particularly, although by no means exclusively, of Mexicans living and working in this country.

The result has been a prevailing perception that Latino/as in U.S. society are primarily undocumented immigrants born in other parts of the hemisphere and, as such, are permanently "illegals," "aliens," or foreigners in the United States. Homogenizing the Latino/a population in these terms and, in this sense, separating them from the general population has allowed for the development of laws and policies ostensibly aimed at protecting "us" from "them." This has, in turn, overtly or otherwise negatively impacted the constitutional rights of all U.S. residents—citizens and noncitizens alike (Oboler, 2006, 3-30).

Thus, despite the fact that more than half (59.8 percent) of all Latinos in the United States today are native-born citizens (Fry and Hakimzadeh 2006), the perception of Latinos as inherently foreign to the very image and idea of "being an American" has now become deeply ingrained—to such an extent that early on in the 2008 presidential campaign, *The Christian Science Monitor* noted that "the touchy subject" of immigration had "become a political minefield for '08 contenders." "Pundits," the newspaper continued, "dub the immigration issue 'a minefield,' 'a new third rail,' as well as a 'megaissue'" (Marks 2007). Indeed, one of the prospective presidential candidates, Colorado Representative Tom Tancredo, saw it fit to base his platform and "debate points" almost exclusively on the issue of immigration and border control, explicitly tying Latino/a immigrants to the "war on terror": "I am 100 percent opposed to amnesty. . . . I will secure our borders so illegal aliens do not come and I will eliminate benefits and job prospects so they do not stay." Moreover, Tancredo "also routinely tie[d] the broken immigration system to the terrorist threat" (Marks 2007).

The above state of social anxiety and violent response to the presence of immigrants in the United States, however, is not without precedent. As David Hernández's makes clear in his chapter, it is worth recalling that, historically, borders, like border controls, in the United States have long marched in step with detentions and deportations. The criminalization of the "other," has often occurred under the guise of the imperative to increase "national security" as well as of (re)constructing or creating new notions of who is "illegal" (Ngai 2005; De Genova 2006). Equally important is the historical recourse to xenophobic and racializing responses to "otherness," including linguistic, social, gendered, and sexual factors. These responses in turn ensure the approval, tacit or otherwise—if not the indifference—of mainstream public opinion toward the fate of those who, like the majority of the ancestors of U.S. citizens of European descent, have been forced to leave their homelands for a variety of reasons in search of a better life for themselves and their children in this country. Particularly in the last few decades, societal responses to otherness have reinforced, in a fundamental way, the perception of Latino/as as "criminal" and therefore as "disposable" people, as "unworthy" of benefiting from the democratic and moral values that are presumed to underlie US society's insistence on fairness and justice for all.

As is often noted, history repeats itself, although, as Marx aptly stated, first as a tragedy, then as a farce. Therefore, historical examples are essential both as records of past injustices and as a measure of how far a nation has moved, or not, in the direction of becoming more humane and just. In his chapter, Alan Eladio Gómez tells the story of Chicanos and Puerto Rican *Independentistas* imprisoned in the Leavenworth Federal Penitentiary in Kansas during the 1970s. He discusses the efforts of the Latinos at Leavenworth to create alliances with others, particularly African Americans and Native Americans; to educate themselves about the U.S. criminal justice system; to understand and address the society that created it; and to make the connections and comparisons to the practices and implications of carceral institutions in other parts of the world, especially Latin America and Africa. In the process, his chapter describes the ways that this self-education empowered and "armed" those like raúlrsalinas "with knowledge and truth," hence leaving the poet-activist "with his dignity intact." Gómez also assesses the ways that this empowerment contributed to their efforts to reform the system, whether through the prison newsletter, through informing those on the outside about the conditions within, or through court suits directly challenging the system's brutality and inhumanity. Noting that there was a 500 percent increase in the U.S. prison system (including a 2,800 percent increase in the number of women in state and federal prison or local jails) between 1972 and the mid-1990s, Gómez concludes that

> the political analysis of Latino prison activists uncovered how the intricate calibrations of violence within the prison regime were related to law, race, and social control outside prison, an important theoretical understanding when trying to untangle the political ideology of law and order as it relates to race, incarceration, and white supremacy (Rodriguez 2006). Incarceration—functioning as "incapacitation"—for a surplus army of labor of women, men, immigrants, criminalized by their mere existence, is directly implicated in the acceptance of preventative detention with regard to racial, ethnic, and, in a post 9-11 world, national and religious minorities.

As José Luis Morín states in his chapter, "Latinas/os, like African Americans, are perceived as a class of poor people of color that pose a threat to the social order, and thus must be controlled and dominated." Victor Rios directly addresses this perception in his chapter, through his discussion of its consequences in the juvenile justice system. His contribution to this volume provides a case study of the way that the politics underlying the introduction of tougher sanctions against both Latino and African American youth increasingly relies and plays on public anxieties about the supposed link of race with crime, hence reinforcing the harmful prejudice.

Several of the authors in this anthology emphasize that although Latinos have long been part of the history, society, culture, and economic development of this country, it is still deplorably the case that they are too-often consigned to a collective space of nonbelonging, regardless of their citizenship status and, again, largely as a result of racial, language, social, and xenophobic discrimination. Together with the collective solidarities and alliances they create among themselves, Latino/as, as the contributors to this anthology attest, draw upon their culture and language background, their ongoing learning, the experiences of their past, and the endless creativity of the human spirit—even behind bars—to face up to and resist the violent and brutal experience of the U.S. prison system.

In her chapter, Laurie Schaffner focuses on how Latina juvenile delinquents use language and culture as a way of establishing a sense of solidarity in prison as well as a way of unsettling what Schaffner refers to as "the orderly flow of the punitive surveillance." Schaffner notes that the findings she presents run counter to traditional narratives of juvenile delinquency, which often reinforce the image of juvenile delinquents as alienated.

At the same time, the simultaneous "inclusion/exclusion" swings in public attitudes and discussions about "what is to be done with *them*" continue apace with the complicated history of U.S. relations with the rest of the hemisphere. As a result, the country and polity is deprived of a sustained discussion, one free of intermittent sensationalisms about the latest wave of immigrants and their undeniable, multiple contributions to this society. Similarly, any dialogue concerning the ongoing exclusion of U.S.-born Latino/as from the polity through their rapidly rising rates of incarceration and consequent loss of the right to vote and to exercise their full citizenship also continues to be silenced. As Juan Cartagena observes in his chapter, "the prison industrial complex continues to sustain itself by misguided political ploys regarding so-called 'drug wars' and 'tough-on-crime' politicians to the point that crime is generally at record lows, while imprisonment is at historic highs. Latinos' collective political strength is directly affected: lost are the votes that are taken from our communities upon incarceration; skewed are the counts of fictitious 'residents' that inflate the relative political strength of these prison towns; and unemployed are the hundreds of former prisoners who face statutory impediments to finding a decent job."

Pointing out that the *Voting Rights Act* is the most important single piece of civil rights legislation in U.S. history, Cartagena notes that all but one *Voting Rights Act* challenge to the discriminatory nature of felon disfranchisement, brought up by Latino, African American, and Native American prisoners, have been rejected by the courts. These court challenges, he argues, "are critically important in understanding the contours of racial discrimination because they lie at the intersection of voting discrimination and discrimination in the criminal justice system today."

Collectively, the contributors to this anthology seek to exemplify, in various ways, *why* it is imperative today that more attention be devoted to the connections between Latino/as and the rest of U.S. society, specifically from the perspective of the causes and implications of the rising rates of incarceration, the conditions under which Latino/as survive inside the prisons, and their subsequent, disempowered lives as both private individuals and citizens once they are released. Looking inside the conditions of the incarceration of Latino/as, including their pre- and postprison experience, can serve to bring to light the socioeconomic, political, and cultural contexts from which they come, and key moments in their historical and current experiences. Just as importantly, these conditions serve as an eloquent reminder of the contributing role played by society's ongoing passivity and indifference to the injustices of social and economic deprivation in Latino/a communities throughout the country.

The Lived Experience

Several of the authors in this anthology draw specifically on their own daily professional lives and experiences working with Latino/as caught in the labyrinth of the criminal justice system, and, in so doing, provide valuable insight into the full implications of the workings of the system for Latino/as in US society. The ongoing perception of Latino/as as a "threat to the social order" is amply exemplified by Mercedes Castillo in her essay describing the Los Angeles Police Department's total disregard for Latino/as' basic constitutional and human rights and the consequent treatment and indignities to which Latino/as are subjected whenever they demand the very right to uphold their rights. Similarly, Laura Garcia's chapter points out the painful irony of the self-incriminating implications of Latino/as' reliance on a common language and cultural background as they seek to communicate and explain their predicament to Spanish-speaking officers at the time of their arrest.

Erik Camayd-Freixas made international headlines with the poignant account in his chapter of the two weeks he spent as an interpreter for the hastily set up federal court in Postville, Iowa, in May of 2008. Breaking the strict rules of silence and confidentiality to which interpreters are held, Camayd-Freixas provides a rare, detailed disclosure and analysis of the workings of the federal courts against undocumented immigrants. He describes the legal procedures in the immediate aftermath of the raid in Postville, Iowa, and the subsequent detentions and deportations of the undocumented workers. The majority of the latter were indigenous people whose lack of knowledge of Spanish and English during their appearance in the courts, only served to further highlight the abusive and surreal nature of their courthouse experience. A chilling warning of the threats posed by the current bureaucratization of justice in the United States, Camayd-Freixas's essay emphasizes the broader immoral and inhumane consequences of the war on terror in shaping the extent to which the rulings of federal immigration judges are now determined and constrained by the (il)legalities still in force, of the Bush administration's national security doctrine. In so doing, Camayd-Freixas denounces the criminalization of workers and deconstructs the totalitarian agenda of immigration enforcement and the politics of intolerance of what he defines as "a dark period in American history."

Latino/as' struggle for survival within the confines of prison walls, their efforts toward self- and group education, the construction of alliances and group solidarities across national as well as racial lines, and under extremely adverse conditions, for their part, refocus attention on their lives and thoughts far beyond the confines of specific prisons and their impact on themselves as well as on their families and communities.

Dicxon Valderruten describes his work in the prisons as both a health education facilitator and as a mentor to incarcerated men in upstate New York. His chapter discusses the ways that, in addition to their educational value, the use of health, and particularly AIDS, education programs can serve to empower prisoners and prepare them in a variety of ways to confront the difficulties of recreating their lives once on the outside. As Valderruten forcefully argues, the existence and role of mentors who help Latino/as once they leave prison is essential for the process of prisoner reintegration.

A recent article about the conditions of women in detention facilities describes a study conducted by the Southwest Institute of Research on Women and the James E. Rogers College of Law at the University of Arizona. As the *New York Times* reported, "The study concluded that immigration authorities were too aggressive in detaining the women, who rarely posed a flight risk, and that as a result, they experienced severe hardships, including a lack of prenatal care, treatment for cancer, ovarian cysts and other serious medical conditions, and, in some cases, being mixed in with federal prisoners" (Frosch, 2009, A23).

In her chapter, Marcia Esparza discusses the need for mentors to help women in their reentry process and focuses on the pedagogical and personal issues entailed by both herself and her students in the course of training them to mentor recently released Latinas. Noting that many of her students come from the same social backgrounds as the women they mentor, Esparza stresses the need to acknowledge mentors' own individual and cultural strengths and self-awareness and her consequent shift to a pedagogy that reflects a more equal, horizontal relationship with her students. This approach, she argues, provides the latter with a new sense of their own authority, making them more effective in fulfilling their objective to become bridges between the incarcerated women they work with and the society into which the latter reenter.

The Art of Resistance

Art, Victor Sorell argues, is both a form of resistance and a significant means for the incarcerated trying to cope with the profound misery of life in prison. His chapter in this anthology describes a particular form of prison art painted on *paños*, or handkerchiefs, contextualizing his critical analysis of this form of artistic production in the histories of both prison art and the international history of art. Through the words and works of six incarcerated Latino artists, Sorell describes their sense of urgency to create, analyzing their depictions of daily life in prison, invoking the depth of their feeling, the hopes and fears their artistic work contains, the personal and political resistance it expresses, and its boundless capacity for redemption. Also included in Sorell's chapter is a discussion of the artistic production of Leonard Peltier, the renowned Native American activist, author, artist, and "related prisoner of conscience/political prisoner" to whom the poet and activist raúlrsalinas, himself a former prisoner, forcefully pays homage in his two poems in this anthology, Peltier 1 and Peltier 2. Like the works of the Latino/a artists discussed by Sorell, Peltier's artwork—whose own patently unjust incarceration in 1977 continues to this day—manifests, too, the solidarities among Latino/as, African Americans, and Native Americans behind bars.

Alan Gomez's interview with raúlrsalinas in this anthology reinforces the solidarities across racial and national groups. Providing us with a powerful description of the extent to which their realities and resistance art helped both to educate incarcerated Latino/as and their allies and to openly explore and share their experiences, raúlrsalinas describes how art served as both a learning and an organizing tool during the 1970s prison rebellions.

Similarly, in his interview in this anthology, Puerto Rican nationalist and former political prisoner Rafael Cancel Miranda narrates his experience behind bars in Alcatraz, Leavenworth, and Marion prisons, detailing his response to the inhumanity of incarceration through principled activism and solidarity as well as through his poetry. His interviewer, Gabriel Torres Rivera, is himself a lifelong community activist who at one time was imprisoned with Cancel Miranda and who, since his release, has continued to fight for the human and citizen rights of all incarcerated people. The dialogue between Cancel Miranda and Torres Rivera reveals the revolutionary nature of Cancel Miranda's lifelong activism as a Puerto Rican nationalist. As both his interview and his poem, *La alegría de tener vergüenza*, included in this anthology, convey, it is a life that has always been grounded in the art of a resistance that emphasizes human dignity and integrity as the stance from which to respond to the oppressive and dehumanizing conditions of the U.S. prison system.

The Way Forward

There is no doubt whatsoever that further research of Latino/as in prison is greatly needed—indeed, there is a serious dearth of available accounts and analyses. While a few autobiographies, letters, academic essays, newspaper articles, poems, and artwork by and about incarcerated Latino/as have recently been published and have therefore reached a wider public, the issue of how to research and do justice to the intimate and often incommunicable and devastating experience of suffering and despair that the authors document here remains wide-open. How to avoid distorting that experience while providing a voice that speaks for the voiceless is the subject of Juanita Díaz-Cotto's chapter. Her essay provides an in-depth analysis of the available literature and reviews researchers' motivations for conducting their studies, the major questions they pose, their work methods, findings, and conclusions, and their interrelationships. Díaz-Cotto concludes that different approaches and methods specific to prison research can yield quite different findings, results, and conclusions. She thus makes several suggestions for future research, specifically from the perspective of a methodology that ensures a more comprehensive and critical understanding of the Latino/a prison experience, including a comparative analysis with other incarcerated populations and criminal justice institutions in both the United States and abroad.

There is a pressing need for further exploration of the implications of mass confinement and its impact on the fundamental rights of all prisoners and detainees, as well as on free citizens, insofar as all are members of national and international communities and histories. Thus, this anthology emphasizes Latino/as' long and multiple struggles against injustice—the inhumanity of border controls; the raids against immigrants; the detention, internment, and deportation of immigrants; family separations; the failures of the U.S. justice system; the workings of the prison system and its aftermath; the policies of control and subversion of the rights of people of Latin American descent in US society; and the narratives of formerly-imprisoned Latino/as' own resistance and struggles to affirm their dignity and humanity both during and after their incarceration. In so doing, the articles in this volume ultimately seek to highlight current conditions in the prison system of the United States and simultaneously contextualize and insert it within a broader transnational framework. Collectively, these chapters underscore the fact that prison writings did not come to an end somewhere in the late 1960s and the early 1970s; rather, they continue to reveal specific aspects of the interconnections among nations, societies, citizens, noncitizens, and human rights that can no longer be ignored. Together, they drive home the point that imprisonment has a profound bearing on many aspects of life, society, and community for millions of people beyond the individuals immediately affected.

The political rhetoric and grossly distorted discourses associated with immigrants, crime, national security, and fear provides much of today's mainstream justifications for the increased "warehousing" of Latino/as, African Americans, Native Americans, and other racialized poor populations in the United States. Moreover, there is no doubt whatsoever that these justifications, like our own inaction, dehumanize us all, for as Ruth Wilson Gilmore (2007, 243) has argued, "dehumanization is also a necessary factor in the acceptance that millions of people (sometimes including oneself) should spend part or all of their lives in cages." Not surprisingly, the shameful indifference of the richest and most powerful nation in the world toward those who are less fortunate in our society—and the willful neglect of the ravages of poverty and racial discrimination, the long-term consequences of inadequate housing, the unacceptable educational and recreational facilities, and the deteriorating neighborhoods in which large sectors of the Latino/a population grow up and live their entire lives—account for much of the lack of societal and institutional support. The creation of societal and institutional support networks could easily prevent the growing incarceration of large numbers of Latino/as, both young and old, as well as the criminal neglect and disregard of their human rights once in prison. As Dixon Valderruten's chapter suggests, this support could and—where it exists—*does* contribute toward easing the reentry of those who have been released.[3] This support also empowers them and helps them to redirect their lives and the lives of those in the communities to which they return.

There are no simple solutions to the issues highlighted by the judicial confinement of what Gómez estimates to be 2.5 million people (including immigrant detainees), over 60 percent of whom are blacks and Latino/as in U.S. federal and state prisons (Harrison and Beck 2006).[4] To the extent that today, as B. V. Olguín points out in his chapter, "the War on Crime has converged with the War on Terror through the deliberate subversions of international treaties and protocols to which the United States is a signatory," it is essential that a two-prong struggle against the government's practice of willful imprisonment of Latino/as be launched. The first approach involves the restoration of the U.S. government's respect for the rule of law both at home and abroad, which is clearly fundamental to the claim and well-being of this society's democracy. In this respect, the various laws enacted since September 11, 2001, have served, as Olguín succinctly states in his essay, to

> collectively curtail constitutional freedoms of speech, association and information; infringe constitutional rights to legal representation, a timely public trial and protection from unreasonable searches; and also allow for the use of extrajudicial imprisonment and secret military tribunals for citizens and non-citizens accused of aiding or abetting terrorism.
>
> Perhaps more importantly, the war on terror has introduced the category of "enemy combatant," a classification unique in American jurisprudence because it situates its designee in the interstices of domestic and international law.

It is this infringement of both U.S. constitutional traditions and the Geneva Conventions, as suggested in Olguín's forcefully argued and documented chapter, that justifies the second approach for addressing the issues discussed above; that is, the shift of the locus of debates on imprisonment in the United States firmly to the international sphere and specifically under the jurisdiction of international human rights standards. Olguín primarily focuses on the incarceration of Latino/as and other people of color to draw attention to and address the full implications of the rejection by the United States of international human rights protocols. Similarly, his focus emphasizes the insistence of the US on the "might is right" argument in the context of the prerogatives that the sole superpower on the planet exercises whenever it deems fit. These include the exclusive right to adhere to or ignore international agreements according to its unchallengeable priorities, justifying human rights abuses and violations—documented by Amnesty International, to cite but one example—irrespective of commitments to the rule of law and justice in international relations. Arguing that the issue at hand is "the treatment of human beings, not simply prisoners per se," Olguín calls for the use of the courts, mass mobilizations, and, while keeping them local, the simultaneous internationalization of prisoner rights campaigns. "We must show" he argues, "that the new U.S. carceral is in fact inhumane and in regular and deliberate violation of international treaties and norms."

Ultimately, then, the focus on Latino/as and prisons invites careful and nuanced analyses and discussions that call into question the current rhetorical, opportunistic, and problematic responses to the pressing problem of an unjust and unequal criminal justice system, which, for so long, has violated the human rights of those it imprisons, often—as raúlrsalinas attests in his interview with Alan Gómez—with full impunity. Salinas's interview and his poems about the still-imprisoned Native American activist Leonard Peltier, like Gabriel Torres Rivera's interview with Rafael Cancel Miranda, and the latter's poem, are eloquent and moving testimonies.

Moreover, as the authors in this anthology suggest, the full import of the arguments and data they present can only be comprehended within a broader framework that conceptualizes and questions political and social institutions in the United States (Wilson Gilmore 2007). This includes the government's current emphasis on national security, immigration, the militarization of border controls, the policing, and abuse of power against both Latino/as and other minorities.

The demonization of individuals and groups, specifically of Latino/as, is intimately related to the fact that the U.S. government's recent policies tend to pursue injustice rather than justice, to leave inhumanity unchecked, to choose xenophobic enclosure over its traditional ideals of human dignity and the right of all human beings to have rights. How to deal with an enemy is one of the cornerstones of all human legal systems—whether ancient or of the most modern variety—for it is the reverse side of the same mirror in which a community contemplates its own identity. The definition and treatment of the "enemy" or of "guilt" and "blame" are but the corollaries of our understanding and experience of humans living together. It is in view of this that Aristotle (1983)—the eternal foreigner in the most celebrated of all democracies, Athens, from which he was exiled in old age—claimed justice to be "what holds the city together" and a quintessentially human task.

Today, we are confronted with the very disturbing reality that the United States builds walls with little if any public debate on what it is walling in and what it is walling out. This book seeks to make a critical contribution in this regard, for once this reality is fully acknowledged, and its implications better understood, we then must mobilize to tear down the many wrongful separations. The only "wall" that a genuine democracy must build, and one that guarantees its true existence, is a safeguard against injustice in all its dimensions, while guaranteeing rights to all its people, including Latinas and Latinos in the United States.

With a few exceptions, the articles and essays included in this anthology were first presented at the conference entitled "Behind Bars: Latinos and Prison," sponsored by the journal *Latino Studies* and held at the University of Illinois at Chicago (UIC), in October of 2006. The papers were part of a special double issue of *Latino Studies* published in 2007, and are now being published, with several new additions, in this anthology. I want to thank the University of Illinois at Chicago for hosting the journal's conference. I want to give special recognition and appreciation to Karen Benita Reyes, the managing editor of *Latino Studies*, whose assistance in organizing the conference was invaluable to me and certainly key in ensuring its success. A special *muchas gracias* also goes to Marta E. Ayala, Community Affairs Specialist for the Department of Latin American and Latino Studies at UIC for her firm support and enthusiasm, and multiple contributions during the conference.

I thank Elitza Bachvarova and Anani Dzidzienyo for their incisive comments and suggestions for this introduction and for their consistent support of my work. As always, to both of you, *muito obrigada*! Last, but by no means least, to all the participants of the conference and the contributors to this anthology: your wonderful collegiality and friendship, unyielding commitment and dedication, and strong support during the entire process of this project made this book possible. Muchas gracias a todos ustedes!

Notes

1. For a compendium of data and analysis of the status of Latino/as in the criminal justice system, see Walker et al. (2004).
2. According to Mauer and King (2007), African Americans are incarcerated at nearly six (5.6) times the rate of whites; and Hispanics are incarcerated at nearly double (1.8) the rate of whites.
3. For an authoritative discussion of much needed reforms and public policies pertaining to prisoner reentry, see the pioneering work of Travis (2005).
4. The headline of a December 5, 2007, press release from the U.S. Department of Justice, Office of Justice Programs, Bureau of Statistics, conveys the stark fact that "One in Every 31 U.S. Adults Was in a Prison or Jail or on Probation or Parole at the End of Last Year." http://www.ojp.usdoj.gov/bjs/pub/press/p06ppus06pr.htm (accessed September 9, 2008).

References

Aristotle. 1983. *Nicomachean ethics*. Oxford: Oxford University Press.

Chavez, Leo R. 2008. *The Latino Threat. Constructing Immigrants, Citizens and the Nation.* Stanford: Stanford University Press.

De Genova, Nicholas. 2006. The legal production of Mexican/migrant "illegality." In *Latinos and citizenship: The dilemma of belonging*, ed. Suzanne Oboler, 61–90. New York: Palgrave.

Elsner, Alan. 2006. *Gates of injustice: The crisis in America's prisons*. Upper Saddle. 2nd edition. River, NJ: Prentice Hall.

Frosch, Don. 2009. Report Faults Treatment of Women Held at Immigration Centers. *The New York Times*, January 21, A23.

Frost, Robert. 1914. *Mending wall*. In *North of Boston*. London: David Nutt.

Fry, Richard, and Shirin Hakimzadeh. 2006. A statistical portrait of Hispanics at mid-decade. *Pew Hispanic Center*. http://pewhispanic.org/reports/middecade/.

Glassner, Barry. 1999. *The culture of fear: Why Americans are afraid of the wrong things*. New York: Basic Books.

Guerra-Thompson, Sandra. 2007. Immigration and the law. *Noticias* 5 (1). Center For Mexican American Studies, University of Houston. http://www.tache.org/pdfs/5520 _CMAS_noticias_last.pdf (accessed January 3, 2008).

Harrison, Paige M., and Allen J. Beck. 2006. *Prisoners in 2005*. U.S. (NCJ 215092). Washington, D.C.: U.S. Department of Justice: Bureau of Justice Statistics. www.ojp.usdoj.gov/bjs/pub/pdf/p05.pdf

Lopez, Mark H., and Michael T. Light. 2009. *A rising share: Hispanics and federal crime*. Report. Pew Hispanic Foundation. February, 18.

Marks, Alexandra. 2007. Immigration issue could make or break presidential candidates. *Christian Science Monitor*, November 19. http://www.csmonitor.com/2007/1119/p01s02-uspo.html (accessed February 19, 2009).

Moore, Solomon. 2009. Study shows sharp rise in Latino federal convicts. *New York Times*, February 18. A14 http://topics.nytimes.com/top/reference/timestopics/people/m/solomon _moore/index.html?inline=nyt-per.

Mauer, Marc, and Ryan S. King. July 2007. Uneven justice: State rates of incarceration by race and ethnicity. The Sentencing Project. http://www.sentencingproject.org/PublicationDetails.aspx?PublicationID=59 (accessed January 9, 2008).

Ngai, Mae M. 2005. *Impossible subjects: Illegal aliens and the making of modern America*. Princeton: Princeton University Press.

Oboler, Suzanne, ed. 2006. *Latinos and Citizenship: The Dilemma of Belonging*. New York: Palgrave.

Stumpf, Juliet P. 2006. The crimmigration crisis: Immigrants, crime, & sovereign power. Berkeley Electronic Press, Legal Series. http://law.bepress.com/expresso/eps/1635

Travis, Jeremy. 2005. *But They All Come Back: Facing The Challenges Of Prisoner Reentry*. Washington D.C. The Urban Institute Press.

Walker, N., J. M. Senger, F. Villarruel, and A. Arboleda. 2004. *Lost opportunities: The reality of Latinos in the U.S. criminal justice system*. Washington, D.C.: National Council of La Raza.

Wilson Gilmore, Ruth. 2007. *Golden gulag: Prisons, surplus, crisis, and opposition in globalizing California*. Berkeley: University of California Press.

Part I

The Issues

I

Latino/as and U.S. Prisons

Trends and Challenges

José Luis Morín

Already the country with the highest rate of incarceration in the world, the United States continues to steadily increase its prison population on an annual basis (Harrison and Beck 2006b). At year-end 2005, persons held in all U.S. federal and state prisons, territorial prisons, local jails, immigration facilities, military facilities, jails under Native American jurisdiction, and juvenile facilities totaled 2,320,359 (Harrison and Beck 2006b, 1). Concomitant with the alarming expansion of the U.S. prison population is the issue that the drive to incarcerate most adversely affects communities of color, including Latino/as (Mauer 1999; Human Rights Watch 2002; Sentencing Project 2003; Walker et al. 2004; Morín 2009). While the overall percentage of the adult population in state or federal prisons increased dramatically between 1971 and 2001, Latino/as experienced a ten-fold increase in incarceration (Bonczar 2003, 5). Based on data from the U.S. Justice Department's Bureau of Justice Statistics (Harrison and Beck 2002), the Sentencing Project (2003, 1) points out that "Hispanics are the fastest growing group being imprisoned."[1]

Like African Americans, Latino/as emerge as trapped by the phenomenon known as "*mass imprisonment*" (Garland 2001a). Many factors appear to converge to produce the increasing number of Latino/a prisoners. As with African Americans, the construction of race in the United States provides fertile ground for the unequal treatment of Latino/as within the criminal justice system. While not identical, the Latino/a experience in the United States tends to mirror many patterns of domination and subordination endured by African Americans. Adverse perceptions and policies toward anyone considered nonwhite have been prevalent throughout U.S. history. It is an ignominious past that has harmed many groups, including Latino/as. As is the case with African Americans, Latino/as have suffered the indignities of *de jure* segregation and today high levels of *de facto* segregation across the nation. Latino/as, arguably, are also affected by hyperincarceration and the symbiotic relationship between prison and the ghetto that Wacquant (2001) identifies when examining the mass incarceration of African Americans.

The formulation of public policy around crime and the fear of crime—like the role of the media in promoting fear and negative images— are both influential in producing high incarceration rates that unfavorably affect persons of color (Beckett and Sasson 2004; Western 2006; Simon 2007). As many analysts point out (e.g., Beckett 1997; Garland 2001a, 2001b; Harris 2002; Haney López 2003), examining the conventional operation of the court, law enforcement, and the criminal justice systems provides insights into the production of the racial and ethnic disparities evident in the penal system.

As is the case with African Americans, common misconceptions associating Latino/as with criminal behavior must be challenged. But differences between Latino/as and African Americans also exist, most notably that Latino/as are subject to myths linking criminality to immigrant status. The fear of crime as a driving force in criminal justice policy making and persistent negative media images of Latino/as and immigrants in relation to crime pose formidable obstacles to the implementation of long-overdue, meaningful, and sensible changes in the prison and criminal justice systems. Ultimately, comprehensive efforts to engage many sectors of society will be necessary to help reverse the trends in Latino/a incarceration in the United States.

The Latino/a Prison Population Upsurge

The Latino/a presence in the U.S. prison population today is troubling, especially in view of the dramatic increases over the last twenty years. In 2004, the rate of Latino/a incarceration in state and federal prisons was 2.6 times greater than for whites (1,220 per 100,000 compared to 463 per 100,000 (Harrison and Beck 2005). As Walker et al. point out (2004, 105), "one in four federal prison inmates is Latino, even though fewer than one in eight U.S. residents is Latino." However grave these statistics appear, the severity of the problem of Latino/a incarceration becomes evermore evident when one considers the exponential increase over the last two decades.

In concluding that Latino/as are "the fastest growing minority group being imprisoned," the Bureau of Justice Statistics found that from 1985 to 1995, "the number of Hispanics in prison rose by 219%, with an average 12.3% increase each year" (Mumola and Beck 1997, 9). While Latino/as represented 10.9 percent of all state and federal inmates in 1985, by 1995, the percentage had grown to 15.5 percent. Since then, annual growth in the Latino/a prisoner population has continued. The total percentage of Latino/a prisoners in state and federal jurisdictions had increased to 19.2 percent by the end of 2004 (Harrison and Beck 2005, 8–9).

As Simon (2007, 141) observes, mass imprisonment in the United States has not produced "racially uniform" results.[2] In 2001, approximately 7.7 percent of Latino males were current or former state or federal prisoners—almost three (2.65) times the number of white males. In a lifetime, Latino males, at 17.2 percent, are also nearly three times as likely to go to prison as white males (5.9 percent) (Bonczar 2003, 5, 8).

When examining Latina incarceration rates for 2004, the Bureau of Justice Statistics finds that "female incarceration rates, though substantially lower than male incarceration rates at every age, reveal similar racial and ethnic disparities" Although African American women experienced an incarceration rate four times that of whites (170 per 100,000 compared to 42 per 100,000, respectively), at 75 per 100,000, Latinas were not far behind at nearly twice the rate of white women (Harrison and Beck 2005, 8).

In a state-by-state look at Latino/a incarceration, the racial/ethnic disparities are strikingly severe. Incarceration rates of Latino/as as compared to whites can be summarized as follows:

- In nine states, between 4 and nearly 8% of adult Latino men are incarcerated.
- In 12 states, between 2 and 4% of Hispanic adults (men and women) are incarcerated.
- In 10 states, Latino men are incarcerated at rates between five and nine times greater than those of white men.
- In eight states, Latina women are incarcerated at rates that are between four and seven times greater than those of white women.
- In four states, Hispanic youths under age 18 are incarcerated in adult facilities at rates between seven and 17 times greater than those of white youth. (Human Rights Watch 2002, 2)[3]

A major contributor to the rise in Latino/a imprisonment rates is the phenomenon of *mass imprisonment*. As defined by Garland (2001a, 1, 2), mass imprisonment is characterized by unprecedented high rates of incarceration that are "markedly above the historical and comparative norm for all societies of this type" and by "the systematic imprisonment of whole groups of the population" rather than of individuals. With respect to this phenomenon, the United States far surpasses other comparable countries, such as those in Europe and Scandinavia, with an incarceration rate six to ten times higher (1). Additionally, Latino/as increasingly appear to meet the criterion of a group systematically subjected to disproportionately high levels of imprisonment.

Citing LaFree, Drass, and O'Day (1992) and Sampson and Lauritsen (1997), Loïc Wacquant (2001, 82) points out that racial inequality in the penal system becomes most discernible when one considers how the ethnic composition of prisoners in the United States reverses dramatically, "turning over from 70 percent white at the mid-century point to nearly 70 percent black and Latino today, although ethnic patterns of criminal activity have not been fundamentally altered during that period." Focusing on the African American experience, he posits that the current ethno-racial makeup of the prisons is part of a continuum that can be traced to the institutions that have historically provided the means for dominating and dividing persons based on race and ethnicity. Moreover, Wacquant argues (2001, 83–84) that just as the institutions of slavery and Jim Crow provided the means to keep "African Americans 'in their place,' i.e., in a subordinate and confined position in physical, social, and symbolic space" in earlier times, the ghetto and the ever-expanding prison system in the United States in the post-civil-rights era form "a *carceral continuum* that ensnares a supernumerary population of younger black men, who either reject or are rejected by the deregulated low-wage labor market, in a never-ending *circulus* between the two institutions." Wacquant posits that a symbiotic relationship between ghetto and prison exists that "enforces and perpetuates the socioeconomic marginality and symbolic taint of the urban black subproletariat, feeding the runaway growth of the penal system that has become a major component of the post-Keynesian state" (84). He further asserts that this symbiosis "plays a pivotal role in the remaking of 'race' and the redefinition of the citizenry via the production of a racialized public culture of vilification of criminals" (84).

If applied to Latino/as in the United States, Wacquant's thesis resonates as similarly true, given the historical and present-day Latino/a experience and place in U.S. society. Regarding the question as to which groups would be most vulnerable to incarceration at present, it is worth noting that, in addition to African Americans, other groups considered "nonwhite" were typically subordinated and targeted for discrimination in U.S. history. As early as 1740, the South Carolina Slave Code identified "the people commonly called negroes, Indians, mulattos and mestizos have [been] deemed absolute slaves, and the subjects of property in the hands of particular persons the extent of whose power over slaves ought to be settled and limited by positive laws so that the slaves may be kept in due subjection and obedience" (quoted in Hall, Wiecek, and Finkelman 1996, 37). Indeed, as the institution of slavery evolved in the United States, a person considered a mulatto or a person "of mixed race" raised the presumption of slavery (191). This history is instructive as to how Latino/as would be regarded in later years, since persons of mixed racial backgrounds—as many Latino/as are—have been, and often continue to be, viewed with disdain and subject to discrimination by the dominant "white" social structure. Consonant with Wacquant's analysis, Latino/as, like African Americans, are perceived as a poor class of people of color that pose a threat to the social order and thus must be controlled and dominated.

Historically, race has played a central role in defining U.S. laws and policies having to do with Latin Americans and subsequently with Latino/as in the United States. Premised on the ideology of the racial, religious, and cultural superiority of Anglo Americans known as Manifest Destiny, in 1848, at the end of the U.S.-Mexican War, the United States wrested approximately half of Mexico's land base, an area that now comprises roughly one-third of the continental United States (Stephanson 1995; Perea et al. 2000, 248; Morín 2009). Indeed, as Horsman (1981, 208) notes, "the catalyst in the overt adoption of a racial Anglo-Saxonism was the meeting of Americans and Mexicans, in the Southwest the Texas Revolution, and the war with Mexico." Advancing the image of Latin Americans as racially "other" and the white Anglo American as superior was key in justifying the U.S. imperial enterprise of the 1800s, including, in addition to its conquests in Mexico by 1848, the subsequent colonization of Puerto Rico and of other islands and peoples in 1898 (Morín 2009, 19–48).

In addition to justifying Anglo-American territorial expansion and hegemony, the racially negative depiction of Latin Americans played a crucial role in securing Anglo-American power and control over the conquered territories and the peoples

of those territories. Although the Treaty of Guadalupe Hidalgo of 1848 was supposed to afford U.S. citizenship and equal rights under U.S. law to Mexicans in the
conquered territories, contrary to international law, Mexicans were not granted
equal rights and full protections. "Whiteness" became the standard for deciding
who is or is not deserving of equal rights of U.S. citizenship. The characterization
and categorization of Mexicans in the newly conquered territories as mongrels,
barbaric, and inferior provided abundant justification for their subordination and
unequal treatment (Horsman 1981).

Similarly, under present U.S. law, Puerto Ricans in their own homeland do not
benefit from full rights under the U.S. Constitution even though they were made
U.S. citizens through a unilateral act of Congress in 1917. As peoples of a territory
colonized by the United States, Puerto Ricans cannot vote for the President of
the United States, who is empowered to recruit and order them to fight U.S. wars.
Moreover, they have no voting representation in the U.S. Congress, a body that legis-
lates on all of the most fundamental aspects of their political, economic, social, and
cultural lives (Perea et al. 2000, 246–366; Morín 2009, 19–48). Supreme Court decisions known as the *Insular Cases—which* form the legal framework that has helped
justify the separation of the right to political participation from citizenship for the
people of Puerto Rico as well as of Guam and the Virgin Islands—still operate today
in a manner that casts Puerto Ricans as a form of "second-class citizens" (Rivera
Ramos 2001, 160–61). In fact, in *Balzac v. Porto Rico* [sic], 258 U.S. 298 (1922), the
U.S. Supreme Court made clear that in spite of having been accorded "citizenship,"
Puerto Rico is not considered "part" of the United States, and thus basic constitutional rights, including fundamental rights to a trial by jury under the U.S. Constitution, are not automatic but can only be accorded if granted by the U.S. Congress.

Conquest and the undermining of basic rights have led some analysts, such as
Angel Oquendo (1996), to point out the parallel experiences of Puerto Ricans and
Mexicans in ways that help define the concept of what it is to be "Latino" in the
United States. Post-1848, Mexicans and many other Latino/a groups have continued to be disempowered and discriminated against, as U.S. laws and the criminal
justice system were readily infused with racialized portrayals of Latino/as as "other"
or as dangerous "aliens." As Bender (2003) points out, the stereotype of Latino/a as
"criminally inclined" has persisted in U.S. law, media, and society from the earliest
period of Anglo-American conquest to the present. Alfredo Mirandé (1987) has
characterized the long trajectory of unequal treatment of Latino/as under the U.S.
legal and criminal justice systems as "gringo justice." The racialization of Latino/as
within U.S. society and its criminal justice system helped to establish and advance
a system premised on biases that have continued to empower and favor whites
over Latino/as and other people of color.

The 1855 "Greaser Act"—an anti-vagrancy law enacted in California that
defined vagrants as "all persons who are commonly known as 'Greasers' or the
issue [children] of Spanish and Indian blood"[4]—was a deliberate use of criminal
law to specifically target persons of Latin American descent based on "racial" criteria. By the 1940s, Mexican Americans in Los Angeles had been relegated to the
socioeconomic margins of society, as manifested by their poverty and segregation
into *barrios* in a city that used to be a part of Mexico.

In an early example of the systematic racial profiling of Latino/as, military and law enforcement personnel singled out for attack Latino youths who defiantly wore zoot suits as a form of self-identity and expression. Today, the 1943 Zoot Suit Riots are remembered as emblematic of a legal and criminal justice system predisposed to characterize Latino/a youths as criminals in order to maintain Latino/as subordinate to the dominant white society (Escobar 1999; Acuña 2007, 201–205).

Like African Americans, Latino/as, too, have suffered the indignities of *de jure* segregation. In fact, the practice of school segregation of children of Latino ancestry was legal and common until the 1940s, when it was challenged in *Mendez v. Westminster School District of Orange County* in 1947[5]—a case that served as a precursor to the landmark 1954 *Brown v. Board of Education* case. In *Hernandez v. Texas*, 347 U.S. 475 (1954), decided by the U.S. Supreme Court three weeks before *Brown*, the court struck down the practice of excluding persons of Mexican descent from service as jury commissioners, grand jurors, and petit jurors. In its decision, the court acknowledged the many years during which Mexicans suffered Jim-Crow-type treatment, including school segregation, separate bathroom facilities, and restaurants that held signs announcing "No Mexicans Served" (*Hernandez v. Texas*, 347 U.S. 475, 479–480 [1954]; see also Olivas 2006).

The upsurge in anti-immigrant and anti-Mexican sentiment in the 1950s gave rise to yet another law targeting Latino/as: "Operation Wetback." Under the federal program created by this law, growing nativist demands to stop Mexican migration were satisfied through a military operation that purported to deport undocumented Mexicans from the United States. As its derogatory name implies, safeguarding human and civil rights was not a concern. In fact, this law served as a pretext for illegal searches and seizures and resulted in the mass deportation of many Mexicans with U.S. citizenship (Mirandé 1987, 125–29; Acuña 2007, 225–26; Healey 2007, 310). As a result, from 1954 to 1959, Operation Wetback led to the deportation of more than 3.7 million persons of Mexican ancestry, many of whom were U.S. citizens (McWilliams 1948/1990, 315–18; Mirandé 1987, 125–29; Perea et al. 2000, 317).

Today, in the application of contemporary U.S. law and in the operation of criminal justice system, Latino/as most often continue to be relegated to a "racialized" status. The use of abusive language and racial and ethnic slurs by police officers, racial profiling, and the excessive use of physical and deadly force against Latino/as and other people of color has been found to be a regular occurrence (Amnesty International 1998, 17–54; Morín 2009, 49–83; Walker, Delone, and Spohn 2007, 110–38).

Another example of how racialized groups are targeted by law enforcement and discriminated against by the justice system is the common practice of racial profiling. Although illegal, in recent decades, racial profiling remains a problem in law enforcement. Its practice by New Jersey state troopers during the decade of the 1990s, in which at least eight out of every ten cars driven by Latino/as and African Americans were singled out for searches on the New Jersey Turnpike, brought to the fore the systematic and institutionalized discrimination practiced in the day-to-day operations of the criminal justice system (Kocieniewski and Hanley 2000).

Reports issued by the New York State Attorney General and the United States Commission on Civil Rights have provided additional evidence that in New York City, race has frequently been used as the sole criterion in the acts committed by law enforcement agents, making evermore apparent the problem of racial profiling as it affects Latino/as (Spitzer 1999; United States Commission on Civil Rights 2000). The New York City Police Department insisted that the reason Latino/as and African Americans were stopped and frisked at higher rates was because they live in high crime-rate neighborhoods. However, a report by the state Attorney General's office found that even after accounting for differences in crime rates between communities of color and white communities, across all crime categories in New York City, Latino/as were still "stopped" by police officers 39 percent more often than whites (Spitzer 1999, x).

Studies conducted in other cities reveal a similar pattern of illegal racial profiling by the police. In a study conducted in Chicago, 80 percent of African American high school students and 62 percent of Latino/a high school students reported being stopped by police, with 62 and 63 percent, respectively, reporting that, when stopped, they were treated disrespectfully by the police (Freidman and Hott 1995, 111). The pattern of racial profiling and "stops" by law enforcement officials strongly point to a continuation of longstanding stereotypes of Latino/as and other people of color as a criminal element in society. This pattern—along with other aggressive police tactics, stricter sentencing laws, and the practice of selective prosecution—appears to play a part in elevating the number of Latino/as and other people of color ending up in the prison system.

Consistent with Wacquant's (2001) hypothesis, many Latino/as in the United States have experienced patterns of ghettoization similar to African Americans in the post-1960s' civil rights era. Many often live in highly segregated and mostly poor areas in cities such as Los Angeles or New York, where they have been most often susceptible to abuse by law enforcement officers and the criminal justice system (Morín 2009). Indeed, Wacquant (2001, 101), citing Ellis (1993), observes that by "the late 1980s, three of every four inmates serving a sentence in the prisons of the entire state of the New York came from only *seven* black and Latino neighborhoods of New York City which also happen to be the poorest areas of the metropolis, chief among them Harlem, the South Bronx, East New York, and Brownsville."

The experience of many Latino/as who have lived under de facto segregation since the middle of the twentieth century is similar to that described by Wacquant (2001, 84), having gone from living in ghettos that resemble prisons to prisons that are now like ghettos. It should not come as a surprise, then, that analysts have concluded that Latino/as manifested their dissatisfaction and disillusionment with the criminal justice system through their participation in the unrest following the acquittal of the white police officers involved in the Rodney King verdict in 1992, with a majority of those arrested being Latino/a and a considerable amount of damage occurring in areas where Latino/as live (Martínez 1993; Pastor 1993).

Crime Policies and Their Impact on Latino/as

As mentioned earlier, the formulation of public policy around the fear of crime and the enormous role of media in driving crime policies based on the fear are also influential in producing incarceration rates skewed against African Americans and Latino/as (Beckett and Sasson 2004; Western 2006; Simon 2007). Given that national data show a decline in the number of crimes committed since the 1990s, it appears that "crime rates themselves may not have driven the prison boom, but long-standing fears about crime and other social anxieties may form the backdrop for the growth in imprisonment" (Western 2006, 48). As Beckett (1997) notes, since the 1960s, politics and policymaking shifted from the "war on poverty" to the "war on crime" and the "war on drugs," often linking poverty with crime, especially poverty in "minority" communities. Notions about rehabilitation through the penal system gave way to a bourgeoning "culture of control," with fear-filled images of criminals as virtually irredeemable "'career criminals', 'drug addicts', 'thugs' and 'yobs'" (Garland 2001b, 135). Coupled with this imagery is a profoundly racialized victim—"not all victims, but primarily white, suburban, middle-class victims, whose exposure has driven waves of crime legislation" (Simon 2007, 76). Moreover, modern crime legislation has come to represent victims in many powerfully symbolic ways, even when victims may not be referenced in the legislation, and thus even

> police are often portrayed in such legislation as victims themselves, not only of criminals, but of defense lawyers, soft-on-crime judges, misguided parole and probation officers, and so on. Prison cells, meanwhile, are the purest expression of the public's embrace of and promise to protect the victims, and potential victims, of crime. (Simon 2007, 76)

Although crime dropped by almost one-third between 1993 and 2000, it continues to dominate both the news and entertainment media (Beckett and Sasson 2004, 43, 100). To the extent that the media's influence on public policy can be measured, it appears to "encourage punitive attitudes, especially when the offenders depicted are African American" (101). Hence, the power of the media lies not only in its ability to project fear but also its capacity to convey a highly racialized picture of crime to the public.

Fear of violent crime has been a primary reason for adopting stiffer penalties that aim to incarcerate violent offenders. But it has not generally been the case that the vast majority of those imprisoned are there for committing violent offenses. In fact, the percentage of persons sentenced for nonviolent drug offenses constituted the largest group of federal prisoners, at 55 percent in 2003 and 60 percent in 2002 (Harrison and Beck 2006b, 10).[6] Of the prisoners held in state facilities from 1995 to 2003, violent offenders have most often constituted only half of those incarcerated: 46.5 percent in 1995, 49 percent in 2001, and 51.8 percent in 2003 (Rennison and Rand 2003, 1; Harrison and Beck 2006b, 9).

Many analysts point out that current policies formulated on the fear of crime frequently produce racial or ethnic inequalities in the prison system (e.g., Beckett

1997; Garland 2001a, 2001b; Harris 2002). "Get-tough" antidrug strategies, commonly referred to as the "war on drugs," amount to "the single greatest force behind the growth of the prison population" (Human Rights Watch 2003, 1). It is a strategy that has been increasingly recognized as a "war" being fought almost entirely in Latino/a and African American communities, based mainly on a mistaken perception that communities of color bear most of the responsibility for drug-related crime in the country (Donziger 1996; Cole 2001; Human Rights Watch 2003; Walker, Delone, and Spohn 2007).

Contrary to conventional perceptions, Latino/as have not been shown to be any more inclined to engage in illegal drug activity than whites. Citing the 2002 National Survey on Drug Use and Health, the Office of National Drug Control Policy (2003, 1) makes plain that "the lowest rate of lifetime illicit drug use was among Hispanics (38.9%) and Asians (25.6%)," while whites had a 54 percent rate of drug use over a lifetime, followed by African Americans at 43.8 percent. Moreover, the data show whites abusing certain drugs at higher levels. The Office of National Drug Control Policy found that "of 12th graders, whites tended to have the highest rates of use for a number of drugs, including inhalants, hallucinogens, LSD, ecstasy, heroin without a needle, amphetamines, sedatives (barbiturates), tranquilizers, and narcotics other than heroin" (2).

Despite these statistics, the "war on drugs" waged in communities of color has had the "devastating" effect of skyrocketing drug-related arrests and incarceration rates of Latino/as and African Americans (Donziger 1996, 116). Of a total of 23,784 federal offenders charged with drug trafficking in 2001, most were Latino/a (44.7 percent) while only about a quarter (26.2 percent) were white and 28.4 percent were African American (United States Sentencing Commission, 2001, 14, table 4). For state prisons, the statistics are similarly dire. In 1996, 40 percent of Latino/as sentenced to state prisons were convicted of drug-related crimes (Ditton and Wilson 1999, 6). When one considers the available evidence demonstrating that drug use among whites is as high, and in some instances higher, compared to other racial and ethnic groups, it seems inconceivable that in 1991, Latino/as and African Americans comprised 92 percent of drug arrests in New York City (Donziger 1996, 116).

In the haste to combat the perceived drug problem in communities of color, recourse to racial profiling is common, with Latino/as and African Americans most often being singled out. There are documented instances in which law enforcement personnel have been trained to identify narcotics dealers by looking for "people wearing dreadlocks and cars with two Latino males traveling together." Further, a 1999 Drug Enforcement Agency (DEA) intelligence report identified major heroin traffickers as "Colombian, followed by Dominicans, Chinese, West African/Nigerian, Pakistani, Hispanic, and Indian. Midlevels are dominated by Dominicans, Colombians, Puerto Ricans, African Americans and Nigerians" (Harris 2002, 49).

Drug-courier profiles used by federal agents at airports have included very long lists of seemingly odd and broadly defined categories, such as persons who "made a local call after deplaning . . . made a long-distance call after deplaning . . . carried a small bag . . . carried a medium-size bag . . . carried two bulky garment bags . . . dressed casually . . . left the airport by taxi" and anyone falling under the category of "Hispanics" (Cole 1999, 47–49).

As Georgetown University law professor David Cole (2001, 248) notes, "racial profiling studies . . . make clear that the war on drugs has largely been a war on minorities. It is, after all, drug enforcement that motivates most racial profiling." Racial profiles appear not to correctly reflect the racial background of either illicit drug consumers or of traffickers. U.S. government data about drug use points to whites using drugs at much the same rate as persons from other racial or ethnic groups. In 2001, "the rate among blacks was 7.4 percent, whites 7.2 percent, and Hispanics 6.4 percent" (Substance Abuse and Mental Health Services Administration 2002, 1). Although precise data in this area is difficult to obtain, illicit drug users also report that they typically obtain drugs from persons of the same race, suggesting that Latino/as and African Americans may not necessarily be more involved in illegal drug distribution either (Riley 1997, 1; Cole 2001, 247).

The impact of the "war on drugs" has also adversely affected women generally, and Latinas in particular. As Mauer, Potler, and Wolf (1999, 1, 2) point out, women in the United States have experienced a drastic increase in incarceration rates, nearly double the rate for men since 1980, and "drug offenses accounted for half (49%) of the rise in the number of women incarcerated in state prisons from 1986 to 1996, compared to one-third (32%) of the increase for men." The number of women imprisoned for drug offenses in state facilities increased by 888 percent from 1986 to 1996, and by 129 percent for nondrug offenses (3).

Latinas in prison fare even worse compared to white women, as the following statistics indicate:

- In state prisons and jails, Hispanic females are incarcerated at almost twice the rate of white females (117 persons to 63 persons per 100,000 [persons in the] population).
- Hispanic women are three times as likely to go to prison in their lifetime as compared to white women (1.5% versus 0.5%).
- In the U.S. general population, 9.7% of women are Hispanic. In the U.S. prison population, 15 percent of women state prisoners and 32%t of women Federal prisoners are Hispanic.
- Between 1990 and 1996, the number of Hispanic female prisoners rose 71%.
- In New York, Hispanic women are 41 percent of the state's prison population but constitute 44% of women sentenced to prison for drug offenses. (Sentencing Project 2003, 2)

For Latinas, imprisonment represents more than a temporary a loss of personal liberty. As Díaz-Cotto (2006) points out in her study of Chicanas in prison, Latinas often face discrimination, harassment, and abuse. Moreover, Latinas must also cope with the harmful effects of imprisonment on their children and family life.

The Courts, the Police, and Latinos

The disproportionately high rate of incarceration of people of color has provoked criticism of the laws that have brought changes in sentencing, including strict mandatory minimum sentencing laws, "three-strikes" legislation, and so-called "truth in sentencing" laws, designed to replace indeterminate sentences with clearly defined penalties without the possibility of early release on parole (Jacobson 2005, 45). Whether stricter state and federal sentencing policies have had a discriminatory impact on people of color has been a subject of considerable study (Walker, Delone, and Spohn 2007, 231–80). Some prominent analysts affirm that changes in sentencing guidelines may have worsened the racial divide within the criminal justice system (e.g., Tonry 1995). Others conclude that discrimination occurs and harsher penalties are imposed, but within certain contexts, as when a person of color is accused of a crime against a white person as opposed to another person of color (Walker, Delone, and Spohn 2007, 280).

Studies that specifically look at bias against Latino/as in sentencing reveal a consistent pattern. In analyzing sentencing data collected by the State Court Processing Statistics program of the Bureau of Justice Statistics for the years 1990, 1992, 1994, and 1996, Demuth and Steffensmeier (2004, 1008) found "in general, Hispanic defendants were sentenced more similarly to black defendants than white defendants. Both black and Hispanic defendants tended to receive harsher sentences than white defendants."

In an earlier study examining ethnicity as well as race as a factor in sentencing, Steffensmeier and Demuth (2001), using quantitative and qualitative data gathered on Pennsylvania sentencing practices, show that Latino/as are vulnerable to harsher penalties because of the prevalence of negative stereotypes and biases that associate Latino/as with illegal drugs activities, low intelligence, and the rise in neighborhood crime. Their qualitative data reinforces this conclusion, with one particular Pennsylvanian judge from a county with an expanding Latino/a population stating: "We shouldn't kid ourselves. I have always prided myself for not being prejudiced but it is hard not to be affected by what is taking place. The whole area has changed with the influx of Hispanics and especially Puerto Ricans. You'd hardly recognize the downtown from what it was a few years ago. There's more dope, more crime, more people on welfare, more problems in school" (Steffensmeier and Demuth 2001, 168).

A comprehensive review of bias in the courts confirms the familiar pattern: both Latino/as and African Americans experience bias in sentencing practices and policies, and, as a result, they receive harsher sentences than whites. An examination of forty recent and methodologically sophisticated studies on the effects of race and ethnicity on sentencing—including thirty-two studies of state court decisions and eight studies of federal court decisions—concluded that

> black and Hispanic offenders—and particularly those who are young, male, or unemployed—are more likely than their white counterparts to be sentenced to prison; they also may receive longer sentences than similarly situated white offenders. Other categories of racial minorities—those convicted of drug offenses, those

who victimize whites, those who accumulate more serious prior criminal records, or those who refuse to plead guilty or are unable to secure pretrial release—also may be singled out for more punitive treatment. (Spohn 2000, 481–82)

The *Sentencing Reform Act of 1984* (28 U.S.C. 991 [b][1][B]; Supp. 1993), designed to prevent "unwarranted sentencing disparity among defendants with similar records who had been found guilty of similar criminal conduct," appears not to have eliminated the influence on sentencing decisions of legally irrelevant factors, such as racial and ethnic characteristics and immigrant status. Based on data on 14,189 defendants convicted of drug offenses, Albonetti (1997, 817) points out that in spite of the new federal sentencing guidelines adopted as a result of the *Sentencing Reform Act of 1984*, "judges impose significantly more severe sentences on defendants who are not U.S. citizens and on defendants who are black or Hispanic."

It is also important to note that biased sentencing is possible because federal judges can circumvent strict sentencing guidelines:

Although the federal sentencing guidelines severely constrain judges' discretion in deciding between prison and probation and in determining the length of the sentence, they place only minimal restrictions on the ability of judges (and prosecutors) to reduce sentences for substantial assistance or acceptance of responsibility. Mandatory minimum sentences also can be avoided through charge manipulation. (Walker, Delone, and Spohn 2007, 273)

Overwhelmingly, studies on the effects of judicial and prosecutorial discretion on federal sentencing show that African Americans and Latino/as are treated more harshly in sentencing than whites (Walker, Delone, and Spohn 2007, 273). Most notably, Steffensmeier and Demuth (2000), in examining federal court data gathered by the United States Sentencing Commission from 1993 to 1996, found that the ability under the federal sentencing statute to "depart downward" from the sentencing guidelines resulted in leniency toward white defendants and harsher sentences for Latino/a and African American defendants (722).

In examining the operations of the criminal courts and the treatment of Chicano rights movement members in Los Angeles in the late 1960s, Haney López (2003) puts forth the theory that race often functions as a matter of "common sense" in the courts, as it does in the course of many day-to-day events. He found that white judges even unwittingly tended to privilege those of their own race and socioeconomic background, while placing Mexicans at a disadvantage, basing their decisions on a form of "common sense" that implicitly accepts that white persons like themselves are generally worthy of opportunities, such as serving on a grand jury, above Mexicans (8). Thus, Haney López asserts that such "common sense" practices are illustrative of how, today, race is constructed on a daily basis and functions to the benefit of whites over Latino/as and other people of color in the courts and in society at large.

The subject of whether police treat people of color differently from whites has drawn considerable attention. Regarding police practices on the streets, criminologists have written about the *"racial halo effect,"* "a dynamic whereby being white American, in and of itself, reduces the odds of being viewed with suspicion or being questioned by an officer" (Weitzer and Tuch 2006, 19; see also Weitzer 1999). It has also been said that law enforcement officers are indoctrinated to uphold practices that result in the unequal treatment of people of color. In explaining why even an officer of color may treat persons of his own community unfairly, Anthony Miranda, a former New York City police sergeant and spokesperson for the National Latino Officers Association, states that Latino/a recruits undergo a process of assimilation into a police culture that seeks to separate them from their own communities and identities as Latino/as (Morín 2009, 108-115). In his view, officers—including Latino/a officers—often internalize a "them-versus-us" view of police-community relations, regardless of their race (109-115). Once integrated into the force, police officers typically adhere to the notorious "code of silence" to shield each other from prosecution when facing severe allegations of wrongdoing, abuse, or brutality against persons of color (Amnesty International 1998; Human Rights Watch 1998; Morín 2009, 106-116).

Myths and the Media: Projecting Latino/as as Criminals

A close look at Latino/as and crime in the United States reveals that Latino/as are not necessarily imprisoned at higher rates because they are more prone than whites to commit crimes. As Walker et al. (2004, 4) point out in their study of Latino/as and the U.S. criminal justice system, Latino/as are generally less likely to be involved in violent crime "than their non-Hispanic counterparts."[7] The great majority of incarcerated Latino/as are convicted of minor, nonviolent offensesor or are first-time offenders, or both;[8] Latino/as are also more likely than whites to be arrested and charged for drug offenses even though they are no more likely than other groups to use illegal drugs and less likely to use alcohol. Evidence in support of these facts notwithstanding, major news and entertainment media generally paint a very different picture of crime in the United States, frequently linking Latino/as with criminal behavior (Bender 2003). Invariably, such characterization helps promote attitudes that favor prison expansion as a solution to a perceived crime problem.

Studies show that the major media tend to be saturated with stories that inaccurately represent Latino/as. As reported by the National Association of Hispanic Journalists, 66 percent of network news stories about Latino/as in 2002 focused exclusively on three topics: crime, terrorism, and illegal immigration. José Padilla, the suspected "dirty bomb" terrorist occupied "a central role in the coverage of Latinos . . . with 21 network stories or 18 percent of all stories aired on Latinos" (Méndez-Méndez and Alverio 2003, 3). Moreover, post-September 11 anti-immigrant sentiments and the politically opportunistic use of crime in election campaigns pose a formidable challenge to reversing the relentless drive to incarcerate. In spite of the facts that belie their portrayals by the media, Latino/a youth and Latino/a immigrants in particular are consistently and repeatedly associated with criminality conduct in the media.

Latino/a Youths and Crime

Despite a recent spike in violent crime,[9] the United States has experienced a precipitous drop in violent crime—down 58 percent from 1993 to 2005[10] (Catalano 2006, 1). Nonetheless, polls have shown an increase in the fear of crime as well as an upsurge in its media coverage. As Dorfman and Schiraldi (2001, 3) found, the National Crime Victimization Survey reported violent crime at its lowest in twenty-five years; nevertheless, 62 percent of those surveyed believed that juvenile crime was rising. They note that the fear of being victimized by crimes committed by youth of color was especially strong, even though "Whites are actually three times more likely to be victimized by Whites than by minorities" (4). Dorfman and Schiraldi show that media coverage has tended to present an exaggerated, unbalanced picture of crime: "while Blacks and Hispanics were overrepresented as violent offenders, Whites were underrepresented as violent offenders on the evening news" (15).

Bias in the criminal justice system ostensibly correlates with high rates of incarceration among Latino/a youth (Villarruel et al. 2002; Walker et al. 2004). National data reveal that Latino/a youth are charged with violent offenses at five times the rate of white youth and serve longer sentences than white youth—as much as 143 days longer for violent crimes (Villarruel et al. 2002, 2–3). In Los Angeles, Latino/a youth are incarcerated at rates much higher than white youth—7.3 times as often from 1996 to 1998—and Latino/a youth are prosecuted as adults more often than white youth—2.4 times as often from 1996 to 1998 (Villarruel et al. 2002, 2).

The fear of youth gangs has spawned support for new laws that have had a disproportionate impact on youth of color (Villarruel et al. 2002; Walker, Delone, and Spohn 2007, 386–90). Gang databases, provided for under laws enacted in California and Arizona, for example, have been reported as vehicles for unfairly targeting Latino/a youths and other youths of color (Villarruel et al. 2002, 62; Zatz and Krecker 2003). While seemingly race-neutral, anti-gang laws carry heavier penalties for gang membership and have had a disparate impact on Latino/a youth, who are more readily identified by law enforcement officers as gang members than are whites (Zatz and Krecker 2003, 192).

Latino/a Immigrants and Prisons

In recent years, legislation focused on reigning in immigrants entering the country has spurred anti-immigrant sentiments. In the national media, no one has been as effective and persistent in the proliferation of fear and false information about immigrants as CNN's Lou Dobbs. In a recent exposé in the New York Times, David Leonhardt (2007) revealed that in 2003, Lou Dobbs had falsely stated on one of his broadcasts that "one-third of the inmates now serving time in federal prisons come from some other country—one-third." Contrary to Dobb's assertions, at midyear 2005, noncitizens actually comprise less than one-fifth (19 percent) of all prisoners in federal custody—well below one-third—and noncitizens in federal and state facilities combined comprised only 6.4 percent (Harrison and Beck 2006a, 5). As Butcher and Piehl (2005) point out, immigrants to the United States actually have lower incarceration rates than other groups in the population. While it is assumed that factors such as low education levels and low average wages would predispose immigrants to engage in criminal conduct, in the main, immigrants tend to come to the country highly motivated to use their skills to forge a better life and are not interested in run-ins with the law that would thwart this goal. Thus, Butcher and Piehl find that immigrants are typically self-selecting and are not typical of the general population.

The presumed link between crime and immigrants from Latin America, and from Mexico specifically, has been shown to be unsubstantiated. As an empirical study of Mexican immigrants revealed, "it is currently the case that immigration and criminal justice policies which appear neutral in relation to Hispanic immigrants, actually bias and distort public perceptions of immigration and crime by inflating Hispanic rates of imprisonment" (Hagan and Palloni 1999, 617). In a comparison of noncitizen immigrants and citizens in state prisons, Hagan and Palloni found that after taking into consideration factors such as age and vulnerability to pretrial detention, noncitizen Latin American immigrants are actually *less* likely to be involved in crime than citizens. The study notes that noncitizen Latin American immigrants come to the United States with strong cultural and family traditions that are incompatible with criminal behavior (630–31). In addition to finding that noncitizen Latin American immigrants are not more involved in criminal activity than citizens, they also noted that "by other measures of well-being—including smoking, alcohol consumption, drug use, and pregnancy outcomes—Mexican immigrants are generally found to do well and sometimes better than citizens" (630–31). To the extent that Latino/a cultural strengths serve to deter crime, the study's authors recommend that "we may wish to place the priority in policy formation on ways to preserve, protect, and promote the social and cultural capital that Mexican immigrants bring to their experience in the United States. An increasing reliance on imprisonment detracts from this goal by banishing immigrant males from their families and communities" (631).

The distinction between U.S.-born Latino/as and foreign-born Latin Americans is significant. Rumbaut et al. (2006, 84) make clear that

> both national and local-level findings . . . turn conventional wisdom on its head and present a challenge to criminological theory. For every ethnic group without exception, the census data show an increase in rates of incarceration among young men from foreign-born to the U.S.-born generations, and over time in the United States among the foreign born—exactly the opposite of what is typically assumed. Paradoxically, incarceration rates are lowest among immigrant young men, even among the least educated, but they increase sharply by the second generation, especially among the least educated—evidence of downward assimilation that parallels the patterns observed for native minorities.

Among the challenges Rumbaut et al. (2006, 85) identify for developing well-informed and reasoned criminal justice policy is that contemporary criminology has centered on race mostly along black/white lines, keeping "ethnicity, nativity, and generation out of the analysis."[11] They point out that this is compounded by the national bad habit of lumping individuals into a handful off one-size-fits-all racialized categories (black, white, Latino, Asian) that obliterate different migration and generational histories, cultures, frames of reference, and contexts of reception and incorporation—omitting from scholarly scrutiny the complexities introduced by millions of newcomers from scores of different national and ethnic origins. (Rumbaut et al. 2006, 85)

Further complicating matters, Latin American immigrants are generally recognized as underserved by law enforcement agencies and are susceptible to negative experiences with the criminal justice system. They face numerous obstacles to establishing good relations with police and other law enforcement agencies and many barriers to successfully traverse the criminal justice system, including language barriers and the fear of being subject to immigration law enforcement (Walker, Delone, and Spohn 2007, 107). Moreover, as Johnson (2003, 346) points out, "[j]udicially-sanctioned race profiling is central to the U.S. government's enforcement of the immigration laws," adversely affecting Latino/as, African Americans, and other people of color.[12] Hence, noncitizen immigrants have become more susceptible to aggressive and arbitrary immigration policies and practices.

In the period following the events of September 11, 2001, heightened enforcement of federal immigration laws has rendered Latino/a immigrants increasingly vulnerable to federal detention and imprisonment. The number of persons detained by the U.S. Immigration and Customs Enforcement (ICE) agency "more than doubled between 1995 and 2005," and at year-end 2005, 19,562 persons were being held for immigration violations (Harrison and Beck 2006b, 10). Once in the prison system, there is evidence that persons incarcerated for immigration violations are susceptible to ill-treatment. As Mark Dow (2004) has documented, those in the U.S. immigration prison system are subject to horrific arbitrariness and many forms of abuse by officials and guards for which they are unable to seek adequate redress due to their noncitizen status.

Although organizations such as the Mexican American Legal Defense and Education Fund have vehemently objected to new legislation that would further threaten the rights of immigrants, including proposed laws that would empower state and local police to enforce federal immigration laws (Walker, Delone, and Spohn 2007, 117), in the current climate of anti-immigrant hostility, it is likely that undocumented immigrants will continue to confront new efforts to criminalize their status. As Rumbaut et al. (2006, 84) indicate, the driving forces behind the rates of incarceration of immigrants are the "myths and stereotypes about immigrants and crime [that] often provide the underpinnings for public policies and practices and shape public opinion and political behavior."

Overcoming the Challenges to Change

Tragically, the many factors that contribute to mass imprisonment also present severe challenges toward the adoption of the most sensible reforms and changes in the criminal justice system that would lower incarceration rates in the United States.

The impetus to continue to subordinate and dominate communities of color in U.S. society, the formulation of public policy around crime and the fear of crime, and the role of the media in promoting fear and negative images of Latino/as and other people of color are among the factors that not only favor the trend in prison expansion but work to prevent change. Many proposals and strategies to address the disparate treatment of Latino/as within the criminal justice system remain unimplemented.

Recent studies of Latino/as and the criminal justice system have recommended measures that could help the criminal justice system rid itself of policies and practices that adversely and disproportionately impact upon people of color (Villarruel et al. 2002; Walker et al. 2004; Morín 2009). Broader acknowledgement of the unfair impact of the criminal justice and correctional system on Latino/as could be an important first step toward ending some of the most detrimental facets of the Latino/a experience within the criminal justice arena. Proposals to curtail racial profiling and other practices that lead to harsher and longer sentences for Latino/as and other people of color, as compared to whites, are included among recent policy recommendations. Addressing longstanding inadequacies of the system that have negative consequences on Latino/as—such as inadequate bilingual and culturally competent services—are also among the recommendations found in a number of analyses on Latino/as and the criminal justice system (Villarruel et al. 2002; Walker et al. 2004; Morín 2009).

There are also specific recommendations for reversing the mass imprisonment phenomenon that merit serious consideration and, in many instances, implementation. For instance, Jacobson (2005) stresses the need to recognize that mass incarceration has led to many inequitable results, including the unfair treatment of certain racial and ethnic groups. He calls for the downsizing of the prison system as a solution to the prison population explosion and suggests various seemingly efficacious and cost-effective alternatives. His proposals support sentencing reform, strategies to reduce recidivism rates, job training, and increased community-based services.

Other sensible recommendations and approaches, as advocated by Travis (2005) and Jacobson (2005), seek to address the problems of recidivism and prisoner reentry. Their recommendations include creating or enhancing education opportunities and job training while in prison, the development of programs that help sustain and strengthen family and community ties during incarceration, and establishing projects that in other ways help enable incarcerated persons to become productive upon their release.

Greater dissemination of the accurate information about the realities of Latino/as in relation to the criminal justice and penal systems could prove to be constructive and indispensable in the effort to mobilize communities and political support for the process of achieving substantive change. Comprehensive efforts in Latino/a communities similar to that proposed by Villarruel et al. (2002)—efforts that involve engaging parents, youths, community, law enforcement, and the political process—provide a model for effecting needed and long overdue changes in the prison and criminal justice system—changes that may assist in turning around the dangerous trend toward increased Latino/a imprisonment.

Notes

1. Data collected by the U.S. Justice Department's Bureau of Justice Statistics are cited throughout this article. The Bureau of Justice Statistics uses the U.S. Census Bureau as its collection agent to gather information about the prison population in each of the fifty states and the Federal Bureau of Prisons (Harrison and Beck 2005, 11). Unlike other data collected under four federally recognized racial categories (white, black, Asian or Pacific Islander, and American Indian or Native Alaskan) used by government agencies, including the Uniform Crime Reports from the Federal Bureau of Investigation (FBI), the Bureau of Justice Statistics National Prisoner Statistics program data includes "Hispanics" as a category in gathering information. While inconsistencies in the collection and use of the "Hispanic" designation occur state by state (Walker, Delone, and Spohn 2007, 14–16), the Bureau of Justice Statistics data on the racial and ethnic composition of the prison system is considered among the most reliable information of its kind available and, therefore, it is used widely in criminal justice analyses.
2. Both data consistently show African Americans and Latino/as as having significantly higher incarceration rates than whites. Why African American incarceration rates are higher than Latino requires further study and empirical analysis beyond the scope of this article.
3. Human Rights Watch (2002, 1) based its findings on the U.S. Census 2000 data on race, gender, and age of persons in all forms of confinement facility for the fifty U.S. states. An explanation of the Census 2000's methodology can be found at http://factfinder.census.gov/servlet/MetadataBrowserServlet?
4. The 1855 "Greaser Act was codified in the Act of April 30, 1855, ch. 175, § 2, 1855, Cal. Stat. 217 (quoted in Haney López 1996, 145).
5. The *Mendez v. Westminster School District of Orange County* decision can be found in 64 F. Supp. 544, 549 (S.D. Cal. 1946), aff'd, 161 F.2d. 774 (9th Cir. 1947).
6. The Bureau of Justice Statistics distinguishes between violent crimes, such as homicides and robbery, from nonviolent crimes, such as property offenses (e.g., burglary and fraud), drug offenses, and public-order offenses (e.g., immigration and weapons violations) (Beck and Harrison 2001, 12, table 19).
7. Walker et al. (2004, 4) support this claim based on data from the Bureau of Justice Statistics (2000).
8. Walker et al. (2004, 4) cite evidence provided by Kamasaki (2002) in support for this claim.
9. Preliminary crime figures for January to June 2006 released by the Federal Bureau of Investigation (FBI) show that violent crime rose 3.7 percent compared to levels for the first half of 2005, while property crimes for the same period dropped by 2.6 percent (Federal Bureau of Investigation, 2006). Notwithstanding this recent spike in violent crime, violent crime rates today remain well below the rates registered in 1973, 1983, and 1993 (Bureau of Justice Statistics 2006a, 5).
10. "The overall violent crime rate fell 58% from 51 to 21 violent victimizations per 100 persons age 12 or older between 1993 and 2005" (Bureau of Justice Statistics 2006a, 5).
11. As argued by Moran (1997), the "unique needs and characteristics" of U.S. Latino/as and immigrants from Latin America deserve increased consideration by government officials and policymakers. This author holds, as do Rumbaut et al. (2006), that this is true, but not at odds with an understanding of the ways in which Latino/as and Latin American immigrants have been "racialized" in the U.S. context, resulting in unjust treatment in the administration of criminal justice system and immigration policies and practices.
12. Johnson (2003, 346) cites *United States v. Brignoni-Ponce*, 422 U.S. 873, 886–887 (1973), as the U.S. Supreme Court precedent for making "Mexican appearance a relevant factor" in justifying a border patrol stop.

References

Acuña, Rodolfo. 2007. *Occupied America: A history of Chicanos.* 6th ed. New York: Pearson Longman.

Albonetti, Celesta A. 1997. Sentencing under the federal sentencing guidelines: Effects of defendant characteristics, guilty pleas, and departures on sentence outcomes for drug offenses, 1991–1992. *Law & Society Review* 31 (4): 789–822.

Amnesty International. 1998. *United States of America: Rights for all.* New York: Amnesty International Publications.

Beck, Allen J., and Paige M. Harrison. 2001. *Prisoners in 2000,* NCJ 188207. Washington, D.C.: U.S. Department of Justice, Bureau of Justice Statistics.

Beckett, Katherine. 1997. *Making crime pay: Law and order in contemporary American politics.* Oxford: Oxford University Press.

Beckett, Katherine, and Theodore Sasson. 2004. *The politics of injustice: Crime and punishment in America.* Thousand Oaks, California: Sage Publications.

Bender, Steven W. 2003. *Greasers and gringos: Latinos, law and the American imagination.* New York: New York University Press.

Bonczar, Thomas P. 2003. *Prevalence of imprisonment in the U.S. population, 1974–2001.* NCJ 197976. Washington, D.C.: U.S. Department of Justice, Bureau of Justice Statistics.

Bureau of Justice Statistics. 2000. *Sourcebook of criminal justice statistics, 1999.* Washington, D.C.: U.S. Department of Justice.

Butcher, Kristin F., and Anne Morrison Piehl. 2005. Why are immigrants' incarceration rates so low? Evidence on selective immigration, deterrence, and deportation. Chicago: Federal Reserve Bank of Chicago. http://www.chicagofed.org/publications/workingpapers/wp2005_19.pdf (accessed June 17, 2007).

Catalano, Shannan M. 2006. *Criminal victimization, 2005: National Crime Victimization Survey,* NCJ 2146644. Washington, D.C.: U.S. Department of Justice, Bureau of Justice Statistics.

Cole, David. 1999. *No equal justice: Race and class in the American criminal justice system.* New York: New Press.

———. 2001. Formalism, realism, and the war on drugs. *Suffolk University Law Review* 35: 241–55.

Demuth, Stephen, and Darrell Steffensmeier. 2004. Ethnicity effects on sentencing outcomes in large urban courts: Comparisons among white, black and Hispanic defendants. *Social Science Quarterly* 85: 994–1011.

Díaz-Cotto, Juanita. 2006. *Chicana lives and criminal justice: Voices from el barrio.* Austin: University of Texas Press.

Ditton, Paula M., and Doris James Wilson. 1999. *Truth in sentencing in state prisons: Bureau of Justice Statistics special report (January 1999),* NCJ 170032. Washington, D.C.: U.S. Department of Justice, Bureau of Justice Statistics.

Donziger, Steven R., ed. 1996. *The real war on crime: The report of the National Criminal Justice Commission.* New York: Harper Perennial.

Dorfman, Lori, and Vincent Schiraldi. 2001. *Off balance: Youth, race and crime in the news.* Washington, D.C.: Building Blocks for Youth.

Dow, Mark. 2004. *American gulag: Inside U.S. immigration prisons.* Berkeley: University of California Press.

Ellis, Edwin. 1993. *The non-traditional approach to criminal justice and social justice.* Harlem: Community Justice Center, mimeographed, 8 pages.

Escobar, Edward J. 1999. *Race, police, and the making of a political identity: Mexican Americans and the Los Angeles Police Department 1900–1945.* Berkeley: University of California Press.

Federal Bureau of Investigation. 2006. Preliminary semiannual uniform crime report, January-June 2006. Washington, D.C.: U.S. Department of Justice.

Freidman, Warren, and Martha Hott. 1995. *Young people and the police: Respect, fear and the future of community policing in Chicago.* Chicago: Chicago Alliance for Neighborhood Safety.

Garland, David, ed. 2001a. *Mass imprisonment: Social causes and consequences.* London: Sage.

———. 2001b. *The culture of control: Crime and social order in contemporary society.* Chicago: University of Chicago Press.

Hagan, John, and Alberto Palloni. 1999. Sociological criminology and the mythology of Hispanic immigration and crime. *Social Problems* 46 (4): 617–32.

Hall, Kermit, L., William M. Wiecek, and Paul Finkelman. 1996. *American legal history: Cases and materials.* 2nd ed. New York: Oxford University Press.

Haney López, Ian F. 1996. *White by law: The legal construction of race.* New York: New York University Press.

———. 2003. *Racism on trial: The Chicano fight for justice.* Cambridge, MA: Belknap/Harvard University Press.

Harris, David A. 2002. *Profiles in injustice: Why racial profiling cannot work.* New York: New Press.

Harrison, Paige M., and Allen J. Beck. 2002. *Prisoners in 2001,* NCJ 195189. Washington, D.C.: U.S. Department of Justice, Bureau of Justice Statistics.

———. 2005. *Prisoners in 2004.* NCJ 210677. Washington, D.C.: U.S. Department of Justice, Bureau of Justice Statistics.

———. 2006a. *Prison and jail inmates at midyear 2005.* NCJ 213133. Washington, D.C.: U.S. Department of Justice, Bureau of Justice Statistics.

———. 2006b. *Prisoners in 2005.* NCJ 215092. Washington, D.C.: U.S. Department of Justice, Bureau of Justice Statistics.

Healey, Joseph F. 2007. *Race, ethnicity, gender, and class in the United States: Inequality, group conflict, and power.* 4th ed. Thousand Oaks, CA: Pine Forge Press.

Horsman, Reginald. 1981. *Race and manifest destiny: Origins of American racial Anglo-Saxonism.* Cambridge, MA: Harvard University Press.

Human Rights Watch. 1998. *Shielded from justice: Police brutality and accountability in the United States.* New York: Human Rights Watch.

———. 2002. *Race and incarceration in the United States: Human Rights Watch briefing.* New York: Human Rights Watch. http://www.hrw.org/backgrounder/usa/race/pdf/race-bck .pdf (accessed January 5, 2007).

———. 2003. *Incarcerated America: Human rights watch backgrounder.* New York: Human Rights Watch.

Jacobson, Michael. 2005. *Downsizing prisons: How to reduce crime and end mass incarceration.* New York: New York University Press.

Johnson, Kevin R. 2003. The case for African American and Latino/a cooperation in challenging racial profiling in law enforcement. *Florida Law Review* 55: 341–62.

Kamasaki, Charles. 2002. Testimony on drug sentencing and its effects on the Latino community, February 25, 2002. Presented before the United States Sentencing Commission, Washington D.C. http://search.netscape.com/ns/boomframe.jsp?query=Kamasaki&page=4& offset=0&result_url=redir%3Fsrc%3Dwebsearch%26requestId%3D685b03bdf7716d6 %26clickedItemRank%3D47%26userQuery%3DKamasaki%26clickedItemURN%3Dh ttp%253A%252F%252Fwww.ussc.gov%252Fhearings%252F2_25_02%252Fkamasaki .PDF%26invocationType%3Dnext%26fromPage%3DNSCPNextPrevB%26amp%3Ba mpTest%3D1&remove_url=http%3A%2F%2Fwww.ussc.gov%2Fhearings%2F2_25_0 2%2Fkamasaki.PDF (accessed January 5, 2007).

Kocieniewski, David, and Robert Hanley. 2000. Racial profiling was routine. *New York Times*, November 28.

LaFree, Gary, K. Drass, and P. O'Day. 1992. Race and crime in post-war America: Determinants of African American and white rates, 1957–1988. *Criminology* 30:157–88.

Leonhardt, David. 2007. Immigrants and prison, *New York Times*, May 30. http://www .nytimes.com/2007/05/30/business/30leonside.html?ex=1184299200&en=e350a7f3a74 35f38&ei=5070 (accessed: July 8, 2007).

Martínez, Elizabeth. 1993. Beyond black/white: The racisms of our time. *Social Justice* 20 (1–2): 22–34.

Mauer, Marc. 1999. *Race to incarcerate*. New York: The New Press.

Mauer, Marc, Cathy Potler, and Richard Wolf. 1999. *Gender and justice: Women, drugs, and sentencing policy*. Washington, D.C.: The Sentencing Project.

McWilliams, Carey. 1948/1990. *North from Mexico: The Spanish-speaking people of the United States*. New York: Praeger.

Méndez-Méndez, Serafín, and Diana Alverio. 2003. *Network brownout 2003: The portrayal of Latinos in network television news, 2002*. Washington, D.C.: National Association of Hispanic Journalists.

Mirandé, Alfredo. 1987. *Gringo justice*. Notre Dame, IN: University of Notre Dame Press.

Moran, Rachel F. 1997. Neither black nor white. *Harvard Latino Law Review* 2:61–99.

Morín, José Luis. 2009. *Latino/a rights and justice in the United States: Perspectives and approaches*. 2nd ed. Durham, NC: Carolina Academic Press.

Mumola, Chrisopher J. and Allen J. Beck. 1997. *Prisoners in 1996*. NCJ 164619. Washington, D.C.: U.S. Department of Justice, Bureau of Justice Statistics.

Office of National Drug Control Policy. 2003. *Minorities and drugs*. Washington, D.C.: Office of National Drug Control Policy.

Olivas, Michael A., ed. 2006. *"Colored men" and "hombres aquí": Hernandez v. Texas and the emergence of Mexican-American lawyering*. Houston, TX: Arte Público Press.

Oquendo, Angel. 1996. Colloquium proceeding: Comments by Angel Oquendo. *La Raza Law Journal* 9:43–47.

Pastor, Manuel, Jr. 1993. *Latinos and the L.A. uprising*. Tomas Rivera Center Study, Los Angeles, California.

Perea, Juan F., Richard Delgado, Angela P. Harris, and Stephanie M. Wildman. 2000. *Race and races: Cases and resources for a diverse America*. St. Paul, MN: West Group.

Rennison, Callie Marie and Michael R. Rand. 2003. *Criminal victimization, 2002: Bureau of Justice Statistics National Crime Victimization Survey (August 2003)*, NCJ 199994. Washington, D.C.: U.S. Department of Justice, Bureau of Justice Statistics.

Riley, K. Jack. 1997. *Crack, powder cocaine, and heroin: Drug purchase and use patterns in six U.S. cities*. Washington, D.C.: U.S. Department of Justice, National Institute of Justice.

Rivera Ramos, Efrén. 2001. *The legal construction of identity: The judicial and social legacy of American colonialism in Puerto Rico*. Washington, D.C.: American Psychological Association.

Rumbaut, Rubén, Roberto G. Gonzales, Golnaz Komaie, Charlie V. Morgan, and Rosaura Tafoya-Estrada. 2006. Immigration and incarceration: Patterns and predictors of imprisonment among first- and second generation young adults. In *Immigration and crime: Race, ethnicity, and violence*, ed. Ed. Ramiro Martínez, Jr., and Abel Valenzuela, Jr., 64–89. New York: New York University Press.

Sampson, Robert J., and Janet L. Lauritsen. 1997. Racial and ethnic disparities in crime and criminal justice in the United States. In *Ethnicity, crime, and immigration: Comparative and cross-national perspectives*, ed. Michael Tonry, 311–74. Chicago: University of Chicago Press.

Sentencing Project. 2003. *Hispanic prisoners in the United States.* Washington, D.C.: Sentencing Project. http://sentencingproject.org/pdfs/1051.pdf.

Simon, Jonathan. 2007. *Governing through crime: How the war on crime transformed American democracy and created a culture of fear.* Oxford: Oxford University Press.

Spitzer, Elliot. 1999. *The New York City Police Department's "stop and frisk" practices: A report to the people of the state of New York from the attorney general.* New York: Civil Rights Bureau.

Spohn, Cassia C. 2000. Thirty years of sentencing reform: The quest for a racially neutral sentencing process. In *Criminal Justice 2000, Vol. 3,* 427–80. Washington, D.C.: U.S. Department of Justice.

Steffensmeier, Darrell, and Stephen Demuth. 2000. Ethnicity and sentencing in U.S. federal courts: Who is punished more harshly? *American Sociological Review* 65:705–29.

———. 2001. Ethnicity and judges' sentencing decisions: Hispanic-black-white comparisons. *Criminology* 39:145–78.

Stephanson, Anders. 1995. *Manifest destiny: American expansion and the empire of right.* New York: Hill and Wang.

Substance Abuse and Mental Health Services Administration. 2002. *Results from the 2001 national household survey on drug abuse: Volume 1. Summary of national findings.* NHSDA Series H-17, DHHS Publication No. SMA 02-3758. Rockville, MD: Office of Applied Studies.

Tonry, Michael. 2005. *Maligned neglect: Race, crime and punishment in America.* New York: Oxford University Press.

Travis, Jeremy. 2005. *But they all come back: Facing the challenges of prisoner reentry.* Washington, D.C.: Urban Institute Press.

U.S. Commission on Civil Rights. 2000. *Police practices and civil rights in New York City: A report of the United States Commission on Civil Rights.* Washington, D.C.: U.S. Commission on Civil Rights

United States Sentencing Commission. 2001. *2001 sourcebook of federal sentencing statistics.* Washington, D.C.: United States Sentencing Commission.

Villarruel, Francisco A., and Nancy E. Walker, with Pamela Minifree, Omara Rivera-Vázquez, Susan Peterson, and Kristen Perry. 2002. *¿Dónde está la justicia? A call to action on behalf of Latino and Latina youth in the U.S. justice system.* Washington, D.C.: Michigan State University/Building Blocks for Youth.

Wacquant, Loïc. 2001. Deadly symbiosis: When ghetto and prison meet and mesh. In *Mass imprisonment: Social causes and consequences,* ed. Garland, David, 82–120. London: Sage.

Walker, Samuel, Miriam Delone, and Cassia Spohn. 2007. *The color of justice: Race, ethnicity, and crime in America.* 4th ed. Belmont, CA: Thomson/Wadsworth.

Walker, Nancy, E., J. Michael Senger, Francisco A. Villarruel, and Angela M. Arboleda. 2004. *Lost opportunities: The reality of Latinos in the U.S. criminal justice system.* Washington, D.C.: National Council of La Raza.

Weitzer, Ronald. 1999. Citizens' perceptions of police misconduct: Race and neighborhood context. *Justice Quarterly* 16:819–46.

Weitzer, Ronald, and Steven A. Tuch. 2006. *Race and policing in America: Conflict and reform.* New York: Cambridge University Press.

Western, Bruce. 2006. *Punishment and inequality in America.* New York: Russell Sage Foundation.

Zatz, Marjorie S., and Richard P. Krecker, Jr. 2003. Anti-gang initiatives as racialized policy. In *Crime control and social justice: The delicate balance,* ed. Darnell F. Hawkins, Samuel L. Meyers Jr., and Randolph N. Stone, 173-196. Westport, CT: Greenwood Press.

2

Pursuant to Deportation

Latinos and Immigrant Detention

David Manuel Hernández

Increasingly, the immigration system functions—like the criminal justice system—to socially control through confinement in secure, disciplinary facilities the unpopular and the powerless, which in this case are undocumented people of color.

—Teresa A. Miller (2002, 216)

This essay explores the contemporary terrain of Latino immigrant detention outside of the shadow cast by the events of September 11, 2001,[1] and within the context of a larger genealogy of Latino detention. Although one of the most distinctive features of the post-9/11 era is the continual avowal of its inimitability, immigrant detention in the United States is a long and continuing story that when understood historically and comparatively, more properly contextualizes the alarming trends in immigrant detention today. In so doing, it allows us to move beyond the exceptionalist rhetoric found in the government's construction of the "war on terror" to a clearer understanding of what the *New York Times* termed the "fastest-growing form of incarceration" (Bernstein 2007). Further, this essay seeks to explore the racialized features of immigrant detention, in particular its long-term effects on Latino noncitizens and citizens, who, prior to 9/11, suffered the consequences of immigrant detention as it expanded throughout the last century. Immigrant detention, as a process related to the deportation of noncitizens, is thus part of the larger history of federal, local, and individual practices that criminalize immigrants, especially nonwhite immigrants. The incarceration of noncitizens is thus related to their surveillance, punishment, and overall inequality in the areas of labor, education, public health, political representation, and everyday mobility.

Although the histories of Latinos in detention differ in many respects from the experiences of the racially targeted group of Arabs, Muslims, and South Asians who were detained immediately after 9/11, critical features of their collective detentions, such as racial profiling, legal vulnerabilities stemming from their immigrant status, deplorable and punitive detention conditions, and an unchecked detention authority, reveal commonalities and long-term patterns in detention history. Further, the legal and institutional changes resulting from the "war on terror" have a scope that reaches all noncitizens in the United States, undocumented and documented, and will expand the detention infrastructure for the foreseeable future. The events of 9/11 have inspired new and old forms of enforcement that target immigrants comprehensively, well beyond the "war on terror." As Kevin Johnson argues, "although Arab and Muslim noncitizens felt the brunt of the civil rights deprivations in the immediate aftermath of September 11, *immigrants in general* will suffer the long-term consequences of the many measures taken by the federal government in the name of fighting terrorism" (2003, 849–50; emphasis added). The contemporary expansion of immigrant detention, a key enforcement initiative—especially in the context of national security crises—should be understood within the complex genealogy of noncitizen detention. Latino experiences with immigrant detention in particular pose a unique history—one that is complex, recurring, and escalating today.

Exceptionalism and the War on Immigrants

One of the greatest challenges to the examination of immigrant detention has been the widespread exceptionalism that surrounds 9/11. It became commonplace after 9/11, as the major tenets of the "war on terror" were formulated, to read or hear proclamations from various segments of society that "everything had changed" and that this was a time of crisis without precedent. Attorney General John Ashcroft announced, for example: "On September 11, the wheel of history turned and the world will never be the same" (2001). Similarly, President Bush told the nation, "We have entered a new era, and this new era requires new responsibilities, both for government and for our people" (2001). The post-9/11 construction of "homeland security," which enveloped and expanded the federal authority to detain noncitizens, also necessitated legislative and policy changes, produced new judicial rulings, and triggered changes in governmental bureaucracies designed to meet the challenges of President Bush's "new era." On the surface, many aspects of immigrant detention indeed appeared to be new and catalyzed by 9/11.

While the pace and scope of these changes, like the ensuing debate, drew attention to U.S. immigrant detention practices, such an awareness was long overdue. Prior to 9/11, legal professionals and immigrant advocates engaged with, and provided services to, detainees and confronted the large-scale expansion of the detention infrastructure, especially the rapid growth in detention mandated by antiterrorist and immigration legislation that passed in 1996. Yet, the critical work of this focused group of immigrant advocates was often overshadowed by anti-prison activists and scholars, confronting the mammoth incarceration of over two million persons within the U.S. "prison industrial complex." Moreover, the issue of immigrant detention, often invisible as a transitional space between apprehension and deportation, was also marginalized by the major foci of the national immigration debate: expanding or restricting "legal" immigration, border militarization, undocumented immigration, labor competition, amnesty, and so on. As a result, as much as the post-9/11 antiterror initiatives initiated a "new" awareness of immigrant detainees, the larger history of immigrant detention was burdened with the exceptionalist shadow of 9/11. Any historical perspective about U.S. detention practices and detainees themselves—who, in the fall of 2001, were considered "suspected terrorists"—was overwhelmed by fear and sensationalism as well as by institutionalized and popular hostility and violence. Although detention as a means of effecting racial expulsions has been a cornerstone in U.S. immigration policy and history, what the public did learn about noncitizen detention dealt specifically with the detention of a racially conflated group of Arabs, Muslims, and South Asians, who bore the initial brunt of new antiterrorist programs and institutions.

Whereas widespread knowledge of U.S. detention practices seems to begin on 9/11 and would later, after the invasions of Afghanistan and Iraq, be disproportionately represented by grisly photos and unsettling narrative accounts from Abu-Ghraib prison in Iraq[2] and Guantánamo Bay Naval Base in Cuba, the stigma of criminal foreignness and "illegality"—and what I term the "undue processes" (Hernández 2005) of detention and deportation—are facets of immigration policy that many immigrant communities, in particular, Latino communities, have been intimately acquainted for generations. It is important to stress the continuity of such practices. For instance, six months after 9/11, Roberto Martínez of the American Friends Service Committee told the *Los Angeles Times*, "Muslim detainees are complaining in New York, and that's nothing new for us. They are going through the fear factor that Mexicans have undergone for years" (Serrano 2002). Martínez's observation relates the Mexican immigrant community's longstanding relationship with immigrant detention and highlights the pervasive anxiety that the ever-present possibilities of deportation and detention engender.

Such fears are not limited to noncitizen detainees. As a broad group of racialized persons in the United States, Latino citizens also become fixed to Latino immigrants through their widespread and centuries-old criminalization as "illegals."[3] Contributing to, and in turn affected by, the detention process, examples of criminalization are ubiquitous, occurring in popular culture, administrative and local enforcement practices targeting Latinos, and within the law. The conflation of whole groups of Latinos as criminals occurs despite Latinos' profound diversity of incorporation into U.S. society. According to Renato Rosaldo (1999, 255–56), "by a psychological and cultural mechanism of association all Latinos are thus declared to have a blemish that brands us with the stigma of being outside the law. We always live with that mark indicating that whether or not we belong in this country is always in question." As a result of this criminal "blemish" and categorical racialization, Latino citizens and noncitizens have been central figures in detention history. From lengthy and large-scale detention and deportation operations targeted at Mexican nationals throughout the twentieth century, to the detention of Latin American asylum-seekers in the cold war, to contemporary Puerto Rican U.S. citizen and so-called enemy combatant José Padilla, we can observe that there are many types of detainees meeting at the nexus of Latino racialization and criminalization.

The post-9/11 "war on terror" contributed to the ongoing history of racial discrimination against noncitizens, initiating a variety of legal and administrative changes directly affecting U.S. immigration policy. For example, after 9/11, there was an immediate suspension of asylum adjudications, entrapping some migrants in detention domestically, or abroad, unable to seek refuge from persecution. In addition, it derailed a serious public discussion and bilateral negotiations with Mexico about a potential amnesty or "regularization" of status for then-over ten million undocumented migrants, a discussion that would remain muted for nearly five years. Latino noncitizens and their families and communities were affected by these and other federal and local enforcement initiatives emerging after 9/11. According to Steven Bender (2002, 1153), Latinos' "negative societal construction made their targeting inevitable as the fervent, amorphous war on terrorism took shape." Racial profiling in law enforcement, a practice that had been broadly criticized over the last decade, received a shot in the arm after 9/11 and was used widely to apprehend Arabs, Muslims, and South Asians in the wake of 9/11, with detrimental effects on Latino and African American communities (Bender 2002; Johnson 2003). While racial profiling in immigration enforcement received limited endorsement by the Supreme Court in *U.S. v. Brignoni-Ponce* in 1975,[4] its resurgence after 9/11 signals the return of racial profiling as a "common sense" law enforcement practice that disproportionately affects immigrants and people of color.

The emergent post-9/11 discourse of national security cross-fertilized with existing anti-immigrant sentiment, both of which rely historically on racialized and criminalized constructions of migrants, of whom Latinos, for decades, have represented the prototypical example and overwhelming majority. Much like other national crises in U.S. history, fighting a war against terrorism came to mean fighting immigrants, even though empirical data on the criminality of immigrants has consistently reflected noncitizens' lawfulness. As a result, such fears of immigrant and Latino criminality have been called erroneous and a "myth" by scholars of immigration and crime (Martínez and Valenzuela 2006). According to Rubén Rumbaut and Walter Ewing (2007, 1), "in fact, data from the census and other sources show that for every ethnic group without exception, incarceration rates among young men are lowest for immigrants, even those who are the least educated. This holds true especially for the Mexicans, Salvadorans, and Guatemalans who make up the bulk of the undocumented population." Presumptions of immigrant criminality, however—in particular Latino criminality—are resilient and are maintained by politicians, the media, and a misinformed general public. As a result, the legal statutes, administrative strategies, and popular suspicions of noncitizens—embedded in detention history—serve as a critical prologue to understanding the contemporary detention and deportation of Latino immigrants, which has expanded prior to and after 9/11.

Adding the specter of terrorism to an already contentious immigration debate exacerbated what Juliet Stumpf (2006) has termed the "crimmigration crisis"—that is, the merger of criminal and immigration law. According to Stumpf, "criminal and immigration law primarily serve to separate the individual from the rest of U.S. society through physical exclusion and the creation of rules that establish lesser levels of citizenship" (2006, 381). Margaret Taylor and Ronald Wright echo this criticism, writing, "However badly these two systems operate by themselves, they work even more poorly when they are haphazardly combined" (2002, 2).[5] The domestic "war on terror," while relying on the prosecutorial advantages of immigration law, has also been used to advance a broader war on immigrants. Through the discourse of national security, the "war on terror" has augmented criminal and immigration enforcement at the federal, state, and local levels, drawing these apparatuses closer together after 9/11, duplicating efforts, and doubling the punishment of noncitizens.

Latinos and Immigrant Detention

Several reasons—in addition to the exceptionalist rhetoric of 9/11 and the "war on terror"—help explain the limited knowledge of Latino detention. Because detention by immigration authorities is a liminal process that occurs, or is supposed to occur, as an administrative procedure pursuant to the execution of deportation or exclusion orders, little is known about it or its history. Immigrant detention is further eclipsed by the enormity and severity of the "prison industrial complex" in the United States, or what Angela Davis has called the "punishment industry" (Gordon 1998/1999, 146). Over two million people—two-thirds of whom are nonwhite—are incarcerated in U.S. prisons and jails, representing a tripling of this population since 1982 (Gilmore 1998/1999, 171). While this is clearly cause for widespread concern, immigrant detainees, too, tripled in the 1990s (Solomon 1999), increasing, since then, to over 275,000 annually. Moreover, as a result of existing and proposed legislation, they are scheduled to triple again in this decade. Immigrant detainees, however, are incarcerated outside of the criminal court system and are largely unaddressed by prison literatures. The parameters and conditions of detainees' confinement thus remain obscured and legally ambiguous.

Consider, for example, the recent political and social atmosphere surrounding immigration legislation. Despite the intense criticism and praise that the U.S. House of Representative's 2005 punitive immigration legislation (H.R. 4437) received, and the dramatic nationwide collective action which ensued in the spring and summer of 2006, few have commented on the proposed legislation's detention and due process provisions that would have dramatically increased the government's capacity to detain and deport noncitizens, including legal permanent residents. Many of these detention provisions were also in the U.S. Senate's more "affirmative" immigration law of 2006 (S. 2611) and included: expanding the definition of an "aggravated felony," which mandates detention and deportation proceedings; increasing mandatory detention without relief and removing barriers to indefinite detention; expanding expedited removal without a court hearing; and redefining "alien smuggling" such that it would criminalize family members, neighbors, coworkers, and relief organizations who provide nonemergency aid to undocumented migrants. All these provisions, including making unproven membership in a gang a deportable offense even if the person never committed a criminal act, would have considerably impacted Latino communities and families. Yet the seriousness of these provisions has been overlooked by Democrats and national Latino organizations who offered ambivalent support for Senate Bill 2611 because of its proposed guest worker program (Flores 2006; National Council of La Raza 2006). This blind spot to the issue of detention further obscures one of the key federal authorities and disciplinary functions of immigration policy.

The collective demographic profile of Latinos in the United States contributes to their vulnerability to confinement within the detention infrastructure. Latinos' numerical size, in particular, in migration categories, and their "societal construction as violent, foreign, criminal-minded, disloyal, and as overrunning the border" (Bender 2002, 1154) have contributed to the long history of Latino immigrant detention. Today, Latinos represent the largest group of foreign-born, documented and undocumented migrants, border apprehensions and removals, criminal alien detainees, and the largest minority group in the United States. Researchers estimate a range between 46 and 51 percent of adult Latinos in the United States are first generation immigrants and an additional one-fifth to one-fourth of all Latinos are their children (Mariscal 2005, 39; Pew Hispanic Center 2005, 2). In other words, a majority of Latinos in the United States are immigrants or directly related to immigrants. The complex range of immigrant issues thus affects a majority of Latinos in the United States. In 2005, for example, Latinos represented seven of the top ten foreign-born groups in immigrant detention, and Mexicans comprised half of all immigrant detainees (Siskin 2007, 13). Latinos thus predominate over immigrant detention today and, as we shall see, have been key figures throughout its history.

That immigrant detention threatens millions of Latino families and their communities is cause for alarm and further study, especially the relationship between the detention processes and other forms of structural and cultural inequality affecting Latino citizens and noncitizens. Widespread beliefs about Latino criminality, especially as it relates to the widely bemoaned and sensationalized presence of "illegals" or undocumented immigrants, have led to the routine and popular conflation of Mexican nationals and other Latinos with "illegals." The Department of Homeland Security estimates that Mexicans represent 57 percent of undocumented immigration and that Latinos account for roughly three-fourths of current and new undocumented immigrants (Hoefer et al. 2006). These figures, although significant, contribute to the widespread criminalization of Latinos, while simultaneously obscuring the fact that (1) roughly half of each year's cohort of new undocumented immigrants enter by legal means and have instead allowed their legal entry status to lapse, and (2) that there are undocumented immigrants from a variety of nations residing in the United States. The vast majority of government efforts to halt undocumented immigration, however, are targeted at Mexican and Latino communities at the U.S.-Mexico border. As a result, Mexicans have euphemistically represented, indeed epitomized, "the illegal," dominating deportation and detention categories for many decades (De Genova 2004, 171).

The detention authority plays a significant role in criminalizing Latino noncitizens, duplicating the punishment of the criminal justice system. Detention accentuates not simply the border separating who remains in the United States and who is deported, but the real weight of such processes is felt by the creation of a social class inside the United States but outside its legal protections. The appropriate measure of detention, then, is in the nearly thirty million noncitizens—the largest among them Latino immigrants and legal permanent residents—who are subject to the threat of detention and deportation.

According to Nicholas De Genova (2004, 161), "deportability is decisive in the legal production of Mexican/migrant 'illegality' and the militarized policing of the U.S.-Mexico border, however, only insofar as some are deported in order that most may ultimately remain (un-deported)—as workers, whose particular migrant status has been rendered 'illegal.'" The structural inequalities created by immigrant detention extend beyond the detainees themselves, or even undocumented migrants, and include all noncitizens, their millions of U.S.-born and naturalized children and family members, and their communities. Moreover, the actors criminalizing noncitizens and detainees are not simply the president and attorney general, or Congress and the judiciary. State apparatuses, enforcing detention, function through smaller bureaucrats, border patrol agents, local police, detention center guards, and border vigilantes like the Minutemen, who, along with private prisons and detention centers, exemplify a private version of immigration control.

What is Immigrant Detention?

The *Immigration and Nationality Act* enacted in 1952 and amended to the present authorizes the U.S. attorney general to detain noncitizens, including persons seeking asylum, pending their deportation or exclusion hearings before an immigration judge (*Immigration and Nationality Act*, Section 236). Detention ensures that immigrants will attend deportation hearings, by preventing their ability to abscond, and restricts mobility if the detainee is determined to be a danger to society. In 2004, there were over 23,000 immigrants in detention daily within the United States; over 230,000 immigrants were detained during the fiscal year (U.S. Immigration and Customs Enforcement 2004). Estimates since that time have ranged from between 20,000 and 30,000 detainees daily.[6] While length of stay can range from days to years, the average adult detainee was held in custody 37.6 days in 2007. The annual population of detainees has risen by nearly 100,000 persons since 2001 to 283,115 in 2006. This continual growth is facilitated by the Department of Homeland Security's increased capacity to detain 30,000 persons daily at 330 adult detention facilities nationwide in 2007 (U.S. Government Accountability Office 2007).

In general terms, detention is the practice of incarcerating noncitizens who are apprehended at ports of entry or within the nation's interior. Maintained in custody until they are released, bonded, and paroled, or deported from the United States, detainees consist of undocumented immigrants, lawful permanent residents, and, at times, particular groups of citizens.[7] To maintain the government's claim that detention is an "administrative process"—and not a punitive one—detention is theoretically utilized exclusively as a noncriminal procedure pursuant to deportation. But, in practice, immigrant detention is employed as a tool for law enforcement, and as witnessed after 9/11, the detention authority is used preventively, where immigrants can be detained for the purposes of discovering after-the-fact charges that justify long-term detention and facilitate deportation.

According to Margaret Taylor and Ronald Wright, "in response to the September 11 attacks, the government has relied on immigration enforcement tools as a pretext for investigative techniques and detentions that would be suspect under the criminal rules" (2002, 2). Underscoring this observation, legal scholar Peter Schuck argues, "But the detention authority is more than a programmatic resource, ancillary to the power to exclude and deport. Detention is also an awesome power in its own right" (1998, 36).

Formerly managed by the Immigration and Naturalization Service under the Department of Justice, custody of detainees is administered at present by Immigration and Customs Enforcement's (ICE) Office of Detention and Removal (DRO) within the Department of Homeland Security (DHS).[8] Immigrant detainees are incarcerated throughout the nation in three types of facilities: federal detention centers managed by ICE, privately contracted prison facilities, and state and municipal jails subcontracting bed space for immigrant detainees. The latter two nonfederal sites, comprising over 300 facilities, are responsible for incarcerating the majority of all detainees nationwide. Because of the variance in standards, conditions, and oversight at the different facilities, federal detention policy is implemented unevenly among the sites. According to Timothy Dunn (1996, 49), "The severity of INS detention practices varie[s] widely across its various districts along the border, depending largely on the availability of detention space and immediate budget resources."

Long preceding the emerging evidence of torture and abuses of power associated with post-9/11 detainees, gross mistreatment—from sexual abuse and rape to overcrowding and denial of medical attention and religious freedom—has been registered at all three types of detention of facilities. Yet due to the lack of federal oversight and evaluation, privately contracted facilities and local jails have received the most criticism (Tangeman 2002, 27). "The worst abuses were inflicted in the prisons run by contractors," writes Robert Kahn (1996, 15) in his study of Central American refugee detention in the 1980s. Poor detention conditions have come under increased scrutiny, especially after it was reported in June 2007 that sixty-two persons had died in ICE "administrative" custody since 2004 (Berestein 2005). "They get treatment that you might see in a Third World country, and it's really a stain on our system of justice to treat detainees this way," said Adele Kimmel, attorney for a criminal alien detainee suing ICE for delays in medical treatment that allowed a cancer to spread to his penis, resulting in amputation (Fears 2007).[9]

Among the key reasons for the unevenness in detention conditions are the weak guidelines that establish detention standards for nonfederal facilities, where over 60 percent of detainees are held. According to the Government Accountability Office (2007, 9), "The standards are not codified in law and thus represent guidelines rather than binding regulations. According to ICE officials, ICE has never technically terminated an agreement for noncompliance with its detention standards." The latter point further suggests that violations of detention conditions have negligible consequences for private and contracted detention facilities.

Detainees' experiences with detention are mediated by the unequal treatment at these sites as well as within the immigration court system, affecting access to counsel and visitation, the pace of legal proceedings, and the length of stay in detention. For example, a report by Syracuse University's Transactional Records Access Clearinghouse (TRAC 2006) determined that immigration judges' decisions in asylum cases vary widely: some judges deny asylum as much as 98 percent of the time and some as little as 10 percent. Unlike the criminal courts, the constitutional right to legal counsel is not guaranteed in immigration proceedings. As a result, as few as 11 percent of immigrant detainees have legal representation in the immigration courts (Miller 2002, 215). In asylum court, for example, the failure rate for an asylum-seeker without legal representation is 93.4 percent (TRAC 2006).

Immigrant advocates, citing problems with detainees' access to legal representation and lawyers' access to their clients, insist that detainees' due procedural rights are in turn further denied or infringed upon through numerous administrative mechanisms within the detention apparatus. A recent review of telephone access at detention centers nationwide, for example, revealed "pervasive" problems. The Government Accountability Office (2007) concluded, "Without sufficient internal control policies and procedures in place, ICE is unable to offer assurance that detainees can access legal services, file external grievances, and obtain assistance from their consulates." Ironically, for those detainees fortunate to obtain legal representation—oftentimes legal permanent residents with significant ties to their community—their length of stay in detention is prolonged as they fight deportation.

In considering detention's far-reaching effect on Latino communities, one must also more broadly examine the intersections of race, gender, class, and sexuality in the detention experience. Migration, as we know, is a complex process, and gender, sexuality, race, and class background have an enormous effect on the outcomes and experiences of migration, just as migration reshapes these intersecting factors in the workplace, the family structure, and in the detention experience. When considering Latino detainees, gender, for example, can be located as a factor in immigrant detention, the criminalization of immigrants, the conditions of detention, and in the broader effects on family and community structures that are reorganized due to the absence of detained family members. Among immigrant detainees, it is estimated that 7 to 10 percent of detainees are women, reflecting a gendered profile to the criminalization of male immigrant detainees. Of the 9/11 detentions, for example, the prototypical "suspected terrorist" was an Arab, Muslim, or South Asian man. The predominance of male detainees creates a set of conditions for women in detention in which facilities and services are severely lacking. In addition to the numerous documented cases of sexual abuse (Patel and Jawetz 2007), services for other vulnerable populations of detainees, such as gay-lesbian-bisexual-transgender detainees, detainees with health problems, and children, are often nonexistent or hazardous.[10]

Further complicating matters is the fact that detainees are a transient prison population—"one of the most highly transient and diverse populations of any correctional or detention system in the world," according to the Government Accountability Office (2007). With the exception of a smaller category of long-term detainees called "lifers," they cycle in and out of immigrant detention at various individual rates. As a result, statistics detailing the national origins of detainees, much like prisoners in general, are difficult to obtain. A survey conducted by the American Correctional Association, Inc., and published in its journal, *Corrections compendium* (2006), addressed the difficulties of accounting for the number of foreign inmates in U.S. and Canadian correctional facilities. Confirming that little has changed in determining these figures over the last decade, the survey cited its own conclusion from its previous report eleven years prior: "The statement that summarized the 1995 survey still describes corrections' accounting for foreign inmates: 'Until a reliable information system is developed and uniformly applied across the country, it will be impossible to know how many . . . beds are occupied by foreign nationals and illegal immigrants.'"

Owing to the prominence of Latinos among the undocumented who are subject to investigations and deportations by the Office of Detention and Removal, most experts agree that Latino immigrants, Mexicans in particular, are the vast majority of detainees. Most recently, the Department of Homeland Security's Office of the Inspector General reported that between 2001 and 2004, 345,006 criminal aliens— the largest detainee category[11]—were apprehended by ICE. Over 250,000, or 75 percent, were from Mexico, thus dominating the criminal alien category from which persons are least likely to be released from detention prior to deportation (Office of the Inspector General 2006, 7). In the early 1990s, the U.S. Government Accountability Office (1992, 124) estimated that 51 percent of detainees were Latinos. This figure, a rate for Mexican detention that remains to this day, was estimated before the unprecedented tripling of detention bed space and the considerable leap in annual detention as a result of the "war on drugs" and major immigration legislation in 1996. During this time, funding for detention and removal grew to 37 percent of INS enforcement spending (Dixon and Gelatt 2005, 5).

While the "war on terror" and the increased detentions of Arab, Muslim, and South Asian immigrants has resulted in a significant increase in the detention infrastructure, the majority-Latino category of criminal alien detainees still represents the largest share of immigrant detainees. The Office of Detention and Removal estimates that for fiscal year 2007, there will be 605,000 foreign-born persons admitted to local and state correctional facilities and that half will be removable aliens (Office of the Inspector General 2006, 2). These persons, who include many long-term legal permanent residents, represent *future* detainees who will be reincarcerated on immigration charges after completion of their criminal sentences. The expansion of bed space to accommodate these detainees is central to the long-term expansion of immigrant detention and reflects the increased coordination of the criminal justice system with the immigration court system.

New initiatives and administrative changes within the homeland security and justice departments have increased the capacity to detain noncitizens and have facilitated longer periods of detention. For example, the Office of Detention and Removal's (DRO) "Strategic Plan 2003–2012: Endgame" seeks a "100% removal rate" of deportable immigrants in order "to maintain the integrity of the immigration process and protect our homeland" (Tangeman 2003). Because detention is a central part of any individual or mass deportation effort, "Endgame's" "operational focus on fugitive apprehension," according to former DRO Director Anthony Tangeman (2003, ii, 1–1), "will require significant increases in detention and removal operations and resources." Responding to this need for detention space, Congress approved the addition of 8,000 detainee beds per year from 2006 to 2010 (Llorente, 2005) as part of the *Intelligence Reform and Terrorism Prevention Act* (2004), effectively tripling detention bed space for the second decade in a row. Although the Department of Homeland Security's Office of the Inspector General reported in 2007 that "ICE is not well positioned to oversee the growing detention caseload that will be generated by DHS' planned enhancements to secure the border" (2007, 1), proposed immigration legislation in 2006 and 2007 also included further expansions in detention bed space—an increase of 20,000 detention beds. This expansion, buoyed by the bureaucratic shift to a national security context, occurs even though the majority of detainees—Latino criminal alien detainees— have nothing to do with terrorism.

What Immigrant Detention Is: A Subtext

The only legitimate purpose of immigration proceedings is to remove those aliens who do not have a legal basis for remaining here.... but where an alien poses neither a danger nor a flight risk, his removal may be effectuated without detention, and detention therefore serves no legitimate government purpose.

—David Cole (2002, 105)

Detention, although intended to be used pursuant to the deportation of noncitizens, has instead long been party to other government agendas. In the past, detention has been used to secure or deter immigrant labor, for military objectives, and to prevent the spread of contagion. In today's episode during the "war on terror," detention is being utilized to extract information, to deter asylum claims, and as a form of law enforcement. Most importantly, and following the failed logic and practice of border militarization, immigrant detention is viewed as a strategy for stemming the flow of undocumented immigration. The U.S. Government Accountability Office reported in 1992, "INS believes that its detention efforts are a deterrent to illegal entry. Accordingly, INS is expanding its detention capability in attempting to respond to the increased flow of aliens illegally entering the country as well as the increased number of criminal aliens" (U.S. Government Accountability Office 1992, 35).

As a result of this deterrence strategy, detention has become a growth industry for private corrections companies and a development strategy for local municipalities seeking to contract jail space with the federal government. "Correctional systems therefore have developed a strong financial interest in determining inmates' immigration status," write John Hagan and Alberto Palloni (1999, 620). Indeed, of the government's fifteen largest immigrant detention centers, seven are contracted facilities with newer, private facilities awaiting completion (U.S. Immigration and Customs Enforcement 2006). Private prisons and contracted bed space account for over 60 percent of immigrant detainee bed space nationwide. The success of deterrence strategies, however, "has been difficult to gauge," concluded the Congressional Research Service (Siskin et al. 2006, 54). Although personnel and resources have been devoted to the border for over a decade, apprehensions have not abated and continue to rise steadily, remaining at well over one million per year.

Occurring episodically over the last one hundred years, the federal government's expansive authority to detain noncitizens is another manner in which the government produces "illegality," both in numbers and perceptions, impacting especially racialized noncitizens who are vulnerable to unequal social relations or are specifically categorized as a group as undesirables or enemies of the state. Hagan and Palloni (1999, 617) have argued that "immigration and criminal justice policies which appear neutral in relation to Hispanic immigrants actually bias and distort public perceptions of immigration and crime by inflating Hispanic rates of imprisonment." Furthermore, along with increased federal enforcement, over the last three decades, the government has vastly increased the number of immigrant detainees by expanding the definition of deportable and detainable crimes, mandating detention in numerous situations and eliminating judicial avenues for relief from detention.

Immigrant detainees occupy a limbic legal position between arrest or exclusion and deportation that is steeped in their status as noncitizens, which itself can generate the diminishment of constitutionally protected due procedural rights. While persons charged with crimes are considered innocent until proven guilty, this principle does not apply to migrants never charged with a criminal offense but instead to those who stand accused of administrative offenses, landing them in the immigration courts, which are separate and outside the protections of the criminal justice system. Further, because immigrants are often considered flight risks, they are subject to increased rates of pretrial detention in criminal cases, and postsentence detention as they are transferred from criminal imprisonment to immigrant detention (Hagan and Palloni 1999).

Crucial to the government's practice of immigrant detention is the nineteenth-century legal view that detention and deportation are not considered punishment for criminal activities. In *Fong Yue Ting v. United States* (1893), it was determined that deportation does not constitute lawful punishment for a crime but is instead an administrative process for returning undesirable noncitizens to their countries of origin. Detention, then, is merely part of that administrative process and does not trigger legal protections that would be initiated if one were charged with a criminal offense. The legal fallacy that incarceration in prisons and jails and forced removal from the United States are not punitive is protected by assertions of national sovereignty and, constitutionally, by Congress' plenary power over all immigration matters. As legal scholar Gabriel Chin argues, "where the status of immigrants is concerned, almost anything goes" (2005, 7).

The Supreme Court ruled in *Fong Yue Ting* (1893) that "the power to exclude or expel aliens . . . is vested in the political departments of the government, and is to be regulated by treaty or by act of congress, and to be executed by the executive authority according to the regulations so established." The Court added that noncitizens "remain subject to the power of congress to expel them . . . whenever, in its judgment, their removal is necessary or expedient for the public interest." Critically, and with lasting effect, the Court argued, "The order of deportation is not a punishment for crime. . . . It is but a method of enforcing the return to his own country of an alien who has not complied with the conditions upon the performance of which the government of the nation . . . has determined that his continuing to reside here shall depend." As a result of this ruling, according to legal scholar William Preston, "due process in deportation was smashed on the rock of judicial decision in 1893, never to be put together again" (1994, 11). Three years after *Fong Yue Ting*, the validity and role of detention in the deportation process was more clearly defined in *Wong Wing v. United States* (1896). In that case, the Supreme Court ruled, "We think it clear that detention or temporary confinement, as part of the means necessary to give effect to the provisions for the exclusion or expulsion of aliens, would be valid. Proceedings to exclude or expel would be vain if those accused could not be held in custody pending the inquiry into their true character, and while arrangements were being made for their deportation. Detention is a asual [sic] feature in every case of arrest on a criminal charge . . . but it is not imprisonment in a legal sense" (*Wong Wing* 1896).

As a result of these historic rulings and interpretations, detainees have been situated outside the protections of criminal justice, although they are criminalized in the popular imagination. In short, as one detainee's attorney stated, "You'd rather be charged with a serious murder where you have some rights than a visa overstay. Because it's civil in nature, the safeguards don't apply" (Getter 2001). Especially in periods of national crisis, immigrants' rights are further abrogated in the detention process because they are subject to far more veiled administrative discretion and practices. Evidentiary standards, secret proceedings, filing deadlines, bond regulations, transfers of detainees, and other "undue processes"—such as restricting counsel or limiting judicial review—are imposed upon detainees. And ironically, although detainees remain apart from accused or convicted criminals in terms of their judicial rights, the majority of ICE detainees are housed with the general population of inmates at state and local jails with intergovernmental agreements with ICE (U.S. General Accountability Office 2007).

Ultimately, detention is an expression of the inequality of noncitizens in the United States, in particular, racialized immigrants such as Latinos. Used to discipline and refine the citizenry, it is a feature of the racial hierarchy from which dominant society benefits. The detention of Latinos and other racialized immigrants helps constitute the normative white citizen and white nation. It, along with the government's expansive immigration control apparatus, serves a disciplinary function that consolidates the power of the state and formulates U.S. nationalism and sovereignty by constructing and controlling insiders and outsiders. In addition, a great deal of political currency is derived from detention. For politicians, the appearance of being tough on crime, immigrants, and terror—for the moment all linked—is valuable and draws easily on, and contributes to, popular criminalized perceptions of immigrants. Detaining immigrants, then, assists in creating an illusion of security. In this sense, the noncitizen is an instrument and constitutive factor of our security state, legitimizing its expansion and drawing support from voters and popular opinion. When paired with xenophobia, national crises are used to mobilize a permanent state of emergency, which facilitates the accumulation of state power over racialized immigrants.

A Brief Genealogy of Latino Detention

With its near-mythic status in the formation of the United States as a "nation of immigrants," immigration history, as it is generally known in the United States, has also served as a repository for historical amnesia. Unlike the heralded experiences of European immigrants whose racial inscription was nonexistent or temporary—permitting descendant generations to achieve social advancement—immigration for Latinos has been a far more vexed process in which Latinos' racialization, criminalization, and constant threat of detention and deportation maintain their racialized foreignness before the law and society. In coming to terms with the contemporary detention of Latino immigrants, it is critical to confront this historical erasure and develop a more complex understanding of the continuity of detention policy over the last century. The capacity for the detention of Latino immigrants has been made possible by its genealogical precursors and judicial and legislative precedents. A variety of discourses of exclusion and Latino criminality, reinvented through the detention process, has served to naturalize Latino immigrants' "illegality." As De Genova argues, "Indeed, the legal production of 'illegality' has made an object of Mexican migration in particular, in ways both historically unprecedented and disproportionately deleterious" (2004, 173). Mexican and other Latino immigrants have thus long lived with the consequences of their degraded citizenship status in the United States. Detained as a result of biological reasoning and fears of contagion, for ideological motives as refugees, or persistently as criminalized noncitizens, Latino experiences with detention are recurring and not isolated episodes in the twentieth century. They provide the historical context for understanding today's escalation of detention, deportation, and degradation of Latino immigrant communities.

Medical Detention

Several major episodes in detention history, some of them ongoing and which coincide with the construction of national crises, have led to the large scale detention of Latino immigrants. The first such episode for Latinos occurred between World War I and II, during a time when Mexican immigrants and Mexican Americans contended with what Natalia Molina has called "medicalized nativism" (Molina 2006, 58). Motivated by emerging questions of public health, which were steeped in racialized presumptions about contagious diseases that were believed to inhabit the bodies and cultures of arriving migrants,[12] medical detention and quarantine were instituted along the U.S.-Mexican border from 1917 until the onset of World War II (Stern 2005, 65). Medical detentions occurred at a time when there was no military threat with which to rationalize the scapegoating or detention of Latino migrants. While an entire discourse of contagion specifically targeted at Asian immigrants emerged on the West Coast (Shah 2001), for Mexicans—who were exempt from racial exclusion laws and later the racist national quota system—medical rationales were even more critical to the restriction of Mexican immigration, as the quarantine and medical detention of border-crossers "became the status quo on the border" (Stern 2005, 70), lasting nearly twenty years.

Detention, Repatriation, and Operation Wetback

During the same period as the border quarantine, concerns over Mexican criminality as well as economic competition in the 1930s Depression era led to a nationwide repatriation campaign that effected the removal and voluntary departure of a conservative estimate of one-half million Mexicans and their children, many of them citizens, in what Francisco E. Balderrama and Raymond Rodríguez called "the first major contingent of displaced refugees in the twentieth century" (2006, 329). Mexican "illegality," which was established with the criminalization of undocumented entry in 1929 (Nevins 2002, 54), has dominated public anxieties for three-quarters of a century. Statutory notions of "illegality" are sustained by popular conceptions of criminality, as both the popular and the statutory constructions of "illegality" shape each other. According to Steven Bender (2003, 1), who traces Latino criminalization to the nineteenth-century construction of the Mexican "greaser," "for Latinas/os and certain other groups, stereotypes actually drive their distressing legal and societal treatment."

In the 1950s, concerns about Mexican immigrant criminality would again lead to record-setting detentions and deportations.[13] On June 9, 1954, the INS initiated what was officially termed Operation Wetback, a nationwide deportation campaign to round up, detain, and deport Mexican nationals. The operation led to the highest number of persons ever held in detention by the INS in a single year, at over one-half million (Swing 1954, 31, 36). Although Operation Wetback resulted in outrage from Mexican American communities and organizations regarding harassment of citizens, the breakup of families, and widespread fear of law enforcement, the INS hailed Operation Wetback a huge success. "For the first time in more than ten years, illegal crossing over the Mexican border was brought under control" after "the backbone of the wetback invasion was broken," proclaimed the INS commissioner (Swing 1955, 10, 14, 17).

Refugee Detentions

In the 1980s, the detention of Latino refugees was a distinguishing feature of the decade, set in motion in 1980, when 125,000 Cuban *marielitos* fled Cuba departing through the port of Mariel. In addition, roughly one million Salvadoran, Guatemalan, and Nicaraguan refugees entered the United States during the decade, fleeing political upheaval and violence that was maintained by U.S. cold war policies and extralegal actions in Central America. The exodus from the Caribbean and Central America fueled a racial panic about refugee streams that were feared to be black and Latino, criminal, ideologically Left, and diseased. Fearing a criminal class of Cuban immigrants among the mostly young and male refugees, the United States broke with its former policy of proactive acceptance as several thousand Cubans were detained *en masse* in the early 1980s, leading to severe overcrowding and riots at detention centers in Georgia and Louisiana (Hamm 1995; Welch 2002, 95–97; Bahadur 2004).

Refugees from Central America further clogged detention centers during the decade, especially after the attorney general ordered, in 1981, that all undocumented refugees be detained until the final adjudication of their asylum cases (Kahn 1996, 16). According to historian María Cristina García (2006, 91), "Detention centers along the United States-Mexico border filled to capacity with people the Border Patrol called the OTMs (other than Mexicans)."[14] As a result, the Port Isabel immigration prison in South Texas expanded, through tent construction, its bed capacity from 425 to 10,000 (Kahn 1996, 13). In addition, there was also an expansion of contracted facilities all along the U.S.-Mexico border and a reopening of a federal facility once used to detain Japanese Americans (Kahn 1996, 20). Encumbered with pervasive allegations of human rights abuses—from denial of legal counsel and translated legal material to invasion of private correspondence and sexual abuse—the newly expanded detention infrastructure facilitated cold war foreign policy objectives, defined differently for various countries of origin. While the asylum applications of Salvadorans and Guatemalans fleeing U.S.-backed administrations were rejected 97 to 99 percent of the time, Nicaraguans fleeing a socialist government that the United States opposed were granted either asylum, at rates as high as 84 percent in 1987, or a suspended deportation, leading to a release from detention (Kahn 1996, 21).

Criminal Aliens

While refugees were being detained at ports of entry in the 1980s, domestic criminalization and detention policy initiatives during the "war on drugs" shifted the enforcement focus inside the nation to "criminal aliens." Detained for having been convicted of deportable offenses, "criminal aliens" represent the largest share of all immigrant detainees today. Any noncitizen, whether undocumented or a lawful permanent resident, can be detained as a "criminal alien" and placed into deportation proceedings. Constituting what border expert Timothy Dunn called a "historic change in INS detention practices" (1996, 73), the increased detention of "criminal aliens" resulted from increased policing, the reclassification and expansion of deportable crimes such as drug or gun trafficking, mandatory drug sentencing, and reduction of avenues for relief from detention. According to the Congressional Research Service, by 2002, of the 202,000 immigrants detained, over 51 percent had criminal records (Siskin 2004, 12).

As legal status generated inequality in criminal law in the 1980s and 1990s, the largest group of immigrants, Mexican nationals, suffered disproportionately from "criminal alien" enforcement. Like African Americans, Mexican and Mexican American communities were already targeted for criminal enforcement of drug crimes—contributing to the massive prison expansion—taking place nationwide. Such criminal enforcement has a direct effect on increases in detention, as noncitizens convicted of deportable crimes are placed in detention and deportation proceedings at the completion of their criminal sentences. Noting that Hispanic incarceration rates have risen 43 percent since 1990, Marc Mauer and Ryan King state, "While the disproportionate rate of incarceration for African Americans has been well documented for some time, a significant development in the past decade has been the growing proportion of the Hispanic population entering prisons and jails" (2007, 1–2). As they were in the 1950s, Mexican nationals are again the largest number of detainees held each year, representing 50 percent of persons in detention, or 101,000, in 2002 (Siskin 2007, 12).

A forerunner to the detentions stemming from the "war on terror," this pre-9/11 episode in detention growth in the 1990s transpired by means of a combination of new legislation that targeted immigrants by reducing their due procedural rights and the reintroduction and codification of "national security" in the wake of foreign and domestic terrorism in the mid-1990s. Two laws were passed in 1996 in the wake of the 1995 Oklahoma City bombing that dramatically increased noncitizens' vulnerability to detention and deportation. The *Antiterrorism and Effective Death Penalty Act* (AEDPA), enacted in 1996 near the one-year anniversary of the Oklahoma City bombing, was drafted as antiterrorism legislation but instead had its greatest impact on noncitizen criminal offenders, making them easier to deport and mandating their detention pursuant to their deportation. Five months later, Congress passed the *Illegal Immigration Reform and Immigrant Responsibility Act* (IIRIRA), elaborately facilitating "criminal alien" detention through a sweeping denial of due process to noncitizens. According to Taylor, "IIRIRA amended some of AEDPA's most controversial immigration provisions, but overall made things worse for non-citizen criminal offenders" (2005, 353). By reinforcing "mandatory detentions" for immigrants facing deportation, removing avenues for judicial relief, and expanding the category of "aggravated felony," which triggers mandatory detention and deportation proceedings, IIRIRA is responsible for the tripling of immigrant detention in the 1990s.

The episodic development of Latino immigrant detention discussed above reflects different constructions of national security in a variety of social, political, and historical contexts. Discourses of national security in these eras cross-fertilize with anti-immigrant sentiment and the legal and social inequalities of noncitizens and result in the expansion of immigrant detention during periods of national crisis. National security is threatened, so it is argued, by the very presence of immigrants. From fears of disease and particular ideologies from abroad, to concern about refugees streams, and to the constant fear of criminal activity among immigrants, detention has served as an operational nexus for these fears and the construction of Latinos as criminals and undesirables. As Jonathan Inda has argued, "a variety of immigration 'experts'—social scientists, INS/DHS bureaucrats, policy analysts, immigration reform organizations, and the popular press—have constructed 'illegal' immigrants—typically imagined as Mexican—as anti-citizens incapable of exercising responsible self-government and thus as threats to the overall well-being of the social body" (2006, 63–64). Latino immigrants—with diminished legal rights as noncitizens and limited social benefits as racialized subjects—have borne the lasting burden of expanding detention policies that have articulated the boundaries of Latino citizenship over the last one hundred years.

Contesting Immigrant Detention

This essay has addressed the history of Latino detention from the institutional level, examining the state's constructions of Latino noncitizenship, national crises, and punishment in creating a system for detaining immigrants. My hope is that the analysis of the racial structures of immigrant detention moves us toward a closer examination of detention conditions and detainee experiences not explicitly addressed in this essay. The historical persistence of Latino immigrant detention, flowing from the categorical racialization and criminalization of immigrants, the lesser legal status of Latino noncitizens, and the official construction of detention as a legally "nonpunitive" exercise, sustains the inferior conditions of incarceration suffered by detainees.

Immigration law—in particular, the detention authority—is regularly utilized to address national crises because it is anomalous to normative forms of governmental checks and balances and because immigrants are not provided the constitutional safeguards of criminal law when they face deportation proceedings. And historically, when immigration law and the international laws of war and human rights present procedural obstacles to government enforcement initiatives utilized by detainees and their lawyers, the United States repeatedly pushes detention into ambiguous and indeterminate legal territories in order to confound and prevent oversight or obstruction of its detention goals.

One must remember that the post-9/11 detention of so-called enemy combatants at Guantánamo Bay Naval Base in Cuba was preceded by the detention, at the same site, of Cuban and Haitian refugees and asylum-seekers interdicted at sea precisely because territorial and legal ambiguities created enforcement policy advantages for the government. According to Scott L. Silliman, executive director of the Center on Law, Ethics and National Security at Duke University, "If you move them to the United States there's no question these people [off-shore detainees] will have more legal rights" (Cooper and Glaberson 2007). Detention practices during the "war on terror"—secrecy, discretionary actions of the executive branch, denials of legal safeguards, and invented legal categories—are thus central to the maintenance of "undue process" in detention and have been factors in detention practices since the inception of the Bureau of Immigration in 1891.

It is critical to mention that against the large bureaucratic detention system in the United States, there are three broad levels of opposition and detainee advocacy: juridical, community-based, and the resistance of the detainees themselves. Since noncitizens are denied particular rights, such as the right to vote, to hold certain jobs, and a variety of social benefits, it is imperative that they be protected by the Constitution to which they are held responsible. Especially for individuals in detention, lawyers, community organizations, and fellow detainees oftentimes provide the only avenues of support and advocacy in a very isolating and dismal situation. Although incarcerated and vulnerable to the variety of "undue processes" available to the state, immigrant detainees have historically contested their detention using the most basic means for protection and have done so to bring public awareness to the conditions of detention. In the 1980s, for example, major riots at detention centers took place in Louisiana and Georgia as a result of the indefinite state of detention of Cuban migrants. The strategic prison sieges, which lasted nearly two weeks, were in opposition to the deprivation of due procedural rights for Cuban detainees, and the ensuing negotiations resulted in each detainee receiving a "full, fair, and equitable review." According to Mark Hamm, as a result of the riots, "the detainees were guaranteed more rights in the United States than at any other time since their arrival on the 1980 boatlift" (1995, 176). Violent prison takeovers by detainees, which, in this case, included hostages, are a sign of the desperation of some detainees, especially under adverse conditions of confinement and in the absence of due process.

Community-based protests as a mode of resistance to Latino-detention practices have also occurred throughout the century. Provoked by their concern and fear for immigrants and detainees, community-based organizations have organized a variety of protests in their support, especially those directly saddled with the federal government's antiterrorist strategies and the general public's hysteria and willingness to act against noncitizens in times of national crisis. Prior to the grassroots-driven marches and demonstrations in the spring and summer of 2006—when, nationwide, hundreds of thousands took to the streets on multiple occasions in opposition to punitive immigration legislation—families, communities, and churches created active protest networks and succeeded in directly aiding detainees, maintaining ongoing protests outside of federal and contracted detention centers and keeping immigrant detention in the public eye.

In one such effort, New Jersey detention activists maintained persistent pressure and presence at the Passaic County Jail over a period of ten years, resulting in the dissolution of the jail's federal contract to detain immigrants, in what the New Jersey Civil Rights Defense Committee called "a significant victory for citizen and detainee activists and their supporters" (2006). The sanctuary movement in support of Central American asylum-seekers and detainees in the 1980s also served as what some have called a twentieth-century "underground railroad" and what historian María Cristina García refers to as "one of the most important acts of civil disobedience of the late twentieth century" (2006, 98). Recalling the outset of the medical detentions in the early twentieth century and the border quarantine discussed previously, "excited [Mexican] women" border-crossers, in a 1917 protest, "inveighed against all Americans" in a demonstration on the international bridge between Ciudad Juárez and El Paso. According to the *New York Times*, the women rioted, blocked traffic for several hours, and shouted "Viva Villa!" because they "resented the American quarantine order that all persons of unclean appearance seeking to cross the bridge must take a shower bath and have clothing disinfected" (*New York Times* 1917, 4; *Los Angeles Times* 1917, 11). In addition to the individual struggles of detainees in the form of hunger strikes, sit-ins, and Internet blogs, these collective efforts, and other acts of resistance to the conditions of their confinement, create the risk of retaliation by guards and wardens within detention centers. Moreover, they often transpire as great risks to family members outside the detention center or in the detainees' respective home countries.

In addition to concentrated support for detainees and their families from the existing infrastructure of nonprofit immigrant agencies, community-based organizations, and fellow detainees, one of the most complicated, yet productive, forms of resistance to state detention practices comes from lawyers and legal advocates. Nonprofit organizations, law school legal clinics, individual lawyers working pro bono, and federal public defenders working for all classes of detainees—"criminal aliens," asylum seekers, unaccompanied children in detention, and 9/11 detainees—have taken their clients' cases all the way to Supreme Court, providing a vigorous and public critique of noncitizen detention. In one crucial case, *American Baptist Churches v. Thornburgh* (1991), a coalition of churches and refugee-service organizations reached an out-of-court settlement with the government that overturned over 100,000 politically biased judicial decisions—"more judicial decisions than any other case in U.S. history"—granting Salvadoran and Guatemalan asylum-seekers who had been denied asylum new hearings under more positive conditions (Kahn 1996, 22–23; Coutin 2000, 17). Before and after 9/11, organizations like the ACLU, the Center for Constitutional Rights, or faith-based legal services like Catholic Legal Immigration Network, Inc., have argued individual cases, filed countless *Freedom of Information Act* requests, and have sued the government on behalf of immigrant detainees. Legal counsel is invaluable because, for criminal alien detainees, their incarceration does not result in a robust due process but a diminished set of rights. Even in the most remote of detention centers, at Guantánamo Bay Naval Base, lawyers have managed to argue on behalf of detainees in cases where "some of the detainees don't even know they have attorneys" (Lewis 2005). According to Michael Ratner of the Center for Constitutional Rights, at the outset of the "war on terror," "the only lawyers willing to help were anti-death-penalty lawyers who were used to representing unpopular clients" (Ratner and Ray 2004, xvi). This has slowly changed, and the *New York Times* (Lewis 2005) reported that increasing numbers of lawyers are traveling to Cuba to represent the most ostracized of detainees—"suspected terrorists."

These efforts at resistance to the detention process are filled with challenges. Complicated changes in the legal structure, emerging law enforcement initiatives, and myriad forms of "undue process" all hamper detention activism. One dynamic, which saddled the immigrants' rights movement in the 1990s and divided Latino community activists, was a form of divide and conquer in which some immigrants' rights groups—in an effort to narrow their political losses—sacrificed the defense of the rights of undocumented migrants in exchange for more support for "legal" migrants. Such efforts, which create a "good-versus-bad" dichotomy of immigrants, have been replicated in the defense of immigrant detainees as well. The most common binary situates the majority-Latino category of "criminal aliens," who have been convicted of crimes prior to their detention, against more "innocent" detainees, often refugees and asylum-seekers fleeing persecution. According to Heba Nimr, a Soros Justice Fellow at INS Watch, "Even immigrant rights advocates were less willing to advocate for more reasoned policies regarding noncitizens with criminal records, because that might jeopardize the tenuous rights of 'innocent' noncitizens" (Nguyen 2002, 6). Such dichotomies are misleading because not only are "good" and "bad" detainees often from the same communities, if not the same families, but the undue processes that harm them usually harm all immigrants.

Contextualizing Latino Detention

As briefly articulated at the outset of this essay, it has been useful to disaggregate Latino immigrant detainees from the sensational and extraordinary post-9/11 detention period in order to shed light on the pervasive history of Latinos in detention as well as the key role of immigrant detention in the criminalization, immobilization, and racial expulsion of noncitizens from the United States. These histories are part of a broad and complex set of racist experiences that Latinos have endured at all stages of the processes of immigration and settlement, ranging from policies and practices at the federal, local, and popular levels that impinge on Latinos' civil rights, cultural practices, and economic advancement. This strategic move notwithstanding, I want to suggest that it is critical to understand Latino detention in a comparative racial frame. The detention of noncitizens in the United States, as it has developed over the last one hundred years, has entrapped a variety of racialized groups in very different political and social contexts. This is because the convergence of national security, race, and noncitizenship is an episodic occurrence in U.S. history, and a comparative racial analysis better reveals the systemic arrangements and institutionalized racism in detention policy.

In addressing Latino immigrant detention in this essay, it has been difficult to speak only of Latinos. With a heterogeneous background, Latinos in and of themselves already have a complex and vexed history of incorporation to the United States: as former colonial subjects, as refugees, as victims of direct military conquest, or as persons displaced by U.S. global economic power. Correspondingly, and as I hope this essay has shown, Latinos have inhabited nearly every category of detainee across an entire century, including medical detainees at the border prior to World War II, persons entrapped in large-scale deportation campaigns in the 1930s and 1950s, refugees and criminal aliens detained because of the cold war and "war on drugs," and lastly, as a result of the contemporary enforcement of the "war on terror," we should also include so-named "enemy combatant" José Padilla. As the prominence and complexity of Latino experiences with detention demonstrate, the detention of immigrants can affect all noncitizens and their families and communities, in particular, historically racialized groups.

Immigrant detention thus underscores the structural inequality of all noncitizens in the United States, and, therefore, it is vital that we come to know Latino detainees alongside similarly positioned persons. Critical episodes of immigrant detention also include Chinese and Chinese Americans detained for biological and eugenic reasoning; Japanese and Japanese American citizen detainees during World War II; immigrant laborers occupying the margins of whiteness, detained during the early twentieth-century Red Scare and the cold war; Haitian detainees since the 1970s; and, most recently, 9/11 detainees. These racialized episodes of immigrant detention are related directly and indirectly to contemporary Latino detention because they have created legal prerequisites, diminished legal avenues for relief, and generated the construction and escalation of the detention infrastructure. While this essay centers on the detention of Latino immigrants, the larger scale of its impact occurs beyond detainees and their families and extends to the creation of severe legal inequalities for all noncitizens. As the largest of this group today, Latino immigrants and their families and communities are extremely vulnerable to the hardships created by this process. Unless challenged, Latinos will suffer disproportionately from the government's domestic "war on terror."

The trends of escalating detentions and deportations—in particular, the expansion of the detention infrastructure established with the dramatic changes in immigration and detention law in 1996—have continued into this new century. In the years following 9/11, national security anxieties continue to occupy the popular imagination and serve to generate political energy for politicians invoking the security threat presented by immigration. According to Heather MacDonald, a fellow at the conservative Manhattan Institute, 9/11 was a "freebie" for persons whose real agenda is to halt undocumented immigration. "Talking about security makes it easier to talk about immigration without being called a racist," says MacDonald (Corcoran 2006). Merging traditional arguments for and against immigration, with fears of international terrorism, politicians from both sides of the aisle have reframed the immigration debate, suggesting that immigrants are the cause of the nation's security vulnerabilities. Candidates in both the Republican and Democratic parties have campaigned on the professed links between terrorism, security, and undocumented workers, reinforcing these connections in campaign advertisements and signaling the merger of discourses of immigration control with national security and terrorism (Corcoran 2006).

In today's context of an ever-expanding "war on terror," the provision of "homeland" security substantiates a vast, secretive, and racially driven security state, domestically and internationally. Thus, while terrorism prosecutions have dropped (Eggen 2006; Lichtblau 2006), older methods of enforcement, such as immigrant detention, have intensified as the array of issues surrounding detention, asylum, undocumented immigration, and border security are couched in their so-called threat to national security. According to Border Patrol Chief David V. Aguilar, "the nexus between our post-Sept. 11 mission and our traditional role is clear. . . . Terrorists and violent criminals may exploit smuggling routes used by immigrants to enter the United States illegally and do us harm" (Archibold 2006, 26). This restructuring of immigration control policies and the current and heated struggles over "enforcement-only" legislation testify to the ascendancy of this terror context. As legislative mandates continue to limit the judicial protections and sources of relief for detainees—as well as immigration judges' ability to grant such relief or maintain legal safeguards—the trend in detention policy is to advance a variety of "undue processes" against noncitizens and detainees by depriving them of their due procedural rights, both statutorily and through administrative minutiae.[15]

Latino migrants and U.S.-born Latinos—demographically the largest of all migrant groups and U.S. minority populations—will bear the burden of the increased capacity of the United States to surveil, control, and detain noncitizens and persons perceived to be immigrants. According to Kevin Johnson, "Ultimately, persons of Mexican ancestry—citizens and noncitizens—will be disparately affected by the legal changes triggered by September 11" (2003, 852). Popular sentiment supports this trend, the political currency it generates for politicians and pundits makes it possible, and history has provided the legal precedents and historical trajectory to execute this punitive tendency. As the huge increases in federal funding and private investment that will triple detention capacity by the end of the decade make obvious, the federal government has unbridled its enforcement initiatives in the wake of 9/11, collaborating with local and international governments and the domestic criminal justice system and formulating highly problematic information-sharing networks. These efforts at protecting the "homeland" through scapegoating, burdening, and reducing the rights of immigrants have distorted the meaning of national security, producing long-term challenges and adverse human consequences for a vital and permanent segment of our society.

Notes

1. From this point forward, I will use 9/11 to refer to the terrorist attacks on the United States on September 11, 2001.
2. For a critical discussion of how the spectacle of torture at Abu-Ghraib obscures "the naturalized landscape" and "unspectacular" punishment of persons in U.S. prisons, see Rodríguez (2006, 9–32).
3. For a legal and popular culture analysis of Latino criminal stereotypes, refer to Steven W. Bender (2003).
4. *United States v. Brignoni-Ponce*, 422 U.S. 873 (1975). The Court found that the "reasonable suspicion" requirement is not met "when the *only* ground for suspicion is that the occupants appear to be of Mexican ancestry" (emphasis added).
5. Citing the waste of resources in duplicating the task of trying, convicting, and detaining noncitizens who committed deportable crimes that are subject to two different court systems, Taylor and Wright have suggested empowering the sentencing judge in the criminal trial with the authority of an immigration judge as well in order to "yield less duplication of resources, quicker deportation, and—notably—lower detention costs" (2002, 3)
6. In its January 25, 2007, report, "Immigration-Related Detention: Current Legislative Issues," the Congressional Research Service reported 20,000 detainees in fiscal year 2005, whereas detainee advocate organization Detention Watch Network reports over 27,000 detainees daily in 2007. See http://detentionwatchnetwork.org/dwnmap (accessed August 2, 2007). The *Los Angeles Times* reported that daily detainees surpassed 30,000 nationally (Gorman 2007).
7. The most notorious example of the detention of citizens is that of Japanese Americans incarcerated during World War II. In addition, among immigrant detainees today are persons who do not know they possess U.S. citizenship (usually because their parents naturalized when they were minors, thus naturalizing the noncitizen children as well). Such persons carry the burden of proving this fact to the government. Lastly, U.S. citizen children of detainees are often taken into custody during the apprehension of their parents.
8. On March 1, 2003, the functions of several border and security agencies, including the U.S. Customs Service and the Immigration and Naturalization Service (INS), were transferred to the U.S. Department of Homeland Security (DHS). After years of pressure and anticipation, the INS was "split" into three agencies: the Bureau of Immigration and Customs Enforcement (ICE), the Bureau of Customs and Immigration Services (CIS), and the Bureau of Customs and Border Protection (CBP).
9. The detainee was held at both an ICE detention center and a private detention facility in San Diego. This particular for-profit detention center is at the center of multiple

lawsuits and allegations of rape of women and men by unsupervised private correction officers (Berestein 2005).

10. An escalating problem has been the increased detention of unaccompanied minors who are captured at ports of entry or in the interior of the country. In 2005, 6,460 underage, undocumented migrants from Central America were detained, an increase of 35 percent from the previous year (Aizenman 2006).

11. It is estimated that there are over eleven million undocumented residing in the United States, with 500,000 arriving annually (Siskin et al. 2006, 1). The DHS reports that Mexicans represent the largest portion of undocumented at over six million, or 57 percent, with the next largest groups arriving from El Salvador and Guatemala. These nations account for 65 percent of all undocumented, while South American migrants account for an additional 8 percent. Asia accounts for 12 percent of undocumented immigration (Hoefer, Rytina, and Campbell 2006, 1).

12. The large majority of detainees are criminal aliens who are undergoing removal proceedings (Siskin et al. 2006, 20).

13. Charles M. Goethe wrote in the pages of the American Eugenics Society's journal, *Eugenics*, in 1929, "Eugenically, as low-powered as the Negro, the [Mexican] peon is, from a sanitation standpoint, a menace. He not only does not understand health rules: being a superstitious savage, he resists them." See Charles M. Goethe, "The Influx of Mexican Amerinds," *Eugenics* 2, no. 1 (January 1929): 6–9, cited in Stern (2005, 68).

14. By 1954, Mexican deportations represented 84 percent of all deportation proceedings, and Mexican immigrants were the largest national group in ten of the thirteen deportation categories listed in the INS annual report. The remaining three categories were noncriminal reasons for deportation (Swing 1954, table 24).

15. In July 2007, a federal judge upheld a near-two-decades-old injunction to protect Salvadoran asylum-seekers because of ongoing widespread abuses in detention and barriers to due process. National Immigration Law Center, "Orantes Injunction Upheld: Judge Finds Widespread Abuses in Immigrant Detention," press release, July 31, 2007.

References

Aizenman, Nurith Celina. 2006. Young migrants risk all to reach U.S. *Washington Post*, August 28.

American Baptist Churches v. Thornburgh, 760 F. Supp. 796 (N.D. Cal. 1991).

American Corrections Association, Inc. 2006. Foreign inmates: Survey summary. *Corrections Compendium* 31 (2): 10–21.

Antiterrorism and Effective Death Penalty Act of 1996 (AEDPA). Public Law No. 104–32, 110 Stat. 1214, codified as amended at 28 U.S.C. § 2241.

Archibold, Randal C. 2006. Border patrol draws increased scrutiny as president proposes an expanded role. *New York Times*, June 4.

Ashcroft, John. 2001. Prepared remarks for the U.S. Mayors Conference (speech at the U.S. Mayors Conference, Washington, D.C.). October 25. http://www.usdoj.gov/archive/ag/speeches/2001/agcrisisremarks10_25.htm (accessed June 22, 2009).

Bahadur, Gaiutra. 2004. Boat-lift refugees fighting limbo. *Philadelphia Inquirer*, October 13.

Balderrama, Francisco E., and Raymond Rodríguez. 2006. *Decade of betrayal: Mexican repatriation in the 1930s*. Rev. ed. Albuquerque: University of New Mexico Press.

Bender, Steven W. 2002. Sight, sound, and stereotype: The war on terrorism and its consequences for Latinas/os. *Oregon Law Review* 81:1153–78.

————. 2003. *Greasers and gringos: Latinos, law, and the American imagination.* New York: New York University Press.

Berestein, Leslie. 2005. Woman in detention alleges rape. *San Diego Union-Tribune*, January 18. http://www.signonsandiego.com/news/metro/20050118-9999-1m18assault.html (accessed August 12, 2007).

Bernstein, Nina. 2007. New scrutiny as immigrants die in custody. *New York Times*, June 26.

Bush, George W. 2001. National address before representatives of firefighters, law enforcement officers, and postal workers (World Congress Center). September 11 News.com, President Bush – Atlanta. November 8. http://www.september11news.com/President-BushAtlanta.htm (accessed June 6, 2005).

Chin, Gabriel J. 2005. *Chae Chan Ping* and *Fong Yue Ting*: The origins of plenary power. In *Immigration stories*, ed. David A. Martin and Peter H. Schuck, 7–29. New York: Foundation Press.

Cole, David. 2002. *In aid of removal: Due process limits on immigration detention.* Research paper series in public law and legal theory, research paper #356980. Washington, D.C.: Georgetown University Law Center.

Cooper, Helen, and William Glaberson. 2007. At White House, renewed debate on Guantánamo. *New York Times*, June 23.

Corcoran, Katherine. 2006. Mexican immigrants caught in backlash of terror anxiety. *San Jose Mercury News*, September 10.

Coutin, Susan Bibler. 2000. *Legalizing moves: Salvadoran immigrants' struggle for U.S. residency.* Ann Arbor: University of Michigan Press.

De Genova, Nicholas. 2004. The legal production of Mexican/migrant "illegality." *Latino Studies* 2:160–85.

Dixon, David, and Julia Gelatt. 2005. *Immigration enforcement spending since IRCA.* Report no. 10, Washington, D.C.: Migration Policy Institute, November.

Dunn, Timothy J. 1996. *The militarization of the U.S.-Mexico border: Low intensity conflict doctrine comes home, 1978–1992.* Austin, TX: CMAS Books.

Eggen, Dan. 2006. Terrorism prosecutions drop. *Washington Post*, September 4.

Fears, Darryl. 2007. Illegal immigrants received poor care in jail, lawyers say. *Washington Post*, June 13.

Flores, Hector M. 2006. Statement by LULAC president Hector M. Flores: Senate immigration bill is a solid move in the right direction. Press release, June 1. http://www.lulac.org/advocacy/press/2006/immigrationbill3.html (accessed September 27, 2006).

Fong Yue Ting v. United States, 149 U.S. 698 (1893).

García, María Cristina. 2006. *Seeking refuge: Central American migration to Mexico, the United States, and Canada.* Berkeley: University of California Press.

Getter, Lisa. 2001. Freedom elusive for refugees fleeing to the U.S. *Los Angeles Times*, December 31.

Gilmore, Ruth Wilson. 1998/99. Globalisation and U.S. prison growth: From military Keynesianism to Post-Keynesian militarism. *Race & Class* 40 (2/3): 171–88.

Gordon, Avery F. 1998/99. Globalism and the prison industrial complex: An interview with Angela Davis. *Race & Class* 40 (2/3): 145–57.

Gorman, Anna. 2007. Rise in detainees straining system. *Los Angeles Times*, November 5. http://articles.latimes.com/2007/nov/05/local/me-immig5 (accessed June 22, 2009).

Hagan, John, and Alberto Palloni. 1999. Sociological criminology and the mythology of Hispanic immigration and crime. *Social Problems* 46 (4): 617–32.

Hamm, Mark S. 1995. *The abandoned ones: The imprisonment of the Mariel boat people.* Boston: Northeastern University Press.

Hernández, David Manuel. 2005. Undue process: Immigrant detention, due process, and lesser citizenship. PhD diss., University of California, Berkeley.

Hoefer, Michael, Nancy Rytina, and Christopher Campbell. 2006. *Estimates of the unauthorized immigrant population residing in the United States: January 2005.* Office of Immigration Statistics, Department of Homeland Security.

Illegal Immigration Reform and Immigrant Responsibility Act of 1996 (IIRIRA), Public Law No. 104-208, 110 Stat. 3009, codified at 8 U.S.C. § 1324.

Immigration and Nationality Act of 1952. INA § Section 236, codified at 8 U.S.C. §1226.

Inda, Jonathan Xavier. 2006. *Targeting immigrants: Government, technology, and ethics.* Malden, MA: Blackwell.

Intelligence Reform and Terrorist Prevention Act of 2004 (IRTPA). Public Law No. 108–458, 118 Stat. 3638.able at http://www.bergen.com/.

Johnson, Kevin R. 2003. September 11 and Mexican immigrants: Collateral damage comes home. *DePaul Law Review* 52:849–70.

Kahn, Robert S. 1996. *Other people's blood: U.S. immigration prisons in the Reagan decade.* Boulder, CO: Westview.

Lewis, Neil A. 2005. In rising numbers lawyers head for Guantánamo Bay. *New York Times,* May 30.

Lichtblau, Eric. 2006. Study finds sharp drop in the number of terrorism cases prosecuted. *New York Times,* September 4.

Los Angeles Times. 1917. "Viva villa" shouted in riots at Juarez. January 29.

Llorente, Elizabeth. 2005. Reform plan will escalate detention of immigrants. *The Bergen Record,* Bergen, NJ, January 18.

Mariscal, Jorge. 2005. Homeland security, militarism, and the future of Latinos and Latinas in the United States. *Radical History Review* 93 (Fall): 39–52.

Martínez, Ramiro, Jr., and Abel Valenzuela, Jr., eds. 2006. *Immigration and crime: Race, ethnicity, and violence.* New York: New York University Press.

Mauer, Marc, and Ryan S. King. 2007. Uneven justice: State rates of incarceration by race and ethnicity. Washington, D.C.: The Sentencing Project.

Miller, Teresa A. 2002. The impact of mass incarceration on immigration policy. In *Invisible punishment: The collateral consequences of mass imprisonment,* ed. Marc Mauer and Meda Chesney-Lind, 214–38. New York: New Press.

Molina, Natalia. 2006. *Fit to be citizens? Public health and race in Los Angeles, 1879–1939.* Berkeley: University of California Press.

National Council of La Raza. 2006. NCLR Commends Senate for Historic Immigration Vote. News release, May 25.

Nevins, Joseph. 2002. *Operation gatekeeper: The rise of the "illegal alien" and the making of the U.S.-Mexico boundary.* New York: Routledge.

New Jersey Civil Rights Defense Committee. 2006. Press release. January 2.

New York Times. 1917. Quarantine riot in Juarez. January 29.

Nguyen, Tram. 2002. Detained or disappeared? *ColorLines.* Summer.

Office of Inspector General. 2006. Detention and removal of illegal aliens. Department of Homeland Security.

———. 2007. ICE's compliance with detention limits for aliens with a final order of removal from the United States. Department of Homeland Security.

Patel, Sunita, and Tom Jawetz. 2007. Conditions of confinement in immigration detention facilities. Briefing paper. http://www.aclu.org/pdfs/prison/unsr_briefing_materials.pdf (accessed August 11, 2007).

Pew Hispanic Center. 2005. *Hispanics: A people in motion.* Washington, D.C.: Pew Hispanic Center.

Preston, William, Jr. 1994. *Aliens and dissenters: Federal suppression of radicals, 1903–1933.* 2nd ed. Chicago: University of Illinois Press.

Ratner, Michael, and Ellen Ray. 2004. *Guantánamo: What the world should know.* White River Junction, VT: Chelsea Green.

Rodríguez, Dylan. 2006. (Non)scenes of captivity: The common sense of punishment and death. *Radical History Review* 96 (Fall): 9–32.

Rosaldo, Renato. 1999. Cultural citizenship, inequality, and multiculturalism. In *Race, identity, and citizenship: A reader,* ed. Rodolfo D. Torres, Louis F. Miron, and Jonathan Xavier Inda, 253–61. Malden, MA: Blackwell.

Rumbaut, Rubén G., and Walter Ewing. 2007. The myth of immigrant criminality and the paradox of assimilation: Incarceration rates among native and foreign-born men. Washington, D.C.: Immigration Policy Center.

Schuck, Peter H. 1998. *Citizens, strangers, and in-betweens: Essays on immigration and citizenship.* Boulder, CO: Westview.

Serrano, Richard A. 2002. Arrests on border fall after 9/11. *Los Angeles Times,* March 2.

Shah, Nayan. 2001. *Contagious divides: Epidemics and race in San Francisco's Chinatown.* Berkeley: University of California Press.

Siskin, Alison. 2004. *Immigration-related detention: Current legislative issues.* CRS Report for Congress, Congressional Research Service.

———. 2007. *Immigration-related detention: Current legislative issues.* CRS Report for Congress, Congressional Research Service, January 25.

Siskin, Alison, Andorra Bruno, Blas Nunez-Neto, Lisa M. Seghetti, and Ruth Ellen Wassem. 2006. *Immigration enforcement within the United States.* CRS Report for Congress. Congressional Research Service, April.

Solomon, Alisa. 1999. A dream detained: Why immigrants have become America's fastest-growing jail population. *Village Voice,* March 24–30.

Stern, Alexandra Minna. 2005. *Eugenic nation: Faults and frontiers of better breeding in modern America.* Berkeley: University of California Press.

Stumpf, Juliet. 2006. The crimmigration crisis: Immigrants, crime, and sovereign power. *American University Law Review* 56:367–419.

Swing, Joseph M. 1954. *Annual report of the immigration and naturalization service.* Washington, D.C.: Government Printing Office.

———. 1955. *Annual report of the immigration and naturalization service.* Washington, D.C.: Government Printing Office.

Tangeman, Anthony S. 2002. Immigration detention: The fastest growing incarceration system in the United States. In *In defense of the alien: Proceedings of the 2001 Annual National Legal Conference on Immigration and Refugee Policy,* ed. Lydio Tomasi, 25–30. New York: Center for Migration Studies.

———. 2003. Memorandum for Deputy Assistant Director, Field Operations Division and Field Office Directors: Office of Detention and Removal (DRO) Strategic Plan 2003–2012: Endgame. Office of Detention and Removal, June 27.

Taylor, Margaret H. 2005. *Denmore v. Kim:* Judicial deference to congressional folly. In *Immigration stories,* ed. David A. Martin and Peter H. Schuck, 344–76. New York: Foundation Press.

Taylor, Margaret H., and Ronald F. Wright. 2002. The sentencing judge as immigration judge. Research Paper No. 02-15, Public Law and Legal Theory Research Paper Series, Wake Forest University School of Law.

Transactional Records Access Clearinghouse. 2006. Report: Immigration judges. Syracuse, NY: Syracuse University.

U.S. Government Accountability Office. 1992. Immigration control: Immigration policies affect INS detention efforts. Report to the chairman, Subcommittee on International Law, Immigration, and Refugees, Committee on Judiciary, House of Representatives. Government Accountability Office, June.

————. 2007. Alien detention standards: Telephone access problems were pervasive at detention facilities; Other deficiencies did not show a pattern of noncompliance. GAO-07-875, Government Accountability Office, July.

U.S. Immigration and Customs Enforcement. 2004. Fact sheet: ICE Office of Detention and Removal. May 4.

————. 2006. Public information: Immigration detention facilities. U.S. Immigration and Customs Enforcement, Immigration Detention Facilities. http://www.ice.gov/pi/dro/facilities.htm (accessed September 18, 2006).

United States v. Brignoni-Ponce, 422 U.S. 873 (1975).

Welch, Michael. 2002. *Detained: Immigration laws and the expanding I.N.S. jail complex.* Philadelphia: Temple University Press.

Wong Wing v. United States, 163 U.S. 228 (1896).

3

"Nuestras vidas corren casi paralelas"

Chicanos, *Independentistas,* and the Prison Rebellions in Leavenworth, 1969–72[1]

Alan Eladio Gómez

El mismo enemigo ha querido mutilar, y si posible, hacer desaparecer nuestras culturas, tan parecidas una a la otra, y sin embargo, tanto el Chicano como el Boricua hemos podido salvar nuestra idenitidad cultural, nuestra personalidad . . . [The same enemy has sought to mutilate, and if possible annihilate our cultures, so similar to each other, and nonetheless, both the Chicano and the Boricua have been able to preserve our cultural identity, our personality . . .]

> —Rafael Cancel Miranda, Puerto Rican *Independentista* and former POW

So we emersed ourselves in the Puerto Rican history and united our struggles . . . [,] you know, joined our struggles as one. And so through that connection and the Black Muslims that were coming in, and the Republic of New Africa, and the Black Liberation Army People, we began to talk.[2]

> —raúlrsalinas, Marion Brother (1972), poet and human rights activist

On September 16, 1971—Mexican Independence Day—Chicano, Puerto Rican, black, American Indian, and white prisoners fashioned black armbands and declared a strike in the prison factories at Leavenworth Federal Penitentiary. Their action was in protest of the murder of George Jackson, the revolutionary prison intellectual and field marshall in the Black Panther Party who was shot in the back on August 21 at Soledad State Prison in California. Their action was also in active solidarity with the rebellion at Attica Correctional Facility in New York, which had come to a violent end three days prior when ten guards and twenty-nine inmates

This essay is dedicated to raúlrsalinas. Free all political prisoners!

were killed at the hands of state police who were authorized by Governor Nelson Rockefeller to shoot. Yet the numerous protests across the United States sparked by these incidents were not simply a spontaneous response; many were led by multiracial and multiethnic cadres of inmates—both women and men—who had *already been organizing* against the prison machine (Jackson 1971, 1996; Badillo and Haynes 1972; Wicker 1975; James 2003, 2007; Mendoza 2006).[3]

The Leavenworth strike was organized by Chicanos Organizados Rebeldes de Aztlán (C.O.R.A), a political formation of "*all* 'Latinos' in the Western Hemisphere (in general) and the 'Chicano' inhabitants and civilizers of the Northern Land of Aztlán (specifically)" (C.O.R.A. bylaws 1972; my emphasis).[4] Latinos incarcerated at Leavenworth created C.O.R.A. to work through political ideas that were inspiring prison rebellions across the country as well as social movements across the globe during the late 1960s and early 1970s. Although the members were primarily Chicanos and Mexicanos, C.O.R.A. included *Puertorriqueños,* specifically the Puerto Rican *Independentistas* fighters (Rafael Cancel Miranda, Oscar Collazo, Irving Flores, and Andres Figueroa Cordero). They worked closely with Black Muslims, American Indians, and working-class white inmates, some of whom had been politicized by their involvement in social movements prior to their incarceration or in state jails.

Prison rebellions increased dramatically from 1967 to 1972, skyrocketing from five to forty-eight (Useem and Kimball 1989). At Leavenworth alone there were five strikes during this period that shut down the for-profit brush, furniture, and clothes factories (Vigil 1999, 356).[5] The rebellions at Leavenworth were directed *against* the violent and racist brutality of guards, inadequate health care, arbitrary punishments and administrative transfers, and the disproportionate numbers of nonwhites behind bars. Prisoner organizing *created* the political culture of an organized social movement around a tradition of writ-writers or jailhouse lawyers and political education strategies that included cultural studies classes, art, poetry, and both clandestine and "sanctioned" newspapers that were the medium for critiques of the history of U.S. foreign policy and the role of the criminal justice system in U.S. society.

Grounded in experiences from before and during incarceration—and drawing on the diverse political histories and ideas that were inspiring people across the globe— prison activists organized to change the terms of their incarceration and developed an analysis and critique of the prison system as part of a national-international matrix of organized violence and white supremacy. "As a logic of social organization" (Rodriquez 2006b, 19), and in tandem with foreign military and economic policies, state technologies of racialized colonial violence included the police, courts, prosecutors, jury selection, guards, and the (in)carceral apparatuses of the state. Raúl Salinas, poet, activist, and editor of the Leavenworth prison newspaper *Aztlán,* described the conditions of incarceration for U.S. minorities as a "backyard form of colonialism."[6]

As activist-scholar Dylan Rodriquez (2006b, 19) writes, the repression against "U.S.-based Third World liberation movements during and beyond the 1960s and 1970s forged a peculiar intersection between official and illicit forms of state and state-sanctioned violence. Policing, carceral, and punitive technologies were invented, developed, and refined at scales from the local to the national, encompassing a wide variety of organizing and deployment strategies." Legal battles waged in the state and federal court systems by radical lawyers were buttressed by strikes, riots, petition demands, and the creation and transformation of educational spaces, as well as the support of family members and active citizens. Prison activists across the country deployed the political language of civil and human rights, developed an international political consciousness grounded in ideas of multiracial solidarities and human dignity, and explicitly linked their own struggles inside the "prisons of empire" to progressive and national liberation movements in the United States, the hemisphere, and across the globe (Davis 2004). On a national level, these combined movements questioned the legality and legitimacy of the prison system as part of the larger coercive apparatuses of "law and order" politics. Perhaps most significantly, these struggles were part of a longer history of self-defense against the violation of civil and human rights by police departments, racist jury systems, prison administrators, and guards, as well as by citizens defending white supremacy in the United States.

The rebellions were part of the larger circulation of progressive struggles in the post-World War II period. In the context of open repression against activists in the United States, particularly the Federal Bureau of Investigation's Counter Intelligence Programs (COINTELPRO) and cold war geopolitics in Latin America, Africa, and Asia, social movements in the United States expanded their international connections during the 1960s (Churchill and Vander Wall, 1999). Inspired by anti-colonial and national liberation efforts in Algeria, Cuba, and Vietnam, as well as American Indian struggles for the sovereignty of the "First Nations," many political and cultural organizations in the United States articulated a politics situated in what they defined as a shared experience of U.S. colonialism. By the late 1960s, as anti-Vietnam War demonstrations escalated and the passage of civil rights laws did not necessarily translate into a change in material conditions, the antiwar, women's, gay liberation, and black, brown, yellow, and red power movements overlapped at the local, national, and international levels. What I offer in looking behind prison walls is one element of a "history of histories" (Gosse 2005, 279) made up of global progressive "experimental civil rights" (Davis 2006, 131) and anti-colonial struggles (Ho 2000; Elbaum 2002; Oropeza 2005; Pulido 2006).

This article contributes to an emerging literature on what has come to be called the prison rebellion years, as well as the literature on Latino/a, Chicano/a, and Puerto Rican social movement history, comparative ethnic studies, political identity, and human rights. Emphasizing the relation to larger national and international social movements of the time, it narrates how interethnic (Alvarez 2007) and anticolonial political formations at Leavenworth were linked not only to the larger prisoners' rights and antiprison movement but also to global rebellions against the status quo. It specifically focuses on the political and personal relationships that developed between Chicanos and the Puerto Rican *Independentistas* who, through their organizing efforts, developed a self-identified "Latino" political identity—as political activists—that was also influenced by a class-based identity of people marginalized by capitalism.[7] The article is divided into three sections. The first section, "Frontier colonial violence and the prison rebellion years," situates these political efforts within literatures focusing on multiracial and transnational solidarities of the U.S. third world Left; the struggle for Puerto Rican independence from the United States; and twentieth-century struggles for justice against state violence, historically and disproportionately targeted against people of color. Section two, "From cultural nationalism to Anti-U.S. imperialism: The Chicano-*Independentista* connection," examines the political and cultural exchanges and influences between the Puerto Rican *Independentistas* and Chicano prison activists. Section three, "Pedagogies of dissent," emphasizes the emergence of a Latino politics, focusing specifically on three interrelated political projects: an ethnic studies course entitled "Cultural History of the Southwest"; the production of a politico-cultural newspaper, *Aztlán*; and the political organization C.O.R.A. that would play a central role in the political militancy of the times. The conclusion offers some thoughts on the current crisis of incarceration.

Methodologically, this research draws from published and unpublished letters and essays, prison newspapers, court records, poetry, and interviews (by the author and previously published), as well as secondary literatures. This article also negotiates a variety of restraints: I have not yet consulted the institutional archives on Leavenworth; therefore, with a few exceptions, the perspective of the state *as read through official documents* is secondary to this analysis. Instead, the character of the repressive state apparatus of the prison is reconstructed from the perspective of those in struggle and their political strategies to humanize the incarceration experience by understanding the functions of prisons in a democratic society. A subtle chronology paces the entire article, while the particular focus is on the years 1970 through 1972 at Leavenworth, with the remainder of the decade discussed subsequently in a generalized fashion. Although the number of people I am writing about is relatively small in comparison to the larger prison population incarcerated in Leavenworth at the time, these individuals mobilized the general discontent prevalent at the time into different levels of political involvement. This consideration will raise questions about the different levels of and responsibilities for political participation and the importance of *mass participation*—even if for brief moments of solidarity—as the larger goal of political movements. It also emphasizes the transformation—individual and collective—inherent in political education and shared experiences of organizing, creation, and violent repression. Finally, this article does not specifically focus on identity formation, but it is important to emphasize the intimate, contradictory, and reciprocal ways that political beliefs and alliances affect identity and how identity is formed through political engagement, personal change, and organized struggle (Perez 1999; Sandoval 2000; Lipsitz 2001; Haney López 2003; Alvarez 2007).

Frontier Colonial Violence and the Prison Rebellion Years

As an increasing number of political activists were imprisoned during the civil rights and global freedom struggles, prisons became an extension of these social movements, characterized by internal dynamics grounded not only in the shared experiences of police brutality, racist juries, and a violent incarceration regime *but also* in the prisoners' preincarceration experiences as ethnic or national minorities in the United States or as colonized subjects within the sphere of U.S. influence (Quijano 1998, 2000; Grosfoguel 2003; Grosfoguel, *Maldonado-Torres, and Saldivar* 2005). In order to frame the context and background of the Latino organizing at Leavenworth, it is necessary to briefly contextualize the history of Chicano and Puerto Rican history in relation to U.S. expansionism in the nineteenth and twentieth centuries. For Chicanos, African Americans, and American Indians, the violence of the prison was simply another episode in a long history of legal and extralegal injustices characterizing domestic and foreign policy during the nineteenth and twentieth centuries.

The history of state-sanctioned genocide against American Indians (the reservation system and the so-called Indian Schools, for example) and the antiblack violence in the South (chattel slavery, the convict-lease system, Jim Crow, and lynching) must be understood in relation to ideas of Western frontier justice, such as lynching and deportations, "Mexican" Jim Crow, the select application of vagrancy laws, and exploitative labor contractors. The slave-catchers and lynch mobs of the South have their equivalent in the West, forming a larger historical narrative of racialized and gendered violence against nonwhites (Paredes 1979; Montejano 1986; Castañeda 1993; Perez 1999; Saldivar-Hull 2000; Callahan 2003; Waldrep 2004; Gonzalez-Day 2007).

I propose a reading of the history of the Puerto Rican Independence movement in relation to domestic colonial subjectivity of Chicano/a history and the "backyard colonialism" of the prison (Blauner 1969; Almaguer 1971; Carmichael and Hamilton 1992). The racialized logic of colonial violence etched in the quasi-legal shorthand for Puerto Rico's status vis-à-vis the United States—"foreign in a domestic sense"—was related to territorial conquest and expansion across the West and the colonization of Mexican and indigenous populations. At the same time, it is important to keep in mind that following the post-1898 U.S. imperialist and expansionist territorial law and policy, Puerto Rico was never considered for actual colonization but was simply a juridical space for resource extraction (labor, raw materials, racialized "otherness"; Santiago 2006, 28).

Puerto Rico experienced a brief respite from colonial rule in 1897 during the transfer of power between Spain and the United States following Spain's defeat in the Spanish-American War. For a few months, Puerto Ricans had won some measure of autonomy until the United States invaded the island that same year and "cast its military and economic net over the whole of the Caribbean" (McPherson 2003, 14). Struggles for Puerto Rican independence during the twentieth century have taken a variety of forms, given that the "reorganization of the repressive apparatus [established during Spanish colonial times] was one of the earliest projects undertaken by the military regime established in Puerto Rico after the 1898 invasion" (Paralitici 2006, 76). Since 1898, "not a single decade has passed without the incarceration of some independence advocate, with the possible exception of the 1920s" (Bosque-Pérez 2006, 16). Organized resistance against the U.S. presence on the island in general and specifically against compulsory English in the public schools and compulsory military service was common during the first two decades of the twentieth century. By the 1930s, the Nationalist Party (established in 1922) had been founded, and it was during this decade that, marked by the Ponce Massacre on March 21, 1937, "the human rights of the citizenry were trampled on with the most impunity than in all the history of Puerto Rico" (Bosque-Pérez 2006, 16). Since then, the persecution and imprisonment of its members and other pro-independence groups would continue unabated until the present.

Repression by domestic Jim Crow police and court apparatuses at mid-century against people of color paralleled the repression— in Puerto Rico and in the United States—against the Puerto Rican independence movement. The history of police and sheriff's departments, court officials, correctional and parole systems, and ordinary citizens terrorizing African Americans, Mexican Americans, Asian Americans (Chinese and Japanese), and American Indians across the country during the twentieth century is well known; what remains to be uncovered are the creative histories of defense and resistance (Tyson 1999; Hill 2006).

At mid-century in urban and rural areas, a newly emerging Mexican American civil rights movement made law enforcement (sheriff and police) brutality and misconduct, institutional and individualized racism, and jury bias a centerpiece of their political organizing (Escobar 1993, 2003; Haney López 2003; Olivas 2006; Alvarez 2007). Referring specifically to the terror tactics of the Los Angeles Police Department (LAPD), but with observations that could apply to other major urban areas in the United States, historian Edward J. Escobar links the struggles of African American and Mexican American communities, noting that in both communities, "many came to see the department [LAPD] as a hostile occupying force" (Escobar 2003, 198). As a result, people organized to defend their lives, families, communities, and dignity. Two parallel forces—(1) the organized resistance to police brutality and federal repression of social movements and (2) the police brutality-as-professionalism program—would come to characterize the post-World War II period relations between the state and people of color organizing for civil and human rights (Escobar 2003). These conflicts were a catalyst to politicize and unify Chicanos, Latinos, African Americans and other targets of police repression (Escobar 1993).

Backyard Colonial Rebellions

Political activists organized alliances—some short-lived, others more long-term—across race and national origin and in both men's and women's state and federal institutions across the country. Perhaps most well-known were the aforementioned Attica rebellions and the organizing of George Jackson, the Soledad Brothers, and the San Quentin Six in California (Jackson 1971; New York State Commission on Attica 1972; Cummins 1994). But rebellions broke out across the country in federal institutions at McNeil Island (Washington State) and Atlanta as well as at state institutions like Greenhaven in Pennsylvania, the Tombs in New York City, the women's unit at Alderson in West Virginia, and in Stillwater, Minnesota (Díaz-Cotto 1996; Gómez 2006b; Losier 2007). In many of these movements, creating interethnic coalitions—however short-term, cautious, or self-serving—was key to successfully mobilizing a large number of prisoners.

In what is still the most extensive study on Latina/o prisoner organizing, Juanita Díaz-Cotto (1996) uncovers the everyday intricacies of prison politics, projects for collective organizing, as well as third-party support in New York. Latinos also organized on the West Coast at McNeil Island Federal Penitentiary in Washington State. Mexican American inmates formed the Mexican American Self Help group (MASH). This organization worked closely with support groups from the

University of Washington and the multiracial community center El Centro de la Raza and also established coalitions with African American, Filipino American, and American Indian organizations.[8] At Florence State Prison in Arizona, striking inmates issued their "curriculum for reform," declaring that "this is a unified movement of all convicts for reform of present conditions ... there are committees now representing all of the Black Brothers, White Brothers, Brown Brothers, and Red Brothers" (Mitford 1972, 234). In Texas, Chicano writ-writers like David Ruiz and Fred Cruz challenged the legal basis for guard brutality, biased parole boards, and inhumane conditions. Their combined legal work and the public advocacy of supporters like Frances Jalet Cruz (the "mother of the Texas prison reform movement" who was tried for being a "revolutionary" by a Texas court), Charlie and Pauline Sullivan, and others led to a landmark ruling in *Ruiz v. Estelle*[9] that mandated sweeping changes and resulted in the Texas system being placed under federal control for more than twenty-two years.[10]

Part of a longer history of reform and philanthropic movements, the normalization of prison as the preferred form of punishment is simply the most recent example of a historical trajectory of reform movements redefining the means *and ends* of punishment and death (Friedman 1993; Pisciotta 1999; Blue and Timmons 2006). An increased reliance on rehabilitation predicated on obedience, order, routine, and self-interest-based incentives (imposed through violence or the threat thereof) characterized mid-twentieth-century approaches to incarceration. These issues and institutions would become the fronts of a progressive struggle and inseparable in their broad impact on Latino/a community formation and resistance. As James V. Bennett, a primary administrative architect behind these strategies' social and political punishment, and the first administrator of the Federal Bureau of Prisons (BOP), wrote in 1952, "The whole penal system is a series of contradictions and paradoxes. On the one hand, prisons are expected to punish; on the other, they are supposed to reform. They are expected to discipline rigorously at the same time they teach self-reliance. They are built to be operated like vast impersonal machines, yet they are expected to fit men to adjust to constantly changing community standards ... and so the whole paradoxical scheme continues because our ideas and views regarding the functions of correctional institutions are *fuzzy*."[11]

Bennett set out to "modernize" the running of prisons (at a time during which the LAPD was also modernizing its interactions with communities of color), believing it both "naïve [that] we can reduce to a science the unhappy task of punishing people" and yet absolutely necessary to make a semantic shift for the stereotypical prison with "towers and walls, steel cells and armed guards" and "find some other name ... like the phrase 'prison community'" to describe an "atmosphere, a climate in which failure, self-defeat, apprehension, and tensions can be dissipated."[12]

At mid-century, African American, Puerto Rican, and Mexican American GI's returning from overseas were faced with Jim Crow racism "on the home front." Many joined already existing civil rights organization, or formed new ones, and began demanding equal treatment. Through the emergence and expansion of social movements in the 1950s demanding justice from the police and court systems, the idea of a prison community did not reconcile with the racist apparatuses of police and state control that linked criminality, juvenile delinquency, and race to uphold white community boundaries. As a result, from mid-century on, Bennett's ideas were challenged by hard-line politicians and often-racist prison administrators and guards demanding that prisons reflect the larger push of "law and order" politics. By the time Myrl Alexander took charge of the BOP, serving from 1964 to 1970, "rehabilitation" was being challenged from across the political spectrum.

From Cultural Nationalism to Anti-U.S. Imperialism: The Chicano-Independentista Connection

The Federal Penitentiary at Leavenworth, Kansas, opened on February 1, 1906, the first of three federal institutions (along with Atlanta and McNeil Island) legislated by the *Three Prisons Act of 1891*. Leavenworth was chosen partly because a military prison already existed there that could be conveniently and easily expanded upon, and the current prisoners provided "free labor" to build the structures (Keve 1991). By the late 1960s, Leavenworth Federal Penitentiary, also known as the "Hot House" and the "Big Top," warehoused some 2,100 people from across the country and continent, including approximately 400 Latinos.[13] In addition to Mafia dons, political prisoners, prisoners of war, and CIA-paid terrorist Orlando Bosch (who participated in the Bay of Pigs invasion and founded the violent anti-Castro terrorist group Coordination of United Revolutionary Organizations), there were people convicted for an entire range of criminal statutes violations (Keve 1991; Earley 1992).[14]

In an editorial for the Leavenworth prison journal *New Era*, raúlrsalinas provided an important insight into the daily conditions at Leavenworth: "Insofar as loss of freedom is concerned . . . [w]e feel that more changes are necessary. . . . The prevailing atmosphere of Leavenworth, which both keeper and kept seem to be hung up in, is one of a distinct stagnating and de-humanizing nature. . . . Leavenworth today is witnessing the arrival of a new type of prisoner . . . one who doesn't scurry into the gloomy caverns of idleness and self-defeat at the mere fact that he has arrived at a prison which has the reputation of being the most infamous of all, in this country."[15]

Born in San Antonio in 1937, and raised in Austin, Texas, by 1968, Raúl had spent time in Soledad in California and Huntsville state prison in Texas for low-level drug offenses; he had begun to write poetry and jazz articles for the Huntsville prison newspaper, *The Echo*, in the late 1960s. Transferred to Leavenworth in 1968, he was involved in the underground contraband trade when he and other Chicano inmates came into contact with the *Independentistas* and other politicized prisoners from the American Indian Movement, the Black Liberation Army, and Chicanos alike. Raúl was this "new type of prisoner" that did not back down from the violence of the carceral regime while locating these experiences as central to the process of personal and political transformation. In addition to these domestic influences, the presence and influence of the Puerto Rican *Independentistas*—Rafael Cancel Miranda, Oscar Collazo, Irving Flores, and Andres Figueroa Cordero—added an anticolonial analysis of U.S. imperialism.

The Puerto Rican *Independentistas* were an important inspiration and influence in the development of a political consciousness among the Chicano prisoners and, by extension, the Chicano movement. Raúlrsalinas comments on their presence after first arriving at Leavenworth: "Up to this time [July 1967], I had only read about the Puerto Rican struggle. . . . [Oscar Collazo] had been pointed out by other non-political peers of mine. We spoke of them as mythical figures, in hushed tones. . . . We knew they were important personages, but not why, or for what specific reasons."[16]

Soon the "Cultural History of the Southwest" class would bring these two groups together, particularly over the issue of language and history (Cancel Miranda 1998a). Again, according to Salinas, "Don Oscar Collazo . . . the maestro, was the one who would give us classes in Spanish, but he would use political phrases and sentences." In the context of an emerging political culture in Leavenworth that included members of the major Black Power organizations of the time, as well as American Indians and poor whites, Chicanos improved their verbal, written, and reading skills in Spanish with curriculum materials that drew from social movement history of Latin America and the African diaspora. Language was both personal and political: "Here was a linguist [Collazo] in command of seven languages . . . who taught me *acentuación* [accent marks] in Spanish. . . . He would give classes in Spanish to Chicanos. But las *frases* [phrases] or the sentences were all from Pedro Albizo Campos. . . . We knew Zapata . . . we knew about Che Guevara and we knew about Ho Chi Minh because these are things that are coming into the prison."[17]

This curriculum served to both sharpen and internationalize their analysis and expand their historical knowledge while simultaneously providing the political weapon of bilingualism as a way to subvert the control of the prison regime (O'Hearn 2006).[18] Learning, or maintaining, the Spanish language had been an important struggle in Puerto Rico since the occupation and domination of the United States. For Cancel Miranda, there was a personal element to the struggle over language, as he was continually reprimanded during his school years in Puerto Rico—to the point of expulsion—for refusing to speak English (Cancel Miranda 1999).

According to Cancel Miranda, the Chicano struggle represented another experience of the struggle against U.S. domination: "*Entonces empezó la lucha de los chicanos ¡y me di lleno de esta lucha! Recuerdo un 16 de Septiembre, fecha de la independencia Mexicana, que paralizamos la prision. Fundmaos el periodico Aztlán. . . . También recuerdo que en Leavenworth hubo una huelga grande. Se paralizo la industria de la carcel. Encalabozaron a muchos. Al finalizar la huelga, toda la poblacion penal (negros, blancos, indios, hispanos) piden unicamente que los represente ante los carceleros para sacar de los calabozos a los castigados*" (Cancel Miranda 1998a).[19]

Miranda's recollection of these political mobilizations centered on an emerging political identity as related to a shared cultural identity. Organized in the prison industries, a work stoppage was one of the few, yet perhaps most direct, ways of demonstrating discontent while simultaneously creating a sense of political community. Although Collazo advised him not to get involved (for reasons not stated), the activists who had organized the strike called upon Cancel Miranda's experience to represent their demands. Two months later when an even larger strike took place, he was immediately put in solitary, accused of having organized the strike (Cancel Miranda 1998a, 1998b, 185).

The organizing efforts of Oscar Collazo and Rafael Cancel Miranda, as well as Irving Flores and Andrés Figueroa Cordero, were an extension of the struggle for Puerto Rican independence that had its roots in the nineteenth-century struggle against Spanish domination (Raskin 1978; Gil de Lamadrid Navarro 1981; Lindin 1988; Trias Monge 1999; Caban 2000; Pabón 2002; Bosque-Pérez and Colón Morera 2006). To those ends, on November 1, 1950, Oscar Collazo and Griselio Torresola carried out an armed demonstration at the Blair House, President Truman's residence, as part of the nationalist-led rebellion on the island and in order to bring attention to the colonial status of Puerto Rico. Torresola was killed while Collazo was sentenced to death—in 1952, he was commuted to life in prison. Four years later, Rafael Cancel Miranda, Irving Flores, and Andrés Figueroa Cordero, led by Lolita Lebrón, carried out a second armed demonstration at the U.S. Capitol on March 4, 1954 (Rodríguez-Morazzani 1998; Susler 1998; Cancel Miranda 1998a, 1998b). The armed demonstration was in response to the successful campaign of the United States to have Puerto Rico taken off the United Nations' list of post-World War II territories that were not independent; Puerto Rico's inclusion on the list required the United States to report to the United Nations about Puerto Rico's status, while the U.S. government argued that Puerto Rico was a commonwealth and no longer a colony. The anticolonial and pro-independence politics of the *Independentistas* continued in the courtroom as they refused to recognize the jurisdiction of the U.S. court system and instead demanded that they be tried in an international court as prisoners of war. Five congressmen had been wounded from the shots fired from the spectator's gallery and Miranda, Cordero, and Flores were each sentenced to seventy-five years in prison and were split up: Cordero was sent to Atlanta, Miranda to Alcatraz, and Flores directly to Leavenworth, where he joined Collazo. Lebrón, the actual leader of the group, was sentenced to fifty years and incarcerated in Alderson, West Virginia. By the late 1960s, all the men had been transferred to Leavenworth.

Not only was the political organizing at Leavenworth an extension of the independence struggle within the "prisons of empire"—it also provided the opportunity to imagine a Latino political and cultural identity. In a letter from Salinas to Antonia Castañeda (penned in Marion Prison in October 1972), Cancel Miranda connected the anticolonial histories of Chicanos/as and Boricuas in a note congratulating Castañeda on the recent publication of an anthology of Chicana literature:

> Bueno, hermana . . . Soy Rafael, hijo de la Patria borincana de La Raza. Leí y comprendí "Literature Chicana: Texto y Contexto." Y le digo que quisiera que mi pueblo la leyera, pues leyéndola no solo se realiza la situación del Chicano y los porqués de esa situación, y sí que también la situación del Puertorriqueño y los porqués de su situación. Nuestras vidas corren casi paralelas y quizás por éso, mientras mejor nos conocemos, más cercas nos sentimos unos de los otros. *El mismo enemigo ha querido mutilar, y si posible, hacer desaparecer nuestras culturas, tan parecidas una a la otra, y sin embargo, tanto el Chicano como el Boricua hemos podido salvar nuestra idenitidad cultural, nuestra personalidad,* y "Literatura Chicana: Texto y Contexto," es una prueba de ello! [my emphasis].[20]

For Cancel Miranda, the "parallel" experiences of cultural imperialism and the "mutilation" of their respective pasts linked the present and futures of Chicanos/as and Puerto Ricans. The organizing against segregation and inhumane prison conditions that resulted in interethnic alliances kept Cancel Miranda fighting and alive: "I was never really imprisoned. I never felt defeated. I kept fighting inside prison and always had the hope of getting out—one way or another. When you resign yourself to the idea that you're not going to get out, that is when you become a convict. The prison becomes your world. But none of us resigned ourselves" (Cancel Miranda 1998b, 34).

Chicanos were a central element in the political formations that allowed Cancel Miranda and, by extension, the other *Independentista* fighters, to continue resisting colonialism by linking up with other people in struggle. The political affinities, inspirations, and exchanges that he highlighted did not occur simply because of a shared history, culture, or language, or only because of the shared experience of incarceration or the larger milieu of social movements at the time. Rather, a confluence of these different influences and shared experiences and the conscious effort to develop spaces and projects for political education were central factors in creating both the conditions and will for political action.

While these activists benefited from the engagement with outside political actors, there were sophisticated Chicano organizers and political theorists inside the walls. Among the most influential Chicano political theorists was Ramon Raúl Chacon. Born in Delany, deep in South Texas, on January 5, 1942, Chacon was arrested in 1967 and sentenced to sixty-six months for trafficking a controlled substance.[21] Chacon helped organize the ethnic studies classes and subsequent strikes. In 1976, at a press conference protesting the imprisonment and torture of Chacon in Mexico, Mario Cantú described the upbringing that inspired Chacon's politics: "Chacon was raised among the poor and suffered the consequences: racism, exploitation and oppression that are common . . . to the national minorities in the US He traveled the way of migration, unemployment, and prison . . . He was instrumental, while in prison, in the formation of a newspaper, political and cultural group discussions by and for the prisoners."[22]

According to Salinas, it was through Chacon that "we got to . . . *Wretched of the Earth* by Franz Fanon. Where he got it from, I don't know. Who his peers or his mentors were, in there or out, before he appeared into our midst . . . I guess we never bothered to ask . . . so from Fanon to Amilcar Cabral—the struggle in Guinea Bissau . . . looking at Mao and what was going on down there in Vietnam."[23] Africa, Latin America, and Asia were all on the radar of Chicano activists because of Chacon. Chacon was a self-identified Magonista, follower of the ideas of Ricardo Flores Magón, a Mexican anarchist whose actions, ideas, writings, and the call *Tierra y Libertad*, inspired the Mexican Revolution of 1910. Along with his brother Enrique, they were imprisoned in various prisons in Mexico and the United States.[24] Magon was eventually imprisoned in Leavenworth, and, on November 21, 1924, died from health complications long ignored by prison officials (Gómez Quiñones 1973; Hernández Padilla 1999; Trejo 2005; Bufe and Verter 2006). For the Chicano Movement, Magónismo was part of a larger history of resistance against "Anglo domination," while the perspective on the connected histories of the political struggles of the U.S. working class—particularly Mexicans living in the United States—and revolutionary movements in Mexico further internationalized the Chicano political vision. Combined with the experience of the *Independentistas*, Chacon influenced the political transformation of activists such as Cantú, Salinas, Chacon, and others, as well as the solidarity between Latinos at Leavenworth.

Pedagogies of Dissent[25]

Education formed a central pillar of mid-century penal theories of social control and rehabilitation; their logic posited that through study (of *the Bible*, primarily), prisoners would come to see the error of their ways. The subjection of the liberal ideal of education to a dialectic initiated by prisoners turned these programs on their heads (Cummins 1994). One common project that provided the possibility for the development of an expanded political imagination was history and cultural studies courses taught through institutions of higher education. These classes offered possibilities to develop a political analysis as well as strategies to engage the administration and improve the prisoners' conditions of incarceration (Mohanty 2003, chap. 8). Many of these educational opportunities were a result of post-Attica reforms that state and federal administrators instituted—some with reluctance—during the 1970s (Zahm, Halleck, and Rubenstein 1998).

Preceding Attica by almost eighteen months, in the spring of 1970, the Leavenworth administration sanctioned a course titled "Cultural History of the Southwest."[26] The first class convened on March 15, 1970, and for the next two years, between twenty and thirty students met to study history, culture, international relations, and politics. Professor Francisco Ruiz of Penn Valley Community College in Kansas City led the class and was assisted by Marciano Morales, Oscar Jorge Vigliano, Andy Gutiérrez, and Francisco Chávez. According to class summaries written by the editor raúlrsalinas and published in the newspaper *Aztlán*, a typical Friday class began with "committee business and reports (correspondences, newspapers, grievances, etc.), then, one of our members is selected as main speaker for the evening to talk on whatever is relevant to the Chicano cause." This format allowed for a collective approach to curriculum development while providing the opportunity to practice public-speaking skills and facilitating the participation of the maximum number of students in political "organizational learning" (Payne 1995; Lipsitz 2001, 288). Salinas explained this "pedagogy of dissent":

> Aqui se puede aventar el camarada, a segun su nivel . . . politics, education, revolucion, whatever. Just so it is pertinent to the Chicano cause. Despues se introducen los visitates de la libre—carnales militantes, Chavista luchugueros, tios tacos, professors, y estudiantes. Aveces hay peliculas del calibre de "huelga en Delano" y "Yo Soy Joaquin". Al final, el profe nos da una hora de lecturas en la lengua castellana, y historia de los mayas/aztecas y literatura mejicana. Por medio de papiro estamos en contacto con todos las pintas de Aztlán, safando el animal aquel te platique! De allí, nichis, carnal! But you know that out front, no? Naranjas! [27]

These classes were dynamic and nontraditional. Rejecting the teacher-student relationship based on a "banking system" of education (the teacher makes "deposits" in the minds of students; students are passive recipients of information), they instead created an environment that emphasized collective learning and contributed to creating a counterhegemonic space behind the walls (Freire 1997; James 2003).

During the two years that the class met, the participants not only expanded their knowledge of history, politics, and current events, but like cultural and political gathering spaces across the country and continent, hosted activists, artists and musicians; the musical group *El Chicano*; theater groups like *Los Mascarones* from Mexico and *Teatro Chicano* from the Colegio Jacinto Treviño in South Texas; local members of the Brown Berets, a radical Chicano organization modeled after the Black Panther Party for Self-Defense; leaders from the American Indian Movement; and a wide range of artists and activists from across the *Américas* that shared songs, art, and stories.[28]

Through essays written in preparation for class and published in the newspaper (discussed in section Aztlán: "To Destroy and Rebuild") these activists proclaimed their solidarity with the Chicano Movement as well as movements from across Latin America, particularly Cuba, Puerto Rico, and Mexico. They also engaged Chicano organizations around the issue of prisoners' rights, challenging them to include prisons in their analysis of the Chicano movement. These activists created coalitions and alliances inside the walls, while visitors brought firsthand experiences of similar alliances that were taking shape at national and international levels.

The exchange of experiences with activists outside the walls added to an understanding of social movements based on reading in journals and newspapers about conferences, marches, and other events. As a class, they subscribed to or maintained correspondence with political and cultural magazines and newspapers from across the country and continent.[29] Some of these materials, particularly those focusing on social movements in Mexico and Latin America, were sent from San Antonio, Texas, by a former Leavenworth prisoner, Mario Cantú, whose time in Leavenworth predated the formation of the class. Born Mauro Casiano Cantú, Jr., on April 2, 1937, in San Antonio, Texas, Mario was the son of a small business owner (grocery store). In 1963, he was convicted of drug trafficking and sentence to fifteen years at Leavenworth (Cantú 1980).

Correspondence between Salinas and Cantú highlights the international political imagination that developed: "Nos movio de establecer [una] embajada Chicana en el Terre. Why not one in Chile? O el la isla del barbudo? Argelia? Quiero que sepas que nos quedamos malias despues de haber leido los magacines [sic] ¿Por qué? [Mexico] Estamos al corriente de los sucesos en las sierras de Guerrero y la tragedia fatal del compañero Genaro Vasquez. El material que mandaste sobre el, fue utilizado para un "lecture" en nuestra clase cultural.[30]

The materials that Cantú sent to Leavenworth introduced these activists to political ideas and organizations struggling for civil and human rights as well as revolutionary movements from across the continent and globe. More than declarations of solidarity, these texts anticipated the postincarceration political trajectories of Salinas, Cantú, Chacon, and others who joined many of these movements upon release. Milton Segoviano captured the influences of these movements in an essay titled, "Awareness": Until now, I was ignorant of the hardships that my people have suffered and are suffering. I now have opened my eyes and for this reason my heart cries out. We Mexicans are involved in a search for identity. Because of this internal division our minds are being polluted, our souls are being annihilated and our rights are restricted. So long as this loss of memory remains undisturbed, so will pollution, annihilation and restriction.[31]

These activists were beginning to theorize an interethnic approach to organizing based on shared histories of repression while recovering the memories of resistance. While identifying primarily as Chicanos and looking to the indigenous roots of Mexico for a sense of cultural identity, these foundations allowed them to make connections with other groups in prison, a consciousness that would lead them to create an emerging Latino identity. That is, from their emerging sense of cultural nationalism came a form of "localized internationalism" evidenced by their support of the struggle for Puerto Rican independence, the American Indian movement, and the Black Power movement. Some of these politicized prisoners later joined revolutionary or radical movements upon their release.

Aztlán: "To Destroy and Rebuild"

By May of 1970, the core groups of students that made up the cultural studies class "expresaba la necesidad para una 'voz'" [expressed the need for a voice] and began to produce the politico-cultural newspaper *Aztlán*. An outgrowth of the class, a medium to communicate across the walls, a chronicle of struggle, and a political tool to share stories of struggle, *Aztlán* exclusively published "convict work." According to Salinas, "We try to stress the importance of originality and the nurturing of unknown hidden talents in the arts, poetry, journalism, publications work and public speaking."[32] An unsigned editorial in the first edition, published on May 5, 1970, linked their organizing efforts with the national Chicano movement:

> At the National Chicano Youth Liberation Conference [organized by the Crusade For Justice in Denver, Colorado] . . . it was decided that . . . indeed, the Southwestern states would henceforth be recognized as the nation of *Aztlán*. The Chicano convicts of Leavenworth number approximately 400. By no mere coincidence, the greatest percentage of us come from the aforementioned area. It is with this spirit of our ancestors deeply rooted within us and a pride in our home states that we consider ourselves, behind prison walls, true representatives of *Aztlán*. A miniature nation is, perhaps, more appropriate. Therefore . . . we feel justified in having chosen *Aztlán* as the title for our newspaper.[33]

This document adapted larger cultural and political influences in the Chicano/a movement to the prisoners' specific conditions and emphasized a collective form of indigenous/Mexican cultural nationalism as part of an oppositional identity in the United States. This, in turn, provided a foundation for political solidarity. More than a newspaper, *Aztlán* was first and foremost a political project:

> The goals of our newspaper are twofold: to Destroy and Rebuild. To destroy the myth of the worthless Chicano; the misconception of his non-productivity; the prejudice that exists, for lack of understanding, in the minds of many; the inferior feelings which we may, or may not, be possessed by. To rebuild the image of ourselves in the eyes of others; the dignity to face the world as Chicanos and Men; the sense of pride in who we are. And finally, to establish communication among ourselves and with our people, wherever they may be. We can accomplish these goals because: SOMOS AZTLÁN![34]

Five editions of *Aztlán* were published from May 1970 to February 1972. Members of the editorial collective twice elected Salinas as editor. The newspaper featured poetry, essays, editorials, and reproductions of oil paintings, pen-and-inks, and watercolors by Manuel Aguilera, Tomás Torres, José D. Marín, Jesse Hernandez, Lolo Guerra, Nando Castillo, Jesus Sanchez, and Ruben Estrella. In addition to debuting the poetry of raúlrsalinas, *Aztlán* also published poems by Juan Reyes and Abel Aldrete (San Antonio), Alberto Mares and Daniel Montoya (Denver), Antonio Flores (Mexico), as well the *Independentistas* Andrés Figueroa Cordero and Rafael Cancel Miranda. These different forms of expression focused on issues of identity and social exploitation, the economic conditions of poverty, Anglo society and violence against Mexicans, international solidarity, as well as prison conditions and policy. This was not simply sheets of mimeographed paper (vital as this medium is), but an elaborate, detailed, and vibrant creation infused by a political urgency and political artistry inspired by urban wall murals and rural message boards. No space was left black; color, poetry, and *homenajes* (to George Jackson, Pablo Neruda, Mario Cantú, *El Colegio Jacinto Treviño*) occupied the "negative (white) space."

In one such essay—titled "American: 2nd Class?"—Alfredo Arrellanes offered a critique of class inequality, emphasizing the importance of learning Chicano and Mexican history. Addressing Anglo-Americans and emphasizing the relationship between the "Chicano Revolution" and other national social movements of the time, Arellanes explained, "It has become increasingly clear that too many Anglos are unable or unwilling to understand what the Chicano Revolution is all about. First, ours is a part of, and coincidental to, the great social upheaval the United States is currently undergoing. In the simplest terms, our complaint is a tiredness of second-class citizenship. Equal protection is being denied to Chicanos in schools, employment, military affairs, voting, politics, police stations and the courts."[35]

Emphasizing the contradictions between citizenship, race, and rights, and histories of state violence, white supremacy, and class inequality, Arrellanes posed a series of questions challenging the myth that "the American Dream is for everyone":

> When our members total approximately five percent of the national population, why do we account for 18 percent of the casualties in Vietnam? With numbers sufficient to have twenty representatives in Congress, why do we only have four? Why such disproportionate numbers in the state and federal prisons of Aztlán? Who sliced this pie? In dealing with Chicanos, can you ever disregard their different ethnic and cultural backgrounds and treat them as you do all other? Is it too much to ask that, in being part of the American society, we also be permitted to retain and take pleasure and pride in our inherited culture of Mexico and the Southwest?[36]

The political struggles circulating at Leavenworth and in social movements throughout the United States are clearly visible in this essay, as Arrellanes links the Chicano prisoners' rights organizing to a larger history of struggle, emphasizing Chicano history not only on its own terms but also as a central part of American history. His argument is not about sameness in difference but a call to decolonize the history of the Southwest. What appears to be nascent cultural nationalism—and to be sure, this was at the heart of the transformation of these inmates—he recognizes as the political urgency of solidarity with other third world peoples and poor people in general: "Many of the Chicano complaints are not peculiar to us alone. In addition to other racial and ethnic minorities, there are poor *whites*, students, and the young. What is wrong with the system? Is its hypocritical denial of 'equal protection' to so many of its citizens causing it to crack? Must it destroy itself?" Emphasizing that poverty transcends racial differences, Arellanes ends on a hopeful note, centering prisoners' rights struggles within a national struggle to improve society: "A long-term pinto second-classer would hope that there is somewhere for him to return and attempt to attain full citizenship for himself and his brothers . . . of helping reshape our society to that which was originally intended: Equality and Justice for all." [37] Not only was Arellanes calling for changes within the prison, he was calling attention to the absolute necessity of creating "abolition institutions" to help rehabilitate society (Davis 2006).

Like the cultural history class, *Aztlán* was part of a strategy to push at the limits of incarceration, to reclaim a sense of personal and cultural identity, and, in the process, to create a medium in which to communicate the cultural renaissance and the political organizing as well as a critical analysis of the mechanisms of control and brutality within the carceral apparatus. As *Aztlán* circulated through the activist networks across the country and continent, the perspective, analysis, and artistic works created behind the bars not only presented a burgeoning Chicano prisoners movement but also became an important influence and component in the larger terrain of social struggles.[38]

Chicanos Organizados Rebeldes de Aztlán.[39]

By October of 1970, seven months after the first cultural history course, the influence of the curriculum and the newspaper *Aztlán* led these activists to reorganize the growing political energy as a political cadre: C.O.R.A. A political vehicle capable of organizing direct actions such as strikes, petitions, and retaliations for guard brutality, as well as a nascent antirape movement, C.O.R.A. developed an "analysis in action," actively organizing and creating spaces and possibilities for inmates to directly engage the prison machine.

The objectives of the organization were direct, strategic, and connected to long-term goals. They pledged to work on self-organization by studying history and researching their own conditions, to prepare themselves for post-incarceration life, and to connect with people on the outside. They not only focused on changes within the context of the prison regime but also prepared themselves to "become an asset to all people and our respective community. . . . Dedicated toward fulfilling our objectives so as to gain knowledge pertinent to the betterment of our people which in turn can only be accomplished by a better understanding of our problems" (see endnote 3). The founding language of the organization reflected the cultural and political transformations happening in other Chicano/a-Mexicano/a communities throughout the country. Echoing the introductory editorial in *Aztlán* (cited above), the bilingual manifesto stated, "We, the 'Chicano' temporarily confined in the United States Penitentiary at Leavenworth, Kansas, conscious of the fact that knowledge, freedom, equality, justice and dignity are the legitimate aspirations of all the 'Chicano' peoples in the Western Hemisphere hereby, for the attainment of our own common goals and objectives adapt 'En [sic] Plan Espiritual de Aztlán' as our Constitution and Charter."[40] C.O.R.A members included "all 'Latinos' in the Western Hemisphere (in general) and the 'Chicano' inhabitants and civilizers of the Northern Land of Aztlán (specifically)" (my emphasis). It is important to highlight this construction of "all Latinos" as a political identity reflecting shared but complicated histories of domination and resistance. Rooted within the Chicano nationalism of the time, the anticolonial politics of the *Independentistas*, and the larger terrain of U.S. third world alliances that were forming (Blackwell 2000; Ferreira 2003; Oropeza 2005; Mariscal 2005; Pulido 2006; Young 2006; Prashad 2007), by using the word "Latino," these activists embraced a political idea of solidarity and identity that was grounded in the local and simultaneously international and interethnic, representing the political and cultural solidarity between Puerto Rico, Mexico, Aztlán and Latin America. For C.O.R.A., Chicano was a hemispheric identity, not simply limited to descendents of Mexicans living in the United States. This is significant in that it complicates the relationship between culture, politics, and identity, offering a Latino identity forged through shared histories and the experiences of political education and organizing while also grounded in an emerging, contradictory and contested Chicano, Mexican, or Puerto Rican identity.[41]

In an incisive and eloquent essay written on March 22, 1972, Joe Rubio explained the significance of this political formation: "C.O.R.A. is a conglomeration of minds that have fortunately seen behind the decayed veil of respectable law and order that is applied to the public. C.O.R.A. is that which has *seen that assimilation is synonymous with extinction. That assimilation is but death on the installment plan* transmitted through blows, and has on occasion killed us. C.O.R.A. [is] the apprehension that the structure which passes for western civilization is a wormy (maggoty) mass, dominated by repressions that have taken centuries to calibrate." Rubio then goes on to critique the supposed necessity of sociological categories used for academic research as forms of "legal assassination," that is, civil death, locating C.O.R.A. as a central force in resisting assimilation to the "deathworld" (James 2005, xxxi) of the prison:

> In administrative terminology we are a set of numbers. In social terms we are public enemies, and in sociological jargon we are those committing the necessary evils thereby allowing the social structure to maintain its fragile cohesiveness. We don't deny being any label that you wish to apply to us, but we do affirm that behind each label beats a heart. It is said that certain moral entrepreneurs have even excluded us from being human because we are prisoners, as if it were in their power to do so. All the [above] mentioned definitions are but disguises flying the banner of different vested interests covering the most elucidating academic studies, including repressive law and order.[42]

Critiquing the medicalizing impulse in penology, Rubio exposed the role that social scientists, in categorizing inmates as "numbers," "public enemies," and "statistics," play in the political conflation of race and crime that undergird the logic of forced social assimilation through the medical violence of rehabilitation. Rubio unmasked the categories and definitions used to justify the destruction of a human being, exposing the scientific cruelty of quantified incarceration studies that function to exclude certain people from humanity and accept, without question, any technique that insures that exclusion. He also links behavioral and cultural assimilation to civil and cultural death, critiquing the linear and progressive narrative of the American dream as elusive for nonwhites, for whom violent racial discrimination and class exploitation are instead the norm: "Think about the treatment Chicanos have been afforded in Texas, from El Paso to the Gulf, from the Valley of Tears [South Texas Winter Garden] to the Red River. Wait but one second and reflect, those conditions are what your government calls progress? How do they measure progress?" Localizing the discourse of development and progress to then expose its contradictions, Rubio indicts Western civilization, while affirming the political and cultural possibilities of solidarity based on shared experiences of repression and resistance. Linking the labor of Chicano workers in South Texas to the deception of American democracy and opportunity and as part of a larger critique of the global impact of Western civilization, Rubio locates the experiences of Chicano—in prison, working in the fields, and throughout society—as being based, in part, on a shared economic experience of exploitation and state violence. For Rubio, the place of Chicanos in a global economy, understood through localized experiences of the impact of racism and economic exploitation, reflects a sense of the international in the local, a third-world perspective emerging from experiences in a U.S. federal penitentiary, the political analysis from the "backyard colony" of an emerging "penal democracy" (James 2007).

From 1970 to 1972, through a nascent form of ethnic studies, a publishing project, and an organized political cadre, these activists directly challenge the prison regime; yet by April of 1972, as a result of their political agitation, the class was disbanded, *Aztlán* ceased to be published, and many of the active organizers (including Salinas and Cancel Miranda) were transferred to Marion Federal Penitentiary. They joined other activists transferred from across the country by a Bureau of Prisons betting on incapacitating the movements by extracting the "leaders" and isolating them at Marion where they were exposed to experimental behavior modification programs, powerful psychotic drugs, and torture. Bringing with them experiences from federal prisons across the country, the transferred activists created the Federal Prisoners for Freedom of Expression Committee and the Political Prisoner's Liberation Front, elaborated a detailed study of the then-emerging behavior modification programs, and sent a report to the United Nations outlining their findings and demanding their human rights be protected. They were punished for these acts, locked-down in the infamous "control units" (later to become the Supermax prisons) specifically created for politicized prisoners. Support groups outside the walls played a central role in publicizing the lockdown and providing legal advice and support. For instance, in early September, the Frente Unido por la Defensa de los Presos Politicos Puertorriqueños of New York sent a petition signed by four hundred persons to the administration and Cancel Miranda, demanding his release.[43] A pair of lawsuits filed by the People's Law

Office challenged the constitutionality of the "control units" on Eighth Amendment grounds of "cruel and unusual" punishment, the denial of access to courts, procedural standard for prisoners placed in solitary confinement, and constitutional rights of freedom of religion and speech in the mails. The first resulted in a favorable decision in 1973 (*Adams v. Carlson*) that was soon overturned in 1978 (*Bono v. Saxbe*).[44] *Bono* established the legal precedent that long-term isolation, sensory deprivation and lockdown, and sensory overload, that is, lighting and noise, as well as lockdown for 23.5 hours, seven days a week, was not only constitutional but also rational and necessary (Gómez 2006a, 2006b; McCoy 2006).[45] It was through the People's Law Office that connections were initially strengthened between the *Independentistas*, lawyers, and members of the Puerto Rican communities in Chicago, New York, Philadelphia, and Puerto Rico. Comprised of Puerto Ricans in the United States and in Puerto Rico, solidarity groups, and overseas support, the social movement that rallied behind the legal strategies was directly responsible for eventual freedom of the *Independentista* fighters (Deutsch 2007).

Although this article focused on the late 1960s and early 1970s, the culture of solidarity that developed between Chicanos and Puerto Ricans continued to influence political movements throughout the decade and into the 1980s and 1990s. Whereas in the late 1960s and early 1970s, American Indians, Chicanos/as, blacks, Puerto Ricans, Chinese, Filipino, Japanese, and others established alliances and deep coalitions defining the contours of political cultures of U.S. third world peoples, in California, Illinois, New York, New Mexico, Texas, and other parts of the Southwest, coalitions were established and strengthened in the 1970s around the issues of freedom for the *Independentistas* and the larger struggle for Puerto Rican independence (Rodriguez 1999; Martinez 2002; Mariscal 2002; Blocks 2009). Moreover, activists like raúlrsalinas, Mario Cantú, Alberto Mares and Ramon Chacon continued their political militancy after their release as they sought out radical and revolutionary organizations that provided the opportunity to put their ideas into practice (Santamaría Gómez 1994; Vigil 1999; Gómez 2006a; Mendoza 2006).

Pasts, Presents, Possibilities

The stories about Latino prisoners are only one element within the broader history of connections between Chicano/a, African American, Puerto Rican, American Indian, Filipino, and radical white working-class activists both inside as well as outside the walls. Together, their struggles existed within the larger circulation of global freedom movements. The prison rebellion years were not simply flashpoints, they were the result of shared experiences and the creation of political projects and organizing initiatives. As an intregal element of the larger social movements circulating across the country and globe, they constituted an important element of anticolonial struggles that in turn created a revolutionary praxis and politics of dignity and freedom, a political positioning grounded in the everyday experiences of violent technologies of state control, and the creativity freed when refusing to conform or be broken. The continuities of racialized punishment, suffering, and death within the prison regime highlight that incarceration and violence are historical legacies of colonialism and slavery and that the institution of the modern twentieth-century U.S. prison is founded on colonial-slave power relationships (Davis 1998; Wacquant 2007). Punishment, incarceration, and death are mechanisms for domestic control of racialized citizens and noncitizens as well as geopolitical strategies of control. As a result, they are foundational to modern state power (Blue and Timmons 2006; Rodriquez 2006a, 2006b).

Although prison rebellions continued throughout the 1970s and into the 1980s, 1972 marked both the zenith of large-scale organized rebellions and a steady yearly increase in the prison population since. The politics of "law and order" had, since the 1950s, reinscribed racialized discourses of juvenile delinquency on nonwhite populations that were counter-posed to patriotic (cold warrior) children. This accelerated in the 1960s, when a public relations campaign that conflated race and urban criminality exaggerated threats to personal and national security (Flamm 2006). This resulted in the (re)criminalization of political and social dissent through an expansion of the policing and infiltration of social movements; the scope and power of grand juries; and the tactical use of criminal, judicial, and prison systems that served as the primary strategies of social and political control of racial minorities and progressive, liberal, and revolutionary ideas (Wilson Gilmore 1998/99; Parenti 2000; Ratner and Ratner 2000; Evans 2005).

The lives of millions upon millions of people—increasingly young, of color, female, migrant, poor, incarcerated for drug-related (low-level dealing or consumption) violations, reincarcerated for parole or probation violations—are affected by this war on human life and dignity. This is not for dramatic affect; the statistics, familiar to some, continue to stagger. While from the 1930s to the early 1970s the rate of incarceration remained relatively steady, beginning in 1972 through 1973 (the height of the rebellion years), the prison population rose from 196,000 to 204,000—a 4 percent increase. Since 1972, the national prison population has risen 500 percent from 196,000 to more than 1.2 million in 1997, to 2.5 million today (including persons in immigrant detention centers (Rodriquez 2006b). There were 5,600 women incarcerated in 1970, yet by 2001, there were 161,000, and as of 2005, there were 202,000 women in state and federal prisons or local jails, an increase of 2,800 percent! Twelve percent, or 1 in 8, of black males aged twenty-five to twenty-nine was in prison or jail in 2005. For Latinos, it was 1 in 26 (3.9 percent) and 1 in 59 (1.7 percent) in relation to white males in the same age group. There are more than five times as many citizens locked up as there were three decades ago. In 1973, the infamous Rockefeller mandatory sentencing drug laws were passed. Throughout the 1970s, other states followed suit. Such was the fervor at the state level that by 1984, the *Sentencing Reform Act*—establishing mandatory sentences at the federal level—was passed. But by the early 1980s in large states like California, the crime rate was falling just at the time that the Reagan administration expanded prison building to warehouse the expanding labor surplus incarcerated for not being white, or rich, or connected, or "in a phase"—or, increasingly, a citizen.[46]

We are now in the fourth decade of the most recent state-sanctioned assault on the lives and dignity of poor people, women and people of color that has characterized the twentieth-century wars on poverty, crime, drugs, and most recently, migrants. Given the "severe racial contours"[47] of prisons today, the organizing efforts of Latino prison activists and the coalitions of support networks and movement lawyers are important because they shed light on historical events that offer clues to better understand the current incarceration crisis and the limits to effective political organizing inside and outside the walls (McCarty, 2006).

Grounded in everyday experiences and shared histories of domination and resistance, the political analysis of Latino prison activists uncovered how the intricate calibrations of violence within the prison regime were related to law, race, and social control outside prison; an important theoretical understanding when trying to untangle the political ideology of law and order as it relates to race, incarceration, and white supremacy (Rodriquez 2006a, 2006b). Incarceration functioning as "incapacitation" for a surplus army of labor of women, men and immigrants criminalized by their mere existence, is directly implicated in the acceptance of preventative and indefinite detention and torture with regard to racial - and in a post-9/11 world—national and religious groups targeted by the state (Gilmore 2007; Rodriguez 2006a). This also brings up a whole series of questions about how global incarceration logics refract and reinscribe the racialized violence of U.S. domestic policies at the local level, for example, with regard to school "zero-tolerance" policies or the racial profiling, targeting and incarceration of entire families of migrants. African Americans, U.S.-born Latinos/as, Latin American immigrants, immigrants from the Caribbean, Africa, Asia, and other outposts of American Empire all have a new set of circumstances from which to draw lessons and make political decisions. Given the politically motivated expansion of the prison industrial complex *in anticipation* of the increase in immigrant detentions, and the lead role that lobbyists and conservative politicians have taken to push for stricter immigration policies, the lessons of the prison rebellion years become urgently important: to recover and politically revisit.

It is important to consider that solidarity is created through struggle and that struggle often precedes solidarity. The circulation and exchange of political ideas and personal experiences, and the need to keep and recover a cultural or racial identity, were the last things that the prison administration wanted for inmates or the general public. Creating interethnic alliances across race and culture challenged the foundations of racial control. The cultural studies class, newspaper, and formal and clandestine political formations were part of a Latino prisoner's rights movement, while the essays, poetry, manifestos, and art published in *Aztlán* are part of the political and intellectual history of Latino/a studies and Chicano/a studies as well as narratives of captivity, resistance, and freedom (James 2003, 2005, 2007). The impact of legal strategies at the national and international levels, and the social movements that gave them force, trace a particular history of creative resistance uncovering the legal infrastructure of a colonial state—from court decisions on constitutional issues, to types of offenses that led to prison terms, to international treaty law that served to reinforce the material violence these communities faced. These decolonizing political formations and projects enrich the analysis of self-activity and collective struggle as central elements of human dignity and the processes of recreating more humane social relations.

Notes

1. "Our lives run almost parallel."
2. raúlrsalinas, interview by author, audio recording Austin, Tx., 16 June 2004
3. Prison machine is a play on the title of the collected letters of raúlrsalinas, *My Weapon is the Pen: raúlrsalinas and The Jail Machine*, ed. Louis Mendoza. *Austin, University of Texas Press: 2006.*
4. C.O.R.A. By-Laws, Leavenworth, Kansas, January 1972, 1–2, Box 8, Folder 7, RSP, SPCU. Although the actual founding of the organization occurred in October of 1970, the copy of the constitution, charter, and bylaws in the Salinas archives is dated January 1972.
5. Leavenworth prison activist Alberto Mares estimates the number at five, while raúlrsalinas identified three. Mares refers to the strikes organized by C.O.R.A. but does not mention 1972 specifically, whereas raúlrsalinas specifically refers to three strikes in 1972. The actual number is probably a total of five, with three taking place in 1972.
6. Letter from raúlrsalinas to Michael Deutsch, September 16, 1972, Salinas Papers, Box 6 Folder 20, RSP, SCSU. Sometime in 1970, Raúl R. Salinas began to sign his writings "raúlrsalinas." Unless written otherwise, or when referring only to his last name, I will use the raúlrsalinas spelling.
7. For the purposes of this article, I use the term "political activist" to emphasize that these persons were organizing for political change for political reasons in order to change their conditions of life and recover a sense of human dignity. The differences between political prisoners, prisoners of war, and politicized or social prisoners must be understood in relation to their similar position within a racist, neocolonial justice system. Specificity about individual cases within the larger prisoners' rights and abolition movements is critically important. For example, Erik Olin Wright argues that differentiating between political prisoners and criminal prisoners hides "the meaning of punishment and the political functions it plays in society." See Wright (1973, 23).
8. Cenobio Macias. Notes on the Mexican American History and Culture Class. January 18, 1971. Salinas Papers, box 7, folder 9, SUSC.
9. David RUIZ, Plaintiff v. W. J. Estelle, Jr. et al. Defendants, 503 F.Supp. 1295, United States District Court, S. D. Texas, December 12, 1980.
10. Filed in 1972, the case took eight years to get to trial, with the trial lasting nearly a year, and resulted in a landmark decision in 1980. Presiding Judge William Wayne Morris wrote, "It is impossible for a written opinion to convey the pernicious conditions and the pain and degradation which ordinary inmates suffer within the TDC [Texas Department of Corrections] prisons' walls." Quoted in "Poets and Prisoners." *Texas Observer*, December 2, 2005, 3. The case ended in 2002 after twenty-two years of federal oversight of Texas prisons.
11. James V. Bennett, "Why Fear and Hate Shadow our Prisons," excerpt from *The New York Times Magazine*, May 11, 1952, reprinted in *U.S. Department of Justice, Federal Bureau of Prisons, Federal Prisons Journal: 60 Years of Public Service*, 1930–1990 (Summer 1990), Vol. 1, No. 4, 32.
12. James V. Bennett, "If Not Prisons—What?" Excerpt from paper delivered to the Institute of Illinois Academy of Criminology, Monticello, Illinois, April 2, 1955, reprinted in *U.S. Department of Justice, Federal Bureau of Prisons, Federal Prisons Journal: 60 Years of Public Service*, 1930–1990 (Summer 1990), Vol. 1, No. 4, 32.
13. United States Congress, House Committee on the Judiciary, Subcommittee on Courts, Civil Liberties, and the Administration of Justice, *Inspection of federal facilities at Leavenworth Penitentiary and the Medical Center for Federal Prisoners, Report*, 93rd Cong.,

2nd sess., January 1974 (Washington, D.C.: U.S. Government Printing Office, 1974), 3; the number 400 is cited in Marín (no last name), "Solidaridad," Aztlán, Cinco de Mayo, Número 1, Año 1. Raúlrsalinas personal archives, hereafter referred to as RSPA.

14. On Orlando Bosch, CORU, other CIA assets like Luis Posada Carriles (released from U.S. custody in May 2007), and the spread of U.S.-supported terrorism in Latin America, see the National Security Archive's web resource page, http://www.gwu .edu/~nsarchiv/NSAEBB/NSAEBB202/index.htm.

15. raúlrsalinas, "New Era, Now Era," New Era (Leavenworth, Fall 1970): 4, Box 7, Folder 8, RSP, SCSU.

16. raúlrsalinas, "Notas: Memorias of Sorts," unpublished manuscript, 55.

17. "Una Platica con Raúl Salinas," interview by Ben Olguín and Louis Mendoza, Stanford University, May 5, 1994.

18. In Algeria during the 1950s, imprisoned FLN fighters would use Arabic as a tool for literary and political analysis, and, during the 1970s at the Long Kesh prison in London, Irish Republic Army prisoners of the war studied Gaelic as both a process of recovery and resistance. Soon, position papers were being written in Gaelic, sparking a revival of the language outside of the walls.

19. "So the struggle of the Chicanos began and I was all for it. I remember on September 16, Mexican Independence day, we shut down the prison. We founded the newspaper Aztlán. I also remember there was a big strike at Leavenworth. The entire prison industry was shut down and many were put in solitary. When the strike was over, the entire population (blacks, whites, Indians, Hispanos) asked that I be the one to represent them and try to negotiate the freedom of those put in solitary."

20. "Well, sister . . . I am Rafael, son of the Borinquen land de La Raza. I read and understood 'Chicano Literature: Text and Context.' And I tell you that I wish my people would read it, since by reading it one not only understands the Chicano situation and the whys of that situation, but also the Puerto Rican situation and the whys of their situation. Our lives run almost parallel and perhaps because of this, as we get to know each other better, the closer we will feel to one another. The same enemy has sought to mutilate, and if possible, annihilate our cultures, so similar to each other, and nonetheless, both the Chicano and the Boricua both have been able to preserve our cultural identity, our personality, and 'Chicano Literature: Text and Context,' is proof of this!" Letter from Raúl Salinas to Antonia Castañeda, 23 Octubre 1972, Box 4, Folder 19, RSP, SCSU." Texto Y Contexto, was edited by Antonia Castañeda Shular, Professor Joseph Sommers and Professor Tomas Ybarra, all from the University of Washington-Seattle, and featured Salinas's poem "Un Trip Through the Mind Jail."

21. Security Report, "Estado de Nuevo Leon," Folder 19–36, L-3, DFS, Archivo General de la Nación, Mexico City.

22. Mario Cantú, "Confidencia de Prensa," 1976, San Antonio, Texas, 3, and Box 2, Folder 13 MCP, BLAC; "PPUA Calls Press Conference in the US," English reprint of press release, Bracero: Organo de la Liga Flores Magon, Vol. 1, no. 1 (1976), 3, Box 4, Folder 1, Mario Cantú Paper, Benson Latin American Collection.

23. raúlrsalinas, interview by author, audio recording, Austin, Texas, June 16, 2004.

24. Their persecution was part of the larger repression against immigrant political activists in the United States during the first years of the twentieth century that culminated in the Palmer Raids—repression that also included the emerging nationalist movement in Puerto Rico.

25. It is important to point out that the demand for expanded educational opportunities inside the walls occurred side by side with, and in some cases, in anticipation of, the high school and university students, professors, and communities that were also walking

out, going on strike, and demanding increased access to, as well as changes within, the education system. In their own ways, both prisoners and students demanded significant changes in utility of learning, the use of education, and the meaning of change.

26. To date, I have not been able to confirm whether the actual class was initially proposed by prisoners who were organizing or by the administration; what is clear is that even though the space was clearly "allowed" to exist, prisoners organized to subvert the institutional parameters that might have limited their curricular options, that is, the radical nature of the curriculum. It is important to note that the relationship between Leavenworth and Penn Valley Community College predated the Attica massacre and the post-Attica spread of higher education programs—limited as they were.

27. "Here is when a comrade can get down, according to his ability . . . Afterwards the freeworld visitors are introduced—militant brothers, Chavez Union organizers, uncle toms, professors, and students. Sometimes there are movies like 'Strike in Delano' and 'I am Joaquin.' Finally, the professor gives us an hour of lessons in Spanish, and history of the Mayas/Aztecs and Mexican Literature. Through the paper we are in contact with all the prisons of Aztlán, excluding 'that beast' I told you about before. From that place, zip, Carnal! But you know that out front, no? Nothing came of it!" "Nothing came of it" is the translation of "naranjas," according to raúlrsalinas. raúlrsalinas to Sr. José Angel Aguirre, June 21, 1971, Box 3, Folder 2, RSP, SCSU.

28. raúlrsalinas, interview with author, audio recording, June 16, 2004; raúlrsalinas, "Music for the Masses," Aztlán No.1 Año 2 (21 de Febrero de 1972): 1–2.; "Cultura de Sudoeste," Aztlán Año 1, Número 4, (26 de Julio de 1971): 2; and "Cultura de Sudoeste," (Año 2, Número 1), 21 de Febrero de 1972, signed by "La gente d'este Canton."

29. An incomplete list includes: *Tecolote* (San Francisco), *La Voz de Aztlán* (St Mary's College), *Echo* (Austin), *Portavoz* (San Antonio), *El Gallo* (Denver), *La Raza and Con Safos* (Los Angeles), *Lado* (Chicago), *Chicano Federation* (San Diego), *Ya Mero* (McAllen, Texas), *El Grito del Norte* (Española, Nuevo Mexico), and *Papel Chicano* (Houston). They also received international newspapers like *¿Por Qúe?* (Mexico) and *Claridad* (Puerto Rico), as well as *The Guardian, P'alante, The Black Panther*, and *The Militant*. See Aztlán Año 1, No. 3 (9 de Marzo, 1971), 4; "Cultura de Sudoeste," Aztlán Año 1, Número 4 (26 de Julio de 1971), 7; and Ernesto B.Vigil, *The Crusade for Justice*, 355.

30. Raúl Salinas to Mario Cantú Jr., February 28, 1972, Box 4, Folder 58, Salinas Papers. "You inspired us to establish an embassy at El Terre [Terra Haute, Indiana]. Why not one in Chile? Or on the island of the bearded one? Algeria? I want you to know that we were devastated to read the magazines *¿Por qúe.* We now know what happened in the sierras of Guerrero, Mexico and the fatal tragedy of compañero Genaro Vasquez. The materials that you sent about him were used for a lecture in our cultural class." Genaro Vasquez, a teacher in rural Guerrero was forced into hiding after the state government in Guerrero fired on a peaceful protest for education reform. He formed the Civic Association of National Revolution (Asociación Civica Revolucionaria Nacional, ACNR) and later died in a fatal car accident on 2 February 1972, although the particular events leading up to the crash suggest that he was assassinated.

31. Milton Segoviano, "Awareness," Aztlán Número 2, Año 1 (Leavenworth Federal Penitentiary, June 1970), 2.

32. raúlrsalinas, "Repaso," Aztlán, (Año 2, Número 1), 13; and "On the History of C.O.R.A and Aztlán," March 1972, reprinted in *My Weapon is the Pen*.

33. Aztlán de Leavenworth, Número Uno, Año Uno, 5 de Mayo de 1970. According to Salinas, as the editor, he was the primary author of this document.

34. Aztlán de Leavenworth, Número Uno, Año Uno, 5 de Mayo de 1970.

35. Alfredo Arellanes, "American: 2nd Class?" Aztlán Número 3 Año 1 (Leavenworth Penitentiary, March 9, 1971), 3. Other essays, with titles like "¿Importa Saber Quiénes Somos?"; "The Decade of Awakening"; "Solidaridad"; "Are we Ready?"; "Life and Desire"; "Para Mi Raza"; "Qué has hecho tu por la Raza"; "Resistance"; "El Carnalismo"; and "El Futuro es Nuestro," simultaneously explored political identities and the each author's own material conditions of incarceration.

36. Alfredo Arellanes, "American: 2nd Class?" Aztlán Número 3 Año 1 (Leavenworth Penitentiary, March 9, 1971), 3.

37. Alfredo Arellanes, "American: 2nd Class?" Aztlán Número 3 Año 1 (Leavenworth Penitentiary, March 9, 1971), 3.

38. In my research on interethnic, multiracial, and international elements of the Chicano/a movement, I have interviewed numerous participants who followed the organizing efforts and rebellions throughout the prison system, largely reported through El Gallo (Denver, Colorado) and El Grito del Norte (New Mexico), and particularly the history narrated here as well as work with some of these activists after their release.

39. The name C.O.R.A. (Chicanos Organizados Rebeldes de Aztlán) was suggested by Beto Gudino. To avoid unwanted attention from prison officials, Chicanos Organizados Raza de Aztlán was chosen as the above-ground name of this "unauthorized political and intellectual site." Cora is also an abbreviation of corazón (heart). See raúlrsalinas, "On the History of C.O.R.A and Aztlán," March 1972, reprinted in *My Weapon is the Pen*.

40. The "Plan" is a founding document of the Chicano/a youth and student movement that outlined a set of action-based programmatic ideas and a political ideology that focused on "unity, economy, education, self-defense, culture, and political liberation" (Muñoz 1989).

41. When asked about "Why Latino?" raúlrsalinas responded in an interview, "We were crazy."

42. Emphasis added. José Rubio, "Essay on C.O.R.A," March 22, 1972, 2–3, Box 8, Folder 7, RSP, SCSU.

43. Letter from Raul Salinas to Michael Deutsch, People's Law Office, September 16, 1972. raúlrsalinas personal archives.

44. Letter from Raul Salinas to Michael Deutsch, People's Law Office, September 16, 1972. raúlrsalinas personal archives. Eddie ADAMS et al., Plaintiffs-Appellants v. Norman CARLSON, Director of the Federal Bureau of Prisons, et al., Defendants-Appellees, 488 F2d 619, No. 73-1268, United States Court of Appeals, Seventh Circuit. Argued June 14, 1973. Decided Aug. 23, 1973. As Amended Oct. 4, 1973. Victor BONO et al., Plaintiffs-Appellants v. William SAXBE, Individually and in his capacity as Attorney General of the United States et al., Defendants-Appellees. 620 F.2d 609 No. 79-1327. United States Court of Appeals, Seventh Circuit. Argued Jan. 15, 1980. Decided April 14, 1980.

45. The plaintiffs in Adams included Edward Adams, 32, originally from Chicago; Vernon Thogmartin, 36, of Kansas City; Dillard Morrison, 51, New York; and raúlrsalinas.

46. Julia Sudbury, "Introduction: Feminist Critiques, Transnational Landscapes, Abolitionist Visions," in *Global Lockdown: Race, Gender, and the Prison-Industrial Complex*, ed. Julia Sudbury. New York: Routledge, 2005; The Sentencing Project, "New Incarceration Figures: Growth in Population Continues," December 2006, http://www.sentencingproject.org/PublicationDetails.aspx?PublicationID=430, accessed on December 4, 2006; Bureau of Justice Statistics, Sourcebook of Criminal Justice Statistics 1996, Department of Justice, Washington, D.C., 1997; Bureau of Justice Statistics, "Prison and Jail Inmates at Midyear 1997," 1998, cited in Marc Mauer, *Race to Incarcerate* (New York: New Press, 1999) 1, 9, 19; and Ruth Wilson Gilmore, *Golden Gulag*, 7–9.

47. I owe this phrase to Professor David Manuel Hernández.

References

Almaguer, Tomás. 1971. Toward the study of Chicano colonialism. *Aztlan* 2 (Spring): 137–42.

Alvarez, Luis. 2007. From zoot suits to hip hop: Toward a relational Chicana/o studies. *Latino Studies* 5:53–75.

Badillo, Herman, and Milton Haynes. 1972. *A bill of no rights: Attica and the American prison system*. New York: Outerbridge and Lazard.

Blackwell, M. 2003. "Contested Histories: las Hijas de Cuauhtémoc, Chicana Feminisms and Print Culture in the Chicano Movement, 1968-1973." In Gabriella Arredondo, Aida Hurtado, Norma Klahn, Olga Nájera-Ramirez, and Patricia Zavella (eds.) Chicana Feminisms: A Critical Reader. Durham, N.C.: Duke University Press. Pp. 59-89.

Blauner, Robert. 1969. Internal colonialism and ghetto revolt. *Social Problems* 16 (Spring): 393–408.

Blue, Ethan, and Patrick Timmons 2006. Editor's introduction. In *Punishment and death*, ed. Ethan Blue and Patrick Timmons. Special issue, *Radical History Review* 96 (Fall): 1–8.

Bosque-Pérez, Ramón. 2006. Political persecution against Puerto Rican anti-colonial activists in the twentieth century. In *Puerto Rico under colonial rule: Political persecution and the quest for human rights*, ed. Ramón Bosque-Pérez and Javier Colón Morera. Albany: SUNY Press. Pg. 13-48.

Bosque-Pérez, Ramón, and Javier Colón Morera, eds. 2006. *Puerto Rico under colonial rule: Political persecution and the quest for human rights*. Albany: SUNY Press.

Bufe, Chaz, and Mitchell Cowen Verter, eds. 2006. *Dreams of freedom: A Ricardo Flores Magon reader*. San Francisco, CA: AK Press.

Caban, Pedro A. 2000. *Constructing a colonial people: Puerto Rico and the United States, 1898–1932. Boulder, CO*: Westview Press.

Callahan, Manolo. 2003. Mexican border troubles: Social war, settler colonialism and the production of frontier discourses, 1848–1880. PhD diss., University of Texas at Austin.

Carmichael, Stokeley (Kwame Ture), and Charles V. Hamilton. 1992. *Black power, the politics of liberation*. New York: Vintage Edition.

Cancel Miranda, Rafael. 1998a. *Sembrando Patria y Verdades*. San Juan, Puerto Rico: Cuarto Ideario.

———. 1998b. We came out of prison standing, not on our knees. Interview by Martín Koppel, Rollande Girard, and Jacob Perasso. In *Puerto Rico independence is a necessity: On the fight against U.S. colonial rule*. New York: Pathfinder. Pg. 25-35.

———. 1999. Presentation at Resistencia Bookstore. Video recording, March, in Austin, TX. Copy in author's possession.

Cantú, Mario. 1980. Interview by Linda Fregoso. Audio recording. March 5, 1980. Longhorn Radio Network Mexican American Programs, Special Collections, Benson Latin American Collection, University of Texas at Austin.

Castañeda, Antonia I. 1993. Sexual violence in the politics and policies of conquest: Amerindian women and the Spanish conquest of Alta California. In *Building with our hands: New directions in Chicana studies*, ed. Adela de la Torre and Beatriz Pesquera, . Berkeley: University of California Press. Pg. 15-33.

Churchill, Ward, and J. J. Vander Wall. 1990. *The COINTELPRO papers: Documents from the FBI's secret wars against dissent in the United States*. Boston: South End.

Cummins, Eric. 1994. *The rise and fall of California's radical prison movement*. Stanford, CA: Stanford University Press.

Davis, Angela Y. 1998. From the prison of slavery to the slavery of prison: Frederick Douglas and the convict lease system. In *The Angela Y. Davis reader*, ed. Joy James. Malden, MA: Blackwell. Pg. 74-95.

———. 2004. Law and resistance in the prisons of empire: An interview with Angela Y. Davis by Chad Kautzer and Eduardo Mandieta. *Peace Review* 16 (1): 339–47.

———. 2006. *Abolition democracy: Beyond empire, prisons, and torture*. New York: Seven Stories.

Deutsch, Michael. 2007. Telephone Interview with Alan Eladio Gómez, July 7, 2007, Austin, Texas.

Díaz-Cotto, Juanita. 1996. *Gender, ethnicity, and the state: Latina and Latino prison politics*. New York: State University of New York Press.

Earley, Pete. 1992. *The hot house: Life inside Leavenworth prison*. New York: Bantam Books.

Elbaum, Max. 2002. *Revolution is in the air: Sixties radicals turn to Lenin, Mao and Che*. London: Verso.

Escobar, Edward J. 1993. The dialectics of repression: The Los Angeles Police Department and the Chicanos Movement, 1968–1971. *Journal of American History* 79 (1483-1514): 488.

———. 2003. Bloody Christmas and the irony of police professionalism: The Los Angeles Police Department, Mexican Americans, and police reform in the 1950s. *Pacific Historical Review* 72 (2): 171–99.

Evans, Linda. 2005. Playing global cop: U.S. militarism and the prison industrial complex. In *Global Lockdown: Race, Gender, and the Prison Industrial Complex*, ed. Julia Sudbury, 115–30. New York: Routledge.

Ferreira, Jason. 2003. All power to the people: A comparative history of 'third world' radicalism in San Francisco, 1968–1974. PhD diss., University of California, Berkeley.

Flamm, Michael W. 2006. *Law and order: Street crime, civil unrest, and the crisis of liberalism in the 1960s*. New York: Columbia University Press.

Freire, Paolo. 1997. *Pedagogy of the oppressed*. New York: Continuum.

Friedman, Lawrence. 1993. *Crime and punishment in American history*. New York: Basic Books.

Gil de Lamadrid Navarro, Antonio. 1981. *Testimonio: Los Indómitos*. San Juan, Puerto Rico: Editorial Edil.

Gómez, Alan Eladio. 2006a. From below and to the left: Re-imagining the Chicano/a movement the circulation of third world struggles, 1970–1979. PhD diss., University of Texas at Austin.

———. 2006b. Resisting living death at Marion Federal Penitentiary, 1972. *Radical History Review* 96:58–86.

———. 2008. Feminism, torture, and the politics of U.S. third world solidarity: An interview with Olga Talamante. *Radical History Review Radical History Review* 101 (Spring 2008): 160-178.

Gómez Quiñones, Juan. 1973. *Sembradores: Ricardo Flores Magon y El Partido Liberal Mexicano: A eulogy and critique*. Monograph No. 5. Los Angeles: Chicano Studies Center Publications, University of California, Los Angeles.

Gonzalez-Day, Ken. 2007. *Lynching in the west: 1850–1935*. Durham, NC: Duke University Press.

Gosse, Van. 2005. A movement of movements: The definition and periodization of the new left. In *The movements of the new left, 1950–1975: A brief history with documents*, ed. Van Gosse. New York: Palgrave MacMillan.

Grosfoguel, Ramón. 2003. *Colonial subjects: Puerto Ricans in a global perspective*. Berkeley: University of California Press.

Grosfoguel, Ramón, Nelson Maldonado-Torres, and José Saldivar. 2005. Latino/as and the Euro-American menace: The decolonization of the U.S. empire in the twenty-first century. In *Latinos in the world-system: Decolonization struggles in the 21st century U.S. empire*, ed. Ramón Grosfoguel, Nelson Maldonado-Torres, and José Saldivar. Boulder, CO: Paradigm. Pg. 1-13.

Haney Lopez, Ian. 2003. *Racism on trial: The Chicano fight for justice.* Cambridge: Belknap.

Hernández Padilla, Salvador. 1999. *El Magonismo: Historia de una Pasión Libertaria, 1900-1922.* Mexico City, Mexico: Era.

Hill, Lance. 2006. *The deacons for defense: Armed resistance and the civil rights movement.* Chapel Hill: University of North Carolina Press.

Ho, Fred. 2000. *Legacy to liberation: Politics & culture of revolutionary Asian/Pacific America.* San Francisco: AK Press.

Jackson, George. 1971. *Soledad brother: The prison letters of George Jackson.* New York: Bantam Books.

———. 1996. *Blood in my eye.* Reprint. New York: Black Classic Press.

James, Joy, ed. 2003. Imprisoned intellectuals: America's political prisoners write on life, liberation and rebellion. Lanham, MD: Rowman and Littlefield.

———. 2005. *The new abolitionists: (Neo)slave narratives and contemporary prison writings.* Albany: State University of New York Press.

———. 2007. *Warfare in the American homeland: Policing and prison in a penal democracy.* Durham: Duke University Press.

Keve, Paul W. 1991. *Prisons and the American conscience: A history of U.S. federal corrections.* Carbondale: Southern Illinois University Press.

Lindin, Harold J. 1988, 1991. *History of Puerto Rican independence movements* Vol. 1. Paramaribo-Zuid, Suriname: Waterfront Press.

———. 1991. *History of Puerto Rican independence movements* Vol. 2. Paramaribo-Zuid, Suriname: Waterfront Press.

Lipsitz, George. 2001. *American studies in a moment of danger.* Minneapolis: University of Minnesota Press.

Losier, Toussaint. 2007. "We are one people": The 1970 New York City jail rebellions and the practice of solidarity. Unpublished seminar paper.

Mariscal, Jorge. 2002. Left turns in the Chicano movement. *Monthly Review* 54 (3): 59–68.

———. 2005. *Brown-eyed children of the sun: Lessons from the Chicano movement, 1965–1975.* Albuquerque: University of New Mexico.

Martinez, Elizabeth. 2002. A view from nuevo Mexico: Recollections of the *Movimiento* left. *Monthly Review* 54 (3): 79–86.

McCarty, Heather Jane. 2006. Educating felons: Reflections on higher education in prison. *Radical History Review* 96 (Fall): 87–94.

McCoy, Alfred. 2006. *A question of torture: CIA interrogation, from the cold war to the war on terror.* New York: Metropolitan Books.

McPherson, Alan. 2003. *Yankee no! Anti-Americanism in U.S.-Latin American relations.* Cambridge: Harvard University Press.

Mendoza, Louis, ed. 2006. *Raúlrsalinas and the jail machine: My weapon is my pen, selected writings of Raul Salinas.* Austin: University of Texas Press.

Mitford, Jessica. 1972. *Kind and usual punishment.* New York: Knopf.

Mohanty, Chandra Talpade. 2003. *Feminism without borders: Decolonizing theory, practicing solidarity.* Durham, NC: Duke University Press.

Montejano, David. 1986. *Anglos and Mexicans in the making of Texas, 1836–1936.* Austin: University of Texas Press.

Muñoz, Carlos. Jr. 1989. *Youth, identity and power: The Chicano movement.* London: Verso.

New York State Commission on Attica. 1972. *Attica: The official report of the New York State Special Commission on Attica.* New York: Bantam Books.

O'Hearn, Denis. 2006. *Nothing but an unfinished song: Bobby Sands, the Irish hunger striker who ignited a generation.* New York: Nation Books.

Olivas, Michael A. 2006. *Colored men and Hombres Aquí: Hernandez V. Texas and the emergence of Mexican American lawyering.* Houston: Arte Público Press.

Oropeza, Lorena. 2005. *¡Raza Sí! ¡Guerra No!: Chicano protest and patriotism during the Vietnam era.* Berkeley: University of California Press.

Pabón, Carlos. 2002. *Nación Postmortem: Ensayos sobre los tiempos de insoportable ambigüedad.* Puerto Rico: Ediciones Callejón.

Paralitici, José (Che). 2006. Imprisonment and colonial domination, 1898–1958. In *Puerto Rico under colonial rule: Political persecution and the quest for human rights,* ed. Ramón Bosque-Pérez and Javier Colón Morera. Albany: SUNY Press. Pg. 67-82.

Paredes, Americo. 1979. *With a pistol in his hand: The ballad of Gregorio Cortez.* Austin: University of Texas Press.

Parenti, Christian. 2000. *Lockdown America: Police and prisons in the age of crisis.* London: Verso.

Payne, Charles. 1995. *I've got the light of freedom: The organizing tradition and the Mississippi freedom struggle.* Berkeley: University of California Press.

Perez, Emma. 1999. *Decolonial imaginary: Writing Chicanas into history.* Bloomington: Indiana University Press.

Pisciotta, Alexander W. 1999. *Benevolent repression: Social control and the American reformatory-prison movement.* New York: New York University Press.

Prashad, Vijay. 2007. *Darker nations: A people's history of the third world.* New York: New Press.

Pulido, Laura. 2006. *Brown, black, yellow and left: The making of the third world left in Los Angeles, 1968–1974.* Berkeley: University of California Press.

Quijano, Aníbal. 1998. La colonialidad del poder y la experiencia cultural latinoamericana. In *Pueblo, época y desarrollo: la sociología de América Latina,* ed. Roberto Briceño-León and Heinz R. Sonntag. Caracas: Nueva Sociedad. Pg. 11-26.

———. 2000. Coloniality of power, ethnocentrism, and Latin America. *Nepantla* 1 (3): 533–80.

Raskin, Jonah. 1978 *Oscar Collazo: Portrait of a Puerto Rican patriot.* New York: New York Committee to Free the Puerto Rican Nationalist Prisoners.

Ratner, Margaret, and Michael Ratner. 2000. The grand jury: A tool to repress and jail activists. In *States of confinement: Policing, detention, and prisons,* ed. Joy James, 277–86. New York: Palgrave.

Rodriguez, Victor M. 1999. Boricuas, African Americans, and Chicanos in the "far west": Notes on the Puerto Rican pro-independence movement in California, 1960s–1980s. In *Latino social movements: Historical and theoretical perspectives,* ed. Rodolfo D. Torres and George N. Katsiaficas. New York: Routledge. Pg. 79-110.

Rodríguez-Morazzani, Roberto P. 1998. Political cultures of the Puerto Rican left in the United States. In *The Puerto Rican movement: Voices from the diaspora,* ed. Andrés Torres and José E. Velázques. Philadelphia: Temple University Press. Pg. 25-47.

Rodriquez, Dylan. 2006a. *Forced passages: Imprisoned radical intellectuals and the U.S. prison regime.* Minneapolis: University of Minnesota Press.

———. 2006b. (Non)scenes of captivity: The common sense of Ppunishment and death. *Radical History Review* 96:9–32.

Saldivar-Hull, Sonia. 2000. *Feminism on the border: Chicana gender politics and literature.* Berkeley: University of California Press.

Sandoval, Chela. 2000. *Methodology of the Oppressed*. Minneapolis: University of Minnesota Press.

Santamaría Gómez, Arturo. 1994. *La Política entre México y Aztlán*. Mexico: Universidad Autónoma de Sinaloa.

Santiago, Charles Venator. 2006. From the insular cases to camp X-Ray: Agamben's state of exception and the United States territorial law. *Studies in law, politics, and society* 39:28–44.

Sudbury, Julia, ed. *Global Lockdown: Race, Gender, and the Prison Industrial Complex*. New York: Routledge, 2005.

Susler, Jan. 1998. Unreconstructed revolutionaries: Today's Puerto Rican political prisoners/prisoners of war. In *The Puerto Rican movement: Voices from the diaspora*, ed. Andrés Torres and José E. Velázques. Philadelphia: Temple University Press. Pg. 144-154.

Trejo, Rubén. 2005. *Magonismo: Utopía y revolución, 1910–1913*. Mexico City, Mexico: Cultura Libre.

Trias Monge, Jose. 1999. *Puerto Rico: The trials of the oldest colony in the world*. New Haven: Yale University Press.

Tyson, Timothy B. 1999. *Radio free dixie: Robert F. Williams and the roots of black power*. Chapel Hill: University of North Carolina Press.

Useem, Bert, and Peter Kimball. 1989. *States of siege: U.S. prison riots, 1971–1986*. New York: Oxford University Press.

Vigil, Ernesto B. 1999. *The Crusade for Justice: Chicano Militancy and the Governments War on Dissent*. Madison, University of Wisconsin Press.

Williams, Robert F. 1998. *Negroes with guns*. Detroit: Wayne State University Press.

Wacquant, Loic. 2007. *Deadly symbiosis: Race and the rise of neoliberal penality*. Oxford, GB: Polity Press.

Waldrep, Christopher. 2004. *The many faces of Judge Lynch: Extralegal violence and punishment in America*. New York: Palgrave MacMillan.

Wicker, Tom. 1975. *A time to die: The Attica Prison revolt*. Lincoln: University of Nebraska Press.

Wilson Gilmore, Ruth. 1998/99. Globalisation and U.S. prison growth: From military Keynesianism to post-Keynesian militarism. *Race & Class* 40 (2/3): 175.

———. 2006. Golden gulag: Prisons, surplus, crisis, and opposition in globalizing California. Berkeley: University of California Press.

Wright, Erik Olin. 1973. *The politics of punishment: A critical analysis of prisons in America*. New York: Harper & Row.

Young, Cynthia. 2006. *Soul power: Culture, radicalism, and the making of a U.S. third world left*. Durham, NC: Duke University Press.

Zahm, Barbara, DeeDee Halleck, and Benay Rubenstein. 1998. *The last graduation: The rise and fall of college programs in prison*. New York: Zahm Productions and Deep Dish TV.

4

The Racial Politics of Youth Crime

Victor M. Rios

Prior to joining the gang at age fifteen, Juan had experienced a childhood of struggle: his father abandoned him before he was born; his mother worked two jobs, having limited guidance for him; school had failed him; and police constantly harassed him. At age sixteen, excited about fitting in and living the thrill of "la vida loca,"[1] he drove a group of his homeboys to rival gang territory, no questions asked. He assumed that his homeboys would get out of the car and "throw down some chingadasos"—have a fistfight. But his homeboys had a different kind of fight in mind. As he slowed the car down to confront his rivals, he heard a fury of gunshots firing from inside his car. Instinctually, he sped off. The next thing he remembers is being pulled over by police and being arrested. Juan was still a minor at the time, and while he did not shoot a gun nor was anyone hurt by the bullets fired from his car, he was nonetheless sentenced thirty-five years to life in prison.

Several factors combined to condemn this youngster to a life in prison: adult sentencing (juvenile waiver), an attempted murder gang-enhancement sentence (fifteen years) and an added gun-enhancement (twenty years). Ten years ago, prior to gang and gun-enhancement sentencing, Juan probably would have served seven to ten years for attempted murder if he were tried as an adult. If he had been tried as a juvenile, he probably would have spent two to three years in youth prison.

While Juan's case is an extreme example of recently implemented, punitive criminal and juvenile justice policies, his case also highlights how sentencing laws profoundly impact black and Latino youth who do not commit serious and violent crimes. In today's punitive urban setting, even the typical juvenile transgressor—the truant, the "tagger," the peripherally involved gang member, the small-time drug dealer, and the petty thief—feels the detrimental impact of zero-tolerance policies in his community; young people of color are constantly policed, surveilled, criminalized, and severely punished for even the smallest of transgressions (Feld 1999; Males and Macallair 2000; Ferguson 2001; Chesney-Lind and Shelden 2004; Rios 2006). Juan, for example, was caught tagging a wall with his neighborhood's name (East Side Oakland) at age fourteen, three years before he was sentenced thirty-five years to life.[2] According to Juan, the owner of the building claimed that the damage cost him over $600 to repair, and Juan was charged with a felony. He faced one year in juvenile hall; however, because this was his first offense, the judge gave him three years probation. This incident still resulted in a felony conviction on his record. This conviction, and the fact that he was placed in a gang database after tagging a building, eventually culminated in his thirty-five years to life sentence.

Prior to the passage of California's Proposition 21 in the year 2000—which, for example, made $400 worth of property damage into a felony (previously felony damage had to be in the excess of $50,000)—Juan likely would have been sentenced for a misdemeanor and would not have been placed in a statewide gang database. His punishment may have entailed participation in a community graffiti removal program. Juan's case illustrates how the drastic changes in juvenile justice policy and practices that took place in the 1990s contributed to the exacerbated criminalization and stringent punishment of black and Latino inner-city youth having a detrimental impact on their lives at the dawn of the twenty-first century.

Healthy adolescent development requires that children make mistakes and learn to correct negative behavior (Zimring et al. 2001). Recent juvenile justice policies and practices, however, have criminalized this coming of age process for youth of color. Inner-city black and Latino youth do not have much opportunity for redemption and rehabilitation after acts of delinquency. Instead, punitive policies push youth deeper into the criminal justice system, routing them directly into what the Harvard Civil Rights Project has called the "school to prison pipeline" (Losen and Wald 2003). This punitive pipeline has replaced the idea that youth offenders should be provided a "surrogate parent" (Feld 1999). Today, the ideal response to youth crime has become, as former California governor Pete Wilson stated during his run for president in the late 1990s, "adult time for adult crime." Black and Latino youth are experiencing the brunt of this punitive transformation (Feld 1999; Males and Macallair 2000).

This article examines the intellectual and political discourse that led to the creation of punitive juvenile justice policy in the 1990s. I analyze the racialized ideas and policies that culminated in a national trend to harshly punish juvenile delinquents. I conduct a content analysis to demonstrate how "get tough" legislation specifically targeted black and Latino youth and played on the public's anxieties about race and crime to generate support. Discourse disseminated by intellectuals, policy makers, and the media exacerbated racial anxiety and fear. Specifically, Proposition 21 serves as a case study of how recent "get tough" legislation racializes youth crime and detrimentally impacts youth of color. In a broader context, this study sheds light to how inextricably connected crime and race are in the American conscience.

Methodology

A content analysis is a "multipurpose research method developed specifically for investigating any problem in which the content of communication serves as the basis of inference" (Holsti 1969, 2). Typically, this method is used to categorize group of words and uncover patterns of communication (Weber 1990). In this particular study, California's Proposition 21 and nineteen pieces written in support, or about supporters, of Proposition 21 are analyzed and individually coded to document instances of conflating delinquency with serious crime and crime with race. These pieces were chosen because they communicate messages aimed at convincing voters that a social problem existed and that Proposition 21 would serve as its panacea. By examining pieces of communication with a clear goal, we can uncover the techniques that proponents use to appeal to the masses.

According to Babbie (1986), the best approach in content analysis is when both "manifest" and "latent" content are analyzed. Manifest contest is "the surface meaning of the text" (Holsti 1969). In this study, manifest content refers to those words or phrases that directly address the issue at hand (e.g., "youth violence"). Latent content are the "deeper layers of meaning embedded in the document" (Holsti 1969, 12). For example, the phrase "inner city thugs" may be analyzed as a racially charged message since the inner city is statistically and symbolically a space where blacks and Latinos live. The author utilizes historical studies to flesh out the underlying meanings of phrases used in support of Proposition 21. I have examined both manifest and latent content in order to guarantee validity (Babbie 1986). The bulk of the analysis, however, examines the latent content since it is in the underlying meaning of discourse where racial politics are often enmeshed (Van Dijk 1991, Santa Ana 2002).

The data consist of Proposition 21 and nineteen articles written by supporters, or about supporters, of Proposition 21. Seven of the articles were written by former California governor Pete Wilson, as was Proposition 21. Eleven articles were written by other politicians and interest-group representatives. The argument in the voter's pamphlet in favor of Proposition 21 is written by Maggie Elvey of Crime Victims United of California, a lobby organization that champions harsher crime measures by endorsing hard-line politicians and inculcating the public with stories of extreme crimes experienced by its members.

The texts were coded for three types of references to crime. The first, "delinquency," identifies the most common of juvenile crime, such as graffiti, truancy, gang identification, loitering, and petty burglary. In 1999, one year prior to the passage of Proposition 21, these status and misdemeanor offenses accounted for 74 percent of total arrests (California Department of Justice 1999). The second reference, "serious crime," refers to violent crimes, sex offenses, and other major felonies, which account for 8 percent of total juvenile arrests (California Office of the Attorney General 1999). Lastly, "entangled" references to juvenile crime were coded. Entangled references invoke both "delinquency" and "serious crime," conflating these distinct transgressions into one delinquency with serious violent crime in one phrase. In this case, phrases where delinquency and serious crime were combined were coded. Examples of entangled discourse include defining nonviolent aspects of gang activity as a felony, identifying juvenile delinquents as a predatory social threat, and constructing typical juvenile delinquency as a serious criminal risk to society: "Dramatic changes are needed in the way we treat juvenile criminals, criminal street gangs, and the confidentiality of the juvenile records of violent offenders if we are to avoid the predicted, unprecedented surge in juvenile and gang violence" (Proposition 21, 2).

These phrases are vague enough to web together petty crime with serious crime. Here the reader cannot distinguish between the violent thug and the juvenile pot smoker or the rapist with the petty thief in that they both are a "predicted" risk.

Connections between race and crime were also coded, including words that referenced the race or ethnicity of criminals (manifest) as well as words, phrases, and messages that alluded to race. The theoretical premise behind examining the conflation between race and crime comes from Kinder and Sears's concept of "symbolic racism" (1981), which refers to the subtler forms of intolerance that evolved after the civil rights movement. Symbolic racism is the coded discourse and practices in mainstream society that affect people of color. In today's multicultural, politically correct society, racism is often deployed through covert discourses and practices. Often, because they rarely hear explicitly racist discourse or have de jure racist practices, many Americans believe that racism no longer exists—that it is a thing of the past. However, in recent times, studies have found that race is central to how voters choose and react to policy and politicians (Kinder and Sanders 1996). California's Proposition 21and other recent punitive criminal justice policies that target juvenile crime are prime examples of symbolic racism because they portray youth of color as inherently and violently criminal.

Race and Justice

Punitive criminal justice policies implemented over the past thirty years—legitimized by the war on drugs and other national crime control agendas—have generated a system of mass incarceration impacting blacks and Latinos in particular (Gilmore 1998; Davis 1999; Parenti 2000; Wacquant and Wilson 2000; Garland 2001; Western 2006). In the twenty years between 1982 and 2002, the incarcerated population of the United States increased from approximately 600,000 to 2,200,000. Approximately half of the detainees are black males and one-quarter are Latino (primarily Chicano) males, populations that make up roughly 7 and 7.5 percent, respectively, of the U.S. population (National Council on Crime and Delinquency 2002). Thirty-three percent of all African American men in this country aged –sixteen to twenty-four are either incarcerated or under criminal justice supervision at any give time (Males and Macallair 2000).

As the criminal justice system developed into a draconian punishment machine through the late twentieth century, the juvenile justice system began to mimic its incapacitation ideals (Feld 1999; Mears 2002). Incapacitation, or the transition from reform and rehabilitation to containment as a source of control, assumes that if criminals and even potential criminals are eliminated from society, then crime will decrease. In the one-hundred-year history of the juvenile justice system in America, some of the harshest punitive policies have been integrated within the last two decades (Feld 1999; McCord et al. 2001, Mears 2002).

By the mid-1990s, despite the diverse and autonomous entities of juvenile justice across states, the federal legislature created laws that changed juvenile justice institutions across the country. In 1996, the U.S. legislature passed the "*Violent Youth Predator Act*," offering millions of dollars to states implementing harsh juvenile justice policies. Starting with the sentence, "Today, no population poses a larger threat to public safety than young adult criminals," the *Violent Youth Predator Act* pushed for lowering the adult court waiver age from sixteen to fourteen; federal prosecution for serious violent offenders; and mandatory and minimum sentences for violent youth offenders, among other harsh measures. Essentially, this act set the stage for the passage of Proposition 21 in California.

A combination of political, intellectual, and media exaggeration of the youth crime crisis developed into a national juvenile crime agenda. For example, in the 1990s, the media increased its reports on juvenile crime—on televised news, 68 percent of all stories on violence involved youth, and 53 percent of all stories that discussed youth were about violence—a fourfold increase from the previous decade (Males 1998). Also during the 1990s, conservative criminologists and politicians developed influential ideas and policy recommendations for controlling "superpredator" "teenage time-bombs," a message that the media consistently spread to the public (Males 1998; Chamblis 1999; Elikann 1999).

The Superpredator

The development of punitive juvenile justice policy in the 1990s was influenced by racialized constructions of black and Latino youth as "superpredators" by intellectuals, politicians, and the media. The "superpredator" thesis, created by then-Princeton professor John Dilulio, catalyzed national media coverage and congressional legislation on youth crime and the need for punitive policy. In 1996, Dilulio claimed that "superpredators"—juvenile criminals—were an emerging violent and criminal risk to society and that serious punitive policies had to be generated to "deter" and "incapacitate" them at as early an age as possible (1996a). "Try as we might, there is ultimately very little that we can do to alter the early life-experiences that make some boys criminally "at risk." Neither can we do much to rehabilitate them once they have crossed the prison gates. Let us, therefore, do what we can to deter them by means of strict criminal sanctions, and, where deterrence fails, to incapacitate them. Let the government Leviathan Lock them up and, when prudence dictates, throw away the key." (Dilulio 1996a:3)"

In "The coming of the super-predators" (1995), Dilulio announced to America a "new wave" of juvenile criminals that would terrorize the nation by 2000. The cause of this soon-to-arrive youth crisis was the drastic increase in the urban youth population, specifically black and Chicano youth, many of whom were "still in diapers." Without a new punitive juvenile justice policy, they would inevitably carry out a "bloodbath" of violence.[3]

Pushing the superpredator thesis a step further, former U.S. Secretary of Education William Bennett, along with Dilulio, coauthored *Body count: Moral poverty and how to win America's war against crime and drugs* (1996). They introduced the idea of "moral poverty." According to Bennett and Dilulio, "moral poverty" is the failure of parents and the local community to provide children with appropriate training in becoming law-abiding, hardworking, "moral" individuals. According to them, moral poverty stems from the increase in single-parent households and homes where one or more of the parents are "deviant" or "criminal" themselves. Specifically, the authors argue that "in the extreme, it is the poverty of growing up surrounded by deviant, delinquent, and criminal adults in a practically perfect criminogenic environment—that is, an environment that seems almost consciously designed to produce vicious, unrepentant predatory street criminals, that repeats the cycle" (14).

As a solution to moral poverty, they argued for throwing out the idea of juvenile justice as rehabilitative and replacing it with a system that spoke to the problem of moral poverty. Under their proposed system, young people would pay "a price for transgressing the rights of others." Bennet and Dilulio argued that rehabilitation programs were responsible for rewarding, rather than punishing, negative behavior among youth and were therefore merely perpetuating the cycle of moral poverty. The superpredator thesis exacerbated the youth crime problem, leading to the hypercriminalization of black and Latino youth (Rios 2006). Proposition 21 serves as an extension of this draconian philosophy.

Turning Delinquency into Serious Crime

Proponents of Proposition 21 constructed a discourse that converted juvenile delinquency—particularly deviance acted out by youth of color—as a serious criminal threat to society. Proponents of Proposition 21 consistently conflated serious crime (i.e., violence, murder, brutality, shooting, drive-bys) with delinquency (i.e., graffiti, gang involvement, defiance, truancy, theft). Fifty-one percent of phrases coded for "delinquency" or "serious crime" were entangled, blurring the lines between serious crime and juvenile delinquency. Only 22 percent of all phrases that discussed delinquency referenced it in isolation from serious crime. For phrases that referred to serious crime, only 28 percent discussed it in isolation from delinquency.

The words of former California Governor Pete Wilson, the creator of Proposition 21, serve as a crucial example of this discursive conflation. On the heels of the superpredator discourse, Wilson announced in 1994 that "a new and violent upsurge in juvenile crime" was on the Californian horizon. If delinquent youth could be constructed as "irreparable criminals" in the making, then harsh policies that would "incapacitate" them could be implemented to deal with the problem. Even before his formal campaign against youth crime, Wilson had always insisted that youth offenders be punished harshly for their transgressions: "But while we sympathize with children who are tempted by drugs or gangs when, as teenagers or adults, they victimize others, our sympathy must yield to responsibility . . . *we must insist on adult time for adult crime.* (Wilson 1994; emphasis added)"

Wilson's solution to this constructed problem was to present voters, who were already in fear of juvenile crime at the time (Males 1998; Elikann 1999; Parenti 2000), with Proposition 21. This act set the stage for a new era of juvenile justice in California that formalized severe punishment for youth offenders. Proposition 21 brought about three major changes in the way juveniles were sentenced in the courts:

1. It allowed prosecutors to try juveniles as adults when they had committed major crimes.
2. It raised the stakes on crimes once considered youthful and therefore misdemeanor, such as graffiti and vandalism, now considered felonies.
3. It provided the court the power to grant "enhancements," or added sentences, for being involved in a gang.

Proposition 21 intended to systematically attack the California youth violence and gang "crisis." According to Wilson, a "drastic" increase in gang activity and youth violence led him to develop this measure. Although the proposition was advertised by proponents as targeting "the irredeemable, those violent criminals, whether they be juveniles or gang members, that cannot be redeemed through prevention and education" (Pacheco 2000), most of its changes focused on nonviolent juvenile delinquency. These changes included charging gang members with conspiracy to commit a felony if their gang committed a crime, even if the individual had no part in planning or carrying out the deed; requiring gang-involved delinquents to register with their county as "gang members"; and creating a six-month minimum sentence for misdemeanors committed as a gang member.

Wilson insisted that today's (majority nonwhite) juvenile delinquents were different than those (majority white) juvenile delinquents of the early twentieth century:

> Today's juvenile justice system was designed in the 1940's, when "serious" youth offenses included truancy, curfew violations and fistfights, and was intended to deal with "juvenile delinquents" whose most serious offenses where petty theft and vandalism . . . It was never intended or designed to handle *gang murderers with semiautomatic weapons or rapists preying upon innocent women.* (Wilson 2000a, 2000b, 2000c, 2000d; emphasis added)

Wilson's discourse shifted away from the reality of the times—that 92 percent of all juvenile offenses in 1999 could still be characterized by his own definition of the "old" more mild delinquency—nonviolent minor offenses causing little to no harm to society (California Department of Justice 1999). However, to the everyday Californian, this discourse presented a new type of juvenile delinquent: the inherently criminal youth of color. Race played a central role in Wilson's ambitions. In addition to turning juvenile delinquency into serious crime, Wilson and Proposition 21 racialized youth crime.

Race, Solidarity, and Proposition 21

While criminalizing petty juvenile deviance, Proposition 21 also criminalized youth of color. Proponents of the proposition invoked youth of color in code language. They described youth as "superpredators," "predatory gang members," "immoral criminals," "rapists," gang murderers," and "blood-thirsty killers"— descriptions that always alluded to cases where the culprit was a youth of color (in fact, all criminal cases highlighted by proponents of Proposition 21 involved youth of color). For example, the central target of the proposition was the juvenile street-gang member (see Bradbury 2000). Since the majority of gang members in California are youths of color, black and Chicano youth were clearly the targeted population. On page one of the proposition, a major Chicano gang is highlighted as one of the central perpetrators of the youth crisis in Southern California. Citing a report by the *Los Angeles Times*, the proposition argued:

> Criminal street gangs and gang-related violence pose a significant threat to pub-
> lic safety and the health of many of our communities. Criminal street gangs have
> become more violent, bolder, and better organized in recent years. Some gangs like
> the Los Angeles based 18th street gang and the Mexican Mafia are properly analyzed
> as organized crime groups, rather than a mere street gang. (Proposition 21, 1).

As one of the opening paragraphs of Proposition 21, this excerpt demonstrates how proponents of Proposition 21 used racial politics to their advantage. While Proposition 21 was intended to crack down on juvenile criminals, it neverthe-less cited the Mexican Mafia as one of its targets. The Mexican Mafia consists of an elite group of adult members that have influence on many neighborhood gangs throughout the country (Rafael 2007). In reality, juvenile gang members are not directly linked to the Mexican Mafia; instead, they are connected to specific neighborhood gangs that sometimes take orders from Mexican Mafia members. In other words, Pete Wilson utilized the alarming nature of the Mexican Mafia to attack juvenile delinquents. In addition, the signifier "Mexican Mafia" helped Wilson convey to his audience that this particular social problem was an ethnic problem. It was clear that Mexican youth were the moral panic.

While this is one of a few manifest (overt) references to race, Proposition 21 and its proponents made many latent (covert) references to race. In the nineteen articles and the proposition, ninety-four latent references were made to race. This was more than the forty-eight references made to violent crime, even though the proposition claimed to attack violent juvenile criminals. To uncover the latent messages that referred to race, empirical studies that had analyzed the criminaliza-tion of racialized populations as central to the U.S. racial order (Almaguer 1994; Takaki 1994; Lipsitz 1998; Chritianson 2000; Parenti 2000; Santa Ana 2002; Acuña 2004) were utilized. By criminalizing racialized "others," whites have historically accumulated wealth, calmed their fears of the "other," and solved white on white class conflict (see Takaki 1994). Proposition 21 of 2000 was not a unique racial policy but rather one that stemmed from a long-duré history of racial politics to subordinate and control undesirable and dishonored populations.

The rhetoric behind Proposition 21 provided a sense of community and "safety" for the California voting population by constructing an immoral, young, racialized criminal class. It served as a symbolic project for building solidarity at a time when Californians of the 1990s were reeling from the effects of a powerful economic crisis (Landis et al. 1992; Parenti 2000; Gilmore 1998 and felt threat-ened by the ever-growing population that would outnumber whites by the year 2000 (Santa Ana 2002).[4] By creating a sense of solidarity for whites and generating mechanisms for managing an increasing minority youth population, Proposition

21 calmed public anxieties. The biggest anxiety-provoking threat for white Californians at the cultural level was the prediction (and eventual reality) that California would inevitably become a minority-majority state (Santa Ana 2002). Because youth of color were associated with crime and since they were the largest growing population in the state, Proposition 21 asked voters to believe that their increase would inevitably increase crime. Proposition 21 then served as the solution to the increasing population of youth of color or, allegorically, to the increasing population of criminals. Proponents proclaimed, "The problem of youth and gang violence will, without active intervention, increase, because the juvenile population is projected to grow substantially by the next decade" (Proposition 21, 2).

As a policy aimed at "redistributing resources along racial lines," what Omi and Winant (1994) refer to as a "racial project," Proposition 21 would expand criminal justice resources aimed at controlling youth of color as the state faced economic crisis and continued to decrease its education and welfare programs (Gilmore 2007). At the dawn of the new millennium, youth of color faced racial formation—"the process by which social, economic and political forces determine the content and importance of racial categories, and by which they are in turn shaped by racial meanings" (Omi and Winant 1994)—characterized by control, criminalization, containment, and incapacitation. In California, synonymous with race, the poor were constructed as a burden to be controlled. David Garland explains, "In the political reaction against the welfare state and late modernity, crime acted as a lens through which to view the poor—as undeserving, deviant, dangerous, different—and as a barrier to lingering sentiments of fellow feeling and compassion" (2001, 132).

In the California political landscape, many other racial projects aiming to "solve" the economic crisis were implemented. Pete Wilson was a central figure in the formation of these policies. Aiming to solve the crisis of the time, he created many scapegoats—including,—"welfare mothers" who would, according to Wilson, "only lose a six pack of beer a week" due to his proposed welfare cuts, "criminal illegal aliens" that would disappear should anti-immigrant Proposition 187 pass in 1994, and college students of color who were "receiving blank checks to attend college" because of affirmative action. It is no coincidence that all of these scapegoats happened to be poor people of color—the easiest population to target since, historically, they were already perceived as burdens, threats, and criminals (Almaguer 1994; Takaki 1994).

The construction of racialized youth subculture (in this case, gang activity) as a serious criminal threat to society reaffirmed to white society that their children would still benefit from white privilege in a time of economic and demographic demise. In order to define the white, middle-class child as a good, honorable, and hardworking subject that would benefit from her achievements in school, it was essential that deviants exist. Sociologist Emile Durkheim explains the function that a criminal class plays in society: "But so that the originality of the idealist who dreams of transcending his era may display itself, that of the criminal, which falls short of the age, must also be possible. One does not go without the other" (Durkheim 1983, 74).

The white, middle-class public needed to be assured that their children would reap the benefits of white privilege in a time of multiculturalism and white demographic demise (Lipsitz 1998; Olzewski et al. 2000).[5] Tapping into these anxieties, proponents argued that an increase in the population would bring about chaos: "The FBI estimates the California juvenile population will increase by more than 33% over the next fifteen years, leading to predictions of a juvenile crime wave" (Elvey 2000a, 2000b). Politicians and the media soothed white voters by drawing a clear line between "our children" and other people's children who were the deviants (Feld 1999):

> Californians deserve to live without fear of violent crime and to enjoy safe neighborhoods, parks, and schools. This act addresses each of these issues with the goal of creating a safer California, *for ourselves and our children*, in the Twenty-First Century. (Proposition 21, 2; emphasis added)

Treating juvenile delinquents as a serious risk allowed politicians to expand their personal agendas and develop their vision for California. This vision did not include support for the poor. Instead, it intended to get rid of the children of the poor—the bulk of juvenile offenders—by any means necessary.

Instead of focusing on the needs of the poor, or on the risks of the poor, social policy such as Proposition 21 has focused on the poor as criminal risks (Feeley and Simon 1992; Harcourt 2001). Jock Young explains this as a phenomenon throughout Western societies in the late twentieth century:

> Concerned with the calculation of risk rather than either individual guilt or motivation . . . We are interested in neither liability nor pathology, deterrence nor rehabilitation. The focus is prior to the event rather than after the event, on prevention rather than imprisonment or cure . . . it is an exclusionist discourse which seeks to anticipate trouble whether in the shopping mall or in the prison and to exclude and isolate the deviant. (Young 1999, 45)

This misplaced focus on the poor as criminal has solved two problems for the state–: it has created an easy solution for dealing with the poor—containment—and it has generated group cohesion among those who have class and race privilege but notice a drop in their own quality of life (Garland 2001). Proposition 21 brought those law-abiding citizens together by generating a criminal class that created unity by voter approval; a new division of moral deviant (racialized youth) versus law-abider (white, middle-class families) was created. By tapping into the fear of the white population, politicians benefited from the racial politics of youth crime. Attacking violent youth crime became an allegory for developing a racialized youth control complex that would deeply penetrate the everyday lives and life course of young poor males of color (Rios 2006). No longer would delinquent youth be given a chance to redeem themselves for their transgressions. The new control order would hold them strictly accountable. Proposition 21, they argued, "ends the 'slap on the wrist of current law by imposing real consequences" (Elvey 2000b, 2). This crusade to manage a "juvenile predatory threat" allowed Wilson to finalize the distinction between "us" (hard working whites) and "them" (criminal black and Latino youth), placating voters by socially incapacitating young men like Juan—at the extreme, sending them to prison for life.

The Social Incapacitation of Inner-city Youth

Pete Wilson and Proposition 21 in California solidified the racialization of juvenile offenders. His proposition also further constructed youth of color as a threat to society. Nationally, the superpredator thesis and the discourse behind Proposition 21 was the foundation of a new logic for dealing with inner-city youth of color. In the California of the new millennium, the fundamental right of "innocent until proven guilty" no longer applied to youth of color; instead, they had been written off by society as inherently criminal. This racial project was carried out through coded language that, at the manifest level, promised to rid society of criminals while alluding to race in a latent manner. This discourse allowed politicians to pass the most punitive of legislations.

The superpredator thesis and Proposition 21 have created juvenile justice practices that put youth away for severe time even though many have yet to commit serious crimes. Symbolically, society has incapacitated poor young males of color even before they have transgressed the law. Today, like never before, youth of color are serving the most punitive of sentences. Youth who might have changed their lives with an opportunity to reform are now perpetually part of the criminal justice system with little to no opportunity to do so.

Juan's story is a prime example of the problems caused by Proposition 21. As he sits in his cell at St. Quentin State Penitentiary, pondering with me what could have been, he tells me that he wishes he did not drive his car that day. I tell him that I wish society had given him a second chance. He tells me that it is not society's fault that he deserves what he got for being a "fuck up." He seems to have crossed over, internalizing his captor's ideas about him: that he is an irreparable criminal to be permanently incapacitated from society. Knowing that I had been in and out of trouble growing up, having been incarcerated a few times, Juan asks me how I made it out. I tell him that I, too, had been involved in a similar incident as a teenage gang member. "Back then" (in the early 1990s), I told him, "the laws were less stringent. They sent me to a Weekend Training Academy where they made me cut shrubs and dig trenches at a county park where many of my peers socialized. I wore an ugly orange vest and got really dirty as the day progressed. As part of my punishment, the team leader would walk me near other peers who played football, swam and lay out on the beach and say, you see, you little knuckleheads, that could be you hanging out there but you choose this station and this is where the train takes you."

I continued to explain, in my own words, that this reintegrative shaming—one of the many rehabilitation components that the juvenile justice system of the past had emphasized—reminded me, in a productive way, that I did not want be pulled away from society: I wanted to be a part of it. Juan looked puzzled. He looked up through the murky, opaque prison Plexiglas and said, "Funny, I was never given that kind of chance." Like me, had Juan been given a chance after his first or second offense, he might have rehabilitated and become a productive member of society. However, society never gave him this chance. Instead, he was treated as a predatory animal in need of incapacitation, requiring "adult time for adult crime." Accordingly, society locked him up and threw away the key.

Notes

1. The crazy life.
2. For protection purposes I have created a pseudonym for "Juan" and the gang he belonged to.
3. As of 2001, Dilulio had changed his mind. In a February 2001 *New York Times* article, he states, "If I knew what I know now, I would have shouted for prevention programs" (Becker, 2001).
4. For economic and cultural crisis, see Parenti (2000); for demographic crisis, see Santa Ana (2002); for community solidarity, see Durkheim et al. (1983).
5. For a paper that demonstrates these anxieties and hermeneutic crisis (Young 1999), see Ron Unz (1999), "California and the End of White America."

References

Acuña, Rodolfo. 2004. *Occupied America: A history of Chicanos.* New York: Pearson Logman.
Almaguer, Tomás. 1994. *Racial fault lines: The historical origins of white supremacy in California.* Berkeley: University of California Press.
Babbie, Earl R. 1986. *The practice of social research.* Belmont, CA: Wadsworth.
Becker, Elizabeth. 2001. "As ex-theorist on young '"superpredators,'" Bush aide has regrets." *New York Times*, February 9. http://proquest.umi.com/pqdweb?index=0&did=68267173&SrchMode=1&sid=2&Fmt=3&VInst=PROD&VType=PQD&RQT=309&VName=PQD&TS=1181351909&clientId=1563#fulltext (accessed April 25, 2006).
Bennett, William J., John J. Dilulio, Jr., and John P. Walters. 1996. *Body count: Moral poverty—and how to win America's war against crime and drugs.* New York: Simon & Schuster.
Bradbury, Michael D. 2000. "Debate on Proposition 21: More tools are needed to curb juvenile crime: Youths who commit violent adult crimes must be made to face serous adult prison sentences." *Los Angeles Times*, February 29.
California Department of Justice. 1999. "Adult and juvenile arrests reported (table 22), Race/ethnic group by specific offense, by county." *Criminal Justice Statistics Center.* http://ag.ca.gov/cjsc/datatabs.php (accessed April 24, 2006).
Chamblis, William J. 1999. *Power politics and crime.* Boulder, CO: Westview.
Chesney-Lind, Meda, and Randall G. Shelden. 2004. *Girls, delinquency, and juvenile justice.* 3rd ed. Belmont, CA: Wadsworth/Thomson Learning.
Cowart, Greg. 2000. "Letters to the editor: Proposition 21 will help take on gang crime." *San Francisco Chronicle*, February 5. http://www.sfgate.com/cgibin/article.cgi?f=/c/a/2000/02/05/ED4770.DTL&hw=Proposition+21&sn=017&sc=202 (accessed September 9, 2006).
Chritianson, Scott. 2000. *With liberty for some: 500 years of imprisonment in America.* Boston: Beacon.
Contra Costa Times. 2000. "Election 2000: Prop.21-age alone is no defense." February 29.
Davis, Nanette J. 1999. *Youth crisis: Growing up in the high-risk society.* Westport, CT: Praeger.
Delsohn, Gary. 2002. Prop. 21 upheld by high court: The 2000 initiative makes it easier to try juveniles as adults. *Sacramento Bee*, March 1.
Desert Sun. 2000. "Take firm hand on youth crime." February 28.
Dilulio, John J., Jr. Nov. 27 1995. "The coming of the super-predators." *Weekly Standard.*
———. 1996a. "The cycle of poverty produces '"super-'predators.'"" *The Star-Ledger*, June 23.

————. 1996b. "Help wanted: Economics, crime and public policy." *The Quill* (December): 39–43.

————. 1996c. "Stop crime where it starts." *New York Times*, July 31.

Durkheim, Emile. 1982. *The Rules of Sociological Method*. New York: St. Martin's.

Elikann, Peter. 1999. *Superpredators: The demonization of our children by the law*. New York: Insight Books.

Elvey, Maggie. 2000. "Youth is no excuse: Her husband lost his life, but one of the boys who killed him will lose only nine years." *San Francisco Chronicle*, February 27.

————. 2000. "Argument in favor of Proposition 21." *2000 California primary election voter information guide/ballot pamphlet, juvenile crime. Initiative statute.* http://primary2000. sos.ca.gov/VoterGuide/Propositions/21yesarg.htm (accessed May 20, 2006).

Feeley, Malcolm, and Jonathon Simon. 1992. "The new penology: Notes on the emerging strategy of corrections and its implications." *Criminology* 30:449–74.

Feld, Barry C. 1993. *Justice for children: The right to counsel and the juvenile court*. Boston: Northeastern University Press.

————. 1999. *Bad kids: Race and the transformation of the juvenile court*. New York: Oxford University Press.

Ferguson, Ann Arnett. 2001. *Bad boys: Public schools in the making of black masculinity*. Ann Arbor: University of Michigan Press.

Gardner, Michael. 2000. "Authorities split over the merits of Prop. 21; Debate rises over bid to get tough on Juvenile crime." *San Diego Union-Tribune*, February 2.

Garland, David. 2001. *The culture of control: Crime and social order in contemporary society*. Chicago: University of Chicago Press.

Gilmore, Ruth Wilson. 1998. "Globalisation and U.S. prison growth." *Race and Class* 40 (2/3): 171–88.

Harcourt, Bernard E. 2001. *Illusion of order: The false promise of broken windows policing*. Cambridge, MA: Harvard University Press.

Holsti, Ole R. 1969. *Content analysis for the social sciences and humanities*. Reading, MA: Addison-Wesley.

Kinder, Donald, and David Sears. 1981. "Prejudice and politics: Symbolic racism versus racial threats to the good life." *Journal of Personality and Social Psychology* 40 (3): 414–31.

Kinder, Donald R., and Lynn M. Sanders. 1996. *Divided by color: Racial politics and democratic ideals*. Chicago: University of Chicago Press.

Landis, John, Cynthia Kroll, Mary Corley, Sean Stryker, and Allyson Watts. 1992. "*The California recession in perspective*." *Fisher Center for Real Estate & Urban Economics*, Report #0292. http://repositories.cdlib.org/iber/fcreue/reports/0292 (accessed April 24, 2006).

Lipsitz, George. 1998. *The possessive investment in whiteness: How white people profit from identity politics*. Philadelphia: Temple University Press.

Losen, Daniel J. and Wald, Johanna Deconstructing the School-to-Prison Pipeline: New Directions for Youth Development. New York: Walden.

Males, Mike A. 1998. *Framing youth: Ten myths about the next generation*. Monroe, ME: Common Courage Press.

Males, Mike A., Dan Macallair, and Justice Policy Institute. 2000. *The color of justice: An analysis of juvenile adult court transfers in California*. San Francisco, CA: Justice Policy Institute.

McCollum, Bill. "*Violent youth predator act of 1996*." *104th Congress*.

McCord, Joan, Cathy Spatz Widom, Nancy A. Crowell, National Research Council (U.S.), and Committee of Law and Justice. 2001. *Juvenile crime, juvenile justice*. Washington, D.C.: National Academy Press.

Mears, Daniel P. 2001. "Getting tough with juvenile offenders: Explaining support for sanctioning youths as adults." *Criminal Justice and Behavior* 28 (2): 206–26.

———. 2002. "Sentencing guidelines and the transformation of juvenile justice in the twenty-first century." *Journal of Contemporary Criminal Justice* 18 (1): 6–19.

Moran, Greg. 2000. Victims' relatives divided on tougher juvenile crime laws. *San Diego Union-Tribune*, February 28.

———. 2001. Williams prosecutors file Prop. 21 defense. *San Diego Union-Tribune*, April 14. Available: Lexis-Nexis Academic Universe, General News. Accessed July 29, 2006

National Council on Crime and Delinquency. 2002. Oakland, CA. http://www.nccd-crc.org/nccd/n_index_main.html (accessed March 7, 2006).

Office of the Attorney General. 1999. "Criminal Justice Statistics Center." Sacramento: State of California Department of Justice. http://ag.ca.gov/cjsc/spereq.php (accessed March 7, 2006).

Olszewski, Lori, Tanya Schevitz, John Wildermuth, and *Chronicle* staff writers. 2000. "New demographics changing everything; Experts examine rise of state's minorities." *San Francisco Chronicle*, August 31. Available: Lexis-Nexis Academic Universe, General News. Accessed August 16, 2006.

Omi, Michael, and Howard Winant. 1994. *Racial formation in the United States: From the 1960's to the 1990's.* New York: Routledge

Pacheco, Rod. 1999. "Proposition 21 a necessary reform." *Ledger Dispatch*, December 16.

———. 2000. "Proposition 21: YES: crime measure addresses problem." *Press Enterprise*, February 20.

Parenti, Christian. 2000. *Lockdown America: Police and prisons in the age of crisis.* New York: Verso.

Poochigian, Chuck. 2000. "Crackdown on kids? Vote yes on Prop.21; Law enforcement agencies need additional tools to clearly and predictably deter juvenile and gang violence." *San Jose Mercury News*, January 20.

Rios, Victor M. 2006. "The hyper-criminalization of black and Latino male youth in the era of mass incarceration." *Souls* 8 (2): 40–54.

San Diego Union-Tribune. 2000. Ex-governor visits S.D. to boost Prop. 21. February 25.

Santa Ana, Otto. 2002. *Brown tide rising: Metaphors of Latinos in contemporary American public discourse.* Austin: University of Texas Press.

Sasson, Theodore. 1995. *Crime talk: How citizens construct a social problem.* Hawthorne, NY: Aldine de Gruyter.

Takaki, Ronald T. 1994. *From different shores: Perspectives on race and ethnicity in America.* New York: Oxford University Press.

Turpin, James. 1996. "New legislation sets tone for future debate." *Corrections Today* 58 (5): 160.

U.S. Department of Justice. Office of Justice Programs. Bureau of Justice Statistics. 2006. *Corrections facts at a glance.* May 31. http://www.ojp.usdoj.gov/bjs/gcorpop.htm#JailRace (accessed June 15, 2006).

Unz, Ron K. 1999. California and the end of white America. *Commentary* (November). http://www.onenation.org/9911/110199.html (accessed April 17, 2006).

Van Dijk, Teun A. 1991. *Racism and the press.* New York: Routledge.

Wacquant, L. J. D., &and W. J. Wilson. 2000. "The new '"peculiar institution"': On the prison as surrogate ghetto." *Theoretical Criminology* 4 (3): 377–89.

Weber, R. P. 1990. *Basic content analysis.* 2nd ed. Newbury Park, CA.

Western, Bruce. 2006. *Punishment and inequality in America.* New York: Russell Sage.

Western, Bruce, and Becky Pettit. 2000. "Incarceration and racial inequality in 'men's employment." *Industrial and Labor Relations Review* 54 (1): 3–16.

Wilson, Pete. 1994. "A basic goal: Freedom from fear." *San Francisco Examiner*, September 21. Available: Lexis-Nexis Academic Universe, General News. Accessed April 23, 2006.

————. 1997. ""3 STRIKES"' law truly makes California safer." *Daily News of Los Angeles*, March 9, Viewpoint. Available: Lexis-Nexis Academic Universe, General News. Accessed April 23, 2006.

————. 1998. "More needs to be done to stop young criminals." *Daily News of Los Angeles*, July 28. http://www.thefreelibrary.com/MORE+NEEDS+TO+BE+DONE+TO+STOP +YOUNG+CRIMINALSa083831582 (accessed April 23, 2006).

————. 2000. "Yes on Proposition 21." *San Francisco Chronicle*, January 10.

————. 2000. "California needs juvenile justice reform." *San Diego Union-Tribune*, February 23, Opinion. Available: Lexis-Nexis Academic Universe, General News. Accessed April 23, 2006.

————. 2000. "How is juvenile justice served? Outmoded system was designed to deal with less serious crimes." *San Francisco Chronicle*, February 27. Available: Lexis-Nexis Academic Universe, General News. Accessed April 23, 2006.

————. 2000. "We 'can't excuse youth violence." *USA Today*, March 10. Available: Lexis-Nexis Academic Universe, General News. Accessed April 23, 2006.

Young, Jock. 1999. *The exclusive society: Social exclusion, crime and difference in late modernity*. London: Sage.

Zimring, Franklin E., Gordon Hawkins, and Sam Kamin. 2001. *Punishment and democracy: Three strikes and you're out in California*. New York: Oxford University Press.

5

Caught in the Net

Language and Cultural Resistance among Latina Adolescents in Juvenile Detention

Laurie Schaffner

Critical Cultural Studies

Esmeralda sat quietly looking down, inspecting the ends of her long black hair as she recounted a little bit of her family history.[1] She arrived in the United States in 1990 with her mother; her father died during U.S. attacks on El Salvador in the 1980s. Esmeralda explained:

> *Llegamos cuanda era niña*[We got here when I was a little girl], I remember *mi mamá* put me in the bed with my cousins and it was too hot. We hadda come here because it was too much problemas in San Vicente. But I don't like it here, it's OK . . . I stopped going to school at eighth grade—*este año que apenas pasó [This past year]*—I'm 16 now. Why did I quit? Well, all my friends didn't go, *y tu sabes*, we got high, *tu sabes*, I got lazy—I didn't like getting up.

Sitting in a concrete, windowless room in a temporary juvenile detention facility in Los Angeles, Esmeralda was being detained—this time, for tagging gang insignia (marking public or private property with the name of a gang), in this instance, "Mara Salvatrucha." But this charge was actually a violation of probation for her original offense—assault and battery. The original petition was filed because of a fight with her sister.

> I had run away from home because of my stupid sister. But then I went back and crawled through my window to get some of my stuff—clothes and shit. Then my mom filed a report on me for beating her. I know I can't blame all *mis problemas* on my mom, but ever since we came here, I haven't got through all my feelings yet. Cause I blamed *mi madre*. But now I know that she was the only person I could yell at.

Esmeralda attempts to sort out what part of her troubles is "her fault" and what part are the events of her biography. Her reflections are typical of what young Latinas reported in their accounts from secure U.S. juvenile facilities. Based on interviews with, and observations of, detained girls and their caregivers, this article details how Latina juvenile detainees maneuver the detention experience. By highlighting ways that Spanish language and Latino culture worked to provide the young women with a sense of solidarity and support for each other, a path of resistance to the authority of detention personnel comes in to view as they navigate the juvenile legal system.

Research focusing solely on Latina juvenile court involvement is virtually nonexistent. Previous studies of troubled Latina adolescents tend to consider such experiences as their unwed teenage pregnancy rates (Erickson 1998) or, when law breaking, their gang involvement (Harris 1988; Moore 1991; for exceptions, see Miranda 2003; Schaffner 2006). Studies on Latino delinquency generally focus on boys (Pabon 1998; Romero 2001; McCluskey 2002; Villarruel et al. 2002), while those on prison-involved Latinas tend to focus on adult women (Enos 2001; Díaz-Cotto 2006). This article widens those lenses to consider adolescent Latinas caught in the net of the juvenile legal system, with a special focus on strength-based assessments of their narratives (see also Leadbeater and Way 1996; Alford 2006; Denner and Guzmán 2006).

U.S. female adolescent offenders of Latina heritage are marginalized from conventional society in various ways: because they are young in an adult-dominated world because they are female in a male-dominated world, because they are Latinas in a European American dominant society, and because they are court-involved youth stigmatized by those who escape the attention of juvenile authorities. Owing to the lack of familiarity that court personnel and detention-line staff may have with Latinas' language habits or family customs, some unique concerns of Latinas in juvenile detention go unmet.

Conventional scholarship argues that language barriers and their link to difficulties with what are termed acculturation and assimilation are among the key problematic factors confronting Latinas (Mirandé 1985; de las Fuentes and Vasquez 1999; see also Navarro 2003). Language barriers—that is, not speaking standard English—are one reason that some Latino/as experience difficulty assimilating, meaning, fitting into mainstream U.S. culture (Valenzuela 1999). Normative ideas about acculturation—the assimilation paradigm—hold that U.S. residents, whether native-born, immigrant, or migrant, should form a cohesive nation of (preferably light-skinned) English speakers, sharing such traditions as U.S. national holidays, ideals about individuality and family mores, and various customary priorities in order to conform to the notion of a coherent nation-state (Omi and Winant 1994; see also Sabogal, Marin, and Ortero-Sabogal 1987; Marin 1993). Language barriers to acquisition of English and difficulties assimilating to dominant structures in U.S. society form part of the seminal Chicago School's "social disorganization" theory of delinquency (Shaw and McKay 1942).

Family size is widely discussed in demographic and popular literature about Mexican American reproductive habits (e.g., Rivadeneyra 1998; for critiques, see Silliman et al. 2004; Gutiérrez 2008). While the size of Latino/a families is often presented as a problem in comparison with smaller European American dominant U.S. families, the reasons why they tend to be large include remaining close to each other and being inclusive of wider kinship networks, including aunts, uncles, and cousins (Baer, Prince, and Velez 2004). This strong unity of familialism became salient as a protective factor in the narratives of the participants in this study. Hence, this article traces notions of kinship relations and their relevance to the experiences of Latina girls in detention.

Social indicators of well-being among teenaged Latinas in the Unites States reveal very real suffering among this specific population (Williams 1990; National Coalition 1999; Centers for Disease Control and Prevention 2006). Contemporary delinquency studies reveal that some correctional staff consider young women to be manipulative and oppositional (Bond-Maupin, Maupin, and Leisenring 2002; Gaarder, Rodriguez, and Zatz 2004). This study, however, begins from the viewpoint that bringing the voices of the detainees to the fore of the analysis will yield new understandings of girls' actions in the juvenile legal system (see also Gaarder and Belknap 2002). Listening to Latina girls in lock-up reveals them to be working with language and culture to navigate the system pathways, thus challenging notions that Latinas fail due to troubles with language barriers and acculturation or that they are passive and lost adolescent girls (see also Pipher 1994).

This critical perspective opens up a vision of detained girls' agency and resistance.[2] The relationship between agency and resistance, or the concept that female juvenile detainees have the ability to make subtle and overt choices to defy or subvert authority, drives the analysis presented in this article, focusing especially on the culturally specific tools at Latina girls' disposal.

Culturally specific or nonwhite ethnic European American standpoints allow views of how this agency is enacted. A century ago, DuBois observed that the "double consciousness" that African Americans gained by living in a racially divided nation actually served them well as they became leaders in the U.S. political struggle for equality (DuBois 1903). In the 1990s, Collins theorized an "outsider/within" status as an awareness that develops from the work that must be done by members with nonmainstream (read white middle-class) backgrounds to learn the logic of the dominant national culture within which outsiders live (Collins 1992). Applied to the narratives and interactions of Latina juvenile detainees, these perspectives allow a view of the deployment of this cultural capital to the Latina girls' advantage (Yosso 2005).

Whether framed as solidarity, resistance, agency, or support, observing the interactions of embattled and detained Latina girls uncovered the ways that this bilingual and transcultural group of Latinas transformed their use of language and culture, formerly often theorized as shortcomings, into an agency-activated advantage.

Latina Girls in the United States/Latina Girls in Court Involvement

The 2000 U.S. Census found that approximately one in eight people in the United States was of Latino/a origin. Mexican Americans made up the most rapidly growing ethnic group in the United States. Moreover, over one-third (36 percent) of

Latinos/as in the United States were under the age of eighteen, compared to 24 percent of non-Latino/a whites and 30 percent of African Americans (Therrien and Ramírez 2001). Latina girls rank as the largest minority group of girls in the United States (National Coalition of Hispanic Health and Human Services Organizations 1999). Of all girls aged thirteen to seventeen years in the United States, Latinas now make up 17 percent (Puzzanchera, Finnegan, and Kang 2006). Excluding girls who live in Puerto Rico, there are more than 5.5 million Latina girls under the age of eighteen living in the United States (National Coalition of Hispanic Health and Human Services Organizations 1999).

It is difficult to assess how many Latina juveniles are currently in the U.S. juvenile legal system. Any quantitative assessments of Latinas in the juvenile legal system nationally present a research challenge because the FBI arrest data are collected only on the following four categories: "black," "white," "Asian," and "Indian." In addition, juvenile justice system data in general, particularly data reflecting the experiences of Latinas, can be unreliable and misleading, largely because jurisdictions nationwide are not evenly represented and reporting is nonstandardized (Snyder and Sickmund 2006). Data specifically focused on the experiences of Latina minors in the system have not been collected nationally, definitions of ethnicity vary (see Hurtado 2003), and, most importantly, many data sets do not disaggregate data by race, ethnicity, and gender.

Since the 1980s, criminologists have been documenting the trend toward what they term the disproportionate minority representation (DMR) of adolescents with juvenile authorities (Snyder and Sickmund 2006). Between 1979 and 1995, Latino/a juveniles held in custody experienced a stunning fourfold increase in their numbers (Smith 1998). The rate at which Latina teenage girls in particular were held in juvenile custody in detention, correctional, and shelter facilities for violent offenses rose dramatically in the 1990s (Smith 1998). Moreover, a 2003 Illinois study found that there is a disproportionate representation of "Hispanic females" in the Cook County Juvenile Temporary Detention Facility (Stevenson et al. 2003). According to a one-day census count in U.S. residential placements in mid-October of 2003, Latinas comprised approximately 15 percent of girls overall in secure facilities (Sickmund, Sladky, and Kang 2005).

However, a closer look at the data from such states as California, Colorado, Arizona, and New Mexico reveal another picture. In 2002, 18 percent of juveniles in the United States were of Hispanic ethnicity (Snyder and Sickmund 2006). Although these states did not disaggregate their juvenile system population data by gender, the disproportionate representation of youth of color in the juvenile legal system has been attributed to a variety of causes, including the growth of the population of youth of color in the general public, the side effects of the "war on drugs," and institutional racism (see also Hsia et al. 2004).

Another crucial and undertheorized factor possibly affecting recent DMR of Latina adolescents involved in juvenile legal systems may be the reinvigoration of the linkages between immigration and criminal systems, including the threat of deportation by the Department of Homeland Security. The *Illegal Immigration Reform and Immigrant Responsibility Act of 1996* stipulates that non-U.S. citizens convicted of aggravated felonies must be deported after they serve their sentences

(*Illegal Immigration Reform Act 1996*). The Bureau of Citizenship and Immigration Services (BCIS) deports minors convicted of felonies in adult courts (Shepherd 2000).[3] According to the Immigration and Customs Enforcement (ICE), ICE removed 187,513 "illegal aliens" from the nation in 2006, with the current number of funded beds at 27,500 for immigration detainees awaiting deportation (Immigration and Customs Enforcement 2006). Even though it is not likely that girls are deported at the same high rates as boys for adult criminal offenses—because the majority of juveniles convicted in adult courts are boys of color—the rapid growth of DMR in juvenile jurisdictions may be affected by concordance between the immigration and criminal systems (Tanton and Lutton 1993; Snyder and Sickmund 2006).

"Cuéntame lo que piensas": Research among Detained Girls

Between 1994 and 2004, I collected one hundred interviews with young women in various juvenile court and community settings around the nation. The girls were interviewed in English or Spanish, depending on their preference. Of the one hundred minors in the sample, forty-one self-identified themselves using such terms as "Latina," "Hispanic," "from Nicaragua," "Puerto Rican," "Chicana," "Mexican," "El Salvador," "Mexican-American," one parent Asian-one parent Hispanic, one parent African American-one parent Hispanic, and so on. Approximately one-third of the interviews were conducted entirely in Spanish and another third in *mitad-mitad* (half English and half Spanish).

The young women of Latina backgrounds who participated in interviews for this study hailed from all over the United States as well as several Central and South American nations. They were interviewed in California, Massachusetts, Colorado, and Illinois. Their median age was fifteen years old; they ranged from thirteen to eighteen years of age. Because I speak Spanish, I requested to speak with young women who wanted to speak Spanish in an interview. Fourteen percent of the young women reported that they were not citizens of the United States; 36 percent preferred to speak in Spanish.

Similar to other reports reflecting the troubled lives of detained young women (Owen and Bloom 1997; Acoca and Dedel 1998), the youth who participated in this research came from depleted and disadvantaged backgrounds: 58 percent had already dropped out of school; 46 percent reported having experienced some form of physical abuse; 40 percent reported sexual harm due to interpersonal violence; and 83 percent claimed to self-medicate or were substance-dependent. As other researchers have found, the conditions for many young women in detention continue to form a tragic and dramatic hidden example of a crisis in policy failure (Belknap and Holsinger 1998; Dohrn 2004; Schaffner 2006).

The interview conversations and participant observations took place in detention facilities. The same fixed interview protocol was used with all participants, containing modules with probes regarding family, school, work, health, sexuality, friends, and favorite activities. Interview questions were open-ended, inviting life-history narratives. Interviews lasted approximately two hours; many detainees confided that they preferred sitting in the interview room and talking to being in the detention units.

The juvenile halls where these data were collected consisted of structures often attached to a local county juvenile court. Holding anywhere from twenty to three hundred youth, girls lived in separate units from boys. A typical living unit consisted of ten or twenty individual rooms (cells) with windows on the doors so that staff can easily make eye contact with residents. In newer facilities, each room might have its own stainless steel seamless toilet and sink, with a concrete bed frame bolted to the wall. Some units were organized dormitory style but the individual room configuration was more common in the facilities visited for this research. Girls were generally allowed to congregate in a living area with book-shelves, tables and seats, and a television set during after-school or after-dinner periods but the threat of "room time" was never far.

The girls' temporary detention stays averaged ten days to three months depending on the status of their case. Sometimes young women were awaiting court dates, transfer to long-term placements, or a trip to a local county hospital. Others were actually designated to serve their dispositional outcome (sentence) in the county facility.

Studying children's lives, specifically girls' experiences with trouble and violence, raises myriad methodological concerns, which challenges the essence of ideas about power and positivism (Fine 1992; O'Connell, Davidson, and Layder 1994; Tolman and Brydon-Miller 2001). My intention in this research was to learn more about the nuanced processes of meaning-making that young women undertake as they are adjudicated delinquent in the U.S. juvenile legal system. One of these processes evolved from noticing when and under what circumstances Latina participants evoked cultural references (to food, music, or fashion styles) or code-switched into Spanish (see also Myers-Scotton 1993; Stavans 2004). Focusing in on coding such exchanges opened a view of those interactions as specific sites of rebellion against detention authorities as well as signals of support for each other.

Resistance and Solidarity in their Own Words

In the United States, official terms such as "English language barriers" and "limited English proficiency" signify the significant challenge that learning English presents to new arrivals (Baker et al. 1996; Riley 1998). Some voters' sense of threat over immigration issues reached a visible peak when California passed its "English-only" Initiative, Proposition 227, in June of 1998. This zealous attempt to end bilingual education in California's public schools occurred even though English is already the first language in the United States. Even so, as of the 2000 census, 20 percent of the U.S. population spoke a language other than English at home (approximately 47 million residents; U.S. Census Bureau 2000).

Language worked in the experiences of Latina minors in detention in various ways. Some pretended that they did not speak English at all; others spoke Spanish under their breath or to each other in ways that staff could not understand;

still others translated for each other and (leaving some things out) for detention authorities. Elsewhere, language has been theorized as a strategy of resistance (e.g. Britton 1999; de Certeau 2002). Similarly, being bilingual served as a survival strategy for detained Latinas in this study as well. In addition to being a way to communicate with each other, having what was in effect a secret language afforded them privacy and a form of resistance to being ordered to speak only English, or to be ordered not to speak at all, which seemed to them to be unnecessarily arbitrary. Being bilingual also gave them the opportunity to help other Spanish monolingual detainees.

> GIRL ONE, whispering: *Oye, Mari, no se lo digas a nadie, le vi a tu primo ayer.* [Hey Mari, don't tell anyone—I saw your cousin yesterday.]
> GIRL TWO: *A donde? Aquí?* [Where? Here?]
> GIRL ONE: *Sí. Estaba saliendo de la iglesia cuando nuestra unit estaba entrando.* [Yeah, he was leaving the church when our unit was entering.]
> COUNSELOR (GUARD): Ladies! I told you I don't like you speaking that jibber-jabber! I'm not havin' it! English only—this is America in here!

The prohibition of open communication among residents (detainees) is common in many secure establishments. Increasingly, girls are segregated from boys in girl-only classrooms, exercise areas, detention units, and court calendars. Security and legal considerations proscribe that "crime partners" not be housed together. Not surprisingly, adolescents feel an urgent need to communicate with and about each other for a variety of reasons, so talking is often the site of contention and rebellion for staff and detainees. Enjoying knowledge of a language other than English served to facilitate some Latina girls' subverting of the rules.

Young women would say things under their breath in Spanish that the counselors in charge could not understand. I overheard many such exchanges, for examples:

> [Under her breath] *"Esa cabrona puede irse a la chingada* [This bitch can go fuck herself]. Yes, ma'am, I going now" (seventeen, Mexican national-African American, weapons offense)
> Can I please go to the bathroom? [Under her breath] *Pnche pendeja [Stupid idiot]* . . . (fifteen, Chicana, drug sales).

These minor expressions of slang and expletives in Spanish, a language not understood by the guards, displayed an opposition to the detention personnel's total control over them as well as belied the common misperception of the quiet, acquiescent Latina girl (e.g., Pipher 1994; see also Taylor, Gilligan, and Sullivan 1995).

Others were truly at a loss, asking me in Spanish, Do you know where my baby is?":

> *Qué chingados estoy haciendo aquí? No entiendo por qué me llevaron por aca. Estoy in la carcel para qué? Por cuanto tiempo? No entiendo nada!* [What the fuck am I doing here? I don't know why they brought me here. I'm in jail for what? For how long? I don't understand any of this.] (sixteen, Mexican national, drug offense).

This young mother was sitting in a U.S. juvenile facility because she had been arrested with two other peers (unwittingly, she claimed) transporting three kilos of marijuana in the trunk of the car across the San Ysidro-Tijuana border. I found it alarming to think that this adolescent, incarcerated mother would feel compelled to ask any passing stranger who spoke Spanish, such as the random researcher, for assistance with her case. When monolingual Spanish speakers found other young women in the detention facilities that spoke both English and Spanish, they tried to get answers for each other from court personnel.

Language itself became salient as a topic of conversation during this research at different times—in response to my question, "What language do you prefer to speak?" 36 percent said "Spanish." A few girls said something like "I don't speak Spanish or English good—just half and half." For some young women, it was true: they literally spoke neither Spanish nor English.

> Yo no sabía that the car had mota en el trunke [I didn't know there was pot in the trunk]. Yo solamente estaba [I was just] driving it over to a friend's house for my compadre. Yo sé que [I know that] they don't believe me, pero deveras, te juro, yo no sabía [but, for real, I swear, I didn't know](seventeen, Mexican national, federal felony charges for transporting drugs across the U.S.-Mexican border).
>
> These little putas think they can fuck with me in here, pero, sabes que? Chinga su madre! [You know what? They can go fuck themselves!] I don't like anybody frontin' me like that. Out here, you gotta come right out y chingarse la madre si tu quieres [and fuck with them if you want to] make it out here on these streets (fifteen, Salvadoran, aggravated assault).

This last example was from a girl born in the United States of parents who fled Central America in the 1980s. Everyone at home spoke mostly Spanish. At school, everyone spoke mostly English. With friends, she, too, said she spoke mitad-mitad.

While among each other, or when talking to other bilingual people, this slippage in and out of both English and Spanish, with heavy usage of slang in both languages, did not pose a problem. But in one facility in Northern California, girls could get extra room time, locked in their individual cells, for speaking Spanish. Stepping into interactions and translating for adults transformed into moments of both resistance and an opportunity to show support and provide protection for each other.

> Mira [Look], Mrs. Jamison, she din't know about standing with her toes on the line. She say she sorry for talking Spanish, Mrs. Jamison. We teach her the rules, Mrs. Jamison, please! (detainee)

In addition to trying to protect their friends, detainees who spoke out also broke an unwritten detention code, "every man for himself" [sic], evident in girls' as well as boys' facilities. Insofar as animosity among girls (sometimes fueled by staff) reigns in many facilities, risky demonstrations of sisterhood are noticeable.

Others who were fluent in Spanish and English related that they felt that being bilingual was a source of pride and gave them confidence. They told of how they had to translate for each other, for court personnel, and for their families. One fourteen-year-old girl spoke in a peculiarly formal fashion.

> My mother and I study together on weekends. Sometimes I help the other girls in my class with their homework. In here, these young ladies don't seem to be ableto speak either English or Spanish properly. I help when I can, but I don't want any trouble (fourteen, Nicaraguan-African American, petty theft: shoplifting).

She enunciated all the words in her accounts with a comfortable use of a wide vocabulary. After talking with her for awhile, I asked her if she switches her speech habits around her friends. She said that they all tease her "for talking proper." But she said it was because her mother, who is from Nicaragua, spoke English "carefully and well" and pressed it upon her daughter, for whom she held "high hopes."

Others demonstrated how they translated only certain parts of the events in order to protect themselves in their families.

> OK, I got into a fight with my girl, but I told *mi mama* that I was just fighting back from a girl at school. I don't want her to find out I'm gay—she will kick me out of the house! (fourteen, Salvadoran, aggravated domestic battery)Here, this young woman was in the midst of cognitive work to give meaning to the idea of the difference between domestic violence as intimate partner abuse and the common portrayal of girls as "girl fighters" who assault each other physically over boys or jewelry or other trivial items. Navigating a filial relationship with her mother that was important to her and sorting out how to survive in a homophobic heteronormative environment, she deployed her knowledge of English and Spanish to her advantage by drawing on bilingual skills to hide the fact from her mother that she was being adjudicated delinquent, not for a random assault but for domestic violence—a different statute and with different implications altogether.

Being bilingual was a strength that court-involved young women used as a developmental edge over their monolingual English counterparts. But I cannot recall even one counselor, probation officer, or judge praising a girl for maintaining her bilingual skills or encouraging her to practice. Although it is rarely framed as a source of strength or an advantage for "at-risk" youth, this use of bilingual skills, as other research has shown, is seen as a developmental strength that can build a sense of connection and improved academics among other samples of youth (Matute-Bianchi 1986).

Sharing cultural experiences played an important role as a tool Latinas used to survive day-to-day life in lock-up. Girls communicated who they were to adults and each other by expressing their opinions of norms of sexuality, beauty, favorite food and music, and family relations. While there is no monolithic homogenous Latino culture per se (De Genova and Ramos-Zayas 2003), Latino/a tradition, or Latinidad, like most cultural traditions, includes intensive family protectionist norms (Madriz 1997; Garcia, Hurwitz, and Fraus 2004). Studies have found that family-mediating protective factors—such as parental supervision, low parent-child conflict, social support, and religious practices—work to provide positive well-being among adolescent immigrants (Ybarra 1983; McLoyd et al. 2000;

Harker 2001). Latina teenagers in particular are more likely to seek help from parents, family members, or friends than professionals (Rew, Resnick, and Blum 1997; see also Roberts and Sobhan 1992). Other research describes "familialism" as a core characteristic in Latino/a culture. These scholars argue that during and after acculturation, examining the many meanings of family is crucial to understanding Latino/a culture (Zambrana and Logie 2000; see also McHaney 2004, Minugh 2004). In my research, court-involved young Latinas, like their schoolgirl counterparts, reported more than problems and abuse in their family lives. One young woman talked about how her mother raised her and her brothers: "Oh, *mis hermanos* walk me everywhere, I never have to worry about getting around. *Así lo hacemos en mi familia [That's how we do it in my family]*." Study participants shared how they were able to access protection from danger by asking for help from their parents, siblings, cousins, aunts, and other family members.

Among Latinas in the juvenile legal system, relationships with other girls mattered, but in the next example, culture trumped gender—actually, culture trumped sexuality.[4] About 7 percent of this sample self-identified as bisexual or lesbian. One young Latina was a gang-identified girl who was also comfortable in her sexual identity as lesbian. Long hair tied in a ponytail, she said she wore over-sized clothes—baggy jeans, running shoes, and a sports-practice starter shirt—in her life outside the facility. In one part of each interview, I asked young women to describe themselves, "If I had to meet you somewhere, like at a McDonald's, how would I recognize you?" In her case, she replied:

> Oh, I'm cool, *chevere*. I got my hair done like this, my bangs all out and shit. My Filas, and my 49ers starter shirt nice and big over my Ben's. I'm kinda short, but cute! (fifteen, African American-Puerto Rican, assault and battery).

In lock-up, all girls in the unit wore the same khaki pants and colored sweat-shirts. In some places, they wore gray jumpsuits.

> I'm cool hanging' with my homies. They jus' treat me like one of them, anyway. Mira, me bein' gay is no real big thing with them, once they could feel me, know what I'm sayin'?
>
> OK, pero hijole, when them other girls come in here lookin' all crazy? *Ni madres!* I am not down with that, know what I'm sayin'? I mean, I am not tryin' to get with that at all, know what I'm sayin'? *Ni madres!*

This young woman was referring to a group of youth advocates who came in to deliver a gender-specific program to girl detainees that focused on "teen health" but was really about lesbian sexuality. The group, from a local peer-led nonprofit agency that serves gay teenagers, were white, mostly dressed in torn clothes, with spiked hair dyed in bright colors, big army boots, safety pins all over their clothes, and a lot of facial piercing. Even though many of these youth shared lesbian or bisexual identities, observing the interactions between the young gang-identified Latina lesbian and the white, privileged, punk rocker, queer youth revealed that in a given setting, at times, ethnic identity, not sexual identity, became more salient for some system-involved girls.

As discussed earlier, girls of color are disproportionately represented among various stages of juvenile legal system populations (Hsia et al. 2004). It is not uncommon to listen to Latinas talk among themselves, comforting, taunting, and regaling each other with tales of home-cooked food and their favorite music.

> GIRL ONE: *Sabes que?* You don't even know, girl. *En mi casa, siempre comemos tamales que mi abuela hace* [In my house, we always eat the tamales my grandmother makes]
>
> GIRL TWO: *Ni modo, hombre! Alla con mi tía, como me gustan las enchiladas! Aray!* [Oh man, over at my uncle's—I love the enchildadas!] God, I wish I could go home.
>
> GIRL THREE: Shit, if I was home, I'd be kickin' it with my homies and a can of Tecate. *Oye—te gustan escuchar* Shakira [Do you listen to Shikira] ? She got a new CD.
>
> GIRL TWO: Fuck Shakira! That's dyke music.

Through food and music, girls identify themselves, aligning with certain identities and ruling out others. The other girls who do not speak Spanish or who like other kinds of food and music often chime in with their opinions. It is at this point that guards usually announce that "talk is dead!" This English-language-only command signaled that all talking was instantly no longer allowed. Anyone who uttered any audible syllable would be immediately sent to serve "room time," a word-phrase that the monolingual Spanish-speaking detainees learned upon pain of solitary confinement.

Sixteen percent of the Latinas in this sample had experienced the death of one of their parents. For example, one sixteen-year-old was in detention in Southern California for crossing the U.S.-Mexican border with marijuana in the trunk of the car. While she was in detention, she found out that her father had passed away. She was grieving the death of her father and was inconsolable. Because of her incessant sobbing, guards placed her on a suicide watch, which required her to be alone in a cell. One of her main complaints was that the detention facility staff would not give her a roommate. She said she was "going crazy" because she did not want to sleep alone. Unfortunately, because cultural specificity was not taken into consideration in this case, the system was actually doing more harm than good.

Anthropologists note different family styles of social distance (Sault 1996). In the United States, sleeping alone is considered desirable and necessary for privacy. But in many cultures around the world, privacy and familial warmth are configured such that co-sleeping arrangements in which several people share the same rooms, beds, or sleeping mats is a desired and expected norm. When visiting relatives or friends arrive, they may join others of the same gender in sleeping in rooms together (Sault 1996). In these cultural contexts, sleeping alone is considered lonely and unpleasant. The young woman whose father had died missed her sisters, aunts, and the comfort of cousins and family members to help her in her grieving.

Language and Family Ideals as Survival Tools

Governmental bureaucracies such as juvenile court authorities are not required by law to provide bilingual services at all times when minors are in their custody. Latinas in secure juvenile facilities may specifically experience the English-only government mandates. In confined juvenile settings, for example, monolingual Spanish-speaking youth in an English-speaking dominant system can be doubly harmed. Not only do girls form a minority in majority-male institutions, if a girl speaks only Spanish or prefers Spanish as her first language, there may be no one on the staff in any given shift in that facility who is bilingual in Spanish and English. Quite literally, then, monolingual detainees may not have a conversation for eight hours, until shift change, as evidenced by the quote above from an interview with the sixteen-year-old Mexican girl concerned because she did not even know where her baby was.

Another unique challenge for some Latinas in the United States is the stigma of speaking nonstandard English or English with an accent. Not understanding what is happening around them due to language and communication challenges can be a frightening experience. As one young journalist framed it, for first or second generation immigrant youth of Latino/a descent, the journey of immigration is not only a journey of nation but also a journey of language: coming to the United States was "a journey from Español to Spanglish" (Jimenez 1998; see also Colgrove 1998, New American Youth Initiative 2001). This is compounded in a juvenile legal setting where language is tied to security issues.

As the quotes cited earlier reveal, young court-involved Latinas reported using language skills to accomplish various tasks, including signaling support for each other, helping each other out by translating questions, concerns, and key terms in order to avoid punitive attention of juvenile authorities, as well as through feigning limited English proficiency (see also Olmedo 2003).

For some Latinas, being proficient in both Spanish and English, having "good" accents in both, and familiarity with slang in both Spanish and English was an asset. "On the outs," these Latina adolescents understood the unwritten social and cultural rules in both the barrio and the mall. In terms of navigating the juvenile court system, for the young women in this sample, bilingualism, in their case, made them outsiders, within in the most beneficial sense of the term, in both the barrio and the courtroom.

Dislocation resulting from immigration and forced migration form another set of experiences framed by mainstream sociological scholarship as challenges to Latino/a youth (Yans-McLaughlin 1990; Marin 1993). The intense experience of transnational relocation during childhood may stimulate adverse social, educational, and health outcomes. Traditionally, forced immigration has been linked to psychological disjuncture in identity development for children (Burnham et al. 1987; Rumbaut 1994, 1997). Disruptive international mobility was found to be detrimental in educational attainment among U.S. adolescents (Gibson and Ogbu 1991), a factor closely correlated with court involvement.

Girls in detention expressed longing for familiar customs such as wanting more culturally sensitive approaches, as evidenced by examples such as the comments made by the young woman grieving the passing of her father. One of the experiences brought up in many of the accounts of the young women in this sample was a sense of dislocation from being "from" somewhere else and moving to the United States at early ages. Other studies of young Latinos who found themselves involved with juvenile legal authorities struggled with such cultural disconnection (Lutton 2001).

Girls and women experience the relocation and resettlement of their families differently than boys and men: processes of transnational dislocation are gendered (Hondagneu-Sotelo 1996; George 2005). Acculturating to the particulars of the gender-sex hierarchy in the United States may present challenges to teenaged immigrant Latinas. For example, one study found that psychosocial stress may arise for some young women as they work to acculturate to a dominant culture that presents definitions of women's roles that differ from those familiar to the immigrant Latina mother (Zayas and Solari 1994).

In other research with adolescent Latina females, young women expressed that there were moments when they felt they could not turn to their mothers for advice about navigating an "American" adolescence (Hurtado 2003). According to one study, acculturation for Latina girls can signal imperatives to adopt attitudes and beliefs that actually bring them harm, such as early sexual behavior or dropping out of school (National Coalition of Hispanic Health and Human Services Organizations 1999; Harker 2001). Research finds that having parents who were born in Spanish-language nations, or who speak a primary language at home other than English, may diminish the imperative for respect towards parental authority among children now living in English-speaking nations (National Coalition of Hispanic Health and Human Services Organizations 1999). These kinds of research results—feeling disconnected from school and not being able to turn to mothers for family support—are represented in the accounts of the court-involved young women in this sample as well, such as Esmeralda, who, sitting in lock-up, felt disconnected from school and family, displaying allegiance to her Salvadoran gang friends.

While adolescent self-destructive behavior is well documented among court-involved Latinas, other kinds of responses to being transcultural—including agency in terms of implementations of strength, self-definition, and resistance—can also be documented by spending time with Latinas in juvenile facilities. As this research shows, Latina girls use cultural concepts to convey their solidarity with each other and in rebellious response to harsh treatment in the system. Other scholars have noted that high levels of leadership skills can result from participation in more than one culture (Garza and Gallegos 1994).

From Victimization to Volition

Young Latina women in this sample demonstrated that claiming Latino/a culture, tradition, and language generated positive feelings of being special and as having something to which to belong. Young women would refer to culture through mentions of specific beliefs, holidays, habits, foods, and fashions that they enjoyed:

"Latinas wear Fila, Black girls wear Nike." In such ways, system-involved Latinas held on to an identity that was separate from that of "criminal." As Latinas in multicultural settings, they used cultural symbols both to communicate with each other and to anchor their sense of self.

In incarcerated settings where even talking is controlled, such minor infractions as speaking Spanish to authorities who do not know the language, or requesting tortillas with a meal, can be seen as subtle attempts to unsettle the orderly flow of the punitive surveillance. Solidarity among the adolescent detainees was evidenced through the signaling of their connection to each other by even their most minimal use of terms of endearment in Spanish.

In contrast to the stream of distressing news both in the statistics and in the public imagination, I found that Latina teenagers in detention drew upon resources at hand as they traversed the system. In interviews, many young women reported that family loyalty was strong among their communities of kin. Some talked about feeling protected by their brothers. Young women interviewed for this project reported that even if they disobeyed their mothers, they felt a strong love from them and for them. Teenage girls of Latina descent in the United States face unique challenges due to their specific location in the gender-sex system and cultural hierarchy in dominant society. Concerns such as language barriers and acculturation may present special challenges for young women caught in juvenile court involvement. However, listening to their accounts and noticing the strategies deployed by Latinas in juvenile detention revealed strengths derived from being bilingual and transcultural, offering counternarratives to conventional delinquency literature that sees only dislocated and alienated Latino/a delinquents.

Notes

1. These data are part of a larger study (Schaffner 2006). All interviews were conducted with informed parental or guardian consent and juvenile assent. All names and identifying details have been slightly altered in order to protect confidentiality. This article draws from research supported by the Woodrow Wilson Foundation Grant in Children's Health and the Office of Social Science Research at the University of Illinois at Chicago.

2. For analyses of the tension between agency and structure, cf. Sewell (1992), and of resistance as a deployment of the power of the powerless, cf. Havel (1985) and Scott (1989).

3. According to the BCIS, the INS deports an average of almost 4,000 noncitizens per week, an annual total of 176,000 in 1999. Among them are 1,100 convicted persons per week, for an annual total of 62,359 in 1999. Mexican nationals accounted for 83 percent of all removals and 77 percent of criminal deportations (INS 2000).

4. Elsewhere, scholars working in critical race, radical feminist, and postcolonial theories, such as Chandra Mohanty (1984), Gloria Anzaldua (1987), and Kimberle Crenshaw (1991), provide rich analyses of the crucial role that theories of intersectionality play for understanding the experiences of marginalized populations. Working with young Latinas in detention requires that same vigilance against making monolithic claims of the universality of "the Latina experience."

References

Acoca, Leslie, and Kelly Dedel. 1998. *No place to hide: Understanding and meeting the needs of girls in the California juvenile justice system.* San Francisco, CA: National Council on Crime and Delinquency.

Alford, Sue. 2006. *The sexual health of Latina adolescents—Focus on assets.* Washington, D.C.: Advocates for Youth.

Anzaldua, Gloria. 1987. *Borderlands/La Frontera: The new mestiza. 2nd ed.* San Francisco, CA: Aunt Lute Books.

Baer, Judith, Jonathan Prince, and Judith Velez. 2004. Fusion or familialism: A construct problem in studies of Mexican American adolescents. *Hispanic Journal of Behavioral Sciences* 26 (3): 263–73.

Baker, David W., Ruth M. Parker, Mark V. Williams, Wendy C. Coates, and Kathryn Pitkin. 1996. Use and effectiveness of interpreters in an emergency department. *Journal of the American Medical Association* 275:783–88.

Belknap, Joanne, and Kristi Holsinger. 1998. An overview of delinquent girls: How theory and practice have failed and the need for innovative changes. In *Female offenders: Critical perspectives and effective intervention, ed. Ruth T.* Zaplin, 31–64. Gaithersburg, MD: Aspen Publishers.

Bond-Maupin, Lisa, James Maupin, and Amy Leisenring. 2002. Girls' delinquency and the justice implications of intake workers' perspectives. *Women and Criminal Justice* 13:51–77.

Britton, Celia. 1999. *Edouard Glissant and postcolonial theory: Strategies of language and resistance. Richmond*: University of Virginia Press.

Burnham, M. Audrey, Richard L. Hough, Marvin Karno, Javier I. Escobar, and Cynthia A. Telles. 1987. Acculturation and lifetime prevalence of psychiatric disorders among Mexican Americans in Los Angeles. *Journal of Health and Social Behavior* 28:89–102.

Centers for Disease Control and Prevention. 2006. *Youth risk behavior surveillance, United States, 2005.* Atlanta, GA: Centers for Disease Control and Prevention.

Colgrove, James. 1998. Immigrant youth and the journey across cultures. *Bridges* 4:1–7.

Collins, Patricia Hill. 1992. *Black feminist thought: Knowledge, consciousness, and the politics of empowerment.* New York: Routledge.

Crenshaw, Kimberle. 1991. Mapping the margins: Intersectionality, identity politics, and violence against women. *Stanford Law Review* 43 (6): 1241.

de Certeau, Michel. 2002. *The practice of everyday life.* Berkeley: University of California Press.

De Genova, Nicholas, and Ana Y. Ramos-Zayas. 2003. Latino rehearsals: Racialization and the politics of citizenship between Mexicans and Puerto Ricans in Chicago. *Journal of Latin American Anthropology* 8 (2): 18–57.

de Las Fuentes, Cynthia, and Melba J. T. Vasquez. 1999. Immigrant adolescent girls of color: Facing American challenges. In *Beyond appearance: A new look at adolescent girls,* ed. Norine Johnson, Michael Roberts, and Judith Worrell, 131–50. Washington, D.C.: American Psychological Association.

Dennner, Jill, and Bianca L. Guzman, eds. 2006. *Latina girls: Voices of adolescent strength in the United States.* New York: New York University Press.

Diaz-Cotto, Juanita. 2006. *Chicana lives and criminal justice: Voices from el barrio.* Austin: University of Texas Press.

Dohrn, Bernardine. 2004. All Ellas: Girls locked up. *Feminist Studies* 30 (2): 302–23.

DuBois, William Edgar Burghardt. 1903. *The souls of black folks.* New York: Penguin Classics.

Enos, Sandra. 2001. *Mothering from the inside: Parenting in a women's prison.* Albany, NY: SUNY Press.

Erickson, Pamela. 1998. *Latina adolescent childbearing in East Los Angeles.* Austin: University of Texas Press.

Fine, Michelle. 1992. *Disruptive voices: The possibilities of feminist research.* Ann Arbor: University of Michigan Press.

Gaarder, Emily, Nancy Rodriguez, and Marjorie Zatz. 2004. Criers, liars, and manipulators: Probation officers' views of girls. *Justice Quarterly* 21 (3): 547–78.

Gaarder, Emily, and Joanne Belknap. 2002. Tenuous borders: Girls transferred to adult court. *Criminology* 40 (3): 481–517.

Garcia, Lorena, Eric L. Hurwitz, and Jess F. Fraus. 2004. Acculturation and reported intimate partner violence among Latinas in Los Angeles. *Journal of Interpersonal Violence* 20 (5): 569–90.

Garza, Raymond T., and Placida I. Gallegos. 1994. Environmental influences and personal choice: A humanistic perspective on acculturation. *Hispanic Journal of Behavioral Sciences* 7:365–79.

George, Sheba. 2005. *When women come first: Gender and class in transnational migration.* Berkeley: University of California Press.

Gibson, Margaret, and John Ogbu. 1991. *Minority status and schooling: A comparative study of immigrant and involuntary minorities.* New York: Garland.

Gutierrez, Elena. 2008. *Fertile matters: The politics of Mexican-origin women's reproduction.* Austin: University of Texas Press.

Harker, Kathryn. 2001. Immigrant generation, assimilation, and adolescent psychological well-being. *Social Forces* 79 (3): 969–1004.

Harris, Mary G. 1988. *Cholas: Latino girls and gangs.* New York: AMS.

Havel, Vaclav. 1985 [1978]. The power of the powerless. In *The power of the powerless: Citizens against the state in central Eastern Europe, ed.* John Keane. London: Hutchinson.

Hondagneu-Sotelo, Pierrette. 1996. *Gendered transitions: Mexican experiences of immigration.* Berkeley: University of California Press.

Hsia, Heidi, George Bridges, and Rosalie McHale. 2004. *Disproportionate minority confinement, 2002 update.* Washington, D.C.: Office of Juvenile Justice and Delinquency Prevention.

Hurtado, Aida. 2003. *Voicing Chicana feminisms: Young women speak out on sexuality and identity.* New York: New York University Press.

Illegal Immigration Reform and Immigrant Responsibility Act of 1996, Pub.L. 104-208, Div. C, 110 Stat. 3009-546.

Immigration and Customs Enforcement. 2006. ICE Office of Detention and Removal fact sheet. Washington, D.C.: U.S. Department of Homeland Security.

Jimenez, Eduardo. 1998. From *Espanol* to Spanglish. *YO! Youth Outlook*, April 22, 325.

Leadbeater, Bonnie Ross, and Niobe Way, eds. 1996. *Urban girls: Resisting stereotypes, creating identities.* New York: New York University Press.

Lutton, Linda 2001. A world of difference for Mexican American kids. *Youth Today* (May), 17–19.

Madriz, Esther. 1997. Latina teenagers: Victimization, identity, and fear of crime. *Social Justice* 24 (4): 39–55.

Marin, Gerardo. 1993. Influence of acculturation on familialism and self-identification among Hispanics. In *Ethnic identity: Formation and transmission among Hispanics and other minorities,* ed. Martha Bernal and George Knight, 181–96. Albany, NY: SUNY Press.

Matute-Bianchi, Maria. 1986. Ethnic identities and patterns of school success and failure among Mexican-descent and Japanese-American students in a California high school: An ethnographic analysis. *American Journal of Education* 95:233–55.

McLoyd, Vonnie C., Ana Mari Cauce, David Takeuchi, and Leon Wilson. 2000. Marital processes and parental socialization in families of color: A decade review of research. *Journal of Marriage and the Family* 62:44-1070-93.

McCluskey, Cynthia Perez. 2002. *Understanding Latino delinquency*. New York: LFB Scholarly Publishing.

McHaney Danner, Ruth. 2004. Family talk: Multicultural families embrace their heritages through languages. *Spokane Spokesman-Review*, November 8.

Miller, Jody. 2000. *One of the guys*. Oxford: Oxford University Press.

Minugh, Kim. 2004. Multicultural—And proud of it. *Sacramento Bee*, December 16.

Miranda, Marie. 2003. *Homegirls in the public sphere*. Austin: University of Texas Press.

Mirande, Alfredo. 1985. *A Chicano experience: An alternative perspective*. Notre Dame, IN: University of Notre Dame Press.

Mohanty, Chandra T. 1984. Under western eyes. *boundary 2* 12 (3): 333–58.

Moore, Joan. 1991. *Going down to the barrio: Homeboys and homegirls in change*. Philadelphia: Temple University Press.

Myers-Scotton, Carol. 1993. *Dueling languages: Grammatical structure in code-switching* New York: Oxford University Press.

National Coalition of Hispanic Health and Human Services Organizations. 1999. *The state of Hispanic girls*. Washington, D.C.: National Coalition of Hispanic Health and Human Services Organizations. www.cossmho.org.

Navarro, Mireya. Redefining Latino: This time in English: language divides Hispanic culture in U.S. *New York Times*, June 8, 2003.

New American Youth Initiative. 2001. *Health and mental health issues: Immigrant youth and families in New York*. Report no. 2. Winter, NY: The Center for New York City Affairs, New School University.

O'Connell Davidson, Julia, and Derek Layder. 1994. *Methods, sex, and madness*. New York: Routledge.

Olmedo, Irma. 2003. Language mediation among emergent bilingual children. *Linguistics and Education* 14 (2): 143–62.

Omi, Michael, and Howard Winant. 1994. *Racial formation in the United States: From the 1960s to the 1990s*. 2nd ed. New York: Routledge.

Owen, Barbara, and Barbara Bloom. 1997. *Profiling the needs of young female offenders: Final report to the executive staff of the California Youth Authority*. Washington, D.C.: National Institute of Justice.

Pabon, Edward. 1998. Hispanic adolescent delinquency and the family: A discussion of sociocultural influences. *Adolescence* 33:941.

Pipher, Mary. 1994. *Reviving Ophelia: Saving the lives of adolescent girls*. New York: Ballantine Books.

Puzzanchera, C., T. Finnegan, and W. Kang. 2006. Easy access to juvenile populations. http://*www.ojjdp.ncjrs* (accessed December 1, 2005).

Rew, Lynn, Michael Resnick, and Robert Blum. 1997. An exploration of help-seeking behaviors in female Hispanic adolescents. *Family and Community Health* 20:1–15.

Riley, Richard W. 1998. *Improving opportunities: Strategies from the Secretary of Education for Hispanic and Limited English Proficient Students*. Washington, D.C.: National Clearinghouse for English Language Acquisition. http://www.ncela.gwu.edu (accessed March 16, 2005).

Rivadeneyra, Lucia. 1998. ?De Verdad Dos Son Mas Felices que Uno?: El Numero de Hijos en Las Familias Mexicanas. *Fem* 22 (181): 14–19.

Roberts, Robert E., and Mahboob Sobhan. 1992. Symptoms of depression in adolescence: A comparison of Anglo, African and Hispanic Americans. *Journal of Youth and Adolescence* 21 (6): 639–51.

Romero, Mary. 2001. State violence and the social and legal construction of Latino criminality: From el bandido to gang member. *Denver University Law Review* 78:1081–1118.

Rumbaut, Ruben G. 1994. The crucible within: Ethnic identity, self esteem, and segmented assimilation among children of immigrants. *International Migration Review* 28 (4): 748–94.

Rumbaut, Ruben G. 1997. Assimilation and its discontents: Between rhetoric and reality. *International Migration Review* 31 (4): 923–60.

Sabogal, Fabio, Gerardo Marin, and Regina Ortero-Sabogal. 1987. Hispanic familism and acculturation: What changes and what doesn't? *Hispanic Journal of Behavioral Sciences* 9:397–412.

Sault, Nicole. 1996. Many mothers, many fathers: The meaning of parenting around the world. *Santa Clara Law Review* 36 (2): 395–408.

Schaffner, Laurie. 2006. *Girls in trouble with the law.* New Brunswick, NJ: Rutgers University Press.

Scott, James. 1989. *Weapons of the weak: Everyday forms of peasant resistance.* New Haven: Yale University Press.

Sewell. William. 1992. A theory of structure: Duality, agency, and transformation. *American Journal of Sociology* 98 (1): 1–29.

Shaw, Clifford, and Henry McKay. 1942. *Juvenile delinquency and urban areas.* Chicago: University of Chicago Press.

Shepherd, Robert E., Jr. 2000. Collateral consequences of juvenile proceedings. *Criminal Justice Magazine* 15 (3): 59.

Sickmund, Melissa, T. J. Sladky, and Wei Kang. 2005. *Census of juveniles in residential placement databook.* http://www.ojjdp.ncjrs.org/ojstatbb/cjrp.

Silliman, Jael, Marlene Gerber Fried, Loretta Ross, and Elena Gutierrez. 2004. *Undivided rights: Women of color organize for reproductive justice.* Boston: South End Press.

Smith, Bradford. 1998. Children in custody: 20-year trends in juvenile detention, correctional, and shelter. *Crime and Delinquency* 44 (4): 526–73.

Snyder, Howard, and Melissa Sickmund. 2006. *Juvenile offenders and victims, 2006 national report.* Washington, D.C.: Office of Juvenile Justice and Delinquency Prevention.

Stavans, Ilan. 2004. *Spanglish: The making of a new American language.* New York: Harper-Collins/Editorial Rayo.

Stevenson, Phillip, Timothy Lavery, Kimberly Burke, Megan Alderden, Christine Martin, Mark Myrent, Kelly Marzano, and Tracy Pasold. 2003. *A study of disproportionate minority representation in the Cook County juvenile justice system.* Chicago: Illinois Criminal Justice Information Authority.

Tanton, John, and Wayne Lutton. 1993. Immigration and criminality in the U.S.A. *Journal of Social, Political, and Economic Studies* 18:217–34.

Taylor, Jill McLean, Carol Gilligan, and Amy Sullivan. 1995. *Between voice and silence: Women and girls, race and relationships.* Cambridge, MA: Harvard University Press.

Therrien, Melissa, and Roberto Ramirez. 2001. *The Hispanic population in the United States: Population characteristics, March 2000.* Current Population Reports P20-535. Washington, D.C.: U.S. Census Bureau.

Tolman, Deborah, and Mary Brydon-Miller, eds. 2001. From subjects to subjectivities: A handbook of interpretive and participatory methods. New York: New York University Press.

United States Bureau of the Census. 2000. *Profile of general demographic characteristics*. Washington, D.C.: U.S. Census Bureau.

United States Bureau of the Census. 2004. Current population survey, March 2004. Washington, D.C.: U.S. Census Bureau.

Valenzuela, Angela. 1999. *Subtractive schooling: U.S.-Mexican youth and the politics of caring*. Albany, NY: SUNY Press.

Villarruel, Francisco, Nancy Walker, with Pamela Minifee, Omara Rivera-Vazquez, Susan Peterson, and Kristen Perry. 2002. *Donde esta la justicia? A call to action on behalf of Latino and Latina youth in the U.S. juvenile system*. Institute for Children, Youth, and Families. East Lansing: Michigan State University.

Williams, Norma. 1990. *The Mexican American family: Tradition and change*. Dix Hills, NY: General Hall.

Yans-McLaughlin, Virginia. 1990. *Immigration reconsidered: History, sociology, and politics*. Oxford: Oxford University Press.

Ybarra, Lea. 1983. Empirical and theoretical developments in the study of Chicano families. In *The State of Chicano Research on Family, Labor, and Migration*, ed. Armado Valdez, Albert Camillo, and Tomas Almaguer. Stanford, CA: The Stanford Center for Chicano Research.

Yosso, T. J. 2005. Critical race theory in education: Whose culture has capital? A critical race theory discussion of community cultural wealth. *Race Ethnicity and Education* 8 (1): 69–91.

Zambrana, Ruth E., and Laura A. Logie. 2000. Latino child health: Need for inclusion in the U.S. national discourse. *American Journal of Public Health* 90 (12): 1827–51.

Zayas, Luis H., and F. Solari. 1994. Early childhood socialization in Hispanic families: Culture, context, and practice implications. *Professional Psychology: Research and Practice*, 3.

6

Lost Votes, Lost Bodies, Lost Jobs

The Effects of Mass Incarceration on Latino Civic Engagement

Juan Cartagena

Images/*Imagenes*. Snapshots and visualizations. I recall a number of them as prelude to these thoughts on the effects of mass incarceration on the civic life of Latino communities across this country:

- Cheo seemingly ignores the plea of voter registration volunteers on the sidewalk outside the Melrose Job Center in the Bronx. Actually, he is circling to tell the young woman in a quiet moment that it is not that he does not care about politics; it is that he cannot vote because of a drug conviction in his past. He is mistaken, she assures him. And so begins another attempt to undo decades of misinformation about who is entitled to exercise what we assumed was a basic citizenship right—the right to vote.
- Steven writes from prison to learn more about his court challenge to felon disfranchisement in New York. His pen recounts another illogical policy in the way the state metes out political power. You see his Latino body is counted as a resident of the upstate, white, rural community he is housed in; not his home community. For political redistricting, his "representative" in Albany benefits from his body count without having to cater to his opinions, for he is disfranchised.
- Fifty percent is a nice round number. It was splashed in a number of newspapers as part of a report by the Community Service Society in 2004. A full 50 percent of black men in New York City were jobless. The number that was barely noticed was 44 percent. A full 44 percent of Latino men in the city at the same time were also jobless. The black-white binary of racial discourse and economics was in full bloom again.

- The faces in the first post-Rose Garden reception after the signing of the Fannie Lou Hamer, Rosa Parks, and Coretta Scott King Voting Rights Reauthorization and Amendments Act of 2006 by President Bush in August 2006 signaled a glorious day for the African American community—particularly its old guard veterans of the civil rights struggles of the 1960s; and deservedly so, because they led the reauthorization of the most important piece of civil rights legislation in our lifetime. The leadership among our Latino representatives was muted, however. Yet Latino political power today, like black political power, is tied to the success of the *Voting Rights Act*[1].
- A municipal court judge in New Jersey sits in his courtroom, where hurried consultations between defendants and court-appointed attorneys are commonplace. A young Puerto Rican female announces that she is prepared to plead guilty to a low-level drug offense. The judge, also Puerto Rican, does his duty and explains the fines and the short-term jail sentence. The young woman is whisked away. Years later, the judge regrets his role on the so-called war on drugs.

Latino community leaders and organizations have yet to fully understand the ramifications of the criminal justice system on their ability to overcome obstacles to meaningful civic engagement. But the numbers are simply too big to ignore now. The prison industrial complex continues to sustain itself by misguided political ploys regarding so-called drug wars and tough-on-crime politicians to the point that crime is generally at record lows, while imprisonment is at historic highs. Latino collective political strength is directly affected: lost are the votes that are taken from our communities upon incarceration; skewed are the counts of fictitious "residents" that inflate the relative political strength of these prison towns; and unemployed are the hundreds of former prisoners who face statutory impediments to finding a decent job. Civic engagement—what I loosely call the ability of individuals and communities to invest social capital and networks (Putnam 1995) to extract public benefits in the exercise of political strength and economic self-determination—is thus compromised in our *barrios*. These issues and how they intersect are particularly relevant in New York—home to over a million Latinos.

Mass Incarceration as a Latino Issue

National data on mass incarceration reveal troubling trends that are collectively manifested in Latino communities. The rate of incarceration in the United States (751 per 100,000) surpasses the rate of every other country in the world (International Centre for Prison Studies 2008). When viewed from the prism of adults only, the rate of incarceration is a startling one in 100 in the United States; for whites, it is one in 194; for blacks, it is one in 29; and for Latinos, it is one in 64 (Pew Center on the States 2008). This national data obscures the effects of mass incarceration at the state level where Latino imprisonment is grossly disproportional to white imprisonment. White incarceration never surpasses the national average of 751 per 100,000 residents, but in Pennsylvania, Idaho, Connecticut,

Massachusetts, Arizona, New Hampshire, and Colorado, the incarcerations rates are over 1,000 for every 100,000 Latino residents, while North Dakota, Montana, Utah, Texas, Oklahoma, California, New York, Iowa, Kentucky, and Nebraska have rates for Latinos that exceed the national average (Paige and Beck 2006).

In turn, state data obscures the devastating effects of mass incarceration at the community level where, in urban centers like New York City, for example, the phenomenon is best described not as mass incarceration but as massive prison and jail migration. New York City accounts for 40 percent of the state's population but contributes close to two-thirds of the total state prison population. Drilling down further, we learn that fourteen of the city's community districts are home to only 17 percent of the city's adult population but account for over 50 percent of the adults sent to prison every year (Cadora 2007). Government expenditures to jail, imprison, return, and reimprison these populations of persons of color reveal the perversity of this migration when 150 individual "million dollar blocks" can be identified in New York City; that is, New York expends, in a city block, more than one million dollars to remove and return residents to and from prison each year (Cadora 2007). In communities marked by concentrated poverty this overinvestment in criminal justice responses as the primary mode of governance questions whether public safety is really achieved. This somewhat counterintuitive notion has been documented by the work of Todd Clear and others: "High levels of incarceration concentrated in impoverished communities has a destabilizing effect on community life, so that the most basic underpinnings of informal social control are damaged. This, in turn, reproduces the very dynamics that sustain crime" (Clear 2002, 193). At a minimum, it cries out for more effective, sustainable investments over time. The reality is, nonetheless, that there is an overconcentration of persons with former criminal records in many of New York City's Latino neighborhoods.

Lost Votes

The effects of the use of mass incarceration as a social tool in urban communities cannot be measured solely by the harms they cause on the individual prisoners or the disruption and dislocation they produce for families, as important as those may be. The "punishment industry," as Angela Davis (2003) calls it, also suppresses the political voice of prisoners and former prisoners, renders voiceless the home communities from which they came and still live in, and dilutes the collective voting strength of Latinos as a whole.

Felon disfranchisement is the amalgamation of a series of state laws that remove the basic badge of citizenship—the franchise—from a segment of our population in some cases going back over a hundred years. Presumably still citizens, persons with felony convictions become even more invisible and excised from society by these laws. Civil death, as the concept is known in Anglo-Saxon jurisprudence, removed political rights and even property from those guilty of serious crimes. This was also reflected in the societal norms of Greek and Roman civilizations that removed political rights from those who committed transgressions against customary law. After the Revolutionary War, the newly independent states rejected the property forfeiture of civil death but maintained the civil disabilities that accompanied the commission of "infamous" crimes (Pettus 2005). This became the foundation of felon disfranchisement as it is practiced today in the United States. Currently, forty-eight states engage in some combination of eliminating the franchise to prisoners, probationers, and parolees; eleven states permanently disfranchise any citizen convicted of a felony. Only Maine and Vermont allow prisoners to participate politically from their cells, as does Canada to the north and Puerto Rico to the south. Voter qualification and disqualification is not the exclusive province of federal laws in this country, as was painfully obvious when the Bush-Gore election of 2000 made everyone expert in the nuances of Florida election law. The "dual citizenship" consequences of our deference to states' rights and federalism nurtures a "double polity" (Pettus 2005) that prevents, at least in today's hyperpartisan environment, any immediate resolution of important national concerns like the dismantling of the electoral college, the establishment of a national norm for vote tabulation, the quest for statehood for Washington, D.C., and the elimination of felon disfranchisement in all elections.

Recent developments in the courts, especially foreign courts, have condemned this inequitable practice, but felon disfranchisement is, nonetheless, common in the Americas. Within the last decade, the highest courts in Canada, South Africa, and Israel, and the European Court of Human Rights, have decisively and eloquently outlawed incarceration disfranchisement—the loss of voting rights during the period of physical incarceration.[2] Chief Justice McLachlin, in the Canadian court opinion, was particularly insightful: "Denial of the right to vote to penitentiary inmates undermines the legitimacy of government . . . It countermands the message that everyone is equally worthy and entitled to respect under the law— that everybody counts . . . It is more likely to erode the respect for the rule of law than to enhance it, and more likely to undermine sentencing goals of deterrence and rehabilitation than to further them."[3] Similarly, in Puerto Rico, voting is extended to all duly qualified voters, including prisoners who have voted through absentee ballots since at least 1980 and whose vote is pivotal in close elections.[4] Puerto Rico, however, is clearly the exception within the Latino nations of Central and South America and the Caribbean, as evidenced by a recent petition for a hearing on felon disfranchisement practices before the Inter-American Commission on Human Rights. No other country in the Americas—indeed, the world—is as punitive and retrogressive in its felon disfranchisement policies as the United States, further marginalizing our election systems as models of inequality. The United States is the only country in the Americas that permanently disfranchises its citizens across broad categories of crimes; the twelve other countries that disfranchise voters postincarceration do so for limited periods or for limited offenses. Incarceration disfranchisement is the most common form of disfranchisement in the Americas, but a number of countries follow the U.S. practice of extending the period of disfranchisement. The Latino nations that appear to most closely approximate, though never replicate, the United States in these policies include Chile, Costa Rica, Cuba, Dominican Republic, Mexico, and Uruguay. Conversely, the Latino nations that have adopted only incarceration disfranchisement are Panama, Paraguay, Peru, and Venezuela (The Sentencing

Project and the International Human Rights Law Clinic at Washington College of Law, American University 2007).

So ingrained is the practice of felon disfranchisement in places like New York—which adopted it in 1821—that even persons who are no longer subject to its reach believe they are disqualified from voting because of a prior criminal conviction. The Community Service Society ran successful street voter-registration campaigns for years, registering more than a quarter of a million voters.[5] Yet many otherwise qualified voters—those no longer on parole—were victims of decades of misinformation about voter eligibility. Community education efforts by various nonprofit organizations were insufficient to rectify blatantly false information that county boards of elections furnished to prospective voters who were previously incarcerated. In numerous cases, prospective voters who were no longer serving parole were illegally advised that they were ineligible or were required to produce unnecessary documentation to prove their eligibility. Uniformity was nonexistent as sixty-two county boards devised their own exclusionary policies. In 2003, advocacy and the threat of litigation from attorneys at the Community Service Society, the Legal Action Center, and the Brennan Center for Justice—all based in New York City—resulted in the first-ever meeting of officials from the Department of Corrections, the Division of Parole, and the New York State Board of Elections. Ultimately, in October 2003, the Board of Elections issued a statewide policy prohibiting the demand for additional proof because it "has the effect of disenfranchising people, and we are in the business of enfranchising people"—surprisingly refreshing words from an agency that refused to act in decades (New York State Board of Elections 2003). Implementation, however, is still at issue.

Much of the discussion to date has focused on the effects of felon disfranchisement on the America's black community, and rightfully so, since blacks remain disproportionately found among the prison and parolee population in numbers that are inconsistent with propensity for crime in general or propensity for illegal drug use and trade in particular. Latinas and Latinos are also disproportionately saddled with these disabilities, but because their numbers are not as stark as blacks, or because data collection is woefully inadequate and mired in a black-white binary (Walker et al. 2004),[6] or because Latino civil rights and advocacy organizations have yet to fully understand the devastating effects of a discriminatory criminal justice system on Latino community life, the debate has not fully incorporated Latino voices of concern.[7]

In the courts, however, Latino prisoners have been catalysts in the movement challenging the unlawfulness of felon disfranchisement, starting with the example laid down by Mr. Abrán Ramírez in California—a former prisoner whose Equal Protection Clause challenge to felon disfranchisement went all the way to the Supreme Court and lost. His case, *Richardson v. Ramirez*,[8] was brought by formerly incarcerated Latinos before the Supreme Court, which rejected the constitutional challenge by ruling that felon disfranchisement is sanctioned by the Fourteenth Amendment to the Constitution. The court thus converted a section of that amendment intended to politically penalize states that came into the Union after the Civil War that insisted on disqualifying former slaves, into a sword against full black and Latino political empowerment. Not until the passage of the Fifteenth

Amendment were states directly prohibited from denying the vote on the basis of race. The *Ramirez* case is significant on a number of levels. The majority opinion echoed the dual citizenship framework of state sovereignty and federalism when it dismissed Mr. Ramirez, and essentially his call to protect his rights as an American citizen, by insisting that states were well within their traditional role of defining the limits of the franchise (Pettus 2005). The dissent by Justice Thurgood Marshall, on the other hand, presaged the rationale of the international tribunals cited above when it noted that disfranchisement hinders the goal of rehabilitation and, in equally declarative language, struck at the heart of the objection to voting by the formerly incarcerated based on suppositions about their opposition to the political views of the status quo: "The process of democracy is one of change . . . The ballot box is the democratic system's coin of the realm. To condition its exercise on support of the established order is to debase that currency beyond recognition."[9]

Following this lead, Latino prisoners were major players in three out of the four major lawsuits filed in this decade.[10] *Farrakhan v. Washington*[11] is a pending *Voting Rights Act* challenge to the discriminatory nature of felon disfranchisement in Washington State brought by black, Latino, and Native American prisoners. *Hayden v. Pataki*[12] is a pending constitutional law challenge to New York's felon disfranchisement laws brought by black and Latino prisoners and parolees. Finally, *New Jersey State Conference NAACP v. Harvey*[13] was an unsuccessful state constitutional law challenge to felon disfranchisement and its effects on black and Latino parolees in New Jersey. The fact that the only two pending court challenges to felon disfranchisement were prisoner-led distinguishes these efforts in the courts from Latino advocacy efforts in general. In both Washington and New York, prisoners acting as their own attorneys *pro se* filed the actions, and public interest law attorneys subsequently followed the call.

What these prisoners assert, in large part and often with no response, is that the number of lost votes in Latino communities in a handful of critical states in the country demands attention from Latino advocates and all students of political empowerment. The states of California, Texas, New York, and Florida are illustrative in this regard. They each rank among the top four states with the largest Latino populations and also among the top four states with the largest number of prisoners in the country. If the hypothesis is that felon disfranchisement directly affects Latino voting strength by robbing potential votes from Latino neighborhoods, one would expect to find this pattern in the states with the largest numbers of Latino residents.

California

California has the largest number of Latino residents in the United States and ranks second in the largest number of prisoners of all races—166,532 in 2005 (Paige and Beck, 2006). Felon disfranchisement operates in California in a way to deprive the vote from prisoners and from parolees until the completion of their parole. Recent estimates (Demeo and Ochoa 2003) indicate that while Latino residents comprise 28 percent of the state's voting-age population, they comprise 37 percent of all persons subject to felon disfranchisement. In 2003, this represented over 100,000 potentially lost Latino votes. This estimate does not account for citizenship. Estimates for 2006 show that California—at 30 percent—is slightly above the national noncitizenship average and is 29 percent for Latinos as a whole (United States Hispanic Leadership Institute, 2008); thus, the number of lost votes is still significant.

Texas

Texas ranks first, unquestionably and decidedly, in the number of prisoners incarcerated within its borders. The United States ranks first in the world in the rate of incarceration, a ranking fueled by Texas. In 2005, the prison population in Texas was 171,338 (Paige and Beck 2006). Texas is also the state with the second highest number of Latino residents in the United States. All persons convicted of a felony in the Lone Star State are disfranchised while in prison or while on probation or parole. In 2003, 30 percent of all persons subject to felon disfranchisement in Texas were Latino—just slightly higher than the Latino proportion of the voting age population. With the breadth of the "punishment industry" in full bloom in Texas, this translates as over 156,000 potentially lost Latino votes (Demeo and Ochoa 2003). Accounting for noncitizenship, Texas, at 25 percent, has the lowest rate of Latino noncitizens than any of the four states highlighted herein (United States Hispanic Leadership Institute, 2008), thus ensuring a deeper loss of potential Latino voting strength due to felon disfranchisement policies.

New York

New York's Latino population ranks third in the country, and its total prison population ranks fourth in the United States with 62,963 persons in prison in 2005 (Paige and Beck 2006). Similar to California, only those persons with felony convictions still in prison or on parole are subject to felon disfranchisement laws. New York's felon disfranchisement laws go back to 1821 at a time when the state constitution imposed higher property requirements on "men of color" as a condition for voting. It took the Civil War and the passage of the Fifteenth Amendment to the U.S. Constitution to nullify racial suffrage but New York went ahead and made felon disfranchisement mandatory in 1894 (Cartagena, Nelson, and Gibbs 2003). Unlike any of the four states highlighted here, however, Latinos in New York are severely and disproportionately disqualified by the state's criminal and election law policies. In 2003, Latinos comprised 34 percent of all persons disqualified because of felon disfranchisement, while they represented only 14 percent of the state's voting age population (Demeo and Ochoa 2003). As a result, over 43,000 potentially lost Latino votes are in New York. New York's noncitizenship rate for Latinos (26 percent) is lower than the national average and demonstrates that adjustments for citizenship still result in a loss of tens of thousands of potential votes (United States Hispanic Leadership Institute 2008).

Florida

The Sunshine State's Latino population ranks fourth in the country, while its total prison population ranks third (Demeo and Ochoa 2003). In 2005, its prison population was 87,545 (Paige and Beck 2006). Up until 2007, it had one of the most restrictive felon disfranchisement laws in the country: only a governor's pardon plus the approval of three members of the state cabinet could restore the right to vote of former prisoners, no matter how much time elapsed from the day they left Florida's prisons. Now only persons convicted of certain nonviolent felony offenses can vote without applying to the state's clemency board.[14] While the Latino citizenship voting age population is disfranchised at a higher rate than the total population, Latinos are actually underrepresented in disfranchisement rates when only voting-age population data is analyzed. Nonetheless, approximately 119,100 potential Latino votes were lost in 2002. Applying 2006 noncitizenship rates (United States Hispanic Leadership Institute 2008), the loss of votes in Florida (with a rate of 31 percent for Latinos) is still significant.

Thus, in California, Texas, New York, and Florida, felon disfranchisement creates clear racial markers in the ability of Latino communities to exercise their votes freely and to aggregate them in a way that fairly and fully reflects their voting strength. These obstacles are typically the ones addressed by the *Voting Rights Act*. The courts, however, have turned away every *Voting Rights Act* challenge to the discriminatory nature of felon disfranchisement, save one: the pending challenge by black, Latino, and Native American prisoners in *Farrakhan v. Washington*. The *Voting Rights Act* is the most important piece of civil rights legislation in our history—the 5,132 Latino elected officials in the United States (National Association of Latino Elected Officials 2006) owe their positions to the success of the *Voting Rights Act*. While the number of Latino representatives are at an all-time high, they represent less than 2 percent of the 493,830 elected officials in this country, demonstrating, once again, that more remains to be done to reach electoral parity (DeSipio 2005). In jurisdictions covered by the *Voting Rights Act*, like New York, the need for a continued and vital enforcement effort to implement the promises of the Act is clear to Latino, black, and Asian advocates (Cartagena 2008).

These court challenges—brought by Latino prisoners, among others—are critically important in understanding the contours of racial discrimination because they lie at the intersection of voting discrimination and discrimination in the criminal justice system today. It remains to be seen in the *Farrakhan* case whether the Act will be openly interpreted to outlaw what is a clear electoral practice and procedure that results in Latinos (and blacks) having less of an opportunity to elect candidates of their choice. As the lower court recognized in the *Farrakhan* case, Washington State, like New York State, as depicted by the prisoners in the Hayden case, has a criminal justice system that produces racially skewed results. Every state that sanctions felon disfranchisement conditions the qualifications for the franchise on the operation of its own criminal justice system. When the latter produces discriminatory and biased outcomes, the state then operates, manages, and establishes both arms of governmental activity implicated in felon disfranchisement. Unlike external factors outside the control of the state that produce racially disparate outcomes, in felon disfranchisement, the state controls the electoral apparatus and the criminal justice system. By effectively delegating decision making on who is disqualified from voting to its criminal courts, the state has merely implemented an internal shift in governmental responsibility over a quintessential area of government regulation: the franchise. With that responsibility comes accountability, and, in New York (as in other states), electoral decision making as it affects Latinos with felony convictions, who are otherwise qualified to vote, has been vested in an arm of government that produces racially biased results. This discrimination must end.

Body Counts

New York State is approximately 62 percent white; yet its prison population of over 67,000 inmates is over 80 percent African American and Latino. Moreover, two-thirds of all persons in New York State prisons resided in New York City at the time of their incarceration. Yet all forty-three prisons built in New York since 1976 have been built in upstate New York communities, not in the city (Wagner 2006). These salient facts dictate how prison policies, census counts, and residency affect the political power of Latinos in the Empire State.

Legislative districts for the New York State senate and assembly are redrawn after every decennial census. In addition to ensuring equal opportunity for blacks and Latinos to elect candidates of their choice in the redrawn districts, the initial task of mapmakers stemming from the one-person, one-vote doctrine of constitutional law, is to create districts that are close to equal in total population. New York's practice of following the U.S. Census Bureau policy of counting prisoners as residents of their prison towns and not their home neighborhoods—for the purpose of legislative redistricting—has a direct bearing on the political strength that Latinos wield in downstate, New York City communities.

The policy of the U.S. Census Bureau is to count persons in their "usual residence,"[15] which is defined as where they spend more nights a year than any other place—for prisoners, this means the prison cell. And this policy has not been fully tested in the courts on racial discrimination or *Voting Rights Act* grounds to date. In one case addressing the inclusion of only registered voters in the population base for state senate legislative districts in Hawaii, the Supreme Court noted that the choice to include or exclude transients, short-term residents, aliens, or "persons denied the vote for conviction of crime"[16] in the redistricting base is left to the discretion of the states—yet another echo of the deference to state's rights and federalism.

Effectively then, upstate New York legislative "representatives" depend on bodies snatched, if you will, from New York City streets and placed in upstate prisons to shore up their representational advantage over urban communities. Comparing upstate rural districts with prisons to downstate districts in Queens County, Peter Wagner concluded that census adjustments to reflect home residencies of New York State prisoners would place at least seven current upstate districts at risk of unconstitutionality because their size would be impermissibly below the maximum deviation permitted (Wagner 2002). Correspondingly, Queens County, currently with the largest overpopulated districts and over one-quarter Latino, would also have to be resized to make them smaller, thus potentially adding an additional district downstate. Body counting also benefits upstate rural New York communities economically at the expense of downstate Latino communities of the city. Coxsackie, New York, home to 3,000 inmates that account for over 27 percent of its population, is at a competitive advantage for federal antipoverty funds "because they earn little or no money, prisoners in the town's two correctional facilities . . . drove down the median income on the census and made it eligible to receive more funding from the federal Department of Housing and Urban Development."[17] Lost votes, now lost funding—another consequence for Latinos attributable to the nation's mass imprisonment fixation.

Body counting prisoners as fictitious members of legislative districts in prison towns and the concomitant loss of political strength that it represents for racial and language minorities is not just limited to New York. Texas, a critical state for assessing Latino political power nationally, has nearly half of the twenty-one counties in the country that have over one-fifth of their residents incarcerated, with Harris and Dallas counties providing a disproportionate number of prisoners in the state system (Wagner and Heyer 2004). Like New York, Texas election law establishes that residency in your home community is not lost because of incarceration. The concerns expressed so far focus on the inequities this practice creates for black communities, but Harris County, which supplies over 21 percent of state prisoners in Texas, and Dallas County, which supplies over 15 percent (Wagner and Heyer 2004), are significant Latino counties as well evidencing additional loss of political strength for Latinos collectively.[18] In Florida—another state with import for collective Latino political power—ten of the state's largest cities are located in counties with the highest number of net inmate exports to prisons outside their confines (Stinebrickner-Kaufman 2004). Studying the partisan effects of this policy in Florida only, Stinebrickner-Kaufman concluded that the more inmates a county imports the more likely it is to be a Republican stronghold, and the more Democrat a county is in the Sunshine State, the more likely its strength is diluted by the method of counting inmates in this manner (Stinebrickner-Kaufman 2004, 278).

In New York City, at least two solutions are possible to redress this inequity. At the federal level, the U.S. Census Bureau can adjust census data to account for the home district of all prisoners. This federal fix got a major boost in a report commissioned by the bureau where, in September 2006, the National Research Council called upon the bureau to study how changes can be made in the way the nation counts prisoners, citing as "compelling" the evidence of "political inequities in redistricting" that stem from current practice (Roberts 2006). Unfortunately, this report did not call upon the U.S. Census Bureau to enact an immediate solution for the 2010 census. The second political fix can come from New York itself. Indeed, the New York State Constitution already establishes that, for the purposes of voting, residence is neither gained nor lost because of incarceration.[19] Current legislative proposals in Albany would require the Department of Corrections to notify election officials of the home address of each inmate, and this information, in turn, would be submitted to the U.S. Census Bureau for a true accounting of the residence of all New Yorkers.

In the absence of any solution, Latino bodies will continue to be counted as residents of their upstate prison towns. Combined with felon disfranchisement, they become a captive source of additional political strength for their "representatives," who, in turn, can ignore their political opinions because, by operation of New York law, they have lost their most basic of citizenship rights—the right to vote.

Joblessness

Gabriel Torres Rivera, a former prisoner himself, works at the Community Service Society in New York City on a number of issues affecting Latinos and blacks who were formerly incarcerated. As an organizer and political activist, he continued the work of his colleague in the Young Lords Party, the late Richie Pérez, by organizing nonpartisan voter registration drives at the street level and voter education efforts aimed at community based organizations. Understanding the impact that the formerly incarcerated have on community life in marginalized communities, he advocates for the day when these individuals, and their brothers and sisters behind bars, will be able to vote freely. Their unique perspective on criminal justice, the prison complex, joblessness, and reentry needs to be heard. A series of discussions that he organizes under the banner of the New York Reentry Roundtable in New York City creates a space for advocates and the formerly incarcerated from over fifty organizations to share information on transitional programs and strategies on how to strive for successful reentry. At the top of these issues is joblessness.

Over two million persons are incarcerated in America, but the population of persons with prior felony records is close to 12 million or 8 percent of the domestic labor force (Pager 2003). According to some estimates, approximately 600,000 to 700,000 prisoners will be released every year this decade, representing a fraction of the current U.S. labor force but a sizeable 30 percent of the annual growth of our domestic labor force (Freeman 2003). Given society's collective neglect of our educational system and its abandonment of rehabilitation as a feature of incarceration, it is no surprise that these individuals are saddled with numerous impediments in the job market: lower education levels, less work experience, and a disproportionate incidence of medical problems that impede full employment.

In New York City, disengagement from the labor force runs deep in black and Latino communities. In 2004, the Community Service Society documented that the jobless rate for black men was 50 percent, and for Latino men, it was 44 percent (Levitan 2004). The rate of joblessness is a better measure of economic recession in urban America because unemployment rates issued by governmental authorities only capture those who are actively looking for work, not the persons who have given up because access to work in a recession may be futile. This disconnection from full civic engagement in minority communities starts at much earlier ages as well. Additional research from the Community Service Society demonstrates that the level of "disconnected youth"—those sixteen- to twenty-four-year-olds who are neither in school nor participating in the labor market—has particular racial markers as well. In 2005, estimates put the number of disconnected youth in New York City at 170,000 (today, the estimate is 200,000), with disproportionately high rates for black and Latino men (16.6 percent and 16 percent, respectively) and the highest disconnection rate in the city for Latinas (20 percent; Levitan 2005).

Of course for the formerly incarcerated, the biggest job impediment is the criminal conviction itself. The stigma of criminality, real or perceived, is evident in the job market, and New York City is no exception. Recent test cases with New York City job applicants indicate racial bias in how employers treat applicants with felony convictions, demonstrating that white applicants fare much better than Latino or black applicants (Pager and Western 2005). More importantly, New York law forecloses employment in a number of trades and professions or makes access to such trades more difficult for persons with felony convictions. Over thirty occupations are foreclosed to the formerly incarcerated under New York law and policy-governing licensing authorities (Legal Action Center 2006). Undoubtedly, for some of these professions, the prohibitions are more rationally related: police officer, firefighter, and teacher. But in New York, "good moral character" or "moral turpitude" requirements are also placed on licensure for barbers and hair stylists, plumbers, junk dealers, tow truck operators, and real estate brokers. While New York law does not sanction an absolute prohibition to employment for persons with criminal records,[20] in practice, the reality is something different.

A recent report by the New York City Bar Association highlights the strong correlation between the extent of unemployment and the incidence of crime and recidivism (New York City Bar Association 2008). Acknowledging the fact that between one-fifth and one-third of prisoners were unemployed just prior to incarceration, and that an astounding 89 percent of persons who violate the terms of probation were unemployed at the time of the violation, the report reinforces the truism that economic stability is a positive deterrence to recidivism.

Civic engagement in Latino communities on both labor and political participation fronts reflects similar patterns in the country as a whole: employment and higher incomes correlate positively with voter registration and voter turnout. In the 2004 presidential election, Latinos who were employed or self-employed had higher turnout rates than those who were unemployed or jobless; similarly, Latinos with incomes above $50,000 had much higher turnout rates than those below that benchmark; finally, voter registration rates were consistently higher within the Latino community when labor participation was accounted for (United States Hispanic Leadership Institute 2008). From the perspective of Gabriel Torres Rivera and the members of the Reentry Roundtable, these national trends are reflected in the city's *barrios* as well.

Ultimately, misinformation about the "collateral consequences" of incarceration (Mauer and Chesney-Lind 2002) makes advocacy by groups like the Community Service Society more important today than ever. And the misinformation begins in the courthouse. The collateral consequences of incarceration are not treated as punishment under U.S. law; instead, the courts deem them a form of civil regulation (National Conference of Commissioners on Uniform State Laws 2005). Despite numerous decisions that require that guilty pleas be made knowingly, voluntarily, and intelligently, neither judges, prosecutors, nor defense attorneys routinely engage an accused person in a conversation about the "collateral" consequences of pleading guilty. Thus, joblessness and the number of trades that are foreclosed from the thousands of defendants who cop a guilty plea are never fully explained to unknowing defendants in the criminal justice system. From the law's perspective, the consequences are ancillary or collateral; but from the perspective of the Latina or Latino defendant from the *barrios*, the consequences are real and direct.

Conclusion

Urban America is an important locus for understanding Latino America. To this end, the intersection of criminal justice policies, political power, and joblessness paints the contours of series of phenomena that must be accounted for in any discussion about Latinos and prison. Loïc Wacquaint's use of the term "carceral continuum," while meant primarily for the African American community in the United States, resonates for Latinos as well. Wacquaint speaks to a "carceral mesh" where economic and political forces have reshaped the functionality of ghetto as home to a low-wage work force, thus making the "ghetto more like a prison" and simultaneous phenomena reflected in the inhabitants in our prisons that make the "prison more like a ghetto" (Wacquaint 2000). For Latinos and blacks, the law's prohibitions on full political engagement for prisoners and parolees through felon disfranchisement and census residency rules exacerbate and prove these observations. The additional, unnecessary, and unwise legal restrictions on the licensure of many professions and trades to former prisoners in urban America adds to this continuum by destroying hope for civic engagement as a rehabilitative tool for formerly incarcerated Latinos.

At the heart of change is the threat of power, taken and realized, not merely demanded. Recognizing that Latino collective political strength requires a look at the "punishment industry" and its legacy in our streets today is step that all Latino institutions, activists, academics, and leaders must take in order to wield the political power needed to achieve social justice.

Notes

1. Voting Rights Act, 42 U.S.C. § 1971, et seq. (1965).
2. Canada: *Suave v. Canada* (Chief Electoral Officer, 3 S.C.R. 519, 2002 SCC 68; 2002); South Africa: *Minister of Home Affairs v. National Institute for Crime Prevention and Reintegration of Offenders* (CCT 03/04; 2004); Israel: *Hilla Alrai v. Minister of the Interior* (HC 2757/96; 1996); Europe: *Hirst v. United Kingdom* (Hirst No. 2).
3. *Suave v. Canada* (Chief Electoral Officer), 3 S.C.R. 519, 2002 SCC 68, para. 58 (2002).
4. *Partido Socialista Puertorriqueño v. Comisión Estatal de Elecciones y Administrador General de Elecciones*, 80 JTS 92 [p. 1738] citing 16 L.P.R.A. 3052 to 3242 as amended by Ley Núm. 3 of September 8, 1980. See also Daniel Rivera Vargas (2004).
5. See the Community Service Society of New York (CSS) Web site, http://www.cssny.org (accessed January 19, 2009).
6. As Walker et al. (2004), conclude, any data on Latinos in the criminal justice system must be interpreted with caution because Latinos are specifically undercounted and

reported as white in general. Marc Mauer (2007) notes that eleven states fail to report data on the number of incarcerated Latinos.

7. For example, a recent and comprehensive state-by-state digest of Latino political issues, *The Almanac of Latino Politics*, is silent on the effects felon disfranchisement on Latino voting strength (United States Hispanic Leadership Institute).

8. *Richardson v. Ramirez*, 418 U.S. 24 (1974).

9. *Richardson v. Ramirez*, 418 U.S. 24, 82-83 (1974).

10. The only exception is *Johnson v. Bush*, 405 F.3d 1214 (11th Cir.; 2005) brought only on behalf of African American voters in Florida.

11. *Farrakhan v. Washington*, 338 F.3d 1009 (9th Cir.; 2003).

12. *Hayden v. Pataki*, 449 F.3d 305 (2nd Cir. 2006).

13. *New Jersey State Conference NAACP v. Harvey*, 885 A.2d 445 (N.J. Super A.D. 2005).

14. See http://www.aclu.org/votingrights/exoffenders/ (accessed February 26, 2008).

15. U.S. Census Bureau, Decennial Management Division Glossary. http://www.census .gov/dmd/www/glossary.html#U (accessed April 24, 2008).

16. *Burns v. Richardson*, 384 U.S. 73, 92 (1966).

17. Huling (2002), 211.

18. The Census Bureau reports that Harris County was 33 percent Latino in 2000, while Dallas County was 29 percent Latino in 2000. U.S. Census Bureau, Census 2000 Summary File (SF-1).

19. N.Y. Const. Art. II, § 4.

20. N.Y. Correction Law § 750.

References

Cadora, Eric. 2007. Justice Mapping Center Study for Mayor's Commission on Poverty. http://www.justicemapping.org.

Cartagena, Juan. 2008. "*Voting Rights in New York City 1982–2006*"*Southern California Review of Social Justice* 17:2, 501-576.

Cartagena, Juan, Janai Nelson, and Joan Gibbs. 2003. Felons and the right to vote. http:// www.gothamgazette.com (accessed October 23, 2006).

Clear, Todd R. 2002. The problem with "addition by subtraction": The prison-crime relationship in low-income communities. In *Invisible Punishment: The Collateral Consequences of Mass Imprisonment*, ed. Marc Mauer and Meda Chesney-Lind 181-193. New York: New Press.

Davis, Angela Y. 2003. Are prisons obsolete. New York: Seven Stories.

Demeo, Marisa J., and Steven A. Ochoa. 2003. *Diminished voting power in the Latino community: The impact of felony disenfranchisement in ten targeted states*. Washington, D.C.: Mexican American Legal Defense & Educational Fund.

DeSipio, Louis. 2005. Latino voters: Lessons learned and misunderstood. In *The unfinished agenda of the Selma-Montgomery voting rights march*, ed. the editors of *Black issues in higher education*, with Dara N. Byrne, 135–142. Landmarks in civil rights history. Hoboken, NJ: John Wiley.

Fannie Lou Hamer, Rosa Parks, and Coretta Scott King Voting Rights Reauthorization and Amendments Act of 2006, 42 U.S.C. § 1973b(a)(7), (8) (2006).

Freeman, Richard. 2003. Can we close the revolving door? Recidivism vs. employment of ex-offenders in the U.S. *The Urban Institute Reentry Roundtable Discussion Paper*, May 19. New York University.

Huling, Tracy. 2002. Building a prison economy in rural America. In *Invisible punishment: The collateral consequences of mass imprisonment*, ed. Marc Mauer and Meda Chesney-Lind, 197–213. New York: New Press.

International Centre for Prison Studies. 2008. World prison brief. http://www.kcl.ac.uk (accessed March 2008).

Legal Action Center. 2006. New York State occupational licensing survey. In *Report and recommendations to New York State on enhancing employment opportunities for formerly incarcerated people*, 56–76. New York: Independent Commission on Reentry and Employment.

Levitan, Mark. 2004. *A crisis of black male employment: Unemployment and joblessness in New York City 2003*. New York: Community Service Society.

———. 2005. *Out of school, out of work, out of luck? New York City's disconnected youth*. New York: Community Service Society.

Mauer, Marc. 2007. Racial impact statements as a means of reducing unwarranted sentencing disparities. *Ohio State Jounal of Criminal Law* 5:19, 19-46.

Mauer, Marc, and Meda Chesney-Lind, eds. 2002. *Invisible punishment: The collateral consequences of mass imprisonment*. New York: The New Press.

National Association of Latino Elected Officials. 2006. *2006 National directory of Latino elected officials*. Washington, D.C.: National Association of Latino Elected Officials.

National Conference of Commissioners on Uniform State Laws. 2005. Uniform Collateral Sanctions and Disqualifications Act, November.

New York City Bar Association Task Force on Employment Opportunities for the Previously Incarcerated. 2008. Legal employers taking the lead: Enhancing employment opportunities for the previously incarcerated. New York:New York City Bar Association.

New York State Board of Elections. 2003. Memorandum to county commissioners, October 29, 1993.

Paige, Harrison M., and Allen J. Beck. 2006. *Prison and jail inmates at midyear, 2005*. NCJ 213133. Washington, D.C.: U.S. Department of Justice, Bureau of Justice Statistics.

Pager, Devah. 2003. The mark of a criminal record. *American Journal of Sociology* 108 (5): 937–75.

Pager, Devah, and Bruce Western. 2005. Race at work: Realities of race and criminal record in the NYC job market. Conference paper, NYC Commission on Human Rights and Schomburg Center for Research in Black Culture.

Pettus, Katherine Irene. 2005. *Felony disfranchisement in America: Historical origins, institutional racism, and modern consequences*. New York: LFB Scholarly Publishing.

Pew Center on the States. One in 100: Behind bars in America 2008. http://www.pewcenteronthestates.org (accessed January 19, 2009).Putnam, Robert. 1995. Bowling alone: America's declining social capital. *Journal of Democracy* 6:1.

Rivera Vargas, Daniel. 2004. A contar votos de presos. *El Nuevo Día*, December 21.

Roberts, Sam. 2006. Panel recommends change in census prisoner count. *New York Times*, September 15.

Sentencing Project and International Human Rights Clinic, Washington College of Law, American University. 2007. Barriers to democracy, a petition to the Inter-American Commission on Human Rights for a thematic hearing on felony disenfranchisement practices in the United States and the Americas. Washington, D.C.: The Sentencing Project.

Steinbrickner-Kaufman, Taren. 2004. Counting matters: Prison inmates, population xases, and 'one person, one vote.' *Virginia Journal of Social Policy and the Law* 11:229, 229-305.

United States Hispanic Leadership Institute. 2008. *The almanac of Latino politics*. Chicago: United States Hispanic Leadership Institute.

Wacquaint, Loïc. 2000. Deadly symbiosis: When ghetto and prison meet and mesh. *Punishment & Society* 3 (1): 95–134. London: Sage.

Wagner, Peter. 2006. 2002. Importing constituents: Prisoners and political clout in New York. Northhampton, MA: Prison Policy Initiative. http://*www.prisonpolicy.org* (accessed October 23, 2006).

———. Testimony of Peter Wagner to the New York Assembly Standing Committee on Government Operations, October 17, 2006. On file with author.

Wagner, Peter, and Rose Heyer. 2004. Importing constituents: Prisoners and political clout in Texas. Northhampton, MA: Prison Policy Initiative. http://www.prisonpolicy.org (accessed February 26, 2008).

Walker, Nancy, J. Michael Senger, Francisco Villarruel, and Angela Arboleda. 2004. *Lost opportunities: The reality of Latinos in the U.S. criminal justice system.* Washington, D.C.: National Council of La Raza.

Part II

The Lived Experience

Checkpoint in Montebello

Inciting Riots, Up Against the Wall, and Earning the Right to be on the Street with Signs that Say "*Retén*"

Mercedes Victoria Castillo

In the last year, our communities have seen an increase in raids and driver's license checkpoints as another approach by the repressive police and Immigration and Customs Enforcement (ICE), aka *Migra*, to create fear, to scapegoat our *Raza* as the reason for all of the problems of the United States, and to continue the everlasting relationship of conquerors and conquered.

This is My Land—Show Me YOUR Papers

On July 27, 2007, at approximately 8:00 p.m., my mother, my friend, and I were driving west on Whittier on our way home. We live in the unincorporated parts of East Los Angeles, or East Los, a place where sheriffs rule and houses are too expensive for working-class people to afford.

We passed by a checkpoint on the opposite side of the street. I called and sent text messages to various people to get the word out on the *retén* on Whittier, east of Garfield. Within twenty minutes, we returned to Whittier and Garfield to see how we could help. We drove right through the checkpoint—the officer asked me for my license and asked if I was drunk, to which I replied, "Not yet." He reviewed my license, he laughed, and he waved me through. There were news reporters, about twenty police officers, and tow trucks ready for business. We later discovered that the news reporters were monitoring human rights abuses.

We drove around to Garfield and Whittier to park our car. We were going to walk over and do some "legal observing." At that moment, a woman who was very distraught passed us and said they had taken her car. She was frantically trying to wave others down to tell them not to go through the checkpoint.

I noticed a man at a nearby restaurant throwing boxes away. I went over and started to write *RETÉN* with a sharpie (typical East Los, you are thinking, but actually a man passing by gave it to me!) on various cardboard boxes.

Two community officers came over to ask me what I was doing. I said, "I am making signs." He says, "For what?" I say, "Because I want to." He goes away.

Five minutes later, another man comes up in a truck with cop lights flashing. He says to me, "What are you doing." I say, "We're holding signs." He says, "You can't do that." I say, "Why not?" He says, "Because it's illegal." I say, "Give me the law that says it is." He says, "Oh, you're going to get your law," and drives off.

My friend and I cross the street. We figure that we can get people to turn away from the checkpoint better if we are on the other side of the intersection. Within ten minutes, a policeman in a motorcycle rides up the ramp on the corner, on to the sidewalk, and screams at us to put our signs down.

Put Your Signs Down!

We look at him and say, "No, we have a right to be here."

He yells again, "Put the signs down and step over to the wall!"

At this point, he is not very nice.

My friend puts her sign down.

I don't want to. (I must have problems with authority.) Although I am not going to lie, I was scared.

So then he pulls out his handcuffs. He screams, "Put the sign down or I will handcuff you."

I say, "Am I under arrest? What law did I break?"

He cites California Code 4 something or other and says that I am inciting a riot.

He grabbed my sign and threw it on the floor and told me to get up against the wall. At this point, my friend and I listen. But we don't want to face the wall. So I tell him, "No need to scream at us, can't we talk like adults?"

He responds, "We're going to do things my way. Now get up against the wall or I will handcuff you.

So we do, like alleged criminals, turn around. He places his hand on my lower back. My friend is patted on her jeans' back pockets.

He then asked us to turn around. He then says, "Which one of you is older?" to which I respond, "What is the relevance? Are you arresting us?"

"You are being detained for an investigation. We have reports from people that you are out on the street, yelling and inciting riots. So I am conducting an investigation."

He says this while he is standing on my signs.

This is Bothering Me

He says, "So which one of you is the adult? Which one of you wants to be the spokesperson? Two beautiful young ladies on a Friday night, have better things to do than to be out here holding up signs."

I say, "I have a right to be here and hold up whatever sign I want. I know my legal rights."

At this point the officer was no longer yelling and was sort of surprised that we had stood our ground. Community members were present and watching as the police continued to talk to my friend and me about checkpoints, immigration, and other issues.

He bent over, picked up my sign, and gave it back to me. For the next five minutes, he explained the legal parameters within which I could be on the street (I already knew these things, but he felt he was helping me).

When he left, the community that was there cheered, and some people offered to hold up our makeshift cardboard box signs.

At around 12:00 a.m., the same police officer came by to tell me that the police were shutting down the checkpoint early, due to low traffic.

Success!!!

In all honesty, I do not know the number of cars that turned away. I want to say that if there were 200 cars that passed by our signs, maybe 160 turned away. After the cops had shut down their checkpoint, we drove by the parking lot where they had parked all of the incorporated cars. We could see about twenty to thirty cars waiting to be towed away. Throughout the night, I saw families, mothers, and their children walking away from the checkpoint with their belongings. I saw working-class people, not drunk people, walking away upset because their cars were taken.

On the other hand, I saw my community pass by honking, waving, thumbs up in the air to tell us thank you for the alert.

By law, there are supposed to be warnings prior to the checkpoints. These warnings say, "DUI Checkpoint Ahead, Prepare to STOP." They are diamond-shaped, like the orange construction signs we see in other places. The sad reality is that most of these checkpoints are conducted in barrios where most people may not read English well, if at all.

What Now?

I wanted to write and share what happened because I think it is important that as a community, we respond to these attacks on our community. This is my barrio, this is *mi gente*, and if the police, *la migra, los pinches militares* come in, we need to stand up and say *YA BASTA!*

If we are good enough to work here, picking your vegetables and cleaning your toilets, then we should have the BASIC right to drive to work. Immigrants are not products, objects, items that can be moved back and forth across our illegal borders as if they were expendable. We are human, we are workers, we are mothers, we are struggling to achieve what every person wants for their family.

I encourage anyone interested in being part of la *Frente Contra las Redadas* to contact me and work within our communities to confront the issue of raids and police taking our people away.

Aquí estamos . . . Ésta es mi tierra.

8

The Interpreter as a Bridge

Language Issues in Chicago's Cook County Jail

Laura E. Garcia

I am a Spanish interpreter for the public defender's office in Chicago, where I have been working since 1994. My daily activities comprise interpreting for public defenders and their clients. My duties take me to the eleven divisions of the Cook County Jail, where I spend roughly 50 percent of my time visiting our clients. I also interpret for the families of the relatively few who have any family here in this country. In this essay, I address some of the language issues Spanish-speaking Latinos face once they are caught in the mire of the criminal justice system in Cook County, Illinois.

Language Issues in Cook County

Thousands of foreigners find themselves charged with a crime in the United States, unable to understand the proceedings because they lack English language skills. Spanish-speaking Latinos are no exception. According to the Cook County Sheriff's Web site, the population in Cook County jail averages over 9,000 people (http://www.cookcountysheriff.org/). In 2000, the *Chicago Reporter* noted that in Cook County, one in twenty-six Latino men in their twenties was either in jail, in prison, or parole. At that time, 1,363 Latinos were in jail, 3,714 in prison, and 1,772 on parole in the Cook County Department of Corrections—in other words, one in seventy-three Latinos was caught up in the system. In fact, Spanish speakers account for 85 percent of interpreter services of the interpreter's office of Cook County, making Spanish the predominant interpreting language in the county's department of corrections.

Over the years, I have interpreted for Latinos who face a variety of charges, ranging from traffic violations and misdemeanors to charges of first-degree murder that carry sentences up to life in prison or death. The most difficult moments in my job have been interpreting for young people, ages seventeen to twenty, and informing them that they are facing death, life in prison, or a sentence of forty-five years. Neither the defendants nor their families can conceive that they will be spending the rest of their lives behind bars or that they will be old men or women if and when they are released. One mother I was interpreting for began to cry when told of her son's thirty-year sentence and exclaimed, "I'll be dead by the time he comes out!" And, of course, there is also the sad truth that many prisoners die behind bars. In all, 15,308 prisoners died between the years 2001 and 2005 in American prisons from a variety of causes, including illness, suicide, and AIDS (Political/Congressional Transcript Wire, 2007)

The odds are stacked against Latino defendants from the beginning, particularly since the 9/11 attacks, when terrorism and undocumented immigrant became synonymous.

Where Does the Problem Begin?

A Spanish-speaking person's problems begin the moment he or she is suspected of a crime and is interrogated by the police. In an ideal situation, the police officer should provide a suspect with a professional interpreter. Instead, the following is a more common scenario that Latinos confront when they are brought to the police station. The suspect is transported to the police department by the police officers or by a detective working on the case. Once there, he or she is taken to an interrogation room. These rooms usually have no windows and no clocks, but they do have a metal bench and a metal pole where, if desired, the person can be handcuffed.

This can be a traumatic experience for anyone, let alone for someone who does not speak the English language. People are often frightened and confused to such an extent that when someone does speak to them in their own language, they immediately find some comfort in that person. The fact that the person is police personnel is pushed aside.

The use of police officers or detectives to interpret in the cases they investigate can result in many problems. One is that police personnel are not trained as interpreters. Secondly, since they are interpreting for the case they are working on, the question of neutrality and bias immediately comes to the fore. While this might not stop the suspect from receiving his or her due process under the law guaranteed by the U.S. Constitution to all persons regardless of citizenship, it can certainly cloud the proceedings.

Miranda Rights

Still, even before a person suspected of a crime speaks, there is the issue of the Miranda rights, which guarantee the rights of anyone who has been arrested. They came about as a result of the *Miranda v. Arizona* case (384 US 436,86Ct. 1602) in 1966, when Ernesto Miranda, a rape suspect, was arrested and taken to a police station in Arizona. After two hours of questioning, he signed a written confession and was subsequently found guilty. Miranda appealed his conviction on the grounds that prior to confessing, he had not been informed of his Fifth Amendment right against self-incrimination, or of his Sixth Amendment right, which guarantees his right to counsel. The Supreme Court overturned Miranda's conviction, finding that the coercive nature of detention in a police station necessitated certain safeguards to ensure that suspects do not give up their Fifth and Sixth Amendment rights. The ruling stated that when law enforcement officers take a suspect into custody with the intention of interrogation, they must inform the person of certain fundamental conditions: the right to remain silent; the fact that anything the suspect says can be used against him or her in court; and the right to an attorney. In addition, if the suspect cannot afford one, an attorney must be provided at no charge.

Regardless of how many detective shows they may have seen in TV or movies, many U.S. citizens themselves are not familiar with the law unless they have been arrested or detained. Latinos who only speak Spanish not only lack any knowledge of American laws, but depending on the political context of their country of origin, particularly those governed by military juntas or dictators, they may not feel they have the right to refuse to speak, much less to ask for an attorney or have the government provide one free of cost.

The language factor only compounds the problem. It is not surprising, then, that suspects find some comfort in the person who interprets for them, and often disregard the fact that they are being interrogated by a police officer. Consequently, they often speak freely, even after being advised of their Miranda rights.

There are three actors in a statement rendition: the state's attorney, the police "interpreter," and the accused. Once the person agrees to make a statement, the state's attorney usually starts asking questions, the police "interpreter" interprets for the accused, the accused responds, and the police "interpreter" then interprets the response to the state's attorney. When everything the accused has said has been written in English, the police interpreter sight-translates the written statement back to the accused. The statement rendition ends with the accused signing the statement, hence agreeing to its accuracy.

What is wrong with this picture? First of all, since he is relying on the accusing side to interpret for him, the suspect really does not know if the translated version of his statement is correct and is actually what he or she said. After all, can anyone really ensure the impartiality of the police interpreter? Second, interpreting-translating is a profession: the fact that someone may be bilingual or has spent two years in Spain does not qualify him or her to be a trained interpreter.

In the course of my duties, I have run into incidents whereby the defendants inform their attorneys that what the attorney says to them is not what they actually said, leading the attorney to ask: "But didn't they read this statement to you?" "Yes," the defendant answers, "but what you are saying is not what they read."

Although many motions are filed challenging the statements' accuracy in an attempt to keep them out of court, these motions are hardly ever won. In the end, it is the defendant's word against the police "interpreter."

The Solution

In order to guarantee the above rights of a person who speaks only Spanish, the interpreter must be unbiased and neutral—and not employed by the police department. This is why in Cook County, there is a Court Interpreters' Office, which is under the Chief Judge of the Circuit Court System. This department provides interpreters in as many languages as are needed in the county. Before any court proceedings begin, court interpreters take an oath "to interpret to the best of their ability." Some states have adopted a code of ethics for court interpreters to guarantee a defendant's rights. Although it varies from state to state, the following statement by the National Association of Judicial Interpreters and Translators captures the essence of this code: "Interpreters shall be impartial and unbiased, and shall refrain from conduct that may give an appearance of bias. . . . Interpreters shall render a complete and accurate interpretation or sight translation by interpreting without altering, omitting, or adding anything to the meaning of what is stated or written, and without explanation." In addition, Latinos need to be educated about their Miranda rights. Too many do not exercise their right to remain silent and their right to have an attorney present while being interrogated.

Still, although educating people about their Miranda rights is something both the community and the individual can do, the use of impartial interpreters to guarantee a person's civil rights must be guaranteed by the government. After all, it is the actual interpretation—without altering, omitting, or adding anything to what is stated or written—that guarantees the rights of all people, including those who do not speak English. Interpreters, then, shoulder a big responsibility: he or she is the link between those who do not speak English and the judicial system.

References

Political/Congressional Transcript Wire. 2007. Rep. Robert C. Scott Holds A Hearing On H.R. 2908, The Death In Custody Reporting Act Of 2007. Congressional Quarterly. July 25. http://www.accessmylibrary.com/coms2/summary_0286-32461390_ITM

9

Interpreting After the Largest ICE Raid in U.S. History

A Personal Account

Erik Camayd-Freixas

On Monday, May 12, 2008, at 10:00 a.m., in an operation involving some nine hundred agents, Immigration and Customs Enforcement (ICE) executed a raid of Agriprocessors, Inc., the nation's largest kosher slaughterhouse and meatpacking plant located in the town of Postville, Iowa. The raid—officials boasted—was "the largest single-site operation of its kind in American history." At that same hour, twenty-six federally certified interpreters from all over the country were en route to the small neighboring city of Waterloo, Iowa, having no idea what their mission was about. The investigation had started more than a year earlier. Raid preparations had begun in December. The clerk's office of the U.S. District Court had contracted the interpreters a month ahead but was not at liberty to tell us the whole truth, lest the impending raid be compromised. The operation was led by ICE, which belongs to the executive branch, whereas the U.S. District Court, belonging to the judicial branch, had to formulate its own official reason for participating. Accordingly, the court had to move for two weeks to a remote location as part of a "Continuity of Operation Exercise" in case they were ever disrupted by an emergency, which, in Iowa, is likely to be a tornado or flood. That is what we were told, but, frankly, I was not prepared for a disaster of such a different kind—one which was entirely man-made.

I arrived late that Monday night and missed the 8:00 p.m. interpreters briefing. I was instructed by phone to meet at 7:00 a.m. in the hotel lobby and carpool to the National Cattle Congress (NCC) where we would begin our work. We arrived at the heavily guarded compound, went through security, and gathered inside the retro "Electric Park Ballroom," where a makeshift court had been set up. The clerk of court, who coordinated the interpreters, said: "Have you seen the news? There was an immigration raid yesterday at 10am. They have some

400 detainees here. We'll be working late conducting initial appearances for the next few days." He then gave us a cursory tour of the compound. The NCC is a sixty-acre cattle fairground that had been transformed into a sort of concentration camp or detention center. Fenced in behind the ballroom-courtroom were twenty-three trailers from federal authorities, including two set up as sentencing courts; various Department of Homeland Security buses and an "incident response" truck; scores of ICE agents and U.S. Marshals; and, in the background, two large buildings—a pavilion where agents and prosecutors had established a command center and a gymnasium filled with tight rows of cots where some three hundred male detainees were kept, the women being housed in county jails. Later, the NCC board complained to the local newspaper that they had been "misled" by the government when they leased the grounds purportedly for Department of Homeland Security training.

Echoing what I think was the general feeling, one of my fellow interpreters would later exclaim: "When I saw what it was really about, my heart sank." Then began the saddest procession I have ever witnessed, which the public would never see, because cameras were not allowed past the perimeter of the compound (only a few journalists came to court the following days, notepads in hand). Driven single-file in groups of ten, shackled at the wrists, waist, and ankles, chains dragging as they shuffled through, the slaughterhouse workers were brought in for arraignment. They sat and listened through headsets to the interpreted initial appearance before marching out again to be bused to different county jails, only to make room for the next row of ten. They appeared to be uniformly no more than five feet tall, mostly illiterate Guatemalan peasants with Mayan last names, some being relatives (various Tajtaj, Xicay, Sajché, Sologüí), some in tears; others with faces of worry, fear, and embarrassment. They all spoke Spanish, a few rather laboriously. It dawned on me that aside from their Guatemalan or Mexican nationality, which was imposed on their people after independence, they, too, were Native Americans in shackles. They stood out in stark racial contrast with the rest of us as they started their slow penguin march across the makeshift court. "Sad spectacle," I heard a colleague say, reading my mind. They had all waived their right to be indicted by a grand jury and had instead accepted an *information* or simple charging document by the U.S. attorney, hoping to be quickly deported since they had families to support back home. But it was not to be. They were criminally charged with "aggravated identity theft" and "social security fraud"—charges they did not understand, and, frankly, neither could I. Everyone wondered how it would all play out.

We got off to a slow start that first day because ICE's barcode booking system malfunctioned, and the documents had to be manually sorted and processed with the help of the U.S. attorney's office. Consequently, less than a third of the detainees were ready for arraignment that Tuesday. There were more than enough interpreters at that point, so we rotated in shifts of three interpreters per hearing. Court adjourned shortly after 4:00 p.m. However, the prosecution worked overnight, planning on a 7:00 a.m. to midnight court marathon the next day.

I was eager to get back to my hotel room to find out more about the case, since the day's repetitive hearings afforded little information and everyone there was mostly refraining from comment. There was frequent but sketchy news on local TV. A colleague had suggested *The Des Moines Register*. So I went to Des-MoinesRegister.com and started reading the twenty-plus articles, as they appeared each day, and the fifty-seven-page *ICE Search Warrant Application*. [1] These were the vital statistics. Of Agriprocessors' 968 current employees, about 75 percent were illegal immigrants. There were 697 arrest warrants but late-shift workers had not arrived, so "only" 390 were arrested: 314 men and 76 women comprised of 290 Guatemalans, 93 Mexicans, 4 Ukrainians, and 3 Israelis who were not seen in court. Some were released on humanitarian grounds: 56 women, mostly mothers with unattended children, a few with medical reasons, and 12 juveniles were temporarily released with ankle monitors or directly turned over for deportation. In all, 306 were held for prosecution. Only 5 of the 390 originally arrested had any kind of prior criminal record. There remained 307 outstanding warrants.

This was the immediate collateral damage. Postville, Iowa (population 2,273), where nearly half of the people worked at Agriprocessors, had lost one-third of its population by Tuesday morning. Businesses were empty, amid looming concerns that if the plant closed it would become a ghost town. Beside those arrested, many had fled the town in fear. Several families had taken refuge at St. Bridget's Catholic Church, terrified, sleeping on pews, and refusing to leave for days. Volunteers from the community served food and organized activities for the children. At the local high school, only three of the fifteen Latino students came back on Tuesday, while at the elementary and middle school, 120 of the 363 children were absent. In the following days, the principal went around town on the school bus and gathered seventy students after convincing the parents to let them come back to school; fifty remained unaccounted for. Some American parents complained that their children were traumatized by the sudden disappearance of so many of their school friends. The principal reported the same reaction in the classrooms, saying that for the children, it was as if ten of their classmates had suddenly died. Counselors were brought in. American children were having nightmares that their parents, too, were being taken away. The superintendant said the school district's future was unclear: "This literally blew our town away." In some cases, both parents were picked up and small children were left behind for up to seventy-two hours. Typically, the mother would be released "on humanitarian grounds" with an ankle GPS monitor, pending prosecution and deportation, while the husband took first turn in serving his prison sentence. Meanwhile, the mother would have no income and could not work to provide for her children. Some of the children were born in the United States and are American citizens. Sometimes one parent was a deportable alien while the other was not. "Hundreds of families were torn apart by this raid," said a Catholic nun. "The humanitarian impact of this raid is obvious to anyone in Postville. The economic impact will soon be evident."

But this was only the surface damage. Alongside the many courageous actions and expressions of humanitarian concern in the true American spirit, the news blogs were filled with snide remarks of racial prejudice and bigotry, poorly disguised beneath an empty rhetoric of misguided patriotism, not to mention the insults to anyone who publicly showed compassion, safely hurled from behind a cowardly online nickname. One could feel the moral fabric of society coming apart beneath it all.

The more I found out, the more I felt blindsided into an assignment of which I wanted no part. Even though I understood the rationale for all the secrecy, I also knew that a contract interpreter has the right to refuse a job that conflicts with his moral intuitions. But I had been deprived of that opportunity. Now I was already there, far from home, and holding a half-spent $1,800 plane ticket. So I faced a frustrating dilemma. I seriously considered withdrawing from the assignment for the first time in my twenty-three years as a federally certified interpreter, citing conflict of interest. In fact, I have both an ethical and contractual obligation to withdraw if a conflict of interest exists that compromises my neutrality. Appended to my contract are the *Standards for Performance and Professional Responsibility for Contract Court Interpreters in the Federal Courts*, [2] where it states: "Interpreters shall disclose any real or perceived conflict of interest . . . and shall not serve in any matter in which they have a conflict of interest." The question was: did I have one? Well, at that point, there was not enough evidence to make that determination. After all, these are illegal aliens and should be deported—no argument there and, hence, no conflict. But should they be criminalized and imprisoned? Well, if they committed a crime and were fairly adjudicated. But all that remained to be seen. In any case, none of it would shake my impartiality or prevent me from faithfully discharging my duties. In all my years as a court interpreter, I have taken front-row seat in countless criminal cases ranging from rape, capital murder, and mayhem, to terrorism, narcotics, and human trafficking. I am not the impressionable kind. Moreover, as a professor of interpreting, I have confronted my students with every possible conflict scenario, or so I thought. The truth is that nothing could have prepared me for the prospect of helping our government put hundreds of innocent people in jail. In my ignorance and disbelief, I reluctantly decided to stay the course and see what happened next.

Wednesday, May 14, our second day in court, was to be a long one. The interpreters were divided into two shifts: 8:00 a.m. to 3:00 p.m. and 3:00 p.m. to 10:00 p.m. I chose the latter. Through the day, the procession continued, ten by ten, hour after hour, the same charges, the same recitation from the magistrates, the same faces, chains and shackles, on the defendants. There was little to remind us that they were actually 306 individuals, except that, occasionally, as though to break the monotony, one would dare to speak for the others and beg to be deported quickly so that they could feed their families back home. One who turned out to be a minor was bound over for deportation. The rest would be prosecuted. Later in the day, three groups of women were brought, shackled in the same manner. One of them, whose husband was also arrested, was released to care for her children, ages two and five, uncertain of their whereabouts. Several men and women were weeping but two women were particularly grief stricken. One of them was sobbing and would repeatedly struggle to bring a sleeve to her nose, but her wrists shackled around her waist simply would not reach, so she just dripped until she was taken away with the rest. The other one, a Ukrainian woman, was held and arraigned separately when a Russian telephonic interpreter came on. She spoke softly into a cellular phone while the interpreter told her story in English over the speakerphone. Her young daughter, gravely ill, had lost her hair and was too weak to walk. She had taken her to Moscow and Kiev but to no avail. She was told her child needed an operation or would soon die. She had come to America to work and raise the money to save her daughter back in Ukraine. In every instance, detainees who cried did so for their children, never for themselves.

The next day we started early, at 6:45 a.m. We were told that we had to finish the hearings by 10 a.m. Thus far the work had oddly resembled a judicial assembly line where the meatpackers were mass processed. But things were about to get a lot more personal as we prepared to interpret for individual attorney-client conferences. In those first three days, interpreters had been pairing up with defense attorneys to help interview their clients. Each of the eighteen court-appointed attorneys represented seventeen defendants on average. By now, the clients had been sent to several state and county prisons throughout eastern Iowa, so we had to interview them in jail. The attorney with whom I was working had clients in Des Moines and wanted to be there first thing in the morning. So a colleague and I drove the two-and-a-half hours that evening and stayed overnight in a hotel outside the city. We met the attorney in jail Friday morning, but the clients had not been accepted there and instead had been sent to a state penitentiary in Newton, another forty-five-minute drive. While we waited to be admitted, the attorney pointed out the reason why the prosecution wanted to finish arraignments by 10:00 a.m. Thursday: according to the *writ of habeas corpus*, they had seventy-two hours from Monday's raid to charge the prisoners or release them for deportation (only a handful would be so lucky). The right of habeas corpus, but of course! It dawned on me that we were paid overtime, adding hours to the day, in a mad rush to abridge habeas corpus, only to help put more workers in jail. Now I really felt bad. But it would soon get worse. I was about to bear the brunt of my conflict of interest.

It came with my first jail interview. The purpose was for the attorney to explain the uniform plea agreement that the government was offering. The explanation, which we repeated over and over to each client, went like this. There are three possibilities. If you plead guilty to the charge of "knowingly using a false social security number," the government will withdraw the heavier charge of "aggravated identity theft," and you will serve five months in jail, be deported without a hearing, and placed on supervised release for three years. If you plead not guilty, you could wait in jail six to eight months for a trial (without right of bail since you are on an immigration detainer). Even if you win at trial, you will still be deported and could end up waiting longer in jail than if you just pled guilty. You would also risk losing at trial and receiving a two-year minimum sentence before being deported. Some clients understood their "options" better than others.

That first interview, though, took three hours. The client, a Guatemalan peasant afraid for his family, spent most of that time weeping at our table in a corner of the crowded jailhouse visiting room. How did he come here from Guatemala? *"I walked."* What? *"I walked for a month and ten days until I crossed the river."* We immediately understood how desperate his family's situation was. He crossed alone, met other immigrants, and hitched a truck ride to Dallas, then Postville, where he heard there was sure work. He slept in an apartment hallway with other immigrants until employed. He had scarcely been working a couple of months when he was arrested. Maybe he was lucky: another man who began that Monday had only been working for twenty minutes. "I just wanted to work a year or two, save, and then go back to my family, but it was not to be." His case, and that of a million others, could simply be solved by a temporary work permit as part of our much overdue immigration reform. "The Good Lord knows I was just working and not doing anyone any harm." This man, like many others, was in fact *not* guilty. "Knowingly" and "intent" are necessary elements of the charges, but most of the clients we interviewed did not even know what a social security number was or what purpose it served. This worker simply had the papers filled out for him at the plant since he could not read or write Spanish, let alone English. But the lawyer still had to advise him that pleading guilty was in his best interest. He was unable to make a decision. "You all do and undo," he said. "So you can do whatever you want with me." To him, we were part of the system keeping him from being deported back to his country, where his children, wife, mother, and sister depended on him. He was their sole support and did not know how they were going to make it with him in jail for five months. None of the "options" really mattered to him. Caught between despair and hopelessness, he just wept. He had failed his family and was devastated. I went for some napkins but he refused them. I offered him a cup of soda, which he superstitiously declined, saying it could be "poisoned." His Native American spirit was broken and he could no longer think. He stared for awhile at the signature page, pretending to read it, although I knew he was actually praying for guidance and protection. Before he signed with a scribble, he said: "God knows you are just doing your job to support your families, and that job is to keep me from supporting mine." There was my conflict of interest, well put by a weeping, illiterate man.

We worked that day for as long as our emotional fortitude allowed, and we had to come back to a full day on Sunday to interview the rest of the clients. Many of the Guatemalans had the same predicament. One of them, a nineteen-year-old, worried that his parents were too old to work, and he was the only support for his family back home. Under different circumstances, these Guatemalans would have been refugees with asylum rights. They are the survivors of thirty-six years of an internal armed conflict (1960 through 1996) that left a balance of 200,000 dead and 1.5 million peasants displaced. But to grant them asylum would be to recognize them as victims of our own geopolitical cold war via the dictatorships that, with U.S. support, launched their counterinsurgency dead squads and "scorched earth" campaigns, annihilating entire villages and practicing genocide, torture, and disappearances in the name of anticommunism and the old domino theory. Still today, residual violence continues to threaten that country's present struggle to consolidate its fragile democracy. Even as we proceeded with the hearings during those two weeks in May, news coming out of Guatemala reported farmworkers being assassinated for complaining publicly about their working conditions. Not only have we ignored the many root causes of illegal immigration, we also will never know how many of these displaced workers, the orphans of our contra wars, are last survivors with no family or village to return to.

Another client, a young Mexican, had an altogether different case. He had worked at the plant for ten years and had two American-born daughters, a two-year-old and a newborn. He had a good case with immigration for an adjustment of status that would allow him to stay. But if he took the plea agreement, he would lose that chance and face deportation as a felon convicted of a crime of "moral turpitude." On the other hand, if he pled "not guilty" he had to wait several months in jail for trial and risk getting a two-year sentence. After an agonizing decision, he concluded that he had to take the five-month deal and deportation because, as he put it, "I cannot be away from my children for so long." His case was complicated; it needed research in immigration law, a change in the plea agreement, and, above all, more time. There were other similar cases in court that week. I remember reading that immigration lawyers were alarmed that the detainees were being rushed into a plea without adequate consultation on the immigration consequences. Even the criminal defense attorneys had limited opportunity to meet with clients: in jail, there were limited visiting hours and days; at the compound, there was little time before and after hearings and little privacy due to the constant presence of agents. There were seventeen cases for each attorney, and the plea offer was only good for seven days. In addition, criminal attorneys are not familiar with immigration work and vice versa, but they had to make do since immigration lawyers were denied access to these "criminal" proceedings.

In addition, the prosecutors would not accept any changes to the plea agreement. In fact, some lawyers, seeing that many of their clients were not guilty, requested an *Alford plea*, whereby defendants can plead guilty in order to accept the prosecution's offer, but without having to lie under oath and admit to something they did not do. That would not change the five-month sentence but at least it preserves the person's integrity and dignity. The proposal was rejected. Of course, if they allowed Alford pleas to go on public record, the incongruence of the charges would be exposed and find its way into the media. Officially, the ICE prosecutors said the plea agreement was directed from the Department of Justice (DOJ) in Washington, D.C., that they were not authorized to change it locally, and that the DOJ would not make any case-by-case exceptions when a large number of defendants are being "fast-tracked." Presumably, if you gave different terms to one individual, the others would want the same. This position, however, laid bare one of the critical problems with this new practice of "fast-tracking." Even real criminals have the right of *severance*: when codefendants have different degrees of responsibility, there is an inherent conflict of interest, and they can ask to be prosecuted separately as different cases, each with a different attorney. In fast-tracking, however, the right of severance is circumvented because each defendant already has a different case number on paper, but they are processed together, ten cases at a time. At this point, it is also worth remembering that even real criminals have an Eighth Amendment right to reasonable bail, but illegal workers do not because their immigration detainer makes bail a moot issue. We had already circumvented habeas corpus by doubling the court's business hours. What about the Sixth Amendment right to a "speedy trial"? In many states, "speedy" means ninety days, but in federal law, it is vaguely defined, potentially exceeding the recommended sentence, given the backlog of *real* cases. This served as another loophole to force a guilty plea. Many of these workers were sole earners begging to be deported, desperate to feed their families for whom every day counted. "If you want to see your children or don't want your family to starve, sign here"—that is what their deal amounted to. Their plea agreement was coerced.

We began week two on Monday, May 19. Those interpreters who left after the first week were spared the sentencing hearings that went on through Thursday. Those who came in fresh the second week were spared the jail visits over the weekend. Those of us who stayed both weeks came back from the different jails burdened by a close personal contact that judges and prosecutors do not get to experience: each individual tragedy multiplied by 306 cases. One of my colleagues began the day by saying, "I feel a tremendous solidarity with these people." Had we lost our impartiality? Not at all: that was our impartial and probably unanimous judgment. We had seen attorneys hold back tears and weep alongside their clients. We would see judges, prosecutors, clerks, and marshals do their duty, sometimes with a heavy heart, sometimes at least with mixed feelings, but always with a particular solemnity not accorded to the common criminals we all are used to encountering in the judicial system. Everyone was extremely professional and outwardly appreciative of the interpreters. We developed, among ourselves and with the clerks, with whom we worked closely, a camaraderie and good humor that kept us going. Still, that Monday morning, I felt downtrodden by the sheer magnitude of the events. Unexpectedly, a sentencing hearing lifted my spirits.

I decided to do sentences on Trailer 2 with a judge I knew from real criminal trials in Iowa. The defendants were brought in five at a time because there was not enough room for ten. The judge verified that they still wanted to plead guilty and asked counsel to confirm their plea agreements. The defense attorney said that he had expected a much lower sentence but that he was forced to accept the agreement in the best interest of his clients. For those of us who knew the background of the matter, that vague objection, which was all that the attorney could put on record, spoke volumes. After accepting the plea agreement and before imposing sentence, the judge gave the defendants the right of allocution. Most of them chose not to say anything, but one, who was the more articulate, said humbly: "Your honor, you know that we are here because of the need of our families. I beg that you find it in your heart to send us home before too long, because we have a responsibility to our children, to give them an education, clothing, shelter, and food." The good judge explained that unfortunately he was not free to depart from the sentence provided for by their plea agreement. Technically, what he meant was that this was a binding 11(c)(1)(C) plea agreement: he had to accept it or reject it as a whole. But if he rejected it, he would be exposing the defendants to a trial against their will. His hands were tied but, in closing, he said to them, very deliberately: "I appreciate the fact that you are very hard working people, who have come here to do no harm. And I thank you for coming to this country to work hard. Unfortunately, you broke a law in the process, and now I have the obligation to give you this sentence. But I hope that the U.S. government has at least treated you kindly and with respect, and that this time goes by quickly for you, so that soon you may be reunited with your family and friends." The defendants thanked him, and I saw their faces change from shame to admiration, their dignity restored. I think we were all vindicated at that moment.

Before the judge left that afternoon, I had occasion to talk to him and bring to his attention my concern over what I had learned in the jail interviews. At that point I realized how precious the interpreter's impartiality truly is and what a privileged perspective it affords. In our common law adversarial system, only the judge, the jury, and the interpreter are presumed impartial. But the judge is immersed in the framework of the legal system, whereas the interpreter is a layperson, an outsider, a true representative of the common citizen, much like "a jury of his peers." Yet, contrary to the jury, who only knows the evidence on record and is generally unfamiliar with the workings of the law, the interpreter is an informed layperson. Moreover, the interpreter is the only one who gets to see both sides of the coin up close, precisely because he is the *only* participant who is not a decision maker and is even precluded, by his oath of impartiality and neutrality, from ever influencing the decisions of others. That is why judges in particular appreciate the interpreter's perspective as an impartial and informed layperson, for it provides a rare glimpse at how the innards of the legal system look from the outside. I was no longer sorry to have participated in my capacity as an interpreter. I realized that I had been privileged to bear witness to historic events from such a unique vantage point and that, because of its uniqueness, I now had a civic duty to make it known. Such is the spirit that inspired this essay.

That is also what prompted my brief conversation with the judge: "Your honor, I am concerned from my attorney-client interviews that many of these people are clearly not guilty, and yet they have no choice but to plead out." He immediately understood and, not surprisingly, the seasoned U.S. District Court judge spoke as someone who had already wrestled with all the angles. He said: "You know, I don't agree with any of this or with the way it is being done. In fact, I ruled in a previous case that to charge somebody with identity theft, the person had to at least know of the real owner of the Social Security number. But I was reversed in another district and yet upheld in a third." I understood that the issue was a matter of judicial contention. The charge of identity theft seemed from the beginning incongruous to me as an informed, impartial layperson, but now a U.S. District Court judge agreed. As we bade each other farewell, I kept thinking of what he said. I soon realized that he had indeed hit the nail on the head; he had given me, as it were, the last piece of the puzzle.

It works like this. By handing down the inflated charge of "aggravated identity theft," which carries a mandatory minimum sentence of two years in prison, the government forced the defendants into pleading guilty to the lesser charge and accepting five months in jail. Clearly, without the inflated charge, the government had no bargaining leverage because the lesser charge by itself, using a false social security number, carries only a discretionary sentence of zero to six months. The judges would be free to impose sentence within those guidelines depending on the circumstances of each case and any prior record. Virtually all the defendants would have received only probation and been immediately deported. In fact, the government's offer at the higher end of the guidelines (one month shy of the maximum sentence) was indeed no bargain. What is worse, the inflated charge, via the binding 11(c)(1)(C) plea agreement, reduced the judges to mere bureaucrats, pronouncing the same litany over and over for the record in order to legalize the proceedings, but having absolutely no discretion or decision-making power. As a citizen, I want our judges—not a federal agency—to administer justice. When the executive branch forces the hand of the judiciary, the result is abuse of power and arbitrariness, unworthy of a democracy founded upon the constitutional principle of checks and balances.

To an impartial and informed layperson, the process resembled a lottery of justice: if the social security number belonged to someone else, you were charged with identity theft and went to jail; if, by luck, it was a vacant number, you would get only social security fraud and were released for deportation. In this manner, out of 297 who were charged on time, 270 went to jail. Bothered by the arbitrariness of that heavier charge, I went back to the *ICE Search Warrant Application* (35–36), and what I found was astonishing. On February 20, 2008, ICE agents received social security "no-match" information for 737 employees, including 147 using numbers confirmed by the Social Security Administration (SSA) as invalid (never issued to a person) and 590 using valid social security numbers (SSNs), "however *the numbers did not match the name* of the employee reported by Agriprocessors" (my emphasis). Of course they did not match –they were made-up numbers, and the employees were using their own real names. There was no evidence of identity theft. For this reason, the document immediately turned hypothetical: "*This analysis would not account for the possibility that a person may have falsely used the identity of an actual person's name and SSN*" (my emphasis). This is a blatant admission that their so-called analysis was nothing but a smoke screen. No-match letters are in fact counterevidence of identity theft, because real theft would require the names and numbers to match. Therefore, the undersigning agent had to concoct a hypothetical ground for suspicion: "In my training and expertise, I know it is not uncommon for aliens to purchase identity documents which include SSNs that match the name assigned to the number." Yet, ICE agents checked Accurint, the powerful identity database used by law enforcement, and found that 983 employees that year had non-matching SSNs. Then they conducted a search of the FTC Consumer Sentinel Network for reporting incidents of identity theft. "The search revealed that *a person who was assigned one of the social security numbers* used by an employee of Agriprocessors *has reported his/her identity being stolen*" (my emphasis). That is, out of 983, only one number (0.1 percent) happened to coincide, by chance, with a reported identity theft. The charge was clearly unfounded and the raid, a fishing expedition. "On April 16, 2008, the U.S. filed criminal complaints against 697 employees, charging them with unlawfully using SSNs in violation of Title 42 USC §408(a)(7)(B); aggravated identity theft in violation of 18 USC §1028A(a)(1); and/or possession or use of false identity documents for purposes of employment in violation of 18 USC §1546."

Created by Congress in an act of 1998, the new federal offense of identity theft, as described by the Department of Justice website,[3] bears no relation to the Postville cases. It specifically states, "knowingly uses a means of identification of another person with the *intent to commit any unlawful activity or felony*" (my emphasis) [18 USC §1028(a)]. The offense clearly refers to harmful, felonious acts, such as obtaining credit under another person's identity. Obtaining *work*, however, is not an "unlawful activity." No way would a grand jury find probable cause of identity theft here. But with the threat of jail time, the promise of faster deportation, their ignorance of the legal system, and the limited opportunity to consult with counsel before arraignment, all the workers, without exception, were pressed to waive their

Fifth Amendment right to grand jury indictment on felony charges. Waiting for a grand jury meant months in jail on an immigration detainer, without the possibility of bail. So the attorneys could not recommend it as a defense strategy. Similarly, defendants have the right to a status hearing before a judge, to determine probable cause, within ten days of arraignment, but their plea agreement offer from the government was only good for seven days. Passing it up meant risking two years in jail. As a result, the frivolous charge of identity theft was assured to never undergo the judicial test of probable cause. Not only were defendants and judges bound to accept the plea agreement, there was also absolutely no defense strategy available to counsel. Once the inflated charge was handed down, all the pieces fell into place like a row of dominoes. Even the court was banking on it when it agreed to participate because if a good number of defendants asked for a grand jury or trial, the system would be overwhelmed. In short, "fast-tracking" had worked like a dream.

It is no secret that the Postville ICE raid was a pilot operation, to be replicated elsewhere, with kinks ironed out after lessons learned. Next time, "fast-tracking" will be even more relentless. Never before has illegal immigration been criminalized in this fashion. It is no longer enough to deport them: we first have to put them in chains. At first sight, it may seem absurd to take productive workers and keep them in jail at taxpayers' expense. But the economics and politics of the matter are quite different from such rational assumptions. A quick look at the *ICE Fiscal Year 2007 Annual Report* shows an agency that has grown to 16,500 employees and a $5 billion annual budget since it was formed under the Department of Homeland Security in March 2003 "as a law enforcement agency for the post-9/11 era, to integrate enforcement authorities against criminal and terrorist activities, including the fights against human trafficking and smuggling, violent transnational gangs and sexual predators who prey on children" (17).[4] No doubt, ICE fulfills an extremely important and noble duty. The question is why tarnish its stellar reputation by targeting harmless, illegal workers. The answer is economics and politics. After 9/11, we had to create a massive force with readiness "to prevent, prepare for and respond to a wide range of catastrophic incidents, including terrorist attacks, natural disasters, pandemics and other such significant events that require large-scale government and law enforcement response" (23). The problem is that disasters, criminality, and terrorism do not provide enough daily business to maintain the readiness and muscle tone of this expensive force. For example, "In FY07, ICE human trafficking investigations resulted in 164 arrests and 91 convictions" (17). Terrorism-related arrests were not any more substantial. The real numbers are in immigration: "In FY07, ICE removed 276,912 illegal aliens" (4). ICE is under enormous pressure to turn out statistical figures that might justify a fair utilization of its capabilities, resources, and ballooning budget. For example, the *Report* boasts 102,777 cases "eliminated" from the fugitive alien population in FY07, "quadrupling" the previous year's number, only to admit a page later that 73,284 were "resolved" by simply "taking those cases off the books" after determining that they "no longer met the definition of an ICE fugitive" (4–5).

De facto, the rationale is: we have the excess capability; we are already paying for it; ergo, use it we must. And using it we are: since FY06, "ICE has introduced an aggressive and effective campaign to enforce immigration law within the nation's interior, with a top-level focus on criminal aliens, fugitive aliens and those who pose a threat to the safety of the American public and the stability of American communities" (6). Yet, as of October 1, 2007, the "case backlog consisted of 594,756 ICE fugitive aliens" (5). So again, why focus on illegal workers who pose no threat? Elementary: they are easy pickings. True criminal and fugitive aliens have to be picked up one at a time, whereas raiding a slaughterhouse is like hitting a small jackpot: it beefs up the numbers. "In FY07, ICE enacted a multi-year strategy ... worksite enforcement initiatives that target employers who defy immigration law and the 'jobs magnet' that draws illegal workers across the border" (iii). Yet, as the saying goes, corporations do not go to jail. Very few individuals on the employer side have ever been prosecuted. In the case of Agriprocessors, the *search warrant application* cites only vague allegations by alien informers against plant supervisors (middle and upper management are insulated). Moreover, these allegations pertain mostly to petty state crimes and labor infringements. Union and congressional leaders contend that the federal raid actually interfered with an ongoing state investigation of child labor and wage violations, designed to improve conditions. Meanwhile, the underlying charge of "knowingly possessing or using false employment documents *with intent to deceive*" (my emphasis) places the blame on the workers and holds corporate individuals harmless. It is clear from the scope of the warrant that the thrust of the case against the employer is strictly monetary: to redress part of the cost of the multimillion-dollar raid. This objective is fully in keeping with the target stated in the *annual report*: "In FY07, ICE dramatically increased penalties against employers whose hiring processes violated the law, securing fines and judgments of more than $30 million" (iv).

Much of the case against Agriprocessors, in the *search warrant application*, is based upon "No-Match" letters sent by the Social Security Administration to the employer. In August 2007, the Department of Homeland Security (DHS) issued a final rule declaring "No-Match" letters sufficient notice of possible alien harboring. But current litigation (*AFL-CIO v. Chertoff*) secured a federal injunction against the rule, arguing that such error-prone methods would unduly hurt both legal workers and employers.[5] As a result, the "No-Match" letters may not be considered sufficient evidence of harboring. The lawsuit also charges that DHS overstepped its authority and assumed the role of Congress in an attempt to turn the SSA into an immigration law enforcement agency. Significantly, in referring to the final rule, the *annual report* states that ICE "enacted" a strategy to target employers (iii), thereby using a word ("enacted") that implies lawmaking authority. The effort was part of ICE's "Document and Benefit Fraud Task Forces," an initiative targeting employees, not employers, and implying that illegal workers may use false SSNs to access benefits that belong to legal residents. This false contention serves to obscure an opposite and long-ignored statistics: the value of social security and Medicare contributions by illegal workers. People often wonder where those funds go but have no idea how much they amount to. Well, they go into the SSA's "Earnings Suspense File," which tracks payroll tax deductions from payers with mismatched SSNs.[6] By October 2006, the Earnings Suspense File had accumulated $586 billion, up from just $8 billion in 1991.[7] The money itself, which currently surpasses $600 billion, is credited to, and comingled with, the general

SSA Trust Fund. SSA actuaries now calculate that illegal workers are currently sub-sidizing the retirement of legal residents at a rate of $8.9 billion per year, for which the illegal (no-match) workers will never receive benefits.

Again, the big numbers are not on the employers' side. The best way to stack the stats is to go after the high concentrations of illegal workers: food process-ing plants, factory sweatshops, construction sites, janitorial services—the easy pickings. On September 1, 2006, an ICE raid crippled a rural Georgia town: 120 arrested. On December 12, 2006, ICE agents executed warrants at Swift & Co. meat processing facilities in six states: 1,297 arrested, 274 "charged with identity theft and other crimes" (8). On March 6, 2007, *the Boston Globe* reported that 300 ICE agents raided a sweatshop in New Bedford: 361 mostly Guatemalan workers arrested, many flown to Texas for deportation, dozens of children stranded. As the *annual report* graph shows, worksite raids escalated after fiscal year 2006, signaling the arrival of "a New Era in immigration enforcement" (1). Since 2002, adminis-trative arrests increased tenfold, while criminal arrests skyrocketed thirty-fivefold, from 25 to 863. Still, in fiscal year 2007, only 17 percent of detainees were crimi-nally arrested, whereas in Postville it was 100 percent —a "success" made possible by "fast-tracking"—with felony charges rendering workers indistinguishable on paper from real "criminal aliens." Simply put, the criminalization of illegal work-ers is just a cheap way of boosting ICE "criminal alien" arrest statistics. But after Postville, it is no longer a matter of clever paperwork and creative accounting: this time around 130 man-years of prison time were handed down pursuant to a bogus charge. The double whammy consists in beefing up an additional and meatier statistics showcased in the *report*: "These *incarcerated aliens* have been involved in dangerous criminal activity such as murder, predatory sexual offenses, narcotics trafficking, alien smuggling *and a host of other crimes*" (6). Never mind the char-acter assassination: next year when we read the fiscal-year-2008 report, we can all revel in the splendid job the agency is doing keeping us safe and blindly beef up its budget another billion. After all, they have already arrested 1,755 of these "crimi-nals" in this May's raids alone.

The agency is now poised to deliver on the "new era." In fiscal year 2007, ICE grew by 10 percent, hiring 1,600 employees, including over 450 new deportation officers, 700 immigration enforcement agents, and 180 new attorneys. At least 85 percent of the new hires are directly allocated to immigration enforcement. "These additional personnel move ICE closer to target staffing levels"(35). Moreover, the agency is now diverting to this offensive resources earmarked for other purposes such as disaster relief. Wondering where the twenty-three trailers came from that were used in the Iowa "fast-tracking" operation? "In FY07, one of ICE's key accom-plishments was the Mobile Continuity of Operations Emergency Response Pilot Project, which entails the deployment of a fleet of trailers outfitted with emergency supplies, pre-positioned at ICE locations nationwide for ready deployment in the event of a nearby emergency situation" (23). Too late for New Orleans but there was always Postville. Hopefully, the next time my fellow interpreters hear the buzzwords "continuity of operations," they will at least know what they are getting into.

This massive buildup for the "new era" is the outward manifestation of an internal shift in the operational imperatives of the "Long War," away from the "war

Worksite Enforcement Arrests

Tackling Illegal Employment

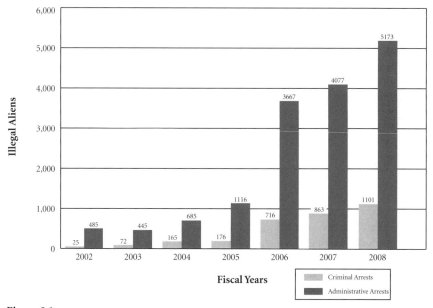

Figure 9.1

Source: Department of Homeland Security (2008)

on terror" (which has yielded lean statistics) and onto another front where we can claim success: the escalating undeclared war on illegal immigration. "Had this effort been in place prior to 9/11, all of the hijackers who failed to maintain status would have been investigated months before the attack" (9). According to its new paradigm, the agency fancies that it can conflate the diverse aspects of its operations and pretend that immigration enforcement is really part and parcel of the "war on terror." This way, statistics in the former translate as evidence of success in the latter. Thus, the Postville charges—document fraud and identity theft—treat every illegal alien as a potential terrorist and with the same rigor. At sentencing, as I interpreted, there was one condition of probation that was entirely new to me: "You shall not be in possession of an explosive artifact." The Guatemalan peasants in shackles looked at each other, perplexed.

When the executive responded to post-9/11 criticism by integrating law enforcement operations and security intelligence, ICE was created as "the largest investigative arm of the Department of Homeland Security" with "broad law enforcement powers and authorities for enforcing more than 400 federal statutes" (1). A foreseeable effect of such broadness and integration was the concentration of authority in the executive branch, to the detriment of the constitutional separation of powers. Nowhere is this more evident than in Postville, where the expansive agency's authority can be seen to impinge upon the judicial and legislative powers. "ICE's team of attorneys constitutes the largest legal program in DHS, with more than 750 attorneys to support the ICE mission in the administrative and federal courts. ICE attorneys have also participated in temporary assignments to the Department of Justice as Special Assistant U.S. Attorneys spearheading criminal prosecutions of individuals. These assignments bring much needed support to taxed U.S. Attorneys' offices"(33). English translation: under the guise of interagency cooperation, ICE prosecutors have infiltrated the judicial branch. Now we know who the architects were that spearheaded such a well crafted "fast-tracking" scheme, bogus charge and all, which had us all, down to the very judges, fall in line behind the shackled penguin march. Furthermore, by virtue of its magnitude and methods, ICE's "New War" is unabashedly the aggressive deployment of its own brand of immigration reform, *without congressional approval.* "In FY07, as the debate over comprehensive immigration reform moved to the forefront of the national stage, ICE expanded upon the ongoing effort to re-invent immigration enforcement for the 21st century" (3). In recent years, DHS has repeatedly been accused of overstepping its authority. The reply is always the same: if we limit what DHS/ICE can do, we have to accept a greater risk of terrorism. Thus, by painting the war on immigration as inseparable from the war on terror, the same expediency would supposedly apply to both. Yet only for ICE are these agendas codependent: the war on immigration depends politically on the war on terror, which, as we saw earlier, depends economically on the war on immigration. This type of no-exit circular thinking is commonly known as a "doctrine." In this case, it is an undemocratic doctrine of expediency at the core of a police agency whose power hinges on its ability to capitalize on public fear. Opportunistically raised by DHS, the sad specter of 9/11 has come back to haunt illegal workers and their local communities across the United States.

A line was crossed at Postville. The day after, in Des Moines, there was a citizens' protest featured in the evening news. With quiet anguish, a mature, all-American woman—a mother—said something striking as only the plain truth can be. "This is not humane," she said. "There has to be a better way."

Notes

1. Immigration and Customs Enforcement, *Application for Search Warrant.* U.S. District Court for the Northern District of Iowa. May 12, 2008. Available at http://www.aila .org/content/fileviewer.aspx?docid=25454&linkid=177821.
2. United States District Courts, *Standards for Performance and Professional Responsibility for Contract Court Interpreters in the Federal Courts. Available at* http://www.njd .uscourts.gov/interp/int-standards-performance.pdf.
3. See http://www.usdoj.gov/criminal/fraud/websites/idtheft.html.
4. See *ICE Fiscal Year 2007 Annual Report, available at* http://www.ice.gov/doclib/about/ ice07ar_final.pdf.
5. See *AFL-CIO v. Chertoff,* Case 3:07-cv-04472-CRB, N.D. Cal. 2007. Available at http:// www.aclu.org/immigrants/workplace/31491lgl20070829.html.
6. See Social Security Administration, Office of the Inspector General, *Congressional Response Report: Status of the Social Security Adminsitration's Earnings Suspense File,* November 2002. Available at http://www.ssa.gov/oig/ADOBEPDF/A-03-03-23038.pdf.

10

Waste Is a Terrible Thing to Mind

Dicxon Valderruten

A mind is a terrible thing to waste.

—United Negro College Fund, advertising slogan

HIV/AIDS and incarceration rank among the most critical problems that have impacted the ethnic minority communities in the United States over the last twenty-five years. New York State (NYS) in particular has the largest number of people living with HIV/AIDS, and its rates of incarceration of Blacks and Latinos are among the top three in the nation. The get-tough-on-crime policies implemented in the 1970s are the primary reason why poor Blacks and Latinos now make up the majority of people incarcerated in NYS. The sale, trafficking, and use of illegal drugs represents the single most important reason why these two groups enter prison at alarming rates; in addition, drugs (intravenous drug use) account for their high rates of HIV infection.

Unless one works in the field of HIV/AIDS or in a prison setting, one would tend to ignore the impact that these two social epidemics (incarceration and HIV) have had on poor communities in NYS. As both a human service provider and a teacher, I have been closely involved in the provision of HIV services for men incarcerated in some of the seventy state facilities that are under the jurisdiction of the NYS Department of Correctional Services. My involvement servicing incarcerated populations in the criminal justice system goes back to 1991, when I became the director of Osborne Association's LIVING-Well, a model case management program that targeted people who were HIV-positive and were being released from prison. Between 1991 and 2001, I worked closely with the NYS Division of Parole and the NYC Human Resources Administration in order to coordinate services for a segment of the prison community who reenters society—they are the casualties of the government-sponsored "war on drugs" and the "war on poverty." Practically all persons to whom the Osborne Association agency has provided HIV services—well over 5,000—over the last twenty-five years are homeless, drug addicts, and people diagnosed, or left undiagnosed, as mentally ill. They are people who have spent a major portion of their lives in and out of the criminal justice system, with little or no support or assistance.

For the last ten years, I have also been directly responsible for the implementation and delivery of several health prevention initiatives (including HIV, hepatitis, sexually transmitted infections, and tobacco) in several men's prison facilities in NYS. No experience has been more empowering and therefore more enlightening than my daily work with men who were members of Prisoners for AIDS Counseling and Education (PACE),[1] while serving time in prison, and who continued the mission of educating themselves and other about HIV prevention. I have worked with some of the brightest minds I have encountered in my twenty-five-year experience as an educator. I encountered them in the school buildings of prisons such as Green Haven, Downstate, Fishkill, and Sing Sing. Working with these people, many of whom have been the victims of a racist and elitist educational system, has required a humility and understanding of their intelligence and potential to contribute to various aspects of society. It has been hard to accept the fact that whether I was teaching a social science course at a senior four-year college like Queens College or at a two-year college like Borough of Manhattan Community College, my students in prison not only came more prepared for their classes but also continued with their educational inquiry well beyond the classroom. Their eagerness to learn made me realize that I needed to create a system of classroom follow-up, where some of the most qualified peer facilitators would conduct one or two additional classes on each topic in order to meet the need of those students who wanted to further their knowledge about each health issue.

PACE members utilize the science of HIV and other infectious diseases as an educational tool that enables them to transform their lives in ways that are seldom seen outside prison. Finding ways of extending the prevention messages to other members of their families, they realize that they would not have bothered to read and learn about new and related issues had it not been for the new information they acquired on issues such as sex, gender, identity, and sexual orientation through learning about HIV/AIDS. Their classroom presentations, which are part of the PACE program, have empowered them to stand in front of people and convey messages that affirm life, not death. In short, in the absence of college courses offered in prison, even the least educated pushed themselves beyond their past experiences. They have utilized HIV education as the foundation for a new form of curriculum that has helped them transform their lives. My health classes do not require that people read and spell well, but what is a requirement is that they try to learn beyond what is reasonable (beyond their reasonable doubt), which means that a good number of my students need to deconstruct what they have been told about themselves (i.e., once a criminal, always a criminal). In my class, they find an increasing fascination with learning. They also learn that negative labels that they received in the past had become permanent roadblocks in their educational journey.

One of the central tenets of my educational philosophy begins with the fact that students need to value their own personal and community experience if they want to be able to transform themselves and therefore transform their communities, including their prison setting. In my classes, I emphasize that an HIV curriculum has a scientific as well as a practical component about some of the challenges that we face in society. In other words, an HIV curriculum is a "curriculum for living" that can serve as a declaration of independence from some of the negative experiences of their past, including their past lifestyles, their engagement with drugs, unprotected sex, money, guns, and violence, and their indifference to crime and its negative consequences. The classroom is not solely the place where we meet in a given building once a week; rather, it is wherever the students happen to be, regardless of time and circumstances. In this process, we all become students and teachers at the same time.

A second important element in my classes in the prisons is that we must utilize any piece of information (or misinformation) and knowledge as a vehicle for transformation. One of the most remarkable experiences I have had in my classes is the way that PACE facilitators at Fishkill Correctional Facility began to deconstruct their concept of manhood and the notion of the macho and were able to move from hating and ignoring gay, bisexual, and transgender men to seeing them as people who have dignity and deserve respect like everybody else, both in the prison setting and outside. During the last training on "Gay, Bisexual and Transgender Issues," the PACE facilitators invited a group of transgender men to share their life experiences with the students in their class. This is not a typical scene in a U.S. prison setting where people create clear divisions between "real men and punks." When they introduced the workshop session, they stated that one of its objectives was to be able to learn from the transgender community and see it as a partner in the prevention of HIV/AIDS. It had taken two years for the PACE group facilitators to take this initiative because in order to be consistent with the messages of HIV prevention, they first had to make the decision to confront their own biases and misinformation. Several people realized that gay, bisexual, and transgender men are discriminated against and despised, just as men who go to prison are devalued because of the crimes they have committed.

Another idea that has been very empowering for many PACE facilitators is the need to transcend the "myth and fact reality" in which they live. Incarcerated men, like prison administrators and employees, see the myth that they could never be able to work together towards a common goal (e.g., servicing people infected with HIV or preventing people from getting infected) as a fact and live it as a reality. The clear distinction between "them" versus "us" is one of the biggest obstacles that PACE members have to overcome in class because it is part of the discourse and, therefore, thinking process in prison. The reality is that if peers are going to learn how to do effective HIV prevention work in prison, they need to see the administration as potential partners in this project. Only in this way can they create channels of communication and intervention strategies through which prison administrative officials and peer educators can seriously communicate towards achieving a common goal. On the one hand, through the HIV class, peer educators learned to identify and value their relationship with other service units within the correctional setting and have transcended their own myths that the administration was not interested in working with them or that it did not value the PACE initiative. Members of the prison medical and rehabilitation units, on the other hand, have changed the way they see the work that PACE members do for the incarcerated community. Another component of the curriculum for living, as I call these health education classes, is the need to promote it as a tool that they can utilize in their own growth, not only in prison but also once they return to their communities. The key to success both inside and outside of the prison setting is the belief that they now have information, knowledge, and skills that they can utilize to promote themselves in the job market once they reenter society and get jobs as service providers for a community of people considered "hard to reach." In this way, their acquired skills can also serve to mentor and educate their children as well as to give back to both their families and communities.

At a recent reunion, for example, several former PACE peers discussed with me their lives on the outside. Some had completed prison sentences ranging from ten to twebty years, while others had left prison only a few days or weeks before. Most are now successfully working in New York City as human service providers, and a few work as clerks. Several noted that were it not for PACE, they would not have been able to acquire the lived experience and the knowledge necessary to communicate more skillfully with their children about such issues as HIV prevention, drug use, violence, and crime.

Moreover, in a context where friendship is difficult to find, PACE had clearly given all of them a sense of community. The preventive mission of the organization had provided guidance, principles, and a commitment to a higher cause while simultaneously ensuring them a certain status within the prison walls. The prison administration looked at PACE as a model program and many facilitators as leaders in the prison community. They are allowed to run HIV-education sessions for newly arrived men as well as for men in the transitional services before they reenter society. They discussed their HIV lessons and emphasized the ways that these contributed to their ability to plan their prevention interventions in the community and to organize successful presentations. As a former peer educator—who is now director of compliance at an alternative to incarceration program—noted, PACE taught him to listen and, equally important, to be patient, skills that he did not previously have. As a result, he listens carefully to men who are mandated to attend court or drug treatment programs and who are often defensive when they first come into his program. He is then able to selectively respond to their sometimes-endless justifications of their wrongdoing.

Other former peer educators talked about the way that PACE helped to transform their thinking and, therefore, their way of relating to their partners. Yet another explained that the program had prepared him to understand the importance of meeting people and of networking in a positive and constructive manner.

Deprived of personal encounters with any one outside of their immediate circle of family and friends, their contact with people who could serve as mentors during their prison terms has also been critically important, in several ways, once they are on the outside. The mentors serve as points of contact and referrals for job opportunities. They are also the people they contact if or when they have crises or unresolved issues. Often having had the experience of mentors who, while in prison, had cared and treated them as friends or partners in their process of transformation rather than as criminals, they feel that they have had a role model who they can now emulate for others. As one former peer educator who went to prison at the age of fourteen and completed a sixteen-year sentence stated, "I realized that

I was ignorant about everything. I thought PACE and other programs were going to give me a fish and what I got was a net and the skills for how to fish."

When I asked the peer educators about their lives today, they said that they enjoy every minute—they enjoy their freedom because they both have and understand the concept of choice. The transformation and freedom that these men now experience is something that "can only work if they give it away." In contrast, all of them commented on how prison life, day in and day out, month after month, year after year, creates the institutionalized mind. It is an existence in which people's basic material needs, such as food, shelter, and clothing, are somewhat satisfied while their intellectual and educational needs are clearly neglected.

Prison education is, by far, one of the most effective forms of reducing recidivism.[2] However, in 1994, the U.S. Congress ended educational practices that would have given people in prison the opportunity to obtain their college education.[3] The irony of this is that in the absence of any kind of educational opportunities in prisons, members of the PACE programs across NYSDOCS have utilized every educational opportunity to improve their educational qualifications through HIV education programs financed by the NYS Department of Health's AIDS Institute. Starting in 1991, under the criminal justice initiative, the AIDS Institute contracted organizations with prior experience servicing prison populations on the outside to enter correctional facilities to provide key HIV services, including education.[4] Yet as these formerly incarcerated men strongly argued, had it not been for the few education programs these and other organizations offered, they would not have benefited from the mentorship that has now allowed them to successfully reintegrate themselves in their communities. They received a few other courses in prison but the various HIV education classes included other skills (i.e., group presentation, outreach, counseling, assessment, networking, and so on).

Now more than ever, these men feel motivated to enter or to continue their college education and to organize themselves and create programs that enrich the lives of men and women in and out of prison. Grounded in the strength that comes from overcoming their past and from the knowledge they gained from their prison experience, they want to be able to positively impact the younger generations so that their communities' youth do not see prison as an inevitable part of their present or future lives. They are determined to share their success stories, for, as one explained, "there is too much emphasis on negative and destructive stories" and very little awareness of the successes of people like them.

When we approached the issue of what they were least prepared for, they commented that they were surprised to see that many of their family and community members are so "laid back" and feel stagnated about their lives. They believe that many of their family members have few aspirations. One described how ill prepared he is to deal with his children's crises and his relationship with their mother. Feeling guilty about his absence from his children's lives, he is both caught up with the need to be responsible and to assist them when they are in crises and simultaneously feeling inadequate, yet unable to say no, when the crisis escalates beyond his control. For some of these formerly incarcerated men, time is the critical factor. They feel they have lost so much time and left so much incomplete, and they are impatient to do today what they had failed to do in the past.

Ultimately, it is important to acknowledge that the crisis created by AIDS has also provided us with the opportunity to rediscover the value of various members of our society. Moreover, it is clear that we need to include and rely on the experience of these men who have so much to give today if we are to find the way of successfully addressing much of the ever-deepening despair and hopelessness in poor, ethnic, minority communities.

Finally, it is time to revisit our government's "get-tough-on-crime" policies and decisions and demand changes that benefit poor communities across the nation.

Notes

1. PACE is a peer-education program in the NYS correctional system for HIV prevention and intervention. It was begun in 1987, in women's prisons, under the name of AIDS counseling and education and has now become the most successful HIV prevention program in the state's correctional facilities. Today, given its success, there are plans to expand the PACE focus on AIDS intervention to other health issues such as hepatitis, tobacco prevention, MRSA, and any future health-related problems that spread from the community to the prison setting.
2. According to the National Institute of Justice Reports to the U.S. Congress, prison education is far more effective at reducing recidivism than boot camps, shock incarceration, or vocational training (cf. Karpowitz and Kenner, n.d.).
3. Before 1995, there were approximately 350 college degree programs (seventy of them in NYS alone) in prisons nationwide. As of now, only a few programs survive (cf. Jeralyn 2005).
4. Some of these organizations included the Osborne Association, the Fortune Society, the Center for Community Alternatives, the Women's Prison Association, and the Prison Ministries. They provide HIV prevention education, HIV treatment education, transitional-discharge planning for people infected with HIV, HIV testing, among other services.

References

Karpowitz, Daniel, and Max Kenner. n.d. Education as crime prevention: The case for reinstating Pell Grant eligibility for the incarcerated. Bard Prison Initiative. Annandale-on-Hudson, NY: Bard College.

Merritt, Jeralyn E. 2005. For whom the Pell tolled: Higher education for prisoners. TalkLeft. The politics of crime. Section Inmates and Prisons. http://www.talkleft.com/story/2005/02/19/061/78055 (accessed January 20, 2008).

11

Closing the Gap

Mentoring Latina Students to
Reach Out to Incarcerated Latinas

Marcia Esparza

"It is very hard to make it out there . . . Now I have a job and I make it day by
day," said Stacey Thompson. She and Linda Soberal, outreach workers from the
Correctional Association Women's Project and former prisoners, spoke movingly
to faculty and students at John Jay College of Criminal Justice in New York City.[1]
They were participants in "Latina Women in Prison," the first seminar held by
Latinas United for Justice (LUJ).[2] Students and I formed LUJ in 2004 to engage
Latina students in political activism and to promote Latina leadership in the criminal justice field by hosting seminars and other events like this one. When Latinas
United for Justice began, I approached my role as mentor in the traditional way,
overseeing students' workloads and guiding research projects. I assumed I would
enforce the accepted faculty-student boundaries by meeting students only in the
classroom or in my office and by talking with them only about their academic
work. Over time, however, I have found that a different kind of mentoring, one
where power relations between students and myself can be leveled off, proves to
be the most authentic and effective way to achieve LUJ's goals. In part this was
because, as a working-class "white Latina" from Chile myself, I am of the same
class and ethnicity as many John Jay students, 40 percent of whom are of Latino
heritage.

The obstacles that Latinas United for Justice confront, are many. LUJ students
are U.S.-born and immigrant Latinas. Many of these women have grown up in
New York City, mainly in working-class families, and are single mothers or financial providers for their relatives. In many cases, their roles as workers and caregivers present significant obstacles to their success in obtaining academic degrees in
fields such as international criminal justice, forensic psychology, or corrections.[3]
Significantly, the members of LUJ's executive committee have fewer economic

responsibilities and are thus able to spend additional time participating in academic life. Generally speaking, John Jay students cope with similar structural constraints, as do increasing numbers of Latina and African American women who are imprisoned every year, largely for nonviolent crimes. At different levels, they feel the effects of the cycles of poverty and deprivation that lead to, and prolong, the current rapid rise in female incarceration.

In a society in which white privilege dominates, students also face stereotypical images, such as the "J-Lo" myth, of Latinas as sexy and docile. In the absence of validated positive role models, these representations undermine Latinas' self-images as thinkers and scholars. "Who are your role models?" I often ask students in class, only to be met with silence.

Mainstream Academia Replicates Cultural Obstacles

Cultural gender stereotypes that place Latinas in a low position in a power hierarchy are perpetuated by the traditional male authority found within academia and by current, widely held conceptions of appropriate teacher-student boundaries. As I shared my views on my approach to mentorship, a few observers frowned on my meeting with students off campus because they saw this as transgressing boundaries. "The [John Jay] administration may not like your approach," they warned. These kinds of pervasive conceptions of student-teacher boundaries that call on faculty to maintain their power over students, in addition to the sexism and racism Latina students experience within a Eurocentric, male academic environment, mirror and reinforce the experiences that shape Latinas' senses of self and identity in the culture.

Having benefited from an open and more equal relationship with my mentors, I draw on my experiences as a guide.[4] During my undergraduate years at Hunter College in New York City, I served as president of the Latino Honor Society under the leadership of Professor Ana Celia Zentella. I also conducted research on New York City Latinas' fear of crime in collaboration with Esther Madriz, a Venezuelan criminologist. Both these mentors often included me in extracurricular activities such as gatherings and panels celebrating the release of a new book. Esther accompanied me to SUNY-Albany when I was visiting prospective graduate schools in 1994. Thus, my relationship with my own mentors serves as a model for me. Zentella and Madriz showed me that the only way to demystify the academic world for students is to make it more accessible to them.

Following my own mentors' example, I have sought to establish bonds of solidarity, supporting LUJ students' acquisition of leadership skills in many different ways. I often meet LUJ executive committee members in venues outside the college to carry out our work. As we plan our organization's activities, we share meals and conversation about our own lives—about our common immigration experiences and heritage, the wider implications of traditional gender roles, the effects of government policies relating to health, and the disadvantages Latinas in academia confront, such as lack of writing skills. As we do so, I watch my students becoming cognizant of their potential and creativity as both analysts as well as carriers of the burdens that mainstream U.S. culture places on them and all Latinas, and in a world where demands for our individual and collective rights often go unheard.

New Authority and Networks Enhance Effectiveness

Over time, I have found that LUJ students' increased networking opportunities and their new sense of their own authority makes them more effective in fulfilling LUJ's goals—including their becoming bridges between the incarcerated women they work with and the society. As students relax outside the John Jay College confines and are more able to openly express strong feelings, the relationships we establish support our struggles to overcome, or at least ignore, the sexism and racism in both the academic environment and the broader society. The strong bonds the students and I develop enhance my own personal and academic life as well, as we go to movies or attend seminars on genocide or war in Latin America, for instance, that relate to our research interests.

A more equal mentorship calls for Latina/o and other faculty to reach out to students, to identify, or at least empathize, with those who share origins as colonized minorities, immigrants, and second-class citizens while at the same time recognizing a shared history of resistance to being categorized as the "other."

To enable students to overcome their intellectual diffidence, we, as teachers and mentors, are called upon to provide them with a cultural and psychological safety net where collegial collaboration can be exercised, bringing us closer to their families and to daily life in their respective communities—communities that are also my own and that include women in prison. After all, people in the communities that should benefit from our academic research—women like Stacey Thompson and Linda Soberal—suffer many of the same social conditions: increasing rates of high school dropout, domestic violence, and Latina incarceration. In New York State, by January 2004, an estimated 75 percent of women in prison were women of color—50 percent of whom were African American, while Latinas accounted for 25 percent of the incarcerated women.[5]

A more equal mentorship also provides students with access to other researchers, colleagues, and friends of mine. By reconfiguring boundaries between students and academic professionals, students are able to reach out to a network of faculty with whom they otherwise would have little contact, particularly in fields such as in sociology or political science, where the number of Latina students is very low. These faculty members help them in many ways, including writing essays, personal statements, and applications for graduate school. By closing the gap between faculty and students, Latinas are also able to get access to inside information on grants and fellowships. Overall, the end result is that students are then initiated and learn to negotiate what is often an alien academic culture.

Barriers to Raising Awareness of Latinas in Prison

Efforts to raise awareness amongst students of the need to conduct research on Latinas in prison and to establish relationships with incarcerated women are met with several obstacles. One of them has to do with students' reluctance to discuss the role played by race and ethnicity in shaping peoples' criminal experiences. This is particularly true for Dominican students (the large majority of whom are Afro-Latinas) whose perceptions of race are embedded in deep-seated views that "others" (mainly Haitians) are of a different race; therefore, racial discussions are kept at arm's length.

A corollary effect of this lack of acknowledgement, and hence discussion of the role played by race in the United States, is the students' own stereotypical views of incarcerated populations. In many ways, students replicate society's understanding of criminalized behavior, as they make assumptions based on racialized motivations, leaving out any analysis of the larger socioeconomic and political causes of incarceration (i.e., unemployment rates for Latinos).

In spite of these obstacles, a more equal mentorship enhances even the initial aim of Latinas United for Justice—to promote Latina leadership within the realm of criminal justice. The mutual relationship of support that creates the context of our meetings and work together raises students' awareness of the importance of their scholarship and their careers in the field. In a broader sense, the construction of an internalized sense of Latina authority gives students a greater ability to reach out to grassroots organizations such as the Correctional Association.[6] My hope is that as they achieve positions of authority, they will in turn aid the organizations in establishing mentoring relationships with other Latinas and thus enhance their effectiveness in serving as bridges between the criminal justice system, incarcerated and formerly incarcerated Latinas, and the larger society.

Notes

1. The Correctional Association Women's Project is led by Tamar Kraft-Stolar in New York City. The project lobbies for the rights of women prisoners.
2. Since then, LUJ has organized seminars on leadership and women in the military. For the Spring 2005 semester, a series of brown-bag luncheons was coordinated. Female faculty from John Jay were guest speakers. Students learned about "survival skills" in academia. A workshop on violence against women in Colombia was then planned for the Spring 2005 semester.
3. Doctoral degrees for Latinos are distributed as follows: "ages 25–29, 6,000 PhDs; ages 30–34, 10,000 PhDs; ages 35–39, 17,000 PhDs; ages 40–44, 8,000 PhDs; ages 45–49, 3,000 PhDs; ages 50–54, 9,000 PhDs; ages 55–59, 10,000 PhDs; ages 60–-64, 7,000 PhDs, and ages 65+, 9,000." See Robles (n.d.).
4. The role played by mentors in Latinas' career life in academia has been acknowledged by Robles (n.d.).
5. See Correctional Association of New York's "Women in Prison Fact Sheet."
6. For a powerful analysis in which adolescents speak openly of their life experiences, which often means entering into unknown, solitary, social territory, see Lyn Mikel Brown (1991).

References

Brown, Lyn Mikel. 1991. Telling a girl's life: Self-authorization as a form of resistance. In *Women, girls and psychotherapy: Reframing resistance,* ed. Carol Gilligan, Annie G. Rogers, and Deborah L. Tolman, 71–86. New York: Harrington Park Press.

Correctional Association of New York, Women in Prison Project. *Women in Prison Fact Sheet.* http://www.correctionalassociation.org/WIPP/publications/Women%20%in%Prison20Fact%Sheet%2004.pdf (accessed March 11, 2005).

Fry, Richard. Latinos in higher education: Many enroll, too few graduate. Pew Hispanic Center. http://www.pewhispanic.org/files/reports/11.pdf (accessed March 13, 2005).

Robles, J. Barbara, Latinas in the academy: Profiling leadership, promoting future scholars. University of Texas at Austin. http://www.utexas.edu/lbj/faculty/robles/research/pdf/latinas.pdf (accessed March 11, 2005).

Part III

The Art of Resistance

Latino Visual Culture Behind Bars

Artistic Inspiration and Redemption
Within the Bowels of Despair

Víctor Alejandro Sorell

When you are there for a long time, you experience a form of death.

—Escobar (1994, 42)

Art, then, becomes the only possibility to rescue and redeem life. Art is the prolongation of life by other means.

—Escobar (1994, 49)

My triumph was only in agony. I spoke the language of anguish and made misery my closest friend.[1]

Refuge and Solace in Words and Images:
The Revelations of Leonard Peña's Paño

The first two of the foregoing epigraphs—written by former political prisoner and Puertorriqueño visual artist Elizam Escobar—address the ultimate effects of prison on the human spirit, the desperation of prisoners within the bowels of despair,[2] and the redemptive power of (all) art. The third fragment is taken from a letter generously shared with me by Texas prison minister Mamie R. Torrez, who received it from a now-deceased Chicano prison inmate, Rudy Ornelas.[3] Ornelas's confession about a visceral existence endured in prison augments Escobar's own first-person testimony. What these snippets of verbal introspection invoke finds visual embodiment or translation in a *paño*, or cloth, entitled *Viaje Atras* [sic] *Viaje* (*Trip After Trip*; January/ February of 2008).

Figure 12.1.   Leonard Peña, *Viaje Atras [sic] Viaje* (2008). India ink & ballpoint pen on cloth [paño], 15.75 inches square.

Photo: Brent Jones. From the collection of V. A. Sorell

A remarkably vivid and complex composition rendered on a ground of 100 per-cent cotton cloth,[4] it captures, in staggering and disturbingly trenchant detail, a vortex of "mind trips" defining the lived experience behind bars (Sorell 2006, 9).[5] Throughout the *paño's* picture plane—a labyrinthine maze notable for its *horror vacui* sense of space—a plethora of anonymous characters engage in the com-edy and tragedy of human drama. Here and there, distinctive individual actors punctuate this visualization of what is largely a tragedy with spiritual overtones. A roughly hewn wooden or stone cross occupies a position of focal centrality in the eye of the vortex. Ironically, this "Calvary" scene is devoid of a crucified Christ. Nonetheless, the cross is iconographically situated in Golgotha, the place associ-ated with a skull mentioned in "all four of the accounts of Jesus' crucifixion in the Christian canonical Gospels."[6] A mesmerizing truncated skull to the viewer's left, adjacent to the cross, locks eyes with onlookers. Arguably, one of these view-ers is a *pinto* (Caló argot for prison inmate) dressed in striped prison garb—the stripes echoing cell bars—about to exit his cell door with a book tucked under his right arm.[7] Depicted within the fabric of the *paño*, this soon-to-be ex-*pinto* is conceivably the artist Leonard Peña (b. 1953) himself, seemingly ready to put a *pinto's* existence behind him and ascend the path leading to the cross and to his own attendant salvation. Buried in the ground by his feet, a face stares from behind bars and serves as Peña's sobering visual reminder of incarceration, resonating with Escobar's two epigraphs.

Undoubtedly, some inmates take redemptive journeys, and religious faith plays a significant role in their lives of captivity (Sorell 2006, 10–12). Peña references the Epistle of Paul the Apostle to the Galatians (Gal. 2:20) as his inspiration for the life he now leads outside of prison.[8] Where he had once been is recorded in the advancing or retreating footsteps registered like tattoos on the extended forearm of the *pinto* executing a *paño* in the lower left quadrant of the drawing—a *paño* within a *paño*. A commanding, nearly three-dimensional and disembodied hand, holding a pencil and suggestively about to break through the picture's own illusory stage unto the physical arena of spectator space, renders this metapicture. Peña's past and new journeys are conflated in this largely autobiographical representation that can be likened to a Bible tract.[9] Peña himself may also be the young, pensive man, partially free of his handcuffs and covered with tattoos, who, from our perspective, occupies a perch to the right of the cross, a pose borrowed from Auguste Rodin's celebrated bronze and marble sculpture, *The Thinker* (1880–1904).[10] The body markings can be read as actual tattoos or, as Peña would characterize them, "life's experiences inscribed on my body,"[11] consistent with what the aforementioned footsteps represent. Below this suspended figure, two disembodied and floating diabolical heads, occupying the lower right quadrant of the *paño*, are depicted with tortured and sinister expressions, probably a reflection on their own disturbing "mind trips." Prison accoutrements and related symbols are dominant in the drawing. Cell bars and doors, keys, handcuffs, hypodermic needles, dice, a smirking court jester,[12] grimacing, menacing and pensive human faces, peacocks (symbolic of inmate pride), serpents, sharks and dragons (symbolic of predatory and fanciful creatures), and spider webs[13] remind us that these *viajes* revolve around incarceration from a host of experiential perspectives. Oblivious to our gaze, a recumbent figure appearing above the just mentioned forearm recalls, for the artist, his once fellow inmates so reclined on their bunks at night. This particular *pinto* may be observing a picture, possibly another *paño*, suspended along his line of vision on the interior wall of an imaginary cell. Tellingly, Chicano artist Leonard Peña executed this *paño* as an ex-*pinto* living in Austin, Texas, on indefinite parole, having already served twenty years of a forty-eight-year sentence. Austin architectural landmarks depicted around the *paño's* vertical center—read by the viewer as left of the central cross—contextualize the artist's current circumstances and place of residence. Clearly, Peña's *paño* depicts palpable images "speaking" with the candor of the voices of our opening epigraphic testimony. No longer confined behind bars, Peña is looking beyond prison. Currently, he is at work on a *paño* depicting Middle Eastern and U.S. election-year subjects.[14]

This chapter foregrounds contemporary visual art executed in prison by Latino inmates, arguing that it is an important means for inmates trying to cope with the "misery" of the carceral experience. The first researcher to discuss prison art as an artistic category was the German psychiatrist and aesthetician Hans Prinzhorn

(1886–1933) in 1926 (Cardinal 1997, xvii–xviii). Against the relatively brief history of prison visual art, the British art critic and academician Roger Cardinal, a pioneering interpreter and promoter of "outsider art," acknowledges an ongoing "tenacity of the human urge to expression" (Cardinal 1997, xiii). Expressive visual culture realized within the asphyxiating and oppressive confines of prison takes many forms—body tattooing, drawing, painting, sculpting, and ceramics arguably constituting the most conspicuous of the media and artifacts. Crafted utilitarian objects are also quite abundant. Objects made of woven paper (*tejido*), occasionally sewn with dental floss for greater durability, include boxes, frames, cup holders, baby shoes, purses, and jewelry articles. Leather belts, bracelets, wallets, and watchbands, as well as miniature furniture and toys, including ships and windmills—constructed with Popsicle sticks or toothpicks—are among other known crafted products discussed only occasionally.

Human blood,[15] coffee grinds, ink removed from the pages of a bible, shoe polish, carbon and letter papers, glossy magazines, newspapers, desk blotters, old calendars, cigarette packages, coarse prison-issued toilet paper, ceramic clay, pebbles and stones, window caulking, soft bread, T-shirts, handkerchiefs, socks, soap, and cold cream may seem unlikely raw materials shaped into prison art or used as visual and tactile elements to embellish different objects. However, *la pinta* (Caló argot for prison) exacts innovation from its would-be artists and similarly innovative materials and practices (Sorell 2004, 630–33). It is also important to account for traditional artistic media when and where they are made available to *pinta* artists: hard lead and charcoal pencils, crayons, pastels, and watercolors, among others.

Escobar himself suggests that it is through artistic creativity that the prisoner rescues and redeems a life suspended between captivity and liberty. Analogously, humanist-scholar W. B. Carnochan contends that prison literature is created through the "interplay of constraint and freedom" (Carnochan 1995, 427). Creative writing, in its many forms, is visual culture's kindred form of expressive culture behind bars. Just how basic but potent the poetic word can become in a prison setting is candidly stated by poet Grady Hillman, who, in 1981, did a creative-writing residency in the Texas prison system through a program called "arts-in-corrections." About that experience, he wrote, "Time has an entirely different meaning in prison. Trust, intimacy. The constructions of identity were highly sophisticated. You learn about both the potential and the tragedy of the human condition. And that's the stuff of art. The one thing I got out of my prison experience is the power of poetry . . . inmates, for whom the creation of a poem was the most important thing in their life" (Burnham and Durland 1998, 255).Scripture appears to provide yet another textual refuge from the "anguish" and harshness of serving time. Interviewed by public artist Jonathan Borofsky in 1985 and 1986 as part of a video documentary entitled "Prisoners" at San Quentin State Prison, African American inmate James Pettaway testified, "One of the things that helps me a great deal is the Bible" (Borofsky 1990, 177). His testimonial calls to mind Peña's sensibility and virtual redemptive journey charted in his emblematic *paño*.

This chapter focuses, in some depth, on seven artists whose work is representative of inmate artists. I profile six Latino cellblock artists: three Puertorriqueños—Oscar López Rivera, Elizam Escobar, and Carlos Alberto Torres; two Chicanos—Leonard

Peña and Camilo Cumpián; and one Cuban, Ángel Delgado. The seventh artist is Leonard Peltier, a Native American prisoner of conscience, whose solidarity with Latino and African American prisoners, and theirs with him, is patently expressed in his art.

The U.S. Prison-Industrial Complex Evolves to the Tune of Slave Songs-Turned Convict Songs-Turned Literature

Tracing the genesis of the American prison in the twenty-first century "from plantation to penitentiary to the prison-industrial complex," H. Bruce Franklin, preeminent cultural historian and recognized leading authority on the subject of American prison literature, rightly examines that literary output in ethnographic and socioeconomic terms. He underscores the extent to which African American history is important, informs our appreciation of slave songs, and, subsequently, of ensuing and related prison literature. How plantation slavery evolved into prison slavery is a pivotal subtext in his compelling argument. He describes, "the vast state prison plantations established . . . where cotton picked by prisoners was manufactured into cloth by other prisoners in prison cotton mills. These (prison) plantations dwarfed the largest cotton plantations of the slave South in size, brutality, and profitability. The transition from a plantation economy to a prison economy saw old plantation slave songs now metamorphosed into the convict work songs of the prison plantations" (Franklin 2000, 1–4). That oral musical tradition, Franklin concludes, helped shape black prison literature from the 1860s until the mid 1960s.

Indeed, the civil rights movement would lend added momentum to literary output both inside and outside prison. In turn, *El Movimiento Chicano/a*, which, like the African American movement, also aimed to secure civil and human rights, would nurture Mexican American prison writers like raúlrsalinas (1934–2008) and Jimmy Santiago Baca (half Chicano and half "detribalized Apache" born in 1952), even as it fostered theater and visual art in the labor context of the United Farm Workers under the leadership of César Chávez and Dolores Huerta (Griswold del Castillo et al. 1990).[16] It is singularly important, particularly in the context of this essay, to recognize that the *pinto* population was never an afterthought among Chicano/a activists. In his "Message to Aztlán," delivered on September 16, 1975, on the steps of Denver's Colorado State Capitol building, Rodolfo "Corky" Gonzales decries the fate of *pintos* left to the capricious devices of an arbitrary justice blatantly at odds with a spirit of redress sought by el *movimiento's* liberating, proactive agenda (Sorell 2006, 4).

African American and Chicano/a social consciousness would also nurture community muralism, the most conspicuous and ubiquitous form of visual culture inside and outside of prison (Barnett 1984, 236ff). The Puerto Rican diaspora in New York City during the sixties and seventies saw the establishment of alternative spaces for artistic production. At *Taller Boricua*, Puerto Rican visual artist and workshop cofounder Marcos Dimas executed posters of Puerto Rican political prisoners like the independence-liberation movement's Lolita Lebrón. (Ramírez

2007, 47ff). In Chicago, another important center of *Puertorriqueño* diasporic activity, artists José Bermudez, Mario Galán, and Hector Rosario, members of the Puerto Rican Art Association, painted the politically strident mural *La Crucifixión de Don Pedro Albizu Campos*, in 1971 (Sorell 1979, 50). Albizu Campos, "The Tiger of Liberty,"[17] and leader of the Nationalist Party for Puerto Rican independence, occupies the mural's actual physical center and pictorial focal point. To his right, he is flanked by a crucified Lolita Lebrón, and to his left, by a corresponding cruci-fied image of Rafael Cancel Miranda (Sorell 1976, 59). Lebrón and Miranda wear the white and black garb symbolic of Puerto Rico's mourning over its colonial captivity and the uniform of the Army of Liberation created on December 17, 1932 (59 ff). Lebrón and Miranda, together with two other partisans, entered the U.S. House of Representatives on March 1, 1954—on the occasion of the open-ing of the Inter-American Conference in Caracas, Venezuela—and wounded five congressmen with a shower of bullets (59). This act led to their incarceration and explains their martyred portraits on the mural's face.

Like their legendary activist predecessors, three of the six Latino artists dis-cussed in this chapter—Oscar López Rivera, Elizam Escobar, and Carlos Alberto Torres—are ideologically invested in Puerto Rican independence, and they, too, were arrested, sentenced, and put behind bars (Félix et al. 2006).

The Anomalous Status of Prison Art

Consistent with Franklin's account of late nineteenth- and twentieth-century developments in U.S. prison literature, Roger Cardinal argues that "the experience of prison has fostered an abundant literature" over time and in a variety of places (Cardinal xv, n.2). But, unlike Franklin, who is silent about prison visual culture, Cardinal acknowledges "the anomalous status of Prison Art." "Whereas there was presumably impromptu instruction in craft skills under regimes sponsoring arti-sanal labor," Cardinal argues, "there seems to have been almost no instruction in, nor encouragement of, artistic practices proper until after the Second World War" (xv, n.2).

Visual Culture in the Name of an Independent Puerto Rico: The Art of Oscar López Rivera, Elizam Escobar, and Carlos Alberto Torres, Prisoners of Conscience

Oscar López Rivera (b. 1943)

Born in the countryside of San Sebastián, Puerto Rico, Oscar López Rivera relo-cated to Chicago in 1957. He served in Vietnam with the U.S. army. Once back in Chicago, he joined the ongoing battle against racism and discrimination. In 1976, his commitment and investment in progressive causes led him to engage in a life of clandestinity. Some five years later, in 1981, López Rivera was arrested and accused of seditious conspiracy and membership in FALN (Fuerzas Armadas de Liber-ación Nacional/the Puerto Rican Armed Forces of National Liberation). He was sentenced to a seventy-year prison term, the first twelve of which he spent in total

isolation (Félix 2006, 34, 46). He would overcome his isolation and "sensory deprivation" by turning to the sister outlets of drawing, painting, and writing (34–35).

Ordained Presbyterian minister Don Beisswenger—formerly a professor in
Vanderbilt University's Divinity School, and incarcerated in April of 2004 for an
act of civil disobedience—reflects on what sort of pastoral care would help inmates
like López Rivera deal with grief in prison. He readily recognizes that "inmates suffer many losses," among them "the daily contact with family," and "community"
(Beisswenger 2008, 71). Surprisingly, it does not occur to this minister to mention
expressive culture, whether literary or visual, as a means of mediating grief (72).
López Rivera, himself, did realize that he "needed to use colors in order to counter
the effects of being locked down in a 6 x 9 foot cell, 23 hours per day, without
access to fresh air, natural light and the colors found in nature" (35). In a rather
diminutive (23" x 17") and sensitive drawing rendered in color pencil and pastel
on paper, Oscar captures, with affection, the likeness of teacher and lifelong activist, Doña Isabel Rosado.

It is an intriguing portrait of this Nationalist leader who, for more than ten
years, was herself in prison for her defense of Albizu Campos when his home came
under attack in 1954 (Beisswenger 2008, 46). Gazing back from behind bars at
the viewer, as though the latter is a visitor to her jail cell, Doña Rosado's gray hair
and deeply furrowed face both attest to, and belie, her steadfast and tenacious
participation over the years in the struggle against the U.S. Navy's occupation of

Figure 12.2. Oscar López Rivera, *Doña Isabel: The Unredeemed Homeland* (n.d.).
Colored pencil and pastel on paper (23"x 17").

Photo: Scott Braley

Vieques. The window-like opening through which she stares is the cartographic silhouette of her beloved island of Puerto Rico. Behind Rosado, we see a lush forest and receding mountainous terrain, all enhanced in subtle pastel hues. A turtle and symbolic *coquís* (little frogs) are depicted in the work's black, shaded foreground. Are we and Doña Rosado meant to hear the distinctive sounds the *coquí* makes? Perhaps the answer resides in Rosado's smile of recognition.

"Katrina's Dome," a painting done in 2006 in acrylic on canvas, comments on the devastation New Orleans suffered in the wake of Hurricane Katrina. Thousands were left homeless and forced to seek refuge in places like the Houston Astrodome, which appears in the painting's background. A proud and stoic family is depicted in the immediate foreground while the criminal inaction of the Bush administration's Federal Emergency Management Agency (FEMA) is denounced billboard-like in the background. López Rivera's own captivity in prison resonates with cruel irony in the fate of these displaced victims, now also held captive by the tragic circumstances that have deprived them of long-term shelter. The family's collective facial expressions and other body language, particularly their accusatory eyes, seem to hold all of us complicit in their displacement and suffering. Notably, the dome's ribbed exterior echoes the verticality of cell bars.

Oscar López Rivera's deeply felt empathy for African Americans is also apparent in an earlier small (18" x 18") painting in acrylic on canvas, *Tribute to Safiyah* (2004). The portrait's subject, Safiyah Bukhari, a former Black Panther, herself a political prisoner and the founding cochair of the Free Mumia Abu-Jamal Coalition, charms us with her captivating smile. So, too, does a splendid acrylic portrait of *Che Guevara* (2006) that best captures López Rivera's artistic virtuosity, especially his handling of color and texture. Such artwork exists in sharp contrast to monochromatic cell environments.[18]

Unlike Leonard Peña, who has infused his drawing with religious inflections, López Rivera deliberately avoids explicit religious content since his tour of duty in Vietnam, where he witnessed a military chaplain's indifference toward a soldier who sought his guidance. That incident made Oscar cynical about his own need for religion.[19]

And, yet, the quiet dignity and serenity that envelop his introspective depictions belie a purely secular approach to painting in captivity. Is there, then, a spiritual aura in Oscar's work, notwithstanding his conscious effort to circumvent religion?

Elizam Escobar (b. 1948)

Painter, poet, and theoretician, Elizam Escobar was born in Ponce, Puerto Rico. He earned a baccalaureate in fine arts at the University of Puerto Rico[20] and then continued his studies at the City University of New York, *El Museo del Barrio*, and the Students' Art League of New York.[21] Between 1979 and 1980, he joined the faculty of the School of Art of *El Museo del Barrio*. He also continued painting, writing poetry, authoring theoretical essays, and studying philosophy. A prolific writer, he published widely in academic journals and books.

On April 4, 1980, Elizam was arrested in Evanston, Illinois, a northern suburb of Chicago, and accused of being a member of the Puerto Rican FALN movement. Elizam and his comrades-in-arms "declared that (they) were combatants in an anticolonial war of liberation against the U.S. government which illegally occupied our homeland" (Escobar 1994 a, 40). He was sentenced to a prison term of sixty-eight years, twenty exceeding Leonard Peña's own harsh sentence (Escobar 1994b, "Notas Biográficas").

Having studied studio art in the academy, Elizam is keenly aware of other artists and their legacy, from the perspective of art history. He admires the Polish-French painter, Balthus; the canonic Mexican *pareja* (couple), Frida Kahlo and Diego Rivera; the melancholy Spanish *maestro* Goya; the creative genius of Picasso, another Spaniard; his fellow-*Puertorriqueño*, Francisco Oller; and many more. Intriguingly, Escobar inverts the traditional subject-spectator relationship, prompting one to ask who is observing whom? (Zavala 1994, 3–4). His approach to the production of visual culture—both as process and end product—should be understood as "*otra forma de pensar, de filosofar, de crear sentido y conocimiento abordando las cosas tanto conceptual como emocional y sensualmente, y no como el* hobby *al que le quieren reducir los carceleros*" (Escobar 1994b, 10).[22] This painter wants to disabuse us of wrong-headed notions about prison as an ideal setting for creativity, "*La noción predominante es que la prisión es un lugar ideal para escribir y pintar. Es todo lo contrario. En la prisión, tal y como yo la he vivido y conocido, la privacidad y la concentración son difíciles de obtener. De hecho, ha sido necesario desarrollar, paulatinamente, poco a poco, una nueva forma de abordar el proceso de pintar para poder superar todo tipo de obstáculos. La necesidad ha hecho esto possible. Para mí, el arte es un acto de liberación, especialmente cuando uno está rodeado de la obscenidad que es la prisión, el arte funge como una salvación, la actividad sagrada de la libertad*" (Escobar et al. 1994, 11).[23]

Escobar sums up his carceral experience with a succinct, yet profound, pronouncement from the vantage point of the imprisoned artist: "the power of art will show its face in spite of the bars" (Escobar 2006, 20).

Evidently, Elizam Escobar attributes something sacred to artistic pursuits, reiterating the essence of the second epigraph cited at the beginning of the chapter.

Parodying the restrictive, systemic nature of prison, where, as Elizam has stated, visual culture is demeaned, he resigns himself to calling his creative space where he paints the "hobby shop." Adopting a more sanguine attitude, he refers to his carceral experience as a whole, as his "season in hell" (Escobar 1994, 41). He is matter-of-fact in his tolerance of interruptions to his painting time, suggesting that such unwanted distractions are "like being awakened while you are just beginning to fall asleep" (35). Elizam was imprisoned at various facilities: initially at Pontiac, Illinois (before 1982), then Menard, Illinois (1982), and, thereafter, Oxford, Wisconsin, and El Reno, Oklahoma, among others. In this latter prison, he painted a provocative painting entitled *La ficción* (The Fiction; 1991).

The artist describes the subject matter: "I portrayed myself as a cadaver in front of the Supreme Court Justices" (Escobar 1994, 44). Elizam then proceeds to explain the symbolic and allegorical dimensions of the striking depiction:

Figure 12.3.   Elizam Escobar, *La ficción* (1991). Oil on canvas, 47" x 72"

Photo: E. Escobar

I am surprised that in a painting like *La ficción* I not only successfully overcame the federal prison system's vigilance and its censorship of delicate subject matter but that I also, unconsciously, reversed the Diego Salcedo legend. According to this legend, a group of Taíno Indians in Puerto Rico, by orders of the *cacique* (chieftain) Uroyoán, drowned this Spanish soldier in 1510 in order to "discover" whether the Spaniards were immortal. Salcedo's body was observed for a number of days to see if he would be resurrected or if he was, in fact, mortal. This legend, of course, was relayed to us through a Spanish/European point of view in order to justify the subsequent suppression of the Taíno rebellion and the conquest that ensued. In *La ficción*, the immediate reference (the Supreme Court Justices) is transcended ("Justice" as fiction, "Justice" as necrophilia . . .). The allegory exceeds itself. The Salcedo legend returns, but this time it is the oppressor questioning the mortality of the oppressed or, on another level, the immortality of art or the artist. (Escobar 1994, 46)

Elizam's corpse in *La ficción* appears again in *Heurística uno* (Heuristic I; 1992), a small (16" x 18.25") mixed-media composition rendered on Masonite. Here, that subject is repeated and assumes more of a sarcophagus-like shape at the center of the work and in the lowest register of the complex composition. The artist's serialized and manipulated self-portrait combined with a stylized and truncated Puerto Rican flag and a repeated supine dead figure together simulate a frame for the picture. The portraits undergo a transformation from a photo likeness of the artist himself to a contorted face done in the manner of the British painter Francis Bacon. The colonization of the Americas and the artist's own imprisonment are referenced by the key dates: 1492, 1992, and 2014 and beyond.

Had Elizam been forced to serve out his original sentence, he would not be scheduled for release until 2048! Fortunately, he was released from federal prison on September 10, 1999, having served nineteen years, five months, and several days. Above the already noted central death scene, Elizam has quoted directly from Picasso and Rivera. He borrows diminutive details from the former's "Minotauro-machia" series and his monumental painting of "Guernica," while, from the latter, he reproduces Emiliano Zapata, the Mexican revolutionary chieftain of the country's southern forces, in the company of his favorite horse, originally depicted in a fresco. The highly luminous bulb that illuminates the aftermath of the bombing of the town of Guernica, as depicted by Picasso, is appropriated by Elizam in his work to accent the desolation of his own prison cell (Zavala 1994, 5).

In 1992, Elizam Escobar paints his own dramatic portrait, *El escondido* (The Hidden One), a 28" x 24" canvas. It is an enigmatic painting of two bodies shown side-by-side in profile, their individual necks intertwined and joined to one head, engaging the viewer in a frontal gaze. To the left of the spectator, a gallows awaits its intended victim. Elizam sheds light on who that victim might be: "Since I frequently employed the image of the gallows and noose, this could be literally interpreted in terms of my own suicidal tendencies" (Escobar 1994a, 48). In one work, *El Ahorcado* (The Hanged One), he depicts his own execution. Elizam explains his choice of subjects, "Paradoxically, as an artist I produce images of martyrdom and death. The irony is that many of those who see me as a symbol and martyr for the cause would like me to produce heroic images of combatants or write optimistic messages and statements, while being, on the other hand, a passively faithful comrade in political terms. Instead, I do the reverse" (50).

Today, Elizam Escobar is a professor in the painting department of the School of Fine Arts (*Escuela de Artes Plásticas*) in San Juan, Puerto Rico (Félix 2006, 20).

Carlos Alberto Torres (b. 1952)

Carlos Alberto Torres is the youngest of the three Puerto Rican prisoners of conscience profiled here. He was born in Puerto Rico and relocated twice, first to New York and then to Chicago. He studied at Southern Illinois University and at the University of Illinois in Chicago, simultaneously dedicating himself to community struggles with seeking improved education, better housing, and jobs. Carlos Alberto also participated in the movement for Puerto Rican independence and, fittingly, given his destiny, in the campaign to free Puerto Rican Nationalist prisoners. In 1976, he was accused of belonging to FALN, which drove him to clandestinity. In 1980, the same year that Elizam was arrested, and about one year before López Rivera's arrest, Alberto Torres was arrested, charged with seditious conspiracy, and sentenced to serve seventy-eight years in state and federal prisons. While there, he earned a baccalaureate degree and became interested in visual culture (Félix 2006, 23–24).[24]

Unlike Elizam and López Rivera, both of whom were offered commutation of their respective sentences by President Bill Clinton, Carlos Alberto did not receive any such offer and will complete his full sentence in 2024 (24). López Rivera refused Clinton's offer that was predicated on his serving an additional ten years (35).

Recalling minister Don Beisswenger's observation about the immediate losses prison inmates mourn, Carlos Alberto Torres recognizes those very same torn tethers to family and community: "Separated from my family and friends, from familiar surroundings, this new social reality would test every part of my makeup" (25).

He sought the therapeutic outlet of self-expression, "I learned that the best approach for me was to allow new interests and perspectives to evolve naturally and seek out and cultivate skills that would permit creative self-expression. I would transform my physical captivity into a time for learning, productive accomplishments and moral victory" (25). At the Federal Correctional Institution in Oxford, Wisconsin, where he was incarcerated until recently, Alberto Torres initially gravitated to the medium of painting in what he characterized as a "well organized art program" (25–26). He would first choose acrylic paints for their fast-drying advantage as well as their range of vivid hues. He later employed oil paints and then transitioned to clay and the art of ceramics (26–27).

Like López Rivera, Alberto Torres does not consider himself a religious person, notwithstanding his Christian upbringing in church coupled with the fact that his own father was a pastor for thirty-five years.[25] He does, however, admit doing an explicitly religious painting, *La resurrección* (The Resurrection, 53" x 42"; 2001), an oil on canvas interpretation of Christ's resurrection, commissioned by the United Church of Christ. Yet the commission called for a crucifixion scene. Explaining why he did a resurrection scene instead, he wrote, "I chose not to paint an execution. I think physical death is certainly every person's ultimate fate. Death is a fact of life common to us all—yet always tragic. The sacrifice and struggle for

Figure 12.4. Carlos Alberto Torres, *Vejigantes Hidden Jar #3* (n.d.). Ceramic jar/pot
Photo: Scott Braley

justice, redeems our valor, suffering and death. It resurrects and gives new life to possibility for justice, which is our hope and dream" (46).

The resurrection of justice is clearly this tender and mystical painting's subliminal message, soothingly conveyed.

Vejigantes (traditional Puerto Rican carnival characters) are among Alberto Torres' favorite subjects conceived in clay (46). Concerning their traditional religious connotations, the artist points out that "*aunque los vejigantes tienen un origen y asociación con celebraciones religiosas, no lo interpreto como una figura religiosa. Más bien es una expression cultura tradicionalista*" (46).[26]

The *vejigante* jars are playful and whimsical ceramic creations flaunting their vibrant palettes in the face of prison's drabness. Beyond its appearance on utilitarian objects, the *vejigante* can also assume the form of a highly animated mask or that of a sculptural freestanding figurine. Arguably, the often open-mouthed *vejigante* becomes the artist's own vehicle through which he projects his human voice, thereby "*alcanza[ndo] más allá de la prisión que me encierra*"[27] (30).

Visual Culture in the Name of the American Indian Movement (AIM): Leonard Peltier (b. 1944), Another and Related Prisoner of Conscience/Political Prisoner

That we now turn our attention to a Native American artist-prisoner is wholly consistent with a *mestizo* frame of reference, with what Chicano/*Nuevomexicano* (New Mexican) land grants activist Reies López Tijerina referred to as "a new breed" (Gardner 1970, 202ff); namely, the offspring of miscegenation between the Spanish colonizers and the native Indian populations residing in the colonized Americas, especially in the American Southwest. The "new breed," or Indo-Hispanos, traced their roots to the sixteenth century, when laws were enacted legalizing matrimony between Spaniards and the native Pueblo Indians (202).[28] Speaking as an Indo-Hispano or *Xicanindio*,[29] Tijerina invoked his kindred status with the Indian, "We have been forced by destiny to adopt two languages; we will be the future ambassadors and envoys to Latin America. At home, I believe that the Southwest is breeding a special kind of people that will bridge the color-gap between black and white. . . . *We are the people the Indians call their 'lost brothers'*" (Blawis 1971, 139–40, 146).[30]In the Midwest, some nine years later, *el Movimiento Artístico Chicano* (MARCH; The Chicano Art Movement) organized an exhibition in 1980 entitled *Anisinabe Waki-Aztlán*, '*una celebración artística de nuestra herencia indígena*' ("an artistic celebration of our indigenous heritage"). The late poet and visual artist Carlos Cortéz Koyokuikatl—himself half Xicanindio and half German and a formerly incarcerated war resister (Bennett 2001, 22ff)—created the linocut print used as a poster for this unique cultural event.

Echoing Tijerina's comment about adopting more than one language—a window unto different views of reality[31]—Leonard Peltier, a citizen of the Anisinabe and Dakota-Lakota Nations and member of the American Indian Movement (AIM), wrote from Leavenworth Prison about his childhood when he participated in migrant farmwork in the potato fields of the Red River Valley while simultaneously becoming fluent in *métis*, a French-Indian mixture, as well as English, some Sioux, and Ojibway (Peltier 1999, 72).

Leonard's own prison poem, "We Are Not Separate," further supports his inclusion in this essay focusing on Latino visual culture behind bars:

We are not separate beings, you and I.
We are different strands of the same Being.

You are me and I am you
and we are they and they are us.

This is how we're meant to be,
each of us one,
each of us all.

You reach out across the void of Otherness to me
and you touch your own soul! (213)[32]

The late ex-*pinto* raúlrsalinas,[33] who effacingly dubbed himself the "cockroach poet,"[34] embodies Peltier's poetic sentiments as reflected in his own work with AIM and the Leonard Peltier Defense Committee, in particular.

Ramsey Clark, counsel to Peltier and former Attorney General of the United States, has no doubt about Leonard's innocence and his unjust incarceration, "I think I can explain beyond serious doubt that Leonard Peltier has committed no crime whatsoever. Even if he had been guilty of firing the gun that killed two FBI agents—and it is certain that he did not—it would still have been in self-defense and in the defense not just of his people but of the right of all individuals and peoples to be free from domination and exploitation" (Peltier 1999, xiv). Peltier once imagined that creating art was the basis for "the most wonderful life." He often "wonder(ed) what (his) life would have been like if [he would] have just gotten that [art] scholarship" he had applied for at an art school in Santa Fe, New Mexico (85).

Peltier's own self-portrait, *POW* (2008), confronts the viewer with an intense gaze, his right eye staring straight ahead with penetrating concentration, while the left eye wanders upward and with no particular focus.

The depiction of prison bars immediately behind Peltier reminds us that he is indeed "a prisoner of (a) war" waged against him and others as Attorney Clark's words contend. Visually, these same bars resist our entrance into the pictorial composition beyond its shallow foreground space bathed in gradations of gray. Only Leonard's face betrays different values of a brown hue. Peltier's prison number (89637-132) appears inscribed on the flap of the pocket of his uniform. Slightly above the number we read the artist-prisoner's signature, subtended by an arrow from which two feathers hang alongside the painting's date of execution. This sympathetic portrait appears to interrogate us as though we are complicit in putting Peltier behind bars.[35] Leonard's resolute presence seems derived from the same expressive vocabulary used the previous year to depict *Medicine Man* (2007) with the same *élan*.

Another painting from 2008, entitled *Horse Doctor*, portrays two corralled horses seemingly deprived of their natural freedom, while *Horses Running* (2007)

Figure 12.5. Leonard Peltier, *POW* (2008). Oil on canvas, 20" x 16"

Photo: Watso, Waban Aki-Odanak

celebrates that splendid animal's freedom to roam unfettered. It would seem that Peltier wants us to appreciate the profound contrast between captivity and liberty. Suffused with primary and secondary colors, the latter two paintings sharply contrast with the largely somber grays of the self-portrait. So, too, does the rich palette of blues and reds evident in the earlier *Family Portrait* of 2002, wherein Peltier towers over two female relatives who flank him on either side.

Indian ritual and ceremony are addressed in other works that we might attribute to any number of traditional Native American artists divorced from the specific context of a federal US prison that, sadly, has garnered, for Leonard Peltier, such attendant prominence and sympathy.

Growing Up in the Shadow of El Movimiento Chicano and The American Indian Movement: The Case of Camilo Cumpián (b. 1976)

Camilo Cumpián, son of Chicago-based Chicano poet Carlos Cumpián, was sentenced to fourteen years in prison for stabbing a romantic rival after months of tense encounters over a love interest. To date, Camilo has served over a decade of his sentence for attempted murder.[36]

Camilo's father was active as a highly *engagé* poet and was also a longtime member of MARCH. In that Chicano cultural *milieu*, Camilo had grown up exposed to many Chicano artists, especially his father's own mentor and dear, lifelong friend, Carlos Cortéz Koyokuikatl. The latter's celebrated woodcut, *La Lucha Continua* (The Struggle Continues; 1986) became the borrowed subject for a mural on which Camilo worked in Chicago's Logan Square neighborhood. His talent reflected in his receipt of several awards for painting in his teenage group category at the Logan Square Summer Art Fest during the 1990s led to the young Cumpián's contribution to another mural directed by Pilsen and South Chicago muralist Francisco Mendoza. While engaged in this mural activity, Camilo adopted the moniker "Fresco" as his street tag. Cortéz's influence also inspired this fledgling artist to do poster art.

Interestingly, inside the Ohio prison where he is currently detained, Camilo has chosen to craft wooden objects, carved versions of metallic spray cans used on the outside for graffiti painting and writing. These simulated "cans" are inscribed with the words "Fresco Reminder," recalling his street tag.[37] Notably, some of these diminutive objects are decorated and embellished with Amerindian-Native American subject matter: Indian figures, ceremonial headdresses, feathers, and buffalo, to name a few.

Camilo's audacious allusion to public and unbridled spray-can art of urban city streets is so removed from the strictly policed cell blocks of the systemic prison environment that, in theory, his art symbolically defies and subverts that authoritarian and controlled private space in which he is doing time.

Figure 12.6.   Camilo Cumpián, *Fresco #3* (2008). Balsa wood, 5" x 3"

Photo: Paul Lee

Cuban Artist Ángel Delgado (b. 1965) Ponders the Dichotomy of Individual Liberty Guaranteed Versus Individual Liberty Denied

"*¿Qué motivos le conmueven a usted para dedicarse a la práctica de su deber artístico dentro de la carcel?*"[38] was the question I posed to Ángel. Like Elizam Escobar, he responded philosophically and affirmed the importance of art behind bars, "*Desde mi estancia en prisión en 1990 (durante 6 meses) por la realización de un performance,*[39] *mi arte gira alrededor de un punto, la libertad del individuo o la falta de esta. Me conmueven la falta de comunicación entre los seres humanos, el destierro, la soledad, el abandono, las restricciones pero sobre todo el encierro en cualquiera de sus variantes físicas o sicológicas. Tratando siempre que el espectador reflexione sobre el tema.*"[40]

Despite what might be interpreted as his existential introspection, this artist and former prisoner confesses to having no religious affiliation.[41] However, he does stop short of denying that he occasionally conveys deliberate religious messages. One of his soap carvings from prison represents the crucifixion of Christ, while another work, a prison handkerchief, depicts a Marian image and the textual inscription, *Ampárame* (Protect Me).

Ángel further observes how visual art benefited him personally while incarcerated, "*Saber pintar, dibujar y esculpir, fue el mayor beneficio que tuve al estar en prisión. Con esta habilidad pude sobrevivir dibujando con lápiz de color y cold cream sobre pañuelos y tallando jabones. Estos "objetos" podía intercambiarlos por cigarros, sábanas, toallas entre otros y en primer termino por comida con lo cual podía resistir el hambre que se pasa en las celdas. Pero sobre todas las cosas me ayudo a ser más humano y comunicarme con los otros, fuera de la prisión.*"[42]

He acknowledges art's value as a means of bartering for food and other things[43] and as a means to communicate with others within prison and beyond its confines. Projecting a humanistic voice beyond the bars that contain him, Ángel strives to speak with the volume of Carlos Alberto Torres's *vejigantes*.

Like Chicano ex-*pinto* artist Leonard Peña, whose *paño arte* was featured in the opening pages of this chapter, Ángel Delgado also chooses to use fabric, both handkerchiefs and bed sheets, as favored media. Two serialized and untitled cotton *pañuelos* (handkerchiefs), inscribed with the artist's initials "AD" in the lower right quadrant of the drawn composition, are quite intriguing and delicately delineated. One serialized and untitled piece dating from 2000, rendered in color pencil with cold cream, displays a centrally placed "bunk-bed" subject extended upward like an architectural construct, rising eight stories or mattresses high. Each mattress has a carefully placed pillow at the head, each shaped a little differently in appearance from its neighbors. Only one featureless, anonymous person appears recumbent on the lowermost bed, alluding, perhaps, to states of exile or loneliness—two of Delgado's thematic interests, as noted earlier. We are prompted to ask what this lone *pinto's* circumstances are and what this individual represents. We are reminded of Peña's own interest in the subject of a prison bed and the memories it stirred. But unlike the congested spatial field depicted in Peña's cloth, Delgado's own *paño* seems to "breathe" with space to spare. The other *paño* I am singling out dates from 2007 and is rendered in mixed media. It revolves around another supine figure, devoid of facial features and with outspread arms, almost in the form of a crucifixion or an allusion to Leonardo da Vinci's iconic *Vitruvian Man*. Delgado has superimposed that figure at the intersection of Concertina wire-topped prison fences. This depiction would seem to capture the artist's notion of liberty denied. A bed sheet drawing from the series *Desde lo horizontal* (From the Horizontal; 2000/2002), done in color pencil with cold cream and soap and measuring 200 x 150 centimeters, also contains coiled Concertina wire surmounting the whole drawing. Below, at the foot of the composition, five human torsos, each with slightly different generalized features, look up, mindful that their liberty is jeopardized.

Ángel Delgado's sculptural compositions complement the textile pieces in their shared prison content. *Sentido impuesto* (Heartfelt Imposition; 2006) is composed

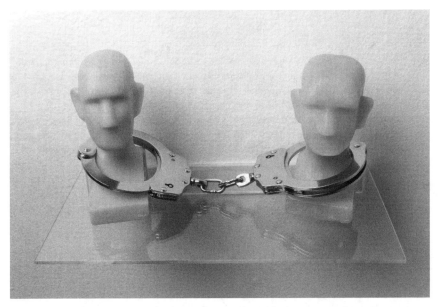

Figure 12.7. Ángel Delgado, *Sentido Impuesto* (2006). Sculpture carved in yellow soap with addition of metal handcuffs, 11 cm. x 20 cm. x 6 cm.

Photo: Nicolas Switalski

of two striking humanoid busts carved of yellow soap and placed on corresponding soap bases attached below their necks.

Joined by metal handcuffs placed necklace-like around their respective sculpted heads, this portrayal of two inmates sharing each other's company may seem like an antidote to loneliness. Yet theirs is an imposed relationship, not a consensual one, as the oxymoronic title would imply. Two more carefully rendered soap sculpture constructions—each a constituent part of a larger composite piece entitled *Memorias acumuladas* (Accumulated Memories; 2004)—are each composed of ten bars of soap encased or shadowboxed in wooden frames. In one composition, the metal links used for joining handcuffs are placed in relief on the recessed surface of the soap bar. Closed padlocks replace the links in the second soap sculpture. The delicacy with which Delgado has executed his pieces belies the context to which they refer and which inspired them. Instead, that delicate touch imbues these works with the feel and appearance of decorative jewelry fashioned with repeated motifs and valued as a memento, consistent with the composite work's overall title.

To foreground the psychological and social desolation of the prison environment and to contrast its sensory deprivation with the palliative effect of Latino visual culture on the inmate population—particularly those engaged in the creative activity documented here—was this essay's basic premise and point of departure. Our journey has introduced us to a number of representative Latino visual artists incarcerated for different reasons, but united in coping with and enduring their captivity by doing artwork inspired and conditioned by their individual and collective circumstances as prisoners.

Notes

1. Letter from Rudy Ornelas to Mamie Torrez (c. 1999, entitled "The Peculiar Woman Under the Bridge"). The letter assumes the form of a confession or *testimonio*, revealing the "miracle of (Ornelas') salvation through Mamie's Ministry." Ornelas' embrace of "misery" (as his) closest friend recalls a line from Lord Byron's narrative poem, "The Prisoner of Chillon" (1816): "My very chains and I grew friends."

2. The prison context is likened to a Siberian prison camp where Fyodor Dostoyevsky spent four years in exile following his conviction for involvement in the Petrashevsky circle. He wrote about his experiences in the novel *The House of the Dead*, published in 1862. Escobar acknowledges his debt to Dostoyevsky (41). The invocation of death also brings to mind the landmark photographic project undertaken by Danny Lyon in the Texas Prison System, *Conversations with the Dead* (1971).

3. According to Torrez, Ornelas died of a drug overdose on May 8, 2006, at the age of forty-five (Mamie R. Torrez, telephone conversations with author, April 17, May 27, and May 30, 2008).

4. Against the socioeconomic and ethnographic backdrop provided by H. Bruce Franklin in his discussion of literary production in prison, the deliberate use of cotton cloth may have more to do with subversive *ends* than readily available *means* for communication.

5. The essence of a "mind trip" is so evocatively conveyed in his canonic poem, "un trip through the mind jail" (1969) by the late raúlrsalinas, Chicano ex-*pinto*, poet, and revolutionary (cf. Sorell 2006).

6. Available at http://en.wikipedia.org/wiki/Golgotha (accessed May 9, 2008).

7. In a telephone conversation of May 9, 2008, Leonard Peña informed me that the book is meant to be the Bible.

8. Leonard Peña, telephone conversation with author, May 9, 2008.

9. "Tracts can effectively spread the gospel to those who are in need of hearing it." Available at http://www.padfield.com/1997/tracts.html (accessed May 12, 2008).

10. Leonard Peña, telephone conversation with author, May 9, 2008.

11. Ibid.

12. A court jester can be likened to a laughing clown. The "intersection of *la vida loca* (the crazy life of the urban streets associated with gang members) and *la pinta* is paved with lamentation, sad memories and regret, arguably best expressed through the masks of comedy and tragedy or laughing and weeping clowns so often delineated on human skin and cloth surfaces inside prison. Such representations echo the New Testament's Gospel according to Luke admonishing the faithful: 'Woe to you who are laughing now for you will mourn and weep' (Luke 6:25)" (Sorell 2006, 7).

13. Spiders and other insects are a recurring motif in Dostoyevsky's *Crime and Punishment*. Refer to Sorell (2006, n.41, 32). A spider can even become an inmate's pet (Cardinal 1997, xx).

14. Leonard Peña, telephone conversation with the author, June 19, 2008.

15. Prinzhorn acknowledges that prison inmates use their own blood as a coloring agent (Cardinal 1997, xviii and xxi). This literally sanguine detail takes a sanguinary turn of its own in the context of the relatively brief history of prison visual art. The Napoleonic Wars are apparently the source for the earliest surviving specimens of prison art in modern times. Small objects carved from meat bones included game paraphernalia like cribbage boards and domino boxes, miniature sailing ships, and mechanical toys. A topical subject among prisoners-of-war then was the rather lurid and macabre public execution artistically represented by bone figures arranged about a guillotine with a functional blade!

16. "The Plan of Delano" (Texas), issued on September 16, 1965, was a proclamation of the United Farm Workers (UFW) and César Chávez, president of the union for the grape strike. The UFW was not exclusively Mexican but rather a national association of all farm workers: "the Negroes and poor whites, the Puerto Ricans, Japanese, and Arabians" (Quirarte 1984, 10).

17. Tiger-like, Don Pedro Albizu Campos delivered a fiercely nationalistic and incendiary speech, "Everybody is quiet but the Nationalist party," before the Lares, Puerto Rico, Municipal Council on September 23, 1950. His carefully crafted argument commemorating the Rising of Lares betrays his legal training. Mindful of his own incarcerations, Albizu Campos acknowledges the surplus jails in Lares as compared to the dearth of bread to feed the hungry (Babín and Steiner 1974, 258).

18. Drawn from O. L. Rivera's letter of March 19, 2008 (1–2), from the medium security prison in which he's presently housed, in Terre Haute, Indiana. His letter came in response to my letter of February 29, 2008, in which I posed nine questions concerning his artwork and artistic motivations behind bars and his interactions with Chicano and Cuban prisoners.

19. *Ibid.*, 3–4.

20. Elizam admits that "in those first college years, (he) was already involved in the independence movement and the student movement on campus" (Escobar 1994a, 37).

21. During these years, Elizam became a member of the Progressive Labor Party (PLP), then a fraternal organization of the Puerto Rican Socialist League. Working for the party's newspaper, he developed ideas for caricatures to illustrate the paper's editorials. He also worked with PLP-front organizations, including guerrilla theater groups (Escobar, 39). His conflicted view that art and politics were different spheres of activity—one "idealistic and useless," the other "practical and realistic" (Escobar, 37)—was being tested. He struggled with the notion of "art-as-instrument-for-something-else" (39).

22. "Another way of thinking, of philosophizing, of creating sense and understanding informing conceptual things as well as emotional and sensual ones, and not as a mere hobby to which the jailers want to reduce it")English translation by author).

23. "The prevailing notion is that prison is an ideal place to write and paint. The very opposite is true. In prison, as I have lived and experienced it, privacy and concentration are difficult to find. As a result, I have had to slowly develop, little by little, a new way of undertaking the process of painting to be able to overcome all kinds of obstacles. Necessity has made this possible. For me, art is an act of liberation, especially when one is surrounded by the obscenity that prison represents. Art functions as salvation, the sacred activity of liberty" (English translation by author).

24. Unless specified otherwise, all citations in the following section are from Félix 2006.

25. Drawn from C. Alberto Torres's letter of March 10, 2008, page 4, written to me from the Federal Correctional Institution (FCI) in Oxford, Wisconsin. His letter was written one day before he would be relocated to the FCI in Pekin, Illinois. His letter was in response to my letter of February 29, 2008. Also, refer to Note 18.

26. "Although the vejigantes originate and are associated with religious celebrations, I don't interpret the subject as a religious figure. More precisely, it is a traditional cultural expression" (letter of March 10; English translation by author).

27. "Reaching beyond the prison in which I'm detained" (English translation by author).

28. The series of decrees (*cedulas*) compiled and published by royal authority since about 1512 culminated in what became known as the *Recopilación de las leyes de los reinos de Indias* (1680–81; Compendium of the laws of the kingdom of the Indies). The *Recopilación* contains 6,377 laws in nine books of uneven length, subdivided into 218 chapters (*títulos*).

29. As the word implies, this reference subsumes both a C(X)icano and Indian identity. Xicanindio Artes, Inc., a contemporary multidisciplinary arts organization in Mesa,

Arizona, presents performances that are reflective of the Latino/Chicano and Indian experiences.

30. Italics for emphasis are added.

31. Peltier suggests that speaking his Indian language was "my [his] first crime" (Peltier 1999, 84).

32. The poem is rendered in italicized form in Peltier's book. The poem's spirit of egalitarianism calls to mind "A Blogspot: Friends of Leonard Peltier" (http://freepeltiernow.blogspot.com/2008/05/fundraising-event-for-puerto-rican.html; and http://freepeltiernow.blogspot.com/2008/11/play-and-salsa-party-for-puerto-ric (accessed 2009/01) that links efforts to secure Peltier's freedom with freedom efforts on behalf of Puerto Rican political prisoners.

33. He adopted fellow writer eecumming's orthographic style, often free of uppercase letters and traditional punctuation.

34. Refer to edited version of article by Alejo Sierra at http://www.raulrsalinas.com/.

35. Recall a similar "visual accusation" in Oscar López Rivera's painting, *Katrina's Dome*.

36. Carlos Cumpián, e-mail communication to author, June 24, 2008. Subsequent information about Camilo and his work is also drawn from the same e-mail.

37. "Fresco" also references freedom by virtue of the shared first three letters in its orthography and the spelling of the word "freedom."

38. "What stimulates you to engage in your art inside prison?"

39. Havana-based art critic, curator, poet, and historian Orlando Hernández describes the performance piece, the outrage it triggered, and the consequences for the artist as follows: "He (Ángel) had defecated on a newspaper during the exhibition *El objeto esculturado* (*The Sculpted Object*, Centro de Desarrollo de las Artes Visuales [Center for the Development of Visual Arts], Havana, 1990). His act was intended to be merely provocative, even artistic (excrement seen as the human sculpture), but the Ministry of Culture and the police saw it differently. They stressed the importance of the newspaper—an issue of *Granma*, the official organ of the Cuban Communist Party—and Ángel was declared guilty of "public scandal," sentenced to six months in jail and incarcerated like a common criminal under the number 1242900" (Hernández 2001, 25).

40. Ángel Delgado, e-mail communication to author, March 10, 2008. Translation: "Since my stay in prison in 1990 (during six months) for having staged a performance piece, my art revolves around one point, an individual's liberty or lack of it. I am moved by the lack of communication between human beings, [a state of] exile, loneliness, abandonment, restrictions; but above all, captivity in any of its physical or sociological variants. I'm always trying to [have] the spectator reflect on the theme" (English translation by author).

41. Ángel Delgado, e-mail communication to author, March 10, 2008: "*No pertenezco a ninguna religión*" ("I am without religious affiliation"; English translation by author).

42. Ángel Delgado, e-mail communication to author, March 10, 2008. Translation: "To know how to paint, draw and sculpt was the greatest benefit I had while in prison. With this skill I was able to survive drawing with colored pencil and cold cream on handkerchiefs and carving soap bars. These objects were exchangeable for cigars, bed sheets, towels, among other (things), and most immediately for food with which I could fend off the hunger one experiences in (prison) cells. But, above all (else), (the art) helped me to be more human and to communicate with others, outside of prison" (English translation by author).

43. For an extended discussion of a prison underground or black-market economy, refer to Pollock (2006), 97, 105, 107, 111–12, 117.

References

Babín, María Teresa, and Stan Steiner, eds. 1974. *Borinquen: An anthology of Puerto Rican literature*. New York: Alfred A. Knopf.

Barnett, Alan W. 1984. *Community murals: The people's art*. Philadelphia: Art Alliance.

Beisswenger, Don. 2008. *Locked up: Letters and papers of a prisoner of conscience*. Nashville: Upper Room Books.

Bennett, Scott H. 2001. Workers/draftees of the world unite! Carlos A. Cortéz Redcloud Koyokuikatl: Soapbox rebel, WWII CO, & IWW Artist/Bard." In *Carlos Cortéz Koyokui-katl: Soapbox artist & poet*, ed. Víctor Alejandro Sorell, 12–56. Chicago: Mexican Fine Arts Center/Museum (now The National Museum of Mexican Art).

Blawis, Patricia Bell. 1971. *Tijerina and the land grants: Mexican Americans in struggle for their heritage*. New York: International.

Borofsky, Jonathan. 1990. Prisoner: James Pettaway. In *Discourses: Conversations in post-modern art and culture*, ed. Russell Ferguson et al., 172–80. New York: Museum of Contemporary Art; Cambridge, MA: MIT Press.

Burnham, Linda F., and Steven Durland, eds. 1998. *The citizen artist: 20 years of art in the public arena (An anthology from High Performance magazine 1978–1998)*. Gardiner, New York: Critical Press.

Cardinal, Roger. 1997. Foreword: A brief history of prison art. In *Cellblock visions: Prison art in America*, Phyllis Kornfeld, xiii–xxi. Princeton, NJ: Princeton University Press.

Carnochan, W. B. 1995. The literature of confinement. In *The Oxford history of the prison: The practice of punishment in western society*, ed. Norval Morris and David J. Rothman, 426–55. New York: Oxford University Press.

De la Garza, Rudolph O., Z. Anthony Kruszewski, and Tomás A. Arciniega. 1973. *Chicanos and Native Americans: The territorial minorities*. Englewood Cliffs, NJ: Prentice-Hall.

Dostoyevsky, Fyodor. 1862/1933. *The house of the dead*. New York: E. P. Dutton.

Escobar, Elizam. 2006. Power/art/prison. In *Not enough space: 25 years behind prison bars*, ed. Jorge Félix et al., 20. Chicago, IL: National Boricua Human Rights Net-Work, in partnership with the Cable Access Network TV of Chicago.

———. 1994. The heuristic power of art. In *The subversive imagination: Artists, society, and social responsibility*, ed. Carol Becker, 35–54. New York: Routledge.

Escobar, Elizam Margarita Fernández Zavala; Iván Silén; and Bertha Husband, contributors. 1994. *Elizam Escobar: Transfixiones*. 10-13. Exhibition catalog (April 9-May 15). San Juan, Puerto Rico: Instituto de Cultura Puertorriqueña (Arsenal de la Marina en la Puntilla).

Félix, Jorge, et al. 2006. *Not enough space: 25 Years behind prison bars*. Chicago: National Boricua Human Rights Network, in partnership with the Cable Access Network TV of Chicago.

Franklin, H. Bruce. 2000. From plantation to penitentiary to the prison-industrial complex: Literature of the American prison. Paper delivered at the Modern Language Association Convention, Washington, D.C. December. Available at http://andromeda.rutgers.edu/~hbf/MLABLACK.htm (accessed April 13, 2008).

Gardner, Richard. 1970. *¡Grito! Reies Tijerina and the New Mexico land grant war of 1967*. New York: Bobbs-Merrill.

Gonzales, Rodolfo "Corky". 2001. [1975]. Message to Aztlán. In *Message to Aztlán*: Selected writings of Rodolfo "Corky" Gonzales. Compiled, with an Introduction by Antonio Esquibel, a Preface by R. C. Gonzales, a Foreword by Rodolfo F. Acuña, and an Editor's Note by Henry A. J. Ramos, 76–81. Houston: Arte Público.

Griswold del Castillo, Richard, et al., eds. 1990. *Chicano art: Resistance and affirmation (An interpretive exhibition of the Chicano Art movement, 1965–1985)*. Los Angeles: The Wight Art Gallery, University of California, Los Angeles.

Hernández, Orlando. 2001. The pleasure of reference. In *Art Cuba: The new generation*, ed. Holly Block, 24–29. New York: Harry N. Abrams.

Lyon, Danny. 1971. *Conversations with the dead*. New York: Holt, Rinehart, and Winston.

Peltier, Leonard. 1999. *Prison writings: My life is my sun dance*. New York: St. Martin's.

Pollock, Joycelyn M., ed. 2006. 2nd ed. *Prisons: Today and tomorrow*. Sudbury, MA: Jones and Bartlett.

Quirarte, Jacinto, ed. 1984. *Chicano art history: A book of selected readings*. San Antonio: Research Center for the Arts and Humanities, University of Texas at San Antonio.

Ramírez, Yasmín. 2007. The activist legacy of Puerto Rican artists in New York and "The art heritage of Puerto Rico." In *ICAA documents project working papers: The publication series for "Documents of 20th-Century Latin American and Latino art,"* ed. María C. Gaztambide, 46–53. Houston: International Center for the Arts of the Americas, Museum of Fine Arts.

Salinas, Raúl R. 1999/1969. *Un trip through the mind jail y otras excursions: Poems*. Houston: Arte Público.

Sorell, Víctor A. 1976. *Barrio* murals in Chicago: Painting the Hispanic-American experience on "our community" walls. *Revista Chicano-Riqueña* 4, no. 4 (Fall): 50–72.

———. 2002. Guadalupe's emblematic presence endures in New Mexico: Investing the body with the virgin's miraculous image. In *Nuevomexicano cultural legacy: Forms, agencies and discourse*, ed. Francisco Lomelí et al., 203–45. Albuquerque: University of New Mexico Press.

———. 2004. Pinto arte. In *Encyclopedia of Latino popular culture*, ed. Cordelia Chávez Candelaria et al., vol. 2 (M-Z), 630–33. Westport, CT: Greenwood.

———. 2006. Illuminated handkerchiefs, tattooed bodies, and prison scribes: Meditations on the aesthetic, religious, and social sensibilities of Chicano pintos. In *Mediating Chicana/o culture: Multicultural American vernacular*, ed. Scott L. Baugh, 2–40. Newcastle, UK: Cambridge Scholars Press.

Sorell, Víctor A., ed. 1979. *Guide to Chicago murals: Yesterday and today*. Chicago, IL: Chicago Council on Fine Arts.

Zavala, Margarita Fernández. 1994. Transfixiones. In *Elizam Escobar: Transfixiones*, contributors. E. Escobar, Margarita Fernández Zavala, Iván Silén, and Bertha Husband, 2–7. San Juan, Puerto Rico: Instituto de Cultura Puertorriqueña (Arsenal de la Marina en la Puntilla).

13

"Troubadour of Justice"

An Interview With raúlrsalinas

Alan Eladio Gómez

Poet, professor, and human rights activist raúlrsalinas is the author of two recent books *My Word is My Weapon Raúlsalinas and the Jail Machine: Selected Writing by Raúl Salinas* (2006), edited by Louis G. Mendoza, and *Indio Trails: A Xicano Odyssey through Indian Country* (2007). In *My Word is My Weapon*, the writings of Salinas, organized by Louis Mendoza, locate the emerging voice of a poet and revolutionary speaking with-and-for struggles from behind the walls. As Mendoza notes, "Though Salinas is renowned in certain literary and political circles, he is *not so exceptional* [my emphasis] a figure that he is known by all. Rather, what we have here is a portrait of someone who is exceptional in his ability to be representative of a good portion of the more than two million people currently caught up in the criminal justice machinery of this nation" (2006, 4)

Exceptional and representative: in these journalistic writings, poetry, and editorials, and in correspondence between Salinas and representatives of the Chicano, Puerto Rican, black, and American Indian social movements of the time, Salinas consistently shares with us the stories of struggle that he was involved in without necessarily focusing on his own role.

Indio Trails: A Xicano Odyssey through Indian Country is a long overdue chapbook or chronicle that includes poems written between 1974 and 1999. As Salinas writes in the preface, "Now it is done—the circle is complete; and so is this collection of writings, both of which were so difficult and painful to finalize." As in previous publications, in these poems, the journey and the writing overlap in Salinas's immediate post-prison experiences in the Pacific Northwest, where Salinas went, in self-imposed exile, "to try out my wings so-to-speak, my political wings; or to see if I was real, to see if it had worked, to see if I wasn't jivin'. They were tests on to myself." These medicine poems narrate his experience during the 1970s: the struggles of the American Indian movement, the Centro de la Raza community center in Seattle, prison organizing and political prisoners, solidarity with Central

American revolutionary movements, and the Leonard Peltier Defense Committee. They also give voice to the intimate relationship between individual and collective transformation and struggle.

Born in San Antonio in 1934, Salinas grew up on the East Side of Austin. From 1957 to 1972, he spent approximately twelve years in four of the nation's most brutal prisons—Soledad State Prison (California), Huntsville State Prison (Texas), Leavenworth Federal Penitentiary (Kansas), and Marion Federal Penitentiary (Illinois). Inspired by the writings and actions of revolutionary theorist George Jackson, the Puerto Rican *Independentista* fighters, and radical Chicanos with whom he organized inside the walls, the prison years marked Salinas's remarkable transformation from individual alienation to political resistance, reflecting the social movements of the 1960s and 1970s, circulating across the globe. Since the 1980s, and after five years of teaching at St. Edward's University in Austin, Salinas has run a bookstore, Resistencia Books, a small press, Red Salmon, in Austin, and has lectured and taught at universities throughout the country.

As poet Joy Harjo has written, raúlsalinas is "a troubadour of justice" who "makes his way through our generation's history with his songs of truth. Some songs are elegies, some love songs, some are howling at the moon, some pure witness."

The following interview was conducted on June 21, 2006, in Austin, Texas.

AG: In a letter to Michael Deutsch, human rights lawyer with the People's Law Office, you explained that the "prison was a backyard for of colonialism." Raúl, can you talk about "backyard colonialism" and the prison rebellion years and how political education was related to engaging with movements outside of the walls, emerging from experiences you had with other inmates inside the walls?

RS: Well, the prison rebellion years . . . Though its not an original term, I am not sure who else used it during that period, other than the people who were in Leavenworth federal penitentiary and, later, those of us that went to the Control Unit in Marion [federal penitentiary]. Maybe five years earlier, the end of the sixties, were some very exciting times socially and politically, everything just exploded, and those were some incredible times that many professors and college people don't like to deal with. In like manner, the prison rebellion years were very exciting times. Even though they were very physically brutal and mentally devastating, they were some very critical highlight moments in history, I would think, in social movements. Because we weren't just challenging the state in an irrational, inane way, but we were very clearly outlining our arena of struggle and what we had to deal with. The fact that people were becoming educated, helping each other to go into higher learning, to read books critically, to become writers and painters and prison barristers or, more commonly known, jail-house lawyers. So, those times were very exciting, very frightening, because there was a transformation taking place. And this was happening throughout the country, no doubt about that. But we were focused on our arena of struggle, which happened to be the federal joint at the time—Leavenworth federal penitentiary, and later, Marion. It was a time of organizing and turning each other on to new materials that we never had the opportunity to hold in our hands, much less read; new languages that we were learning, new concepts, new paradigms, that began to make it clear to us that it was part of a colonial mindset. This is the captives, this is the renegades, these are the ones who will not conform to the reservation or the plantation, and we must deal with them.

So, how did the state deal with us, the feds in this case, but the state overall? The way the state deals with any captive, military or otherwise. It's about brutal, physical assaults to mental pressures, that go into the clinical, which go into the mind-altering drugs, which go into the attempts to deprive one of one's senses and shake-up one's sense of equilibrium, and confusion setting in. These were all tactics that were brought in very calculated by the administration at Marion, which became some of the first models, under the director, Dr. Martin Groder, there at Marion.[1] They tried to domesticate us, to pacify us, to control us, to render us helpless, powerless, but they didn't succeed. And so, those were very rewarding stories that we have to guide us today, that we can share still with the young people, about what the hell struggle is about, what the hell transformation is about. I mean as painful . . . you know, you cry, you hurt, you question, you are confused, you move on, you consult, you sit in communion with your comrades.

AG: You talk about a "we" and an "us." The University of Texas Press has just published a book, edited by Louis Mendoza, Chair of Chicano Studies at the University of Minnesota. It compiles your writings and letters and articles written during these times, the prison rebellion years, that are both giving us the stories that you are talking about but also demonstrating the links that you had with movements outside of the walls. Who is the "we" and "us"?

RS: The "we" and "us" were those individuals that I happened to be part of in those prisons. And because we began to look at this society, and the individualistic nature of this society, and how it's a dog-eat-dog, every man for himself, we saw other people in other lands, in other countries, utilizing other forms, and they seemed to be more humane—even though they were vilified before our eyes in the media. These societies seemed to be more connected to the human spirit, more about sharing, more about including the entire community.

The first thing we learned was there is no such thing as being self-taught. I would be so grossly negligent—aside from being a damned liar—if I fall into the trap and agree when people say I am self-educated. I am not self-educated. I was educated by some brilliant, brilliant minds and they all gave me something of themselves, as I am sure I gave them. So once we challenged the state our numbers were reduced even more, and that was the true test of who the "we" and the "us" was: the people who chose to stand and not allow anyone, including the state which held us captive, to trample on our dignity. And that's who "us" and "we" was, the people that refused to be broken. And so leaving the cage and coming into the larger cage, which the United States is—a prison in and of itself, and people find that odd and strange until you break it down for them. It was only natural that I, and the others like me who survived, begin to seek out like-minded people on the streets as well.

AG: So from Leavenworth and the organizing with the Puerto Rican *Independentistas*, with other Chicanos, blacks, and American Indians, to Marion, where you were a plaintiff in the lawsuit, *Adams v. Carlson*,[2] that challenged the arbitrary long-term punishment of isolation, sensory deprivation, and behavior modification, and then you were released. When you talk about "seeking out like minded people on the streets," what did you take with you from these experiences, when you were looking for comrades on the streets who were involved in similar struggles?

RS: Oh my god. What did I take with me? I felt that I was prepared to live as a totally different man than I had lived when I first went in; that I could contribute to humanity, as opposed to just society, and become some straight, blue-ribbon committee person on the governor's task force or something. It was a matter of coming out and testing what had been learned. So I brought with me a wealth of information and knowledge, some loyalties, some undying friendships that are alive and well to this day, those of us who survived.

These individuals who were out, who made it out, were all involved in some struggle, in their country, in their community. And so I felt I was armed with knowledge and truth, and I was armed with my dignity intact. I came out feeling like I had been washed and cleansed and prepared to be the most productive person that I could be, and that I didn't need to be the godfather or the kingpin or street-corner hustler, ripping people off; I didn't need to do any of that—not that I ever did it before. My reasons for being in prison were slightly different than being a mobster-gangster-terrorizer. And so I was a new person. That's what I brought with me. I was a new person because the "we" and the "us" had given me that new person, as I had helped give them their new personas. So it was a hell of a feeling, and it was a hell of an armor to carry, you know. Strap that one on your back.

AG: You talk about survival and those that got out. *My Weapon is My Pen* ends with a final dedication and declaration: "In honor of those who did not survive the 'prison rebellion' years, and in solidarity with those prison fighters who continue to struggle, I commit the remainder of my life to exposing the inhumanity of the jail machine. La lutta continua." As a survivor yourself, when you are released from Marion, where do you go?

How was that another part of this process of transformation?

RS: Well, I literally went into exile. And I say that in the most nonrhetorical manner because people have problems with the term exile, or they think exile means being cast off in an island by yourself somewhere. The true sense of *exiliado* is also *desterrado*, to displace you, to remove you from your homeland. And since I could not return to Texas because the Rangers were waiting for me—the Texas Rangers, not the baseball team—and California had a life-top on me just for doing what Willie [Nelson] does everyday and gets praise in the press for it, I go to Seattle. Because through my writings, through my poetry primarily, *Trip through the mind jail* very specifically—which is a classic poem, not because I wrote it but because the people have made it so—I had established some correspondence with graduate students and professors at the University of Washington, and they were doing prison work at McNeil Island federal penitentiary. So it was a natural connection, and they begin to correspond with me and they asked me what they could do for me . . . so they helped me obtain my release: the late Dr. Joseph Sommers, along with—now retired from the Rockefeller Foundation—Tomás Ybarra-Frausto and historian Antonia Castañeda, they were very instrumental in getting me to Seattle and enrolled at the University of Washington—a city and state that I had never been to, a university the likes of which I had never set foot in. This was my first taste of university life, although I was taking college courses in prison. But as a result of being in the northwest and ready to try out my wings, so to speak, my political wings; or to see if I was real, to see if it had worked, to see if I wasn't jivin'. They were tests on to myself.

I immediately immersed myself with the prison movement, going into McNeil Island, to Shelton Reformatory in Walla Walla state prison. It was only natural, I guess. My god, I was beginning to understand internationalism and colonialism based on some of the readings I had done, but to look at colonialism and to begin to see how it operated outside and the control over the institutions just made it the perfect arena of struggle for that time. As we always said, "Your arena of struggle is where ever you happen to be at, at that time, that's your arena of struggle," and this was it.

And I began an association with *El Centro de la Raza*, a civil rights, human rights, social service agency that was very much at the forefront of the struggle in the northwest for Chicanos, Latinos, migrants, students, and they occupied an abandoned schoolhouse. And I was taken there by Dr. Sommers to meet the people, and I immediately fell in love with all of them. Men, women, and children who were like, to me, they were in an occupied zone. All the readings I had done, and all of a sudden, here's a village, its occupied, people are guarding it, there is security. All of a sudden it was right there. And of course the people there were very much involved in supporting the [American Indian] fishing rights struggles and the Asian struggles in the Northwest, which had to do with organizing unions around the salmon fisheries [Alaska Cannery Workers]. So we began to involve ourselves with anti-Marcos [Ferdinand] work—Filipino youth, the KDP (*Katipunan ng Mga Demokratikong*), some of the same people who later went back east and merged with the I Wor Kuen.[3] And that brought us in contact with these folks who were engaging Marcos directly. So there we were.

And then there was a youth festival in the Soviet Union, and we sent two delegates. And so we prepared them: political education classes—we began the political studies classes; and all the while, looking at our very specific situation and what our readings and our visits to these other lands told us about what we were doing, or perhaps what we must do. And from there it led us to Cuba. We sent four brigades between '75 and '80. And then, in Chile 1973, the popularly elected government of Salvador Allende was toppled by 800 mil [thousand dollars] by some benefactors in the U.S., and we opposed that. We took on the ITT stockholders meeting in Seattle and disrupted it.

Then, all the while continuing our local work, we moved into solidarity with another union, which is a union of African Americans, very progressive. It was an African American union, which later became a minority union: United Construction Workers. And again, some of those people went with us to Cuba. Then, as a result of the fishing rights struggles, I became acquainted with the American Indian Movement. And that what I have devoted my time to up until returning to Austin, where my work is now mostly youth-oriented, arts work, immigration, environmental.

AG: Your stories about Seattle being a place that brought together different U.S. third world peoples—Chicanos, Asians, blacks, American Indians, and people from the Southwest—for gathering and summits, that is Seattle, as part of this larger network of anticolonial third world struggle in the United States. In 1999, Seattle was again on the world stage with the mobilizations against the IMF, bringing up many of these same issues you are talking about: the analysis based on local conditions, anticapitalist, the inspiration of movements abroad—across the land borders, or across the oceans, or the street. How are these movements related?

RS: First of all, the reason why they are related is that they are under threat by the same system. And whether it's called colonialism or neoliberalism or globalization, globalizing of the economy, it's still the same machine at work, gobbling up humanity. Whether it be in Seattle, or East Austin, or south of the border, south of the river, we're up against the same opposition, and I think all we can do is learn from how they treat us all the same. And "they" meaning the state, the university, the prison system, the military; and people can quibble and talk about "yes-and-no," "but," "aren't you being harsh": people have to also not be afraid to speak what they think rather than what they think others want them to say. There is viciousness upon the citizenry of this land, from that same corporate greed for profit through forced labor. Seems pretty clear to me that some grandma fishing on the river for subsistence is no different than an immigrant taking all kinds of risks to come to make a living for their family. I don't see any difference—they are all linked. We have a common struggle and, at the risk of sounding rhetorical, a common enemy. I'm sorry, there are some evil forces at work out there, and they are not outside of the country.

AG: In the news in the past years, since the wars began against Afghanistan and Iraq, we have heard about torture, murder, rape, and the punishment of war . . . the profit machine and the war of U.S. empire. The prison walls were never borders, but in the political organizing you were part of, you changed those walls into something else. Today, we're in the fourteenth day of the aggression against Lebanon, one that reminds us of the cycles of empire. Given your experience with alliances and solidarity, how do we as people of color in the U.S. understand what is happening?

RS: Again, it is no less difficult a struggle to organize our own communities than it is to go out and just organize. It's very difficult because there is a fear factor at play. A lot of Chicanos and Latinos, out of fear, and denial of that fear, would be cynical, or funny, or not take a position. So we have a lot of work to do to talk to our *gente*—even though we're still dying in such patriotic numbers that the government doesn't care. And it seems like a lot of our *gente* (people) doesn't care to see another youngster coming back in the valley, where, per capita, they are killing more, or in some Appalachian valley community of poor whites. It's not easy to convey to people what is at stake for us, but what is at stake is not going to get any better.

I heard these two guys on NPR today—"One Real Country," "One Right Country," or something—and they're talking about the present administration and how they operate. And he told how there was a press gathering, and he told Bush, "If you want another 9/11, just keep at it the way you are going." And we must not be surprised ever again if we continue to be as arrogant as some of our leaders are in our names, if we allow them to be as arrogant as they are. What we've got to convey to our people is that its not about Jewish people, its about Zionism; its about war machines that are destroying people with no weapons. And homemade rockets are no weapons compared to F-16, or tanks, or bulldozers that destroy your homeland forever. So yeah, we don't want to take sides.

And lets talk about humanity, because that is who is dying, humanity. And I think that for our people, that is where I go. It's about humanity. We start talking about who you are supporting, and who I am supporting, and we are going to get into a fight, an argument, a shouting match, and that is the mood of the country because someone said, "You are either with us or you are with the terrorists." Well, I'm not with the terrorists, nor am I with whoever said it. I'm sorry. Those things need to be said, and they are being said by white folks, they are being said on comedy shows, why can't we say them?

AG: Because we have Condoleezza Rice, Alberto Gonzalez, and, previously, Colin Powell, perhaps the most multicultural imperial formation yet. What have been the effects of this professionalization, or the way that struggles in the 1980s particularly—the decade of the Hispanic—became commodified and emptied of the systemic critique?

RS: We have found now, through history, that that was very calculated. It was a calculated move through the Heritage Foundation at the time of the census. And here is this hype to clean up those rowdy renegades, once again to round up the renegades. Let's bring some of them to the house, into the "second story" [laughter], and we've got it made. So that one is hard to deal with: we've got to convey to our *gente* that we are pawns, we are suckers. One of the most embarrassing moments to me is to see all those beautiful Latina and Latino entertainers who wanted to just be such nice Americans and show their patriotism by singing the national anthem in Spanish, and I was so embarrassed that they were rejected by the power structure of this country. They were vilified for daring to sing the national anthem in Spanish. Two weeks later, I think, Bush was singing "La Cucaracha," or something on Cinco de Mayo, or for the National Council de La Raza.

AG: So you come back to Austin in the early '80s and we are now in 2006. What has changed; what hasn't?

RS: What stayed the same is that people are still going to jail from the east side. In Austin, very few Chicanos are recruited to the University of Texas—it's a building we look at from across the great divide. So, that hasn't changed. The homeland has been bombarded, but there are still pockets of resistance: new languages, new issues, related still to land; more environmental issues being articulated by the Latino community. What has changed is the onslaught of gentrification invading the West Bank—our West Bank; condos galore; affordable housing for anybody, except for the natives that lived there for over sixty years. So those are some of the changes.

AG: Some people would say that's progress. That's what development is supposed to bring.

RS: Well, yeah, of course—those clean Hispanics that probably got a cut out of that land deal. Of course it's good for them. Have them talk to Señora Cásares on 5th Street about the railroad tracks where the villas are at now. Have them talk to the Limón clan about what happened to 5th Street. Yeah, they moved away, yeah, there was upward mobility, yeah, they were hard workers, but a lot of it had to do with not being able to keep the compound where grandma and grandpa, and mom and dad, and all the kids were born. That's very important. So, a lot of those things were gone, but as always, there was struggle.

New issues: immigration, the war in Mexico—the new war in Mexico—and the need to respond to it. Why? Because they are our people. Why? Because they are humans caught in the trap. Why? Because we understood the forces behind all of that, which was empire junior, son of empire—or son of vampire, more like it. Don't print that. No, print what ever. There was a new movement, so to speak. New faces, new language, new concepts to learn. And so I wanted to learn, and so I aligned myself with people who knew—young people, and that being a struggle in and of itself, because I wanted to work with young people, young people wanted to work with me. But we have that big generational divide that both sides perpetuate. A lot of old fogies think youngsters have nothing to contribute, and a lot of the youngsters think they were immaculately conceived and nothing was here before them and everything started with them—kind of like The Chronicle [laughter].[4] These new struggles brought us in contact with new people and a chance to visit those lands where those struggles were being waged; to learn more about why we were supporting, concretely, rather than in a vacuum, as so many people have done before, and as we have done before—without much analysis, just sheer for the hell of revolution, for the hell of it. We knew intuitively, we knew intellectually, we certainly knew as fellow strugglers, what it was about. And then, these new concepts that I am still learning, that young people start bringing, and the discussions and debates, and the ideological struggles that were reminiscent of the 1960s—I didn't have that language. And so, I went out to get it and try to learn it. I am still trying to learn it, because its important that I learn the language that the young people are speaking, that the social movements are addressing their issues in, so that I can be a good communicator amongst them, because that is what I want to do.

You mentioned something about my final words in my book. Again, that is not rhetoric. Some people might read it as rhetoric—who do don't know me. Some people might read it as rhetoric because every youngster on the block who grabs a microphone is into revolution, and I respect that, because it has got to start somewhere. But I'm seventy-two years old, I have not been broken by any system, and I reiterate: I commit the remainder of my days to helping expose that machine that almost ground me up, that tried to grind me up, and that has ground so many of our people up, and that continues to grind them in larger numbers each year.

AG: The recent count is more than 2.5 million people incarcerated; and the number of people in the criminal justice system—either on parole, probation, or other arrangements—is steadily reaching 7 million. Thirty-four years after your release from Marion and fighting against the control unit, behavior modification programs, and torture techniques are now a centerpiece for a sadistic foreign policy, making prisons and torture and war the most profitable exports of the U.S. How do you see the current crisis of incarceration for people of color and, most recently, with immigrants?

RS: A whole new set of prisoners: that is the end result. Who is going to prison today? Young black and brown people, with the larger number of women ever on the rise, and poor white people. That's whose going to prison and filling these jails. One important thing about the war and torture—and we are teaching a class at St. Edward's [University], no hate school here, Jones [laughter]—is that, the methods of torture and the whole introduction of torture as another tool of repression, we are finding out everyday more and more, documented and just visual images, are U.S. imports, are imports from U.S. prisons. Not only are the exports, who run those jails like Abu Ghraib or Guantanamo ex-prison guards, but the methods of torture . . . People say, "America will never be the same," "the day that shocked America"; well, with all due respect to human lives, which we shed tears every day, for thirty some-odd years, we have been crying for people who have died on all sides. The torture that they apply there is nothing new to prisoners in the U.S.—especially politicized prisoners or prisoners of war, who do exist in the U.S. prisons. And so Abu Ghraib, Guantánamo, and Bahgram are all products of yankee-doodle penology. And now, when they come back, either they are rewarded with prison jobs or else they are so shell shocked themselves, that the only place they can find—and we have seen the films—the only places they can find to go work out where they feel secure, is the maximum security prisons of California, the SHU's [Special Housing Units]—what replaced the Control Unit at Marion. Standing on that barrel with the hood, brother, you tell people in Huntsville about that one! Ours was a barrel you stood in. In your tiptoes, handcuffed to the bars all the way up to your tiptoes: that's common in Huntsville, which was the most physically brutal prison I was in, Marion being the most mentally repressive. So yeah, this war, the low-intensity war in Mexico, that's how they move on prison activists. It's a low intensity war. They starve you out, they wedge you into a corner, and then you strap yourself. And then they wonder why you strap yourself. So that's what I meant, I guess, to answer your initial question. That's what a backyard form of colonialism means to me, that all of that is brought home, and all of this here is taken over there as exports—I meant in the larger sense, domestic or internal colonization with all these boot-licking lackeys. We have the neocolonial forces; that's who those clean cut spic-and-span folks are.

Notes

1. Cf. Committee to End the Marion Lockdown (1977) and Gómez (1996, 58–86).
2. Eddie ADAMS et al., Plaintiffs-Appellants v. Norman CARLSON, Director of the Federal Bureau of Prisons, et al., Defendants-Appellees, 488 F2d 619, No. 73-1268, United States Court of Appeals, Seventh Circuit. Argued June 14, 1973. Decided Aug. 23, 1973. As Amended Oct. 4, 1973. Rehearing Denied Oct. 31, 1973. Filed by the People's Law Office in Carbondale against Bureau of Prisons director Norman Carlson on September 11, 1972. *Adams v. Carlson* charged prison officials with cruel and unusual punishment; the denial of access to courts; the denial of procedural standards for prisoners placed in solitary confinement and/or administrative segregation; and the denial of

constitutional rights of freedom of religion and freedom of speech in the mails (see Dayan 2007).

3. I Wor Kuen was an anti-imperialist Chinese and Asian American organization that emerged from the New Left in New York City in November 1969. In Cantonese, I Wor Kuen means "Society of the Harmonious Righteous Fist," drawing their name from the Chinese fighters in their struggle to overthrow imperialism and colonialism during the Boxer Rebellion in 1900. Like the Red Guards in San Francisco, the Brown Berets, the American Indian Movement, and the Young Lords Party, I Wor Kuen were inspired by the survival programs of the Black Panther Party, establishing similar projects on the East and West coasts. On I Wor Kuen and other revolutionary Asian organizations, see Ho et al. (2000) and Pulido (2006).

4. Alternative weekly newspaper in Austin, Texas.

References

Committee to End the Marion Lockdown. 1977. Breaking men's minds: Behavior control and human experimentation at the federal prison in Marion. St. Louis, MO: National Committee to Support the Marion Brothers and the Task Force on Behavior Control and Human Experimentation of the National Alliance against Racist and Political Oppression.

Dayan, Colin. 2007. *The Story of Cruel and Unusual*. Cambridge, MA: MIT Press.

Gómez, Alan Eladio. 1996. Resisting Living Death at Marion Federal Penitentiary, 1972. *Radical History Review* 96 (Fall): 58–86.

Ho, Fred, with Carolyn Antonio, Diane Fujino, and Steve Yip. E, eds. 2000. *Legacy to Liberation: Politics and Culture of Revolutionary Asian Pacific America*. San Francisco: AK Press.

Mendoza, Louis G., ed. 2006. *raúlsalinas and the Jail Machine: Selected Writings by Raúl Salinas*. Austin: University of Texas Press.

Pulido, Laura. 2006. *Black, Brown, Yellow and Left: Radical Activism in Los Angeles*. Berkeley: University of California Press.

Salinas, Raúl. 2007. *Indio Trails: A Xicano Odyssey through Indian Country*. San Antonio, TX: Wings Press.

14

Peltier 1 / Peltier 2

raúlrsalinas

Peltier 1

(LIFE SENTENCES
-2 of them-
is what Peltier's got).

Mientras
Past (persistent)
Parranda partners
Siempre unbelieving
Weaving of
Chongo Rojo/ Indigena
As warrior trenzas
wrapped in Red
further complex
futile reunions
Quizas!
not meant to be.

And so We
aqui in Milwaukee snows
show support for
"Stick-Standing Man"
preso politico
standing trial
while
personas encountered en
previous (un)poetic lives
viven oblivious
de lo obvious
burla

poetas don't grace
covers of time
still being done by the BRO.
Sisters carry on the struggle
Turtle woman awakening
from sleep . . . rest
dreamsmiles
before the courts convene
and we must
stand in solidarity
again.

Milwaukee, Wisconsin
Winter 1978

Peltier 2

Peltier
Sun Dance Man
Warrior/Hunting Man
brings singing
buffalo
       (penetrating sting)
to shatter
babylonian madness
sadness in the song
Crow Dog
       White Coyote
brings thundering rains
conjures
whispering waters
of
ana mae r
rememorings
"i'll speak with you through the rain."

The Deer
Stood
Rooted in his ways
Warriors three
before
the court of
monarchy
tribunal would suppress them
dressed in prison grey
while

relatives
brighten dull courtroom
all in "colors"
in the traditional mode
plus jail cell matrimony.

Bobby's spirit left
dangling in the dungeon
Stencils over urban sprawl call.
From the northwest
"Then Fastest Spray can artist"
comes
to test
graffiti gardens
doing dwelling decorations of the slums
Eagle feather come to those who wait . . .
and work . . .

Los Angeles
Lompoc Escape Trial
Fall 1979
From *Indio Trails*

15

"*Estoy como cuero de jicotea, que ni las balas me pasan*"

An Interview with Rafael Cancel Miranda

Gabriel Torres-Rivera

Rafael Cancel Miranda is a Puerto Rican Nationalist who has fought for the independence of Puerto Rico since his early teens. On March 1, 1954, he and three other Nationalists, including one woman, traveled to Washington, D.C., and assaulted the House of Representative to bring attention to the plight of Puerto Rico and its people. They were captured and their sentences ranged between fifty-six and eighty-four years. While in prison, they consistently refused to attend parole hearings, claiming that as Puerto Rican nationals, the U.S. government lacked jurisdiction over them. In September 1979, after an outpouring of international support, President Jimmy Carter released them.

Rafael spent the first six years of his sentence at Alcatraz Island at a time when political consciousness among prisoners had yet to take hold. As a man who had committed his life to fighting political injustice, he soon assumed his role as activist in Alcatraz—and later in Leavenworth and Marion prisons—fighting for the rights of fellow prisoners by organizing work stoppages and conducting strikes.

Although Rafael, "El Jefe," and I did not meet until 1975, he and the nationalist struggle for the Independence of Puerto Rico were familiar to me when I was a child. I would often listen to my parents rail against Don Pedro and the Nacionalistas. I later learned more about the struggle through my membership in the Young Lords Party in Spanish Harlem, New York. During our time at the federal penitentiary in Marion, Illinois, Rafael and I became closer; we were the only two Puerto Rican prisoners. To him I was always—and still am—a brother, friend, comrade and colleague "*uno de la familia.*"

"*Estoy como cuero de jicotea, que ni las balas me pasan*" (I'm as strong as a tortoise shell, even bullets can't get through me) is a saying I learned from other

Puerto Rican prisoners when I was first incarcerated in 1971 and that I later shared with Rafael. We still use it when describing how we feel.

Throughout his life, Rafael has steadfastly fought for the independence of his beloved Puerto Rico—"*Borinquén*." His politics, poetry, and humanitarian efforts have taught me what it means to be a true Boricua, and I continue to learn from him today. The following interview was conducted on Friday, February 22, 2008. Gracias, Jefe.

Gabriel: How are you, chief? I was telling a friend of mine that I call you "chief," not Rafael.

Rafael: Yes, but from you the "chief" thing is an affectionate term.

Gabriel: Thanks for the interview. Could you tell us a little about the time you were in Alcatraz? Because I remember you told me about a visit, when you and your sister Zoraida were told that you couldn't talk in Spanish. So, how did you deal with that? How did you relate to other prisoners? How did they treat you?

Rafael: Well, during that period, the other prisoners were my family, so I didn't have any problems with them. Some couldn't understand me, and I remember one of them once asked me at the table in the dining room, whether I had been paid to go to Washington for what I did . . . and I said, no, I would pay for the honor, because you know, it was difficult to understand in the kind of society we live in, that someone could do something for nothing just out of good will because he loves his people. That's difficult in this system; it's almost surprising, you know? They couldn't understand it at all; you know the reputation Alcatraz has, that's all I need to say.

Gabriel: Yes, sure, talk more about that.

Rafael: I met human beings there. As you know, prisoners are labeled as criminals, or whatever; they're labeled as if all their thoughts, everything they do were criminal. And it's not like that. In Alcatraz, I met very honest people who I would trust with the keys to my house, with my family inside, because I knew that they would defend the honor of that home. I met human beings like that in Alcatraz.

Gabriel: How did you spend your time? What did you do, more or less, during the day? And could you also tell me a little about the visits? Because I imagine that that must have been hard.

Rafael: Well, first of all, they wouldn't allow me to have visits from my children. I already had two children at that time and they wouldn't allow me to see them. Visits occurred through a glass window, and you could only see part of your visitor's face through a glass and it had to be by a phone that was connected to a central station, where they listened to everything, everything you said, and they demanded that you speak in English because they wanted to know what you were talking about. I remember that my sister tried to talk to me in Spanish, and they ran over and said "No, no; English," because they were listening to our conversations. You remember that there was a work stoppage; I joined it because it was also about the visits, because that was inhumane.

Gabriel: There, in Alcatraz?

Rafael: In Alcatraz. There was a strike, and I remember that they kept us locked up for nine days, without a shower, without anything.

Gabriel: All the prisoners that participated?

Rafael: They did a lockout to the entire prison, but lockouts were normal because by five in the afternoon, you were already locked up until the following day. But that time it was the whole day. I remember that they gave us peanut butter sandwiches to eat in the morning, peanut butter in the afternoon, peanut butter at night, for nine days, and a glass of water at night. And since prisoners have to overcome these things, it reminded us of that song, "sugar in the morning, sugar in the evening."

Gabriel: Yeah, I remember . . .

Rafael: But one can always overcome circumstances if you have a good sense of humor and a strong will.

Gabriel: Yes, chief. But at that time, didn't the other prisoners also have political consciousness?

Rafael: No, because George Jackson wasn't there yet and Attica and political consciousness came years later, when the George Jackson episode took place.

Gabriel: Did they take you to Marion after Alcatraz?

Rafael: After Alcatraz, after the six years in Alcatraz, they sent me along with other prisoners, all of us handcuffed and chained to each other, and transferred by train to Leavenworth prison. But before Alcatraz, I was in prison for two years, because I didn't want to kill Koreans.

Gabriel: In Tallahassee?

Rafael: In Tallahassee. I was eighteen years old, and I turned twenty at the Tallahassee prison. I was incarcerated while I was student in Puerto Rico, an active student. They wanted me to join the U.S. army. How could I be part of the army, if they invade my people, kill my people, murder my people, try to humiliate my people? So I refused to be part of the invading army, and I was sentenced by one of their courts, that they call federal, but it was a court of the main United States, it wasn't Puerto Rican; and they sentenced me to two years and one day. I was in solitary confinement for four months and also for nine days because that's where I encountered racism and I had to give a couple *jinguetazos*—a couple of punches to a racist gringo police officer who worked at the prison. They took away my good conduct. They took away the five months of good conduct and left me the full two years and one day; and when I got out, I went back to Puerto Rico and from there I had to go to Cuba.

Gabriel: That's what I was going to ask you. I know you were in Cuba, too.

Rafael: I was in Cuba until Batista also incarcerated me at the Tiscornia detention camp, a kind of prison in Cuba. They put me on an airplane and expelled me from Cuba. That was an honor Batista gave me. A guy like Batista, who doesn't like me, that means there's some good in me.

Gabriel: That's good.

Rafael: However, Fidel hugged me years later when I got out of prison. And even one of Fidel's bunions is worth more than a million Batistas.

Gabriel: Do you remember roughly what year you went to Leavenworth?

Rafael: Yes, they sent me to Leavenworth in 1960.

Gabriel: At the time, was there any sort of movement among the prisoners? How was it? Because I have been told that among Chicano prisoners there was some type of movement.

Rafael: In Leavenworth, when Corky González and the other one, what's his name?

I can't remember . . . Yes, we even organized a newspaper there called *El Aztlan*, which came from the old name for Mexico. We stopped the prison work once, on September 16th, Mexico's independence day. We had an organization, I was with our Chicano brothers, and we participated in various activities, specifically, by the way, in one of the strikes in 1970.

Gabriel: Still there, in Leavenworth?

Rafael: In Leavenworth, in 1970, they abused some prisoners, three prisoners, and we organized a strike that paralyzed the work in the prison. That's when they locked me up in solitary confinement for five months and accused me of organizing the strike, and so they put me in solitary confinement, the *calabozo* in the hole.

Gabriel: In the *calabozo* as Chicanos call it.

Rafael: Yes, about five months eating on the floor, etc., etc. And after five months, they chained me, they tied me up and moved me to Marion Prison as punishment. That was around 1970, about the time you and I met.

Gabriel: So it was with the Chicanos that you first mobilized with other prisoners who were into politics, who had, as they say, political awareness, right?

Rafael: Yes. I did it with other Afro brothers at Marion. That's where I participated in the struggle of the brothers.

Gabriel: Tell me a little bit about that, because I remember that there was a demonstration in Marion, too, right? Where they also locked up other prisoners.

Rafael: Yes, that's where they created the behavior modification program, and they kept me for eighteen months in that program, in which they give you drugs, Thorasine, Prolixin . . . I forgot the other one . . . Valium . . . and other types of drugs.

Gabriel: Tell me more about that, Chief . . . how many people were in the demonstration?

Rafael: The strike happened because some people escaped and one of the people who was able to escape was Jessie López; and when they captured them, they knocked him down and beat him up, they used a *cachiporra* on him. They aren't supposed to do that, and that's why there was a strike.

Gabriel: Explain to us, what is a *cachiporra*?

Rafael: It's a hand weapon, a piece of leather-wrapped metal. It's what the police use, a blackjack.

Gabriel: Yes, yes, it doesn't leave any marks.

Rafael: Yes, it was a blackjack, a *cachiporra*, well, they hit him with it on the head, so then there was a strike. And of course, they accused me of being part of that, too . . . So then, they locked up a hundred of us in the control units. Among us, was a brother from the Republic of New Africa, Akinsiyu.

Gabriel: Yes, I remember him.

Rafael: Akinsiyu, he changed his name from his slave name, and there were other fellow Africans, too. There were also others from the Black Liberation Army, such as Oscar Washington, and others. Leonard Peltier was also in Marion, he's still there, the Native American brother from that land that the Anglos stole, and who's been in prison for more than thirty years now. Herman Bell was also there with me. Well, there we were, they put us in there, and locked up a hundred of us, and finally there were thirty-six of us left. But then lawyers from the People's Law Office took our case to court, and finally one of their courts decided that it was cruel and unusual punishment, and we were let out. Most of the others were sent to other prisons, but they didn't want me at the other prisons . . . so they left me at Marion until the people released us, because it was the people [the lawyers and community people] who got us out.

Gabriel: Could you talk about the People's Law Office? Where was it?

Rafael: In Chicago, and I remember there were many lawyers—they did a lot, they fought hard . . . Michael Deutsch was one of them.

Gabriel: Michael Deutsch. Yes, I know him well.

Rafael: Mara Siegel . . . Dennis Cunningham. It was an office of lawyers dedicated to the struggle for civil rights, for prisoners' rights, in particular.

Gabriel: Let's go back a little. Could you tell me a bit more about how life was in prison, day to day, particularly for a prisoner like you, who landed in prison because of political consciousness.

Rafael: They had us, Oscar Collazo, Irvin Flores, Andrés Figueroa, Lolita Lebrón, and me, they had us on a list that they called the "special monitoring list." The prisoners called it "the Hot List," in other words . . .

Gabriel: The Hot List . . .

Rafael: . . . they dealt with us directly from Washington, they didn't allow us certain things that other prisoners could have, such as visits, etc., and they had more control over our lives. But you know how prison life is.

Gabriel: Now that you mention that, I was remembering, because you met this *Negro de Oro*, Gabriel Torres, yours truly, in 1975.

Rafael: Yes, because he got it into his head that he was my bodyguard.

Gabriel: Well, I wanted to be your bodyguard. Now I feel like laughing. I just remembered, chief, that you talked on the phone with my mother, too, I had forgotten that.

Rafael: Yes, that's true.

Gabriel: Ok, chief . . . how many Boricuas were there in Alcatraz?

Rafael: That I know of, during the six years I was there, there were four of us *Boricuas*. In Leavenworth, there were a lot of Mexicans.

Gabriel: Chief, in your own view, how are things now, in terms of politics, the United States, the people who are in prison? Overall, how do you see the prison system, now that there's a prison in Guantánamo, and all this about homeland security?

Rafael: That's racism.

Gabriel: How do you see it, chief, and how do you see it in the future?

Rafael: Well, for Puerto Ricans, since 1898 when we were invaded . . . First, they bombed us from the high sea on May 12, 1898. . . . they, the U.S. Marines, murdered Puerto Ricans, with bombs in San Juan, and they killed Puerto Rican men, youth, women, and children, and then they turned around and ran away. And then they invaded us that same year, on July 25th, but we Puerto Ricans resisted, confronted them, and ever since then, we've been exploited incarcerated and massacred. On March 21st, 1937, they sent an Anglo General, Blanton Winship, and Colonel Riggs to exterminate all the nationalists. A newspaper headline said, "When in front of Nationalists, shoot to kill." Our fight has always been as if

George Bush were there the whole time, with all those racists they have there. We were also massacred in Rio Piedras and later in Utuado. The incarceration of hundreds and hundreds of Puerto Ricans, among them Albizu Campos, and my father, Rafael Cancel Rodríguez, defenders of independence. My father was a survivor of the Ponce Massacre. OK, but right now, analyzing the torture they're legalizing . . . if you dare do any little thing to them, they label you as an enemy combatant and they put you in prison without even a trial.

Gabriel: Yes, and there was a *boricua* called José Padilla.

Rafael: José Padilla. And we still have three prisoners, who've been incarcerated for twenty-seven years.

Gabriel: What are their names?

Rafael: Oscar López, Carlos Alberto Torres, Haydee Beltrán. And recently, they incarcerated another Puerto Rican patriot, Avelino González Claudio, who they're accusing of being a "Machetero." In other words, for us, there's always been imperialism; it's always been bloody, aimed at ending all resistance in Puerto Rico. The greatness of Puerto Ricans is that, even after a hundred years of holding us captive, we're still fighting. The struggle has always been difficult, and right now, with homeland security, they think that they are authorized to commit any atrocity, and that patriotism which is antipatriotic, is not homeland security, it's stolen land security . . . what they call homeland security is stolen land.

Gabriel: Stolen from who, chief?

Rafael: From the Native Americans . . . and from Mexico.

Gabriel: So, chief, the work I do here at the Community Service Society (CSS), is trying to help people, the formerly incarcerated, people who've just gotten out of prison. Because the vast majority of those released from prison cannot reintegrate because they don't have jobs. For example, they can't get a barber's license; they can't get a plumber's license. So it's a big battle, a struggle for rights for those who are still incarcerated, so they can have access to good health care, to good doctors. How do you see that, chief, in terms of the people who are coming out of prison now?

Rafael: Well, it's like what you're saying, they label prisoners and then, when they get out on the street, they're stigmatized.

Gabriel: Yes, I've already been out for twenty-nine years, and I'm restricted from certain jobs.

Rafael: Imagine others who were incarcerated for whatever reasons. They either know or ask you, why were you in prison? Just for loving your people, for doing things for your people, and for respecting yourself. There are criminals in Washington right now, and they're the ones who should be locked up but they have the keys to the prisons. They should be the ones locked up, because of all the things they're doing in Iraq right now, exterminating men, women, children, over a million people, and they take you and me there, to fight their wars. They don't go. The ones who benefit aren't going. They take you, me, the Hispanics, to die there like idiots, fighting for their oil and to steal the land from the Iraqis.

Gabriel: And there are a lot of Latinos, Chicanos, *Boricuas*, among them.

Rafael: Yes, we're the ones who are dying like idiots over there. If we're going to die, and to fight, let's do it against our real enemy. The Iraqi people are not our enemies. If we're going to fight, do it for our people, not for those who threw our people out in the ocean to be eaten by sharks. They sit back, rubbing their belly. Understand, they don't go to war. They use people's poverty, and since so many are being forced to enlist in the military to survive, they become paid murderers, hired killers.

Gabriel: And a lot of them go into the army because they want to get an education, not because they want to go to war.

Rafael: They're cornered. It's the need that they've created for us.

Gabriel: Chief, let me ask you, we received the sad news about Raúl Salinas's passing. Could you tell us a little bit about him, since I know you knew him?

Rafael: Not only did I know him, but I also loved him very much, like a brother in the struggle.

Gabriel: Could you talk a little about him?

Rafael: He was unlucky, like a lot of us. Life had cornered him and he got into some things that aren't very pleasant to remember. He began to get patriotic in prison; he learned about his people, his own race, his own people, because of where he was, and then he became a fellow fighter, for his people's rights. I remember the last time I saw him in prison; they had us both in behavior modification, and when he got out, he passed by the cell where they had me locked up, to say goodbye, and I gave him a poem. They forbid me to write poems for the outside because they were revolutionary poems. And he was one of the prisoners to whom I gave a poem, so he could send it to my father. And that's how my first book, *Ideario de un puertorriqueño*, was put together. All my friends from prison kept their word. I would give them copies of my poems to send to my father, and my father put together my first book, with the poems my prison friends sent him from their homes. They all kept their word to me, among them, Raúl Salinas.

Gabriel: Now that you talk about behavior modification, I remember that when I was there, I would talk to you from inside my cell while you were in the yard. Do you remember?

Rafael: Yes.

Gabriel: That would raise my spirits. My spirit would fly, and I would get so excited because I could see you, in the yard. Anyway, chief, it's been a real pleasure. Take good care of yourself. I love you very much. Thank you, chief.

16

La alegría de tener vergüenza

Rafael Cancel Miranda

Quisiera vivir en paz con los cielos,
en armonía con la naturaleza
pero no a cambio de hacerme el ciego,
cuando vamos perdiendo la vergüenza.
Y aunque sé que para tantos es de tontos,
eso de vivir con la frente alta,
yo prefiero morir pobre de todo,
a vivir sin lo único que nos realza.
Con eso que nos lleva a vivir,
dignos de ser hijos de algún Dios,
dignos de lo que dicen por ahí,
de que somos la imagen del Creador.

*   *   *

Lo obvio no siempre es lo real.
¿Vanidad? Preferir verse bien a sentirse bien.
Los indignos se someten, los dignos se resisten y combaten.
La victoria solo es un imposible para los que no luchan.
Pueblo sin patria es nave al garete, sin ancla y sin destino propio.
El meollo de la cosa es cómo tener lo más sin dejar de ser lo mejor.
Discusiones de borracho valen lo que un mamarracho.
La felicidad de los dignos no cabe en ningún bolsillo.
¿De qué vale una ciudad llena de luces si no tiene luz propia?

*   *   *

Prefiero que seas mi amigo,
recorrer juntos el camino,
contar estrellas contigo,
forjarnos un mismo camino.
Pero solo como hermanos,

¡jamás como tu sumiso!
pues antes que ser tu esclavo,
¡barro el piso contigo!

* * *

Los hipócritas no tienen amigos verdaderos pues la hipocresía es incapaz de sinceridad; y,
sin sinceridad, no hay verdadera amistad.
El hombre verdaderamente libre quiere que todos lo sean.

* * *

Dicen de un hombre honesto,
que se dejó corromper por los chavos,
digo que era deshonesto,
¡solo que antes era un pelao!

* * *

Son muchos los que prefieren no pensar pues sentirían nausea de sí mismos.
Quien tiene las manos bonitas no necesita de sortijas, así como quien tiene viente/veinte
no necesita de lentes.
El colonizado en estado crónico de coloniaje se desvive por servirle al colonizador y, como
dicen los enamorados, "dejan de ser ellos para ser de ellos".

Part IV

The Way Forward

Chicana(o)/Latina(o) Prisoners

Ethical and Methodological Considerations, Collaborative Research Methods, and Case Studies

Juanita Díaz-Cotto

Race, Ethnicity, and Penal Studies

Reviews of case studies on male (Jacobs 1979) and female (Díaz-Cotto 2000) penitentiaries in the United States reveal the lack of attention historically paid by mainstream social scientists to the role played by race, racism, and ethnic factors in penal institutions. In 1979, James B. Jacobs critiqued this oversight in studies of male prisons up until the late 1970s[1] and traced the first social science study to seriously consider issues of race, and to a lesser extent ethnicity, in a men's facility to former prisoner and academic John Irwin's, *The felon* (1970).[2] Elsewhere, I have critiqued (Díaz-Cotto 2000) how major studies of women's prisons carried out between 1965 and 1998 ignored or downplayed the role of race, racism, and ethnicity in women's facilities and traced the first social science study to seriously consider the role of race and racism in a women's facility to Eloise Spencer's doctoral dissertation, "The Social System of a Medium Security Women's Prison" (1977).[3] How gender discrimination is intertwined with racial and ethnic discrimination in male and female institutions was not discussed until the publication of my book *Gender, ethnicity, and the state: Latina and Latino prison politics* (1996).[4]

Overlooking the roles played by race, racism, and ethnicity is noteworthy not only because people of color have historically been overrepresented in penal facilities throughout the country but also because it is widely known that "prisons have a long history of segregation and racial discrimination" (Jacobs 1979, 1). As Jacobs noted, by the mid-1970s, segregation had been well documented in at least one government report (New York State Special Commission on Attica 1972) as well as in court decisions issued between 1963 and 1974 that declared racial segregation in various state prisons unconstitutional (Jacobs 1979). Numerous articles published in mainstream newspapers also discussed the racial conflicts among prisoners and between prisoners and staff that took place in male institutions throughout the country during the late 1960s and early 1970s (Jacobs 1979).

The omission is also surprising, particularly in the case of male prisons, if one considers that by the late 1950s, prisoners affiliated with the Nation of Islam had already begun to challenge racial discrimination and segregation in prisons (Jackson 1962, 1970; Brown 1965; Malcolm X and Haley 1964; Cleaver 1968; Jacobs 1979). Moreover, during the 1960s and 1970s, prison administrators very actively and publicly engaged in repressing the activities of all prisoners, particularly prisoners of color, who were either politicized while incarcerated or had been imprisoned as a result of their political activism on the outside (Carroll 1977; Jacobs 1979, 1983; Irwin 1980; Díaz-Cotto 1996). Activities chiefly targeted among these were the coalition-building efforts of prisoners, such as the strikes and rebellions that took place in jails and prisons throughout the United States, the publishing of the underground prisoner newspaper *The Outlaw* at San Quentin, and the 1971 Attica prison rebellion in New York (Davis et al. 1971; Badillo and Haynes 1972; Davidson 1974; Cummins 1994; Díaz-Cotto 1996).

Equally significant, by 1970, Claude Brown (1965), Malcolm X and Haley (1964), Piri Thomas (1967), Eldridge Cleaver (1968), and George Jackson (1962) had publicized their prison experiences in their writings. These works were soon followed by other writings by Jackson (1970), Angela Y. Davis et al. (1971), Davis (1974), and Thomas (1974). The writings and activism of prisoners and former prisoners were part and parcel of the civil rights and liberation movements being waged by African American, Chicana(os)/Latina(os) and other oppressed peoples inside and outside the United States.

In view of the above, it appears that the lack of interest in discussing the importance of racial and ethnic factors in major prison studies has been more the result of researchers' own biases rather than a reflection of prisoners' realities or the lack of available data to draw on. When combined with the historical tendency of social scientists to ignore or downplay the experiences of women prisoners, the oppressive role played by penal staff, and the positive role third parties can play on behalf of prisoners, this omission has distorted the realities of prisoners and nonprisoners alike. It has also hindered our ability to discern clearly the strategies and tactics needed to change oppressive social conditions.

This essay compares the major studies carried out by social scientists from diverse fields—anthropology, sociology, and political science—on the experiences of Chicana(o)/Latina(o) *pintas(os)* (prisoners/former prisoners) in New York and California state prisons. The first part of the essay provides a general discussion of the major methodological and ethical dilemmas these researchers confronted. The second part compares how such dilemmas were resolved by each study and explores the main motivations of researchers for conducting their studies, the major questions posed, the research methods used, the findings and conclusions reached, and how these were interrelated. The last part of the essay concludes with a brief review of the major findings and a commentary on the methodologies that help to address a number of underlying concerns such as: What research methods are most likely to yield findings most useful to pintas(os), their barrios,[5] and non-pintas(os) seeking to document pintas(os)' institutional experiences and attempts to change oppressive conditions inside the walls? What methods are more likely to measure the impact preprison experiences have on imprisoned Chicanas(os) as well as the impact imprisonment has on pintas(os) and their barrios? How do prisons reproduce, and therefore reinforce, differential power relationships existing on the outside?

While scholars within the fields of history, psychology, education, literary and cultural studies, geography, and gender and lesbian and gay studies have written about what I call the Prison Industrial Military Complex (Díaz-Cotto 2006), the focus on social science research is emphasized in this essay only because, to date, the major institutional case studies on Chicana(o)/Latina(o) prisoners have emerged from within the social sciences. It is important to note, however, that depending on the researcher, there can be much overlap between the methods and data used and compiled by social scientists and other fields of study and that no one field has a monopoly on reality.

Penal Research on Chicana(o)/Latina(o) Prisoners

During the 1970s, several social scientists published works that examined conflicts taking place between African American, Anglo-European, and Chicano prisoners in California (Irwin 1970; Minton 1971; Pell 1972; Wright 1973; Yee 1973; Jacobs 1977). One studied informal networks created by African American and Latino prisoners in New York State (Ianni 1974);[6] another assessed the participation of Puerto Rican prisoners in the New York City 1970 jail riots and the Attica prison rebellion (Badillo and Haynes 1972).[7] Others investigated Chicanos' participation in a New Mexico prison riot (Saenz 1986) and prison gangs in Texas (Ralph 1992).

To date, however, only a handful of social scientists have significantly documented the institutional experiences of Chicano prisoners in California (Davidson 1974; Moore et al. 1978) and Latino prisoners in New York (Díaz-Cotto 1996). While only one study has explored Chicanas' experience in jail (California; Díaz-Cotto 2006), a second has compared the histories of Latinas and Latinos imprisoned in two New York State penitentiaries (Díaz-Cotto 1996).

This article focuses on reviewing social science case studies on *pintas(os)'* institutional experiences. Having said this, however, it is important to note that it is the works produced directly by *pintas(os)* themselves that have received the most notoriety within the academic and criminal justice fields and particularly within the barrios.[8] *Pintas(os)'* cultural productions have captured the popular imagination because they are accessible to larger audiences and reflect the day-to-day struggles and concerns of many barrio residents. Academics who are politically committed to helping *pintas(os)* change oppressive criminal justice policies and structures are aware of the value of *pintas(os)'* documenting their lives, in their own words and from their own perspectives—hence the growing number of scholars concerned with making the words of Chicana(o)/Latina(o) *pintas(os)* most widely known (Torres 1975, 1981; Olguín 1995, 1997; Rodríguez 2006; Díaz-Cotto 2006; Salinas and Mendoza 2006). Ultimately, access to all sources can help researchers frame new and more realistic research questions, devise more challenging methods of gathering and interpreting data, and arrive at more realistic findings that have practical applications for the communities they study and their allies.

The study of penal institutions is imperative because they are a microcosm of society, that is, they replicate and thus illustrate what is taking place on the outside, the myriad ways power elites attempt to control certain groups, and the manner in which such groups seek to empower themselves. Moreover, they are themselves a means by which societal elites attempt to control the behavior of groups seen as threatening the status quo.

Oral Documentation and Collaborative Research Methods, Some Ethical and Methodological Concerns

Oral Documentation and Collaborative Research Methods

In view of the dearth of scholarly research on the incarceration experiences of *pintas(os)*, one of the key methodological questions is what are the most effective ways social scientists can gather reliable and comprehensive data? Engaging in nonexploitative collaborative research efforts in which oral history research is a main component is one means of achieving this goal.

Collaborative research, as here understood, entails allowing those studied to influence all or part of the research process.[9] The extent of such collaboration is one of the characteristics that differentiate researchers on *pintas(os)* from one another. Overall, intermediaries who have helped prisoners document their experiences and stories have included academics, journalists, filmmakers, attorneys (e.g., Correctional Association of New York), prisoners support groups (e.g., California Coalition for Women Prisoners), civil and human rights organizations (e.g., Amnesty International, Human Rights Watch), legislators (e.g., Badillo and Haynes 1972) and government agencies and commissions (Hispanic Inmate Needs Task Force 1986; New York State Special Commission on Attica 1972).

Oral documentation has been the main source of information for most scholars who have conducted institutional case studies regardless of researchers' race, nationality, or sex, and independently of the time period covered or the facility studied (Clemmer 1940; Sykes 1958; Ward and Kassebaum 1965; Giallombardo 1966; Davidson 1974; Díaz-Cotto 1996, 2006; Owen 1998; Ross 1998). This has been the case even when oral documentation has been part of larger ethnographic or fieldwork studies involving "observation, participation, archival analysis and interviewing" (Reinharz 1992, 46).

Oral sources take diverse forms, including *testimonios* (testimonies or personal declarations) made before penal (Santana 1985) or private agencies or individuals; closed or open-ended interviews; and oral histories in the form of "case studies, in-depth life history reviews, biographical interviews, life histories, and personal narratives" (Reinharz 1992, 129). Katherine Angueira (1988) summarized the functions of *testimonios* as being to "openly defy a system of oppression, unmask existing myths, provide information, inspire others to speak about their own victimization, and validate survivors' fears, insecurities, and preoccupations as normal reactions to the devastating experience they have survived as evident in the similarity in responses with other survivors" (76).

While some *pintas(os)* have had a few select individuals (e.g., attorneys, academics), private organizations (e.g., human rights), and public agencies (e.g., legislative bodies) document their stories while imprisoned, most have been able to provide such information only upon their release. The reasons have been primarily twofold. Prison administrators have tried to control who has access to information about what transpires inside the walls, and they have sought to prevent prisoners, staff, and third parties from informing others about conditions and the treatment prisoners receive. Ultimately, penal policies combined with researchers' own racial, ethnic, and gender biases, and lack of vision have limited the information published about all prisoners.

Ethical and Methodological Considerations

One of the advantages of collaborating with those studied and of conducting oral history research is that researchers are able to obtain more varied and detailed data than they would have access to otherwise. The drawbacks are that some sources may deliberately lie, forget key information, or unwillingly distort information offered.

In cases where *pintas(os)* are interviewed while still incarcerated, the credibility of the information may be compromised by fear of retaliation from other prisoners or penal staff. This may occur even when penal authorities allow the researcher to collect the data without obvious interference or the imposition of conditions requiring the latter to reveal his or her sources. Scholars have sought to avoid such pitfalls by interviewing a combination of prisoners and former prisoners or by interviewing only former prisoners, assuming that *pintas(os)* are more likely to provide reliable information if their anonymity is protected.

Researchers have complemented, verified, and cross-referenced oral data in several ways. They have engaged in field observation, conducted interviews with *pintas(os)*, penal staff, and third parties from different racial and ethnic groups, and have researched statistical data, legal documents, prisoners' and mainstream newspapers, prisoner newsletters, organizational and private documents and reports, prisoners' writings, and previously published books and articles on the subject.

Emphasizing the importance of political prisoners' writing about their own experiences, Barbara Harlow (1992) raises the concern that much of the scholarly literature produced about prisoners directly or indirectly serves to justify their imprisonment. She argues that both prisons and universities "function as complicit parts of the same operational system of dominant state control of dissent and the containment of antisystemic change" (Harlow 1992, 13). Thus, it could be argued that while prisoners are institutionalized physically, most mainstream academics are institutionalized intellectually. Equally important, those carrying out studies within institutions frequently find themselves compromising, even when not outright collaborating, with the goals of penal authorities in order to have access to the institutions. "Even . . . critiques of the prison system, however, too often can be subjected to the consent of that same prison system and its apparent insistence on a language of authority and objective responsibility that requires a complicit compromise from the would-be researcher and attempts to usurp his/her project" (Harlow 1992, 24).

Furthermore, scholars open to incorporating the concerns and voices of prisoners, former prisoners, or their barrios can be denied access to penal facilities. Moreover, should their studies contradict mainstream views within or outside the academy, their research is often labeled "subjective" and therefore biased, while the views of researchers supportive of the status quo are labeled objective and scientific (Zinn 1979).

An underlying question is how "theory" should be generated. As stated by Francis A.J. Ianni and Elizabeth Reuss-Ianni, "Under the classical logico-deductive scheme, theory is first developed, and then taken into the field and examined through the research process" (Ianni and Reuss-Ianni 1972, 183). This view is challenged by other social scientists who argue that "theory should be developed *in* (not before) the process of research, so that it is 'grounded' in the empirical world in which the research is being carried out" (Ianni and Reuss-Ianni 1972, 183; see also Glaser and Strauss 1967). While mainstream social scientists are more likely to support the former view, activist academics are more likely to support the latter.

In view of the diverse ideological and political roles played by academics in supporting or opposing the status quo, a primary ethical concern pertains to the motivations that prompt penal studies. For example, was the researcher initially motivated by political identification with state authorities, prisoners, third parties (Fishman 1990), or was the research the result of other personal motivations, such as the desire to advance professionally? The answers to these questions will influence the agendas of the researchers, whose voices are prioritized in the resulting narrative as well as in the nature of their collaboration with *pintas(os)*, penal staff, and other interested parties.

Consideration must be given to the issue of whose stories are considered the most valid to tell (Becker 1967). Should it be that of criminal justice and other state elites whose personal and political views are widely publicized and whose policies are enforced on a daily basis by a host of government agencies? Should it be the views of the people who are the object of criminal justice policies and who rarely have a venue through which their voices can be heard? Or should one prioritize the voices of academics and others who claim to provide an objective view in their representation of those studied? In the latter case, Alcoff (1995) and others have raised the question of whether anyone, including academics, ever has a right to speak for another, and, if they do, under what conditions it is appropriate for them to do so.

Moreover, in what language, literally and figuratively, should researchers convey their information? Is it ethical for academics who study populations with little access to adequate educational systems, such as non-English speaking peoples and the poor, to produce their work in an academic jargon and in a language not easily accessible to those they write about? Rarely are scholars concerned with these issues.[10]

Of further concern is who will benefit from the information gathered: *pintas(os)* and their communities of origin or penal authorities and other state elites interested in surveilling and controlling prisoners or their barrios? Important, too, is the power imbalance that exists between those who are being studied and the researchers who generally determine the questions asked, the data gathered, the findings and conclusions reached, how the information is conveyed to the public, and the targeted audience for their work (Zinn 1979; Reinharz 1992). It is also scholars who tend to gain the most from the research, in terms of works published, compensation for such work, career advancement, and professional status. Such power differentials are problematic even when both researchers and researched come from similar racial, ethnic, gender, sexual, and/or class backgrounds.

As a result of such disparities, even when Chicana(o)/Latina(o) communities have cooperated with social scientists, most in the barrios have felt that the day-to-day realities experienced by them have been historically distorted by the predominantly middle-class, Anglo-European, female, but primarily male, researchers who have carried out the studies and published their conclusions (Zinn 1979). These, barrio residents frequently feel, at best, do not have a clear understanding of what it is like to live in the barrios and, at worst, use their research to justify the implementation of discriminatory policies. As a result of these and other equally negative experiences with Anglo-European professionals they come in contact with (e.g., criminal justice personnel, case workers, teachers) many Chicanas(os)/Latinas(os), but particularly *pintas(os)*, are hesitant to cooperate with even well-meaning social scientists. As Moore et al. (1978) observed, "the convicts see legitimate research consistently misused in order to label behavior for purposes of control . . . Many such labels are derived from psychological research . . . Most know how they are utilized, and have acquired a strong distrust for batteries of questionnaires. They equally distrust qualitative approaches because of their similarity to the use of informers by law enforcement people . . . There is no reason for my convict—especially for any Chicano convict—to believe assurances of confidentiality (Chicano communities also have their own strong hostility to conventional research"; (4–5).

Within this context, "insiders" (i.e., those who come from the groups being researched) may find it easier than outsiders to gain access to Chicana(o)/Latina(o) communities. As Maxine Baca Zinn has argued, "the unique methodological advantage of insider field research is that it is less apt to encourage distrust and hostility, and the experience of being excluded (e.g., as a white researcher) from communities, or of being allowed to 'see' only what people of color want them to see" (1979, 212).

However, while being an insider may open doors with the individuals and communities studied, insiders' access, like that of outsiders, may depend on several factors, including the transparency of one's personal and political biases; the inclusion or exclusion of voices of the studied throughout the research process (Moore 1977; Reinharz 1992); and whether or not insiders are seen as exploiting their barrios. Age, sex, nationality, class background, language skills, and perceived sexual orientation are additional variables. Acceptance as an insider, however, can place emotional and political expectations on researchers that they may find difficult to meet (Zinn 1979).[11]

Despite the sometimes apparently insurmountable obstacles, a few social scientists have persisted in forming diverse collaborative relationships with *pintas(os)* in order to study the impact criminal justice policies, including imprisonment, have had on them and their barrios. Two possible results of collaboration have been discussed in Marie "Keta" Miranda's (2003) work. Miranda described how the young Chicana gang members she came in contact with struggled with her "around relations of power" and contested not only her research goals and methods but also her presumed right to represent them. In the end, Miranda chose to resolve the methodological and ethical dilemmas she confronted by changing her original research agenda, forming an "alliance" with the subjects of her study and adopting a methodology that involved collaborative research (47–48). In the process, the young women exerted their agency to defend their interests. Miranda nonetheless recognized that as the ethnographer producing the final project, she ultimately maintained the power to represent those studied.

A comparison of studies of *pintas(os)'* incarceration experiences in New York and California will reveal how social scientists tackled the methodological and ethical dilemmas discussed above.

Documenting *Pintas(os)'* Experiences of Imprisonment: Davidson, Moore et al., and Díaz-Cotto At a Glance

To date, there have been three case studies that specifically focus on the institutional experiences of Chicanas(os) or Latinas(os) in New York and California: R. Theodore Davidson's *Chicano prisoners: The key to San Quentin* (1974); Juanita Díaz-Cotto's *Gender, ethnicity, and the state: Latina and Latino prison politics* (1996); and Juanita Díaz-Cotto's *Chicana lives and criminal justice: Voices from el barrio* (2006). While Joan Moore et al.'s *Homeboys: Gangs, drugs, and prison in the barrios of Los Angeles* (1978) is not an institutional case study per se, the information provided on Chicanos imprisoned in California is substantive enough to merit its inclusion in any serious discussion of Chicanos/Latinos and incarceration.[12]

In reviewing these works, it is useful to list common research questions that informed these studies. These questions included: How do *pintas(os)* experience imprisonment? What are *pintas(os)'* major concerns and priorities? What groups do they form while imprisoned? Which of these allow them to exert the most control over their own lives? What relationships do *pintos* have with one another as well as other prisoners, staff, and third parties? How have preprison experiences affected pintas(os)' experience of incarceration? Díaz-Cotto (1996) also sought to compare and contrast the experiences of *pintos* to that of *pintas*.

Davidson, Chicano Prisoners (1974)

In 1974, Davidson published *Chicano prisoners*, the first study of prisoners conducted by an anthropologist and the first major social science work on Chicano *pintos*. *Chicano prisoners* was based on twenty months (June 1966 to February 1968) of observation of male prisoners at California's San Quentin state penitentiary. Davidson began his study while still a Ph.D. student at the University of California, Berkeley, because prison administrators "wanted to see if an anthropologist could determine what subcultural factors were responsible for Mexican-American prisoners being excessively violent and excessively reluctant to participate in rehabilitation activities" (1974, 1).

Davidson initially accepted views held by San Quentin administrators that denied alternate constructions of Chicano prisoners and ignored their participation in formal prisoner groups, that is, groups created by prisoners but "legitimized" by prison administrators and whose goals included rehabilitation. Eventually, his review of government data revealed that *pintos* were in fact not more violent than other prisoners during the period he studied.

Although Davidson was authorized to visit all areas of the facility (except death row), and interview prisoners freely, he was expected to tell staff "if I learned that someone was going to be physically harmed or that the prisoners were going to destroy the prison in some manner" (1). Thus, while he sought to maintain his autonomy as a scholar, ultimately, according to Harlow, penal demands that prioritized the "stability of the prison itself . . . under the ostensibly humanitarian sensitivity for the safety and well being of the anonymous prisoners" required Davidson to make "a complicit compromise" and attempted to "usurp" his project (Harlow 1992, 24, 25).

While Davidson's priority was to study prisoners' behavior, he continued to interview a number of pintos upon their release from the facility. Davidson's primary "informants" were members of small cliques, some affiliated with Family, a Chicano prison gang. His collaboration with these men deepened to the point that by the time the book was published, Davidson claimed that it had been edited by Chicano prisoners. As a result, he argued, "This analysis focuses on those things, which are most meaningful and important to the prisoners themselves, such as *their own* economy, leadership, social control, law, types of prisoners, ethnic divisions, and levels within their culture" (2). Davidson's other sources included penal staff, government reports, earlier studies of male prisoner subculture, and articles published in mainstream newspapers—the *San Quentin News* (the formal prisoner newspaper) and *The Outlaw*. His close collaboration with *pintos* and the oppressive treatment all prisoners received eventually led Davidson to sympathize with prisoners' demands for penal reforms. Subsequently, he was banned from San Quentin for leaking information to prisoners' rights activists and the mass media.

Davidson's study was valuable in that, for the first time, a researcher focused on the experiences of *pintos* and allowed a number of them to speak about their lives and concerns as well as the outside influences that affected how they adapted to prison life. A significant observation was that preprison influences, such as Chicana(o) cultural values, barrio loyalties and rivalries, and racial antagonisms influenced Chicanos' relationships with *pintos* and non-*pintos* alike. These influences, combined with staff racism and cultural isolation, led them to form ethnic-based groups. On the basis of the information Davidson obtained from his informants, he concluded that while some prisoners affiliated with Family participated in formal prisoner groups, they saw these groups as being marginal because they were powerless to effect significant changes on behalf of prisoners. Also, formal prisoner groups could not gain the support of most Chicanos who, because of their experiences with political leaders on the outside, would be naturally distrustful of such "sociopolitical" leaders (152).

According to Davidson, Family controlled the prison through its control of the underground prisoner economy and used its "Chicano Fund" "to help the less fortunate nonmember Chicanos" (99). Davidson also held that, at times, members of Family played key roles in the building of reform-oriented prisoner coalitions and sometimes initiated them. "There are times, however, that Chicano or Family members will covertly (from the staff perspective) use the power and authority they have acquired through economic activities to influence and lead sociopolitical activities inside. And, without Family backing, Chicanos probably would not even press for a protest" (150). The above claims were significant in that they recognized the potential prisoner gangs had to participate in reform-oriented coalitions.

Davidson's conclusions were challenged by *pinto* (Chicano Pinto Research Project 1975) and non-*pinto* researchers and barrio residents who saw his views as resulting from a misunderstanding of barrio values and distorted information he received from those he interviewed. Alfredo Mirandé (1987) critiqued Davidson for seeing Chicano criminality as an extension of Chicano culture, for claiming to provide an "insider" perspective, and for intensifying racism between Chicanos and African Americans: "It seems incredulous that hard-core members of a super-secret organization would bear their souls to an Anglo social scientist, especially one who was commissioned by the administration . . . such cooperation is completely at odds with the convict code. What appears more likely is that those convicts who served as informants told him only those things that they wished to reveal or, perhaps more accurately, what they thought he wanted to hear" (Mirandé 1987, 203).

Moore et al. (1978) also critiqued Davidson's assertions that formal *pinto* organizations were basically useless and Family was a "benevolent and effective" organization (127). It was partly in response to Davidson's arguments that Moore et al. published *Homeboys*.

Moore et al., Homeboys (1978)

In 1978, Joan W. Moore, a sociologist working closely with *pintas(os)* and non-*pintas(os)* in Los Angeles, published *Homeboys*. *Homeboys* (male barrio residents) was informed by a history of collaboration between academics, members of self-help and prisoner service groups, *pintos*/addicts/ex-gang members in East Los Angeles, and middle-class administrative and clerical staff.

Most of the research took place between 1974 and 1975, when Moore et al. secured funding to conduct interviews under the aegis of the Chicano Pinto Research Project. The project followed the lead of Chicanos imprisoned at San Quentin who, distrustful of mainstream researchers, had started to develop their own research materials in the mid-1960s. *Homeboys* also followed the work of the League of United Citizens to Help Addicts (LUCHA), a Los Angeles-based Chicano self-help group composed of ex-pintos that compiled information on the experiences of Chicano addicts. Similarly, the collaborative efforts that gave birth to *Homeboys* were influenced by the community fieldwork tradition that emerged out of the University of Chicago during the 1920s.

Significantly, homeboys from the three Los Angeles barrios studied were not only subjects of the research but also served as interviewers, critics, informants, and analysts. They used the resources and contacts of Chicano self-help groups to conduct interviews with *pintos* inside and outside prisons. Additional data was gathered through questionnaires, surveys, self-surveys, seminars, and informal discussion groups. The collaboration, however, was at times fraught with major conflict both between academics and nonacademics, and within a *pinto* staff comprised of men from sometimes-rival gangs. Conflict between academics and nonacademics emerged as a result of "divergent values" as well as "problems of mutual acculturation and overcoming stereotypes" (184). One major result of the *Homeboys* collaboration was that the research design was modified to include an "oral history approach" as a major source of data (188). Collaboration also led researchers to expand their objectives, the result being the production of "a major body of historical materials" on "the barrios, the gangs, the drug market, and the prison self-help movement" (190).

Like Davidson, Moore et al. noted how preprison experiences and barrio norms and conflicts affected *pintos*' behavior inside penal facilities. Unlike Davidson, who primarily focused on what transpired within the institution, Moore et al. deliberately sought to study the relationship between drug use, barrio gangs, self-help groups, and prison experiences. "Secondarily and indirectly, we are concerned with the racial effect—that is, Chicanos as a minority group within prison" (95).

Moore et al. drew their information about Chicanos' incarceration experience from former prisoners and from questionnaires distributed in four male penitentiaries. However, in order to assess the validity of Davidson's findings, they focused their primary attention on Chicanos' experiences at San Quentin during the same time period covered by Davidson's research. Sharing some of his informants, Moore et al. found that many of them clearly regarded Davidson as an "outsider," frequently and deliberately misleading him (127). While Davidson saw organizations such as Family playing a politically oriented coalition-building role within San Quentin, Moore et al. emphasized the destructive nature of the two Chicano prisoner gangs active within California prisons by the time *Homeboys* was published: Nuestra Familia and "a particularly vicious criminal organization-the Mexican Mafia" (178).

Commenting on Davidson, Moore et al. noted, "It is also odd that he almost dismisses the position of the convict in the formal social structure (job assignment, program, proximity to release) as important in understanding the convict social structure" (127). They emphasized both the positive rehabilitative role played by *pinto* self-help groups and the fact that it was *pintos*, and not prison administrators, who determined the groups' goals and the means to achieve them. Furthermore, Chicano self-help groups played key roles in the building of Chicano solidarity because they emphasized the need for unity and collaboration and offered an alternative to the prevailing gang and barrio rivalries and hostilities. Once released from prison, the positive influence played by such groups could be extended to the barrios.

Penal administrators also recognized the important role ethnically based self-help groups could play in the building of prisoner solidarity. Thus, they used the existence of gangs to construct all Chicano prisoners as violent and "potentially 'revolutionary'" (135–36) as they sought to disband Chicano self-help groups throughout California prisons. Notwithstanding, organizations such as El Mejicano Preparado, Listo, Educado, y Organizado (EMPLEO), formed in 1966 at San Quentin as the first Chicano *pinto* culture group, spread throughout California institutions.

The creation of *pinto* self-help groups on the inside paralleled the creation of such groups on the outside. Chicano self-help groups provided *pintos* one of the most significant sources of support upon their release from institutions, and it was *pintos* involved with self-help groups and other barrio organizations that helped develop the research model that led to the publishing of *Homeboys*.

Moore et al. found other continuities between life on the streets and life inside prisons. One was that most Chicanos emphasized familism, that is, the emphasis on forming family-like relationships with their homeboys and homegirls in the barrios and inside institutions.[13] Other continuities and parallels inside and outside the walls included limited economic, social, and educational opportunities and exposure to multiple forms of discrimination (e.g., economic, social, cultural, and political). These, combined with the targeting of Chicanos for harassment by criminal justice agencies, contributed to their coming in constant contact with "progressively more punitive institutional agencies" (205).

Despite these significant findings and the fact that Moore et al. were able to achieve collaboration between academics and nonacademics, few social scientists will be ever be able to achieve, they—like Davidson—were soon critiqued for presumably blaming Chicano criminality on Chicano culture (Mirandé 1987).

Díaz-Cotto, Gender, Ethnicity, and the State (1996)

In 1996, I published *Gender, ethnicity, and the state*, partly in reaction to the dearth of information on Latinas(os)' prison experiences in the United States. The study examined New York State penal policies from 1970 to 1987, the period preceding and following the 1971 Attica prison rebellion. The impact of the policies were traced through a comparison of the experiences of, and the organizing strategies pursued by, Latina (and non-Latina) prisoners at Bedford Hills Correctional Facility and Latino (and non-Latino) prisoners at Green Haven Correctional Facility. The book measured how race, gender, and ethnicity reinforced one another to generate divergent responses from both penal elites and third parties to prisoners' calls for support and reforms. *Gender, ethnicity, and the state* was one of the first prison studies in the United States carried out by a political scientist, the first to discuss the experiences of imprisoned Latinas, and thus the first to compare these with that of Latinos.

The research emerged from an ongoing political commitment to document the lives and experiences of Latinas(os) in the United States and abroad. I hoped that information gathered would motivate others to support Latinas(os) in their attempts to secure prison reforms, the hiring of more bilingual personnel, and the provision of much needed bilingual programs and services. Likewise, I wanted to illustrate the conditions under which *pintas(os)* (and other prisoners) could wrest significant concessions from the state.

In order to obtain my information and cross-reference the data gathered throughout 1989 and early 1990, I interviewed Latina(o) and African American former prisoners, penal employees, and third parties (e.g., attorneys, feminists, lesbian activists, and members of the Center for Puerto Rican Studies). Additional data was gathered from prisoner and mainstream English and Spanish-language newspapers, prisoners' rights newsletters, court cases, government and private organizational reports, and prisoners' autobiographies (Thomas 1974). In some instances, those interviewed gave me access to their personal, organizational, and institutional files.

Unlike Davidson and Moore et al., I had previously volunteered at both of the institutions I studied years before initiating my research so that I had already met some of the *pintas*, penal personnel, and third parties I would interview. All but a few of those interviewed referred me to additional sources. While I did initially interview a handful of *pintos* at Green Haven, the presence of a Latino staff member throughout the interviews prevented prisoners from being fully honest with me. Lacking connections within the New York State Department of Corrections bureaucracy that would allow me to conduct research free from institutional interference at either facility, I concentrated on interviewing former prisoners. Overall, interviews took place at interviewees' homes, work sites, and at the locales of community organizations.

Fortunately, I was perceived as an "insider" in multiple ways (e.g., woman, Latina, lesbian, prisoners' rights activist, bilingual, of poor and working-class extraction, yet also an academic) and I was open to documenting the experiences of Latina(o) and non-Latina(o) prisoners, third parties, and civilian and security staff. This allowed me to gain the trust of diverse types of populations interested in discussing disparate power relationships at various levels and their experiences of individual and institutional racial, ethnic, gender, and sexual discrimination and abuse on the inside.

While I did not maintain contact with most of the *pintas(os)* I interviewed, I incorporated their observations and analysis directly into the book as quotes. By this means, I sought to give prisoners a direct voice within the context of academia and break with mainstream prison studies. I also offered *pintas(os)* and some attorneys the opportunity to review and comment on the manuscript before it was published.

The data collected illustrated various coalition-building models used by *pintas(os)* and their allies and the conditions under which Latina(o) and other prisoners can coalesce with third parties and progressive penal personnel to win concessions from the state. At Green Haven, Latinos secured a number of concessions from the state when they joined forces with progressive penal staff and radical students and faculty affiliated with the Center for Puerto Rican Studies (CPRS). Although Latinas at Bedford Hills also received support from CPRS, they were able to secure significant concessions only when they joined non-Latina prisoners and prisoners' rights attorneys in filing several class action suits on behalf of all prisoners.

Like Davidson and Moore et al., I discussed the existence of formal and informal prisoner groups. However, I did not pass judgment as to which groups were better equipped to help prisoners survive, thrive, and engage in coalition-building efforts. The reality is that membership in formal and informal prisoner groups overlaps. New York State had no significant prison gangs during the period studied, making such comparisons less problematic than in the case of California. I found, as had Moore et al., that even formal Latino prisoner groups could be targeted for elimination by prison authorities because of their potential to serve as coalition-building organizations. In fact, at both Green Haven and San Quentin Chicano/Latino prisoner organizations were once disbanded due to their coalition-building activities.

Ultimately, my comparison of imprisoned Latinas and Latinos led me to conclude that

> while Latina and Latino prisoners tended to share the same concerns, substantial gender differences existed with respect to how they organized. The variation in organizing strategies was conditioned not only by the priority they assigned to diverse interests but also by the disparate treatment male and female prisoners have historically received from both penal personnel and third parties. Furthermore, the ability of Latina(o) prisoners to have their concerns addressed was affected by their level of organization and unity, the degree to which they were able to mobilize penal personnel and Latina(o) community members on their behalf, and their ability to secure the support of non-Latina(o) prisoners, or at least neutralize their resistance to Latina(o) prisoner concerns. (8–9)

Even with third party and penal staff support, however, Latina(o) prisoners were able to wrest significant concession from state elites only when the state was most divided among itself.

Final Observations

The works of Davidson, Moore et al., and Díaz-Cotto were all groundbreaking studies with respect to the populations documented, the research questions posed, and the methodologies used. Davidson was the first to explore major aspects of the Chicano prisoner experience on the west coast, examining the important role played by informal groups and economic networks. Moore et al. studied the interrelationship between *pintos*' experiences before, during, and after incarceration and the positive and negative influences exerted by formal and informal *pinto* groups. I, in turn, compared Latina prisoners' experiences to that of Latinos on the east coast and documented the types of interactions that took place between prisoners, penal personnel, and third parties. All of us depended on oral sources of information for the bulk of our data. However, while Davidson and Díaz-Cotto included oral sources of information as a major component of their initial research designs, Moore et al. adopted an oral history approach as a primary means of gathering data after they had initiated their study.

Although we all recognized the need to collaborate with those whose experiences we wanted to document, we differed with respect to the types of sources we used and the extent of our collaboration with them. Initially, Davidson's key informants were both penal staff and members of prisoner cliques, primarily Chicanos. As his research progressed, Davidson developed close ties with a small number of *pintos*, some of whom he maintained contact with after their release from prison. Moore et al. developed a collaborative research model that brought together Chicano *pintos*/addicts/ex-gang members and members of self-help and prisoner service groups, all of whom served as sources. They were joined by a middle-class academic and administrative staff. I obtained my data primarily from interviews with Latina(o) former prisoners and third parties, African American former prisoners, and progressive Latina(o) and white penal staff, only a few of which I kept in touch with once the interviews were completed.

The studies also differed in terms of how we first gained access to those interviewed. While Davidson was initially asked by penal administrators to study imprisoned Chicanos, Moore et al.'s research was informed by a history of collaboration between Moore and the *pintas(os)* she worked with. I developed my contacts with those I interviewed primarily as a result of my having volunteered a few years earlier at both institutions I studied. All of us complemented our oral data with additional primary and secondary sources.

All three studies were motivated by the desire to document major aspects of *pintos* and/or *pintas'* experiences in state penitentiaries. However, Davidson's initial motivation to document Chicano prisoners from the perspective of penal administrators, like the nature of the questions he posed, gradually changed as his relationship with his Chicano sources deepened and he received more exposure to the treatment accorded prisoners. Ultimately, he opted to describe the role played by various *pinto* informal groups and economic networks presumably from the perspective of his Chicano informants. Moore et al. sought to examine the continuities that existed between the experiences of *pintos* –pre, during, and postincarceration and the impact of discriminatory penal policies on imprisoned Chicanos. They also wanted to appraise what types of *pinto* groups were more likely to help empower Chicana(o) communities. My primary goals were to explore the organizing strategies pursued by Latina(o) prisoners as they sought to wrest significant concessions from penal elites and to compare the ways in which gender, ethnicity, and racism influenced the goals and strategies pursued by prisoners, as well as the responses of penal personnel and third parties to their calls for support.

All of us confronted ethical and methodological dilemmas during the data-gathering process. I was concerned about how much information I should reveal regarding the organizing strategies pursued by *pintas(os)* and feared that the information I revealed might be used against some of my sources should they be reincarcerated. Davidson's major ethical dilemma surfaced when he felt forced to choose between publicly revealing the conditions and treatment given prisoners or remaining silent in order to enjoy continued access to the facility. For Moore et al., the central dilemmas surfaced as a result of the tensions generated by a collaborative research model that brought together both rival gang members and academics and nonacademics.

Although all of us agreed on the important role preprison experiences and outside forces had on Chicanas(os)/Latinas(os) behavior on the inside, Davidson and Moore disagreed as to whether it was formal (i.e., self-help organizations) or informal prisoner groups (i.e., gangs) that exerted the most significant and positive influences on *pintos* and their barrios. In contrast, I examined the overlapping nature of formal and informal prisoner groups and networks and their potential of the latter to play both positive and negative roles.

Suggestions for Future Research: Methodological Considerations

It is clear that Davidson, Moore et al., and Díaz-Cotto made significant contributions to a host of fields within and without the social sciences. However, much remains to be done if we want to document comprehensively the experiences of Chicanas(os)/Latinas(os) with the U.S. criminal justice system and the institutions in which they have been imprisoned historically (e.g., juvenile detention facilities, local jails, state and federal prisons, military prisons, private prisons, immigration detention facilities, and male and female institutions). Even more remains to be done if we want to compare the realities confronted by *pintas(os)* and other incarcerated peoples in the United States, Latin America, and other parts of the world.

Included below are some methodological suggestions for those seeking to document Chicanas(os)/Latinas(os)' experiences with the U.S. criminal justice system. Some of these might be applicable to research conducted abroad or studies aiming to contrast experiences inside and outside the United States.

As penal institutions are a microcosm of society, research that seeks to compare prisoners' experiences, whether within (e.g., single case studies) or among diverse types of institutions (e.g., comparative studies), to that of their communities on the outside, would contribute much to our understanding of how penal institutions are one of the means by which those in power seek to control the behavior of Chicana(o)/Latina(o) and other populations. Moreover, models that examine both the influence of preincarceration experiences on Chicanas(os)/Latinas(os) and the impact institutionalization has on *pintas(os)* during and after incarceration would allow us to observe the continuities that exist between life inside and outside the walls and the types of formal and informal groups and networks most likely to provide *pintas(os)* mutual support and positive leadership role models. In addition, a multilevel analysis that explores how gender, race, class, ethnicity age, and sexuality interact to reproduce relationships of power and subordination within diverse contexts would provide us a greater understanding of the methods by which such power differentials are perpetuated and the tactics and strategies needed to eliminate them.

Methods likely to yield the most realistic and practical findings are those that are both grounded in the realities of the barrios prisoners come from and seek to promote community empowerment. We should strive to make our research designs and data collection process as interdisciplinary and inclusive as possible in order to access all available information, but particularly the voices and perspectives of barrios residents, including the works produced by *pintas(os)*.

Owing to the scarcity of data on Chicana(o)/Latina(o) prisoners in the United States, an oral history approach would need to be a central component of any future research models seeking to document *pinta(o)* histories. Where possible, institutional studies should include interviews with *pintas(os)*, third parties, and penal personnel. Ethical and logistical dilemmas encountered by researchers who want access to penal institutions could be partially resolved by interviewing former *pintas(os)* and progressive penal staff and by maintaining judicious cordial relations with penal administrators.

While it would be preferable for academics, be they "insiders" or "outsiders," to join forces with *pinta(o)* and non-*pinta(o)* prisoners rights' activists and others in the barrios who have developed research models applicable to Chicana(o)/Latina(o) communities, this option might not be available in the localities researchers wish to study. Under these circumstances, academics and nonacademics might want to explore the possibility of jointly developing such models. The collaborative research method that gave birth to *Homeboys* would seem like a reasonable place to start.

Researchers for whom the development of such broad-based coalition-building strategies might not be feasible might want to study the coalition-building strategies pursued by prisoners in conjunction with progressive third parties and penal personnel (Díaz-Cotto 1996). This would allow them to elucidate the conditions under which such collaboration can be established and perhaps motivate others to engage in similar types of research or coalition-building strategies.

Studies concerning U.S. criminal justice policies should be complemented by studies that compare them to those implemented abroad, particularly when policies, such as the international war on drugs, have been promoted and frequently imposed by U.S. economic, political, and military elites. Such findings could be used to generate international alliances seeking to eliminate disparate power relationships globally.

Ultimately, scholars would do well to well keep in mind that it is research that addresses the concerns of those being studied, incorporates them into the research design, and is carried out in an egalitarian manner that is more likely to gain the trust and support of sources and hence provide the most reliable information and practical applications.

Chapter 17

1. While this essay focuses on institutional case studies, others have analyzed the role race and racism have played in determining who comes in contact with the criminal justice system and their experiences once incarcerated. See Díaz-Cotto's "Reference List" (2006), Prisoners of Conscience Project (1992), Network of Black Organizers Staff (1996), and Morín (2005).

2. Some examined prisoner subcultures or racial conflicts between prisoners in male institutions (Carroll 1977; Jacobs 1977; Irwin 1980).

3. Others discussed how racism influenced the treatment of U.S. prisoners in women's reformatories and state prisons (Rafter 1985; Hicks 1999) and race relations in federal penitentiaries for women (Kruttschnitt 1983).

4. In 1998, Luana Ross published *Inventing the savage: The social construction of Native American criminality*, a groundbreaking case study of the treatment received by Native American women imprisoned in Montana.

5. *Barrios* can refer to a neighborhood, a territory claimed by a gang, or the gang itself.

6. Francis A. J. Ianni's *Black mafia* (1974) discussed the participation of Puerto Rican and African Americans in informal prisoners groups and economic networks at Green

Haven and Attica penitentiaries following the 1971 Attica prison rebellion. Ianni's conclusions were based on information provided primarily by two field assistants, one of whom had been imprisoned at Attica and the other at Green Haven. Ianni believed that the histories of the institutions were so similar that he merged the accounts of both prisons into one narrative. However, the fact that Green Haven was where penal elites experimented with prison reforms and the formation of formal prisoner groups as of 1972 (Díaz-Cotto 1996) makes it unlikely that the experiences of prisoners were so similar in both facilities as to warrant such merging.

7. Lee (1977) provided a profile of Latina(o) prisoners in New Jersey. The Hispanic Inmate Needs Task Force (1986) documented the concerns of Latina(o) state prisoners and staff in New York State.

8. Some examples are Sánchez (1971, 1976, 1983, 1990), Thomas (1974), Piñero (1975), Torres (1975, 1981), Talamantez (1976), Baca (1979, 2001), Santana (1985), Cardozo-Freeman (1991), Olguín (1995, 1997), Salinas (1995, 1999), Peláez (2001), Rodríguez (2006), and Salinas and Mendoza (2006). In 2002, Jorge Antonio Renaud became the first prisoner to write a guide describing the functioning of a major state penitentiary system (Texas) in the United States.

9. Although I use the term "collaboration" to speak about cooperation between *pintas(os)* and non-*pintas(os)*, Dylan Rodríguez and Viet Mike Ngo (the latter imprisoned in California) have argued that "the vernacular of 'collaboration' (or coalition, solidarity, partnership, etc.) exaggerates the political and historical possibilities of those meetings between free and unfree, to the extent that one of the 'collaborators' is categorically immobilized-not at liberty to move, speak, and practice" (Rodríguez 2006, 33).

10. Social scientists who want to make their work accessible to nonscholars also face academic criteria that judges whose work is "scholarly" and "theoretical" and therefore worthy of receiving recognition, financial support, and publishing.

11. Being an insider does not shield scholars from the criticism of other academic insiders who have different viewpoints or are competing for the right to represent the interests of *pintas(os)* and other barrio residents.

12. Although a comparison of *Chicana Lives and Criminal Justice* and *Homeboys* would allow us to gauge the impact preincarceration experiences have on how Chicanos and Chicanas experience their confinement, as well as the impact imprisonment has on *pintas(os)* and their communities, limitations of space do not allow for comparisons of that type at this time. Thus, I limit my discussion here to Díaz-Cotto's *Gender, Ethnicity and the State* (1996).

13. The exception to this pattern is state-raised youths who formed the majority of members of Mexican Mafia and Nuestra Familia.

References

Alcoff, Linda Martín. 1995. The problem of speaking for others. In *Who can speak: Authority and critical identity*, ed. Judith Roof and Robyn Wiegman, 97 – 119. Urbana: University of Illinois Press.

Anguiera, Katherine. 1988. To make the personal political: The use of testimony as a consciousness-raising tool against sexual aggression in Puerto Rico. *Oral History Review* 16 (2): 65–93.

Arnold, Regina. 1994. Black women in prison: The price of resistance. In *Women of color in U.S. society*, ed. Maxine Baca Zinn and Bonnie Thorton Dill, 171–84. Philadelphia: Temple University Press.

Baca, Jimmy Santiago. 1979. *Immigrants in our own land*. Baton Rouge: Louisiana State University Press.

———. 2001. *A place to stand*. New York: Grove.

Badillo, Herman, and Milton Haynes. 1972. *A bill of no rights: Attica and the American prison system*. New York: Outerbridge and Lazard.

Becker, Howard. 1967. Whose side are we on? *Social Problems* 14:239–47.

Brown, Claude. 1965. *Manchild in the promised land*. New York: Macmillan.

Cardozo-Freeman. 1991, Inez. Memoirs of a pinto. *The Americas Review* 19 (1): 74–82.

Carroll, Leo. 1977. *Hacks, blacks, and cons: Race relations in a maximum security prison*. Prospect Heights, IL: Waveland.

Chicano Pinto Research Project. 1975. *Final report*. Los Angeles: Chicano Pinto Research Project.

Cleaver, Eldridge. 1968. *Soul on ice*. New York: McGraw Hill.

Clemmer, Donald. 1940. *The prison community*. New York: Holt, Rinehart, and Winston.

Cummins, Eric. 1994. *The rise and fall of California's radical prison movement*. Stanford, CA: Stanford University Press.

Davidson, R. Theodore. 1974. *Chicano prisoners: The key to San Quentin*. New York: Holt, Rinehart, and Winston.

Davis, Angela. 1974. *Angela Davis: An autobiography*. New York: Random House, 1974. [Reprint edition. New York: International Publishers. 1988.]

Davis, Angela Y., Ruchell Magee, the Soledad Brothers and other political prisoners. 1971. *If they come in the morning*. New York: New American Library.

Díaz-Cotto, Juanita. 1996. *Gender, ethnicity, and the state: Latina and Latino prison politics*. Albany, NY: SUNY Press.

———. 2000. Race, ethnicity, and gender in studies of incarceration. In *States of confinements: Policing, detention and prisons*, ed. Joy James. New York: St. Martin's.

———. 2006. *Chicana lives and criminal justice: Voices from el barrio*. Austin: University of Texas Press.

Fishman, Laura T. 1990. *Women at the wall: A study of prisoners' wives doing time on the outside*. Albany, NY: SUNY Press.

Giallombardo, Rose. 1966. *Society of women: A study of a women's prison*. New York: John Wiley.

Glaser, Barney, and Anselm Strauss. 1967. *The discovery of grounded theory*. Chicago: Aldine.

Harlow, Barbara. 1992. *Barred: Women, writing, and political detention*. Hanover, CT: Wesleyan University Press.

Hicks, Cheryl Deloris. 1999. Confined to womanhood: Women, prisons, and race in the state of New York, 1980–1935. PhD diss., Princeton University.

Hispanic Inmate Needs Task Force. 1986. *Final report, A meeting of the minds*. Correctional Services, Division of Hispanic and Cultural Affairs.

Ianni, Francis A. J. 1974. *Black mafia: Ethnic succession in organized crime*. New York: Simon & Schuster.

Ianni, Francis A. J., and Elizabeth Reuss-Ianni. 1972. *A family business: Kinship and social control in organized crime*. New York: Russell Sage Foundation.

Irwin, John. 1970. *The felon*. Englewood Cliffs, NJ: Prentice-Hall.

———. 1980. *Prisons in turmoil*. Boston: Little, Brown.

Jackson, George. 1962. *Blood in my eye*. New York: Random House.

———. 1970. *Soledad brother: The prison letters of George Jackson*. New York: Bantam.

Jacobs, James. B. 1977. *Stateville: The penitentiary in mass society*. Chicago: University of Chicago Press.

———. 1979. Race relations and the prisoner subculture. *Crime and Justice* 1:1–27.

———. 1983. *New perspectives on prisons and imprisonment.* Ithaca, NY: Cornell University Press.

James, Joy, ed. 2003. *Imprisoned intellectuals: America's political prisoners write on life, liberation and rebellion.* Lanham, MD: Rowman & Littlefield.

Johnson, Paula C. 2003. *Inner lives: Voices of African-American women in prison.* New York: New York University Press.

Kruttschnitt, Candace. 1983. Race relations and the federal inmate. *Crime and Delinquency* 29:577–92.

Lee, Robert Joe. 1977. Profile of Puerto Rican prisoners in New Jersey and its implications for the administration of criminal justice. M.A. thesis, Rutgers University.

Malcolm X, and Alex Haley. 1964. *The autobiography of Malcolm X.* New York: Ballantine.

Minton, Robert, ed. 1971. *Inside prison American style.* New York: Random House.

Miranda, Marie "Keta." 2003. *Homegirls in the public sphere.* Austin: University of Texas Press.

Mirandé, Alfredo. 1987. *Gringo justice.* Notre Dame, IN: University of Notre Dame Press.

Moore, Joan W. 1977. A case study of collaboration: The Chicano pinto research project. *Journal of Social Issues* 33:144–58.

Moore, Joan W., Robert García, Carlos García, Luis Cerda, and Frank Valencia. 1978. *Homeboys: Gangs, drugs, and prison in the barrios of Los Angeles.* Philadelphia: Temple University Press.

Morín, José Luis. 2005. *Latino/a rights and justice in the United States: Perspectives and approaches.* Durham, NC: Carolina Academic Press.

Network of Black Organizers Staff. 1996. *Black prison movements/U.S.A.* Trenton, NJ: Africa World Press.

New York State Special Commission on Attica. 1972. *Attica: The official report of the New York State Special Commission on Attica.* New York: Bantam.

Olguín, Ben V. 1997. Tattoos, abjection, and the political unconscious: Toward a semiotics of the pinto visual vernacular. *Cultural Critique* 37 (3): 159–213.

———. 1995. Testimonios pintaos: The political and symbolic economy of pinto/a discourse. PhD diss., Stanford University.

Owen, Barbara. 1998. *"In the mix": Struggle and survival in a women's prison.* Albany, NY: SUNY Press.

Peláez, Vicky. 2001. Cuando una madre es puesta tras las rejas. *El Diario/La Prensa*, May 13, 2, 3.

Pell, Eve, ed. 1972. *Maximum security: Letters from California's prisons.* New York: Dutton.

Piñero, Miguel. 1975. *Short eyes.* New York: Hill and Wang.

Prisoners of Conscience Project. 1992. *Can't jail the spirit: Political prisoners in the U.S., A collection of biographies.* 3rd ed. Evanston, IL: National Council of Churches of Christ.

Rafter, Nicole Hahn. 1985. *Partial justice: Women in state prisons, 1800–1935.* Boston: Northeastern University Press.

Ralph, Paige Heather. 1992. Texas prison gangs. PhD diss., San Houston State University.

Reinharz, Shulamit. 1992. *Feminist methods in social research.* New York: Oxford University Press.

Renaud, Jorge Antonio. 2002. *Behind the walls: A guide for families and friends of Texas prison inmates.* College Station: Texas A&M University Press.

Rodríguez, Dylan. 2006. *Forced passages: Imprisoned radical intellectual and the U.S. prison regime.* University of Minnesota.

Ross, Luana. 1998. *Inventing the savage: The social construction of Native American criminality.* Austin: University of Texas Press.

Saenz, Adolph. 1986. *The politics of a prison riot: The 1980 New Mexico prison riot, its causes and aftermath.* Corrales, NM: Rhombus.

Salinas, Raúl. 1995. *East of the freeway: Reflections de mi pueblo, poems.* Austin, TX: Red Salmon Press.

———. 1999. *Un Trip through the Mind Jail y Otras Excursiones.* Houston: Arte Público Press.

Salinas, Raúl, and Louis G. Mendoza. 2006. *Raúlrsalinas and the jail machine: Selected writings by Raúl Salinas.* Austin: University of Texas Press.

Sánchez, Ricardo. 1971. *Canto y grito mi liberación.* El Paso, TX: Mictla Publications.

———. 1976. *Hechizospells: Poetry/stories/vignettes/articles/notes on the human condition of Chicanos and Picaros, words and hopes within soulmind.* Chicano Studies Center Publications, Series no. 4. Los Angeles: University of California, Los Angeles.

———. 1983. *Amsterdam Cantos y poemas pistos.* Austin, TX: Place of Herons Press.

———. 1990. *Eagle-visioned/Feathered adobes: Manito sojourns and Pachuco ramblings.* El Paso, TX: Cinco Puntos.

Santana, Luz. 1985. Address before the Hispanic Inmate Needs Task Force. Hispanic Inmate Needs Task Force Banquet, Albany, New York.

Spencer, Eloise Junius. 1977. The social system of a medium security women's prison. PhD diss., University of Kansas.

Sudbury, Julia, ed. 2004. *Global lockdown: Race, gender, and the prison industrial complex.* New York: Routledge.

Sykes, Gresham. 1958. *The society of captives.* Princeton, NJ: Princeton University Press.

Talamantez, Luis. 1976. Life within the heart imprisoned: The collected poems of Luis Talamantez. San Jose, CA: Fidelity.

Thomas, Piri. 1967. *Down these mean streets.* New York: Alfred A. Knopf.

———. 1974. *Seven long times.* New York: Praeger.

Torres, Benjamin. 1975, 1981. *Pedro Albizu Campos: Obras escogidas.* 3 vols. San Juan, Puerto Rico: Editorial Jelofe.

Ward, David, and Gene Kassebaum. 1965. *Women's prisons: Sex and social structure.* Chicago: Aldine-Atherton.

Wright, Erik Olin, 1973. *The politics of punishment: A critical analysis of prisons in America.* New York: Harper & Row.

Yee, Minn S. 1973. *The melancholy history of Soledad prison.* New York: Harper's Magazine Press.

Zinn, Maxine Baca. 1979. Field research in minority communities: Ethical, methodological, and political observations by an insider. *Social Problems* 27 (2): 2.

Toward a Pinta/o Human Rights?

New and Old Strategies for Chicana/o Prisoner Research and Activism

B. V. Olguín

The production of the terrorist as a figure in the American imaginary reflects vestiges of previous moral panics as well, including those instigated by the mass fear of the criminal and the communist. Willie Horton is the most dramatic example of the former. Anti-communism successfully mobilized national—perhaps I should say nationalist—anxieties, as does the so-called war on terrorism today. None of these figures are entirely new, although the emphasis has been different at different historical conjunctures.

—Angela Davis, 2005

Crime, Terrorism, and the New War on Dark Brown Men

The spectacular September 11, 2001, airborne attacks are transforming U.S. society in ways that will only be fully understood after the passage of more time. Some of the ongoing transformations, however, were foreseen by critics of the draconian 1994 Omnibus Crime Bill. They warned against the continued erosion of civil liberties—especially for minorities—under the guise of yet another war on crime that followed former President Reagan's war on drugs in the 1980s and former President Nixon's Crusade Against Crime in the 1960s. The effects of the war on terror have already been much worse than anyone imagined. In the first five years since the September 11 attacks, the 1994 Omnibus Crime Bill was complemented by even more draconian legislation: the 2002 passage of the *USA PATRIOT Act* (the Orwellianesque acronym for "Uniting and Strengthening America by Providing Appropriate Tools Required to Intercept and Obstruct Terrorism"), the subsequent *USA PATRIOT Act II*, and the 2006 *Military Commissions*

Act. These laws collectively curtail constitutional freedoms of speech, association, and information; infringe constitutional rights to legal representation, a timely public trial, and protection from unreasonable searches; and also allow for the use of extrajudicial imprisonment and secret military tribunals for citizens and noncitizens accused of aiding or abetting "terrorism."

More importantly, the war on terror has introduced the category of "enemy combatant," a classification unique in American jurisprudence because it situates its designee in the interstices of domestic and international law. By using this category for U.S. citizens and noncitizens alike, the U.S. government seeks to avoid the protections afforded a "prisoner of war," who has rights outlined by the Geneva Conventions, including access to a legal defense. Even persons charged with sedition and espionage are allowed such access to civilian legal representation. In contrast, an "enemy combatant" is denied access to U.S. courts as well as international tribunals precisely because, according to interpretations of the category, they have no nation-state patron. They exist in a legal and thus civic limbo as prototypical "anticitizens" of the world. Not surprisingly, by the end of 2001, over one thousand Arab, South Asian, and African Muslim males studying or working in the United States had been detained and held incommunicado. Most of the detainees were ostensibly arrested on visa violations but were later imprisoned under suspicion of having terrorist links. The Department of Justice and Department of Defense conduct the detentions through various subordinate agencies and military branches. Both departments refuse to release the names of many past or current detainees or even the details surrounding their alleged offenses to the general public, prospective legal representatives, or even their own families.

In the first two years of this pogrom, at least fourteen U.S. citizens were caught in the dragnet and subsequently held in civilian prisons, military brigs, and once-secret CIA-run prisons abroad with limited or no access to legal representation. All but one of these initial detainees were racial minorities. These domestic "enemy combatants" come from vastly different ethnic backgrounds—Arab, East Asian, African, African American, (mixed-race) Latina/o, and one Caucasian—and include one woman (the African American wife of one of the alleged "ringleaders"). Yet rather than diversify the image of the new twenty-first-century "menace to society," the circumstances surrounding the detention and prosecution of these U.S. citizens further reinforces the new prejudicial racialization of this old antithetical American.

The first and only "enemy combatant" to receive a civilian trial was John Walker Lindh, a white male from an upper-middle-class family in upscale Marin County north of San Francisco, whose father is a wealthy corporate attorney. Lindh was convicted and sentenced to twenty years in prison, with eligibility for early release for good behavior. In contrast, Yasser Hamdi, who was born in Louisiana to Saudi Arabian parents during his father's employment in the oil industry, was held incommunicado for three years in a U.S. Navy brig in Norfolk, Virginia, since his capture in the same Mazar al-Sharif Battle in which Lindh was captured. Hamdi was released and expelled from the country in 2005, only after the U.S. Supreme Court, in *Hamdi v. Rumsfeld* (2004), ruled against the government's right to hold "enemy combatants" indefinitely and incommunicado. The Court further demanded that detainees in the U.S. war on terror must be treated in accordance with Article 3 of the Geneva Conventions, which prohibits "violence to life and person, in particular murder of all kinds, mutilation, cruel treatment and torture" and "outrages upon personal dignity, in particular, humiliating and degrading treatment" (1949).[1] Similarly, six Yemeni Americans arrested in New York City in September 2002, along with four African Americans and one Saudi Arabian-American arrested in October 2002, remained in detention, as late as 2006, without access to legal representation or a courtroom hearing.

These detentions suggest that not all enemy combatants are created equal, and the implications for Latinos are dire. During the first two years of the war on terror, the classification and extended detention of the twelve racial minority males and one black female as "enemy combatants" revealed that race—further darkened by a religion deemed by some to be "foreign"—undergirded the construction of abjection in the arming of the war on terror. Indeed, dark brown bodies have become the nexus at which domestic law enforcement practices converge with U.S. international political and military objectives. As Angela Davis (2005) notes in an interview excerpted in the epigraph at the beginning of this chapter, in the new U.S. government foreign policy at the turn of the twenty-first century, the local neighborhood dark brown American male has become a villain of global proportions.

The initial arming of this war on terror as an extension of the five-decade-old war on crime, targeting dark males, has a particular relevance to Latinos when one considers the case of Jose Padilla. A Puerto Rican born in New York City and raised in a low-income Latino barrio in Chicago, Padilla was a reputed former "gang member" and ex-convict who converted to Islam during a prison stint in Florida. He was arrested on May 8, 2002, under suspicion that he was scouting targets in the United States for a uranium-loaded "dirty bomb" attack and was held incommunicado for four years under military custody. (The U.S. government avoided the application of *Hamdi v. Rumsfeld* by re-charging Padilla in 2006 under domestic criminal statutes that are unrelated to his previous charges as an "enemy combatant," and subsequently convicted him in a federal court in 2007, sentencing him to 17 years in prison.)

Padilla's arrest has been accompanied by an alarmist, racially coded media blitz that has raised the specter of hordes of Latino criminals who convert to Islam in prison to become even more threatening than the old Latino menace to society: internationalized enemies of the United States. For instance, in a June 30, 2002, syndicated story ominously titled "Prison system could be terror breeding ground," journalist Dan Freedman reported that the recent arrest of ex-convict Padilla "could be evidence that prison systems here and overseas have become inadvertent breeding grounds for militant Islamic terrorists." Freedman cites Charles Colson, an aid to former President Richard Nixon and the architect of the inaugural war on crime in the 1960s. Colson observed that "alienated, disenfranchised people are prime targets for radical Islamists who preach a religion of violence, of overcoming oppression by Jihad" (2002). After noting the growing numbers of disenfranchised racial minorities in prison, Colson adds, "it's no accident that Islam's influence is growing behind bars." Coincidentally, this sensationalist report coincides with the nationwide increase in Latina/o conversions to Islam.[2] Reports that a former leader (or "godfather") of the Chicano prison gang "the Mexican Mafia" converted to Islam while in prison, locates Chicano and Chicana prisoners—or *Pintos and Pintas*—within this neocrusade discourse that pits the Christian West with a potentially expanding Islamic East. In the wake of the September 11 attacks, the specter of dark criminal masses reproducing their abjection in U.S. prisons is not just a domestic crisis: it has become a matter of national security. However hyperbolic this representation of a mass uprising of prisoners cum Islamic terrorists may be, it nonetheless foregrounds how domestic law enforcement practices and U.S. foreign policy have begun to converge at the site of the penitentiary.

Relocating the U.S. Carceral onto the International Sphere

The convergence of the war on crime and the war on terror demands, and ironically enables, an alternative, if not altogether new, approach to activist "prison work." U.S. President George W. Bush inadvertently provided an impetus for this new era of prison work on September 7, 2006, when he confirmed the existence of secret U.S. prisons run by the CIA in foreign countries, some of which openly permit the use of torture. This fact, and the U.S. practice of "extraordinary rendition" by which "suspected terrorists" are transported to these secret prisons, had been an open secret since Seymour Hersh first reported on the matter in a *New Yorker* article in May 2004. But Bush's admission—together with the ensuing public debates about the new U.S. Army interrogation manual that still permits the use of "water boarding" (near drowning) and the formal establishment of special military tribunals to try "enemy combatants" to circumvent *Hamdi v. Rumsfeld*—have made the convergence of U.S. foreign policy with domestic policy, and U.S. military protocol with domestic penology, a matter of public record.

Even though the U.S. Congress ratified the *Military Commissions Act* that resulted in the legal elimination of habeas corpus protections—a hallmark of modern jurisprudence that normally permits prisoners to challenge their imprisonment, thereby ensuring (at least theoretically) against unlawful arrest and imprisonment—the fissures of U.S. criminality and penality today are pregnant with possibilities—and, of course, urgency—for prisoner rights activists and scholars. That is, these legal stratagems, debates, compromises, and more stratagems to permit torture and extrajudicial detention have, in effect, linked domestic and international standards for the treatment of prisoners. As noted above, the latest U.S. war on crime has made international prisoners of U.S. citizens like Puerto Rican José Padilla. Likewise, the U.S. war on terror has made domestic prisoners of international citizens (exclusively Muslim males, many of whom still remain unidentified and held incommunicado in U.S. prisons or secret prisons in undisclosed locations).[3] This application of a legal limbo had already been deployed through immigration detention centers prior to the September 11, 2001, attacks and implementation of the war on crime. But now it is formal legal code.

The stripping of both U.S. and non-U.S. citizens of fundamental prisoner rights enshrined in the Geneva Conventions immediately introduces human rights paradigms into the equation. Indeed, even Amnesty International, whose anticommunist bias prevented any critiques of U.S. prisons until the early 1990s, when it began a campaign against the death penalty, has weighed in on the now standard violations of human rights in the new internationalized U.S. carceral. In its widely publicized 2005 annual report, former Amnesty International Secretary General Irene Khan described the U.S. prison at Guantanamo Bay as "the gulag of our time" (Amnesty International 2005). This preliminary intervention of human rights activists has opened a small crack in the heretofore-impenetrable discourse that posits the myth that U.S. prisons are among the world's "best."[4] In this conjunctural moment arising from profound rollbacks of prisoner treatment standards in the United States, I argue that domestic U.S. prison work must retool and readapt to deploy human rights theory and practice both for "common" prisoners as well as for those who are nationally and internationally recognized as "political prisoners." In this new era of the U.S. carceral, the domestic prisoner has become internationalized, and vice versa, and therefore requires a new theory of praxis.

Prisoner Classification as New-Old Battleground

Prisoner classification has always been a battleground—especially regarding race—precisely because of the convoluted and irregular classification methods used by state and federal agencies. For instance, Latina/o prisoners alternately are classified as "Hispanic," "White," "Black," "Hispanic: White," and "Hispanic: Non-White." But the most vexing and politically charged category remains "political prisoner." Officially, the United States has no political prisoners. But former U.S. President Clinton's pardon and release of sixteen Puerto Ricans who had been imprisoned for engaging in insurgent activities to end U.S. colonial domination of the island nation of Puerto Rico revealed the hypocrisy of such a claim. A decade before Clinton sought to free the United States from international scorn for imprisoning Puerto Rican freedom fighters previously classified as "terrorists"— including those held in "preventative detention" without having actually been convicted of armed insurrection—Ronald Fernandez had succinctly argued that the classification of these prisoners as "terrorist" was a political decision that illuminated, rather than effaced, the fact that they were political prisoners (1994). The war on terror—and its attendant legislation permitting "extrajudicial detention," "extraordinary rendition," "coercive interrogation," and secret trials—has exposed a fact that Puerto Rican *independentistas* and other minorities have known all along: there were and still are political prisoners in the United States. According to the Jericho movement, there were approximately 150 political prisoners and prisoners of war in U.S. prisons as of December 1, 2006.[5]

The unprecedented convergence of U.S. law with international standards, and international prisoners of war ("enemy combatants") with U.S. Latinos, confirms what Chicana/o prisoner rights activists have maintained since the nineteenth century: Chicana/o prisoners and incarceration rates must be understood and addressed within an international context. I have shown elsewhere how the incarceration of Chicana and Chicano prisoners such as Modesta Avila, Jimmy Santiago

Baca, Ricardo Sánchez, Raúl Salinas, Fred Gómez Carrasco, Judy Lucero, and Alvaro Hernández Luna, among others, is inextricably linked to colonial domination and the subsequent struggle for material resources in the southwestern United States.

Other scholars, activists, and prisoners themselves have long argued for the reclassification of Mexican expatriates (e.g., the Magón brothers), Puerto Rican *independentistas* (e.g., Rafael Cancel Miranda), black (e.g., Mumia Abu Jamal), and internationalist White (e.g., Marilyn Buck) prisoners as "political prisoners" due the protections and rights delineated in the Third Geneva Convention, "The Geneva Convention relative to the treatment of prisoners of war" (United Nations 1929). Many of these early campaigns to have domestic prisoners reclassified as international, or even political, prisoners failed, primarily due to persistent U.S. government denials of the existence of U.S. political prisoners and prisoners of war. Former U.S. President Clinton's pardon of *independentistas* was unprecedented.

But the war on terror has sufficiently muddled the divisions between the local and the global as well as the domestic and the political. Indeed, the use of terms like "terrorist" and "enemy combatant" in awkward U.S. government attempts to legitimate extrajudicial detainment, torture, and possible summary execution are pregnant with counterhegemonic opportunities. After all, when a U.S.-born Puerto Rican can be classified as an "enemy combatant" and held for two years incommunicado without the rights of habeas corpus, and the U.S. Supreme Court can rule, as it did in *Hamdi v. Rumsfeld* (2004), that a non-U.S. citizen held in the custody of the U.S. military must be afforded both domestic and international rights as delineated in the Geneva Conventions, why can we not reassess the status of all U.S. prisoners within the *de facto* hybrid domestic and international U.S. criminality and penality? The U.S. government itself has inadvertently led the way.

In calling for a broader application of the category of "political" imprisonment to enable human rights paradigms in U.S. prison work, I am not naive about material and subjective conditions in the United States. I know this strategy alone will fail, especially if we are linking prisoner rights to revolutionary critiques of capitalism and imperialist U.S. practices. The United States, after all, is the world's sole superpower and the largest and most powerful empire in the history of the world, whose people, frankly, have been sufficiently mystified into participating in the continued preservation and extension of this regime because of the real and imagined benefits they derive from the empire. Nor am I being insensitive towards the real, day-to-day struggles of prisoners who rely on appeals to limited but nonetheless tried-and-true civil rights discourses to improve their living conditions and, in some cases, to save their very lives. The recourse to the U.S. judicial system, however biased and imperfect it may be, is especially important in death penalty cases, when time constraints become lethal.

These caveats notwithstanding, I am calling for a return to the 1960s and 1970s era of prisoner rebellions so we can redeploy aspects of the internationalist methodologies—if not necessarily the exact language—of prisoner rights movements. I realize that this move to reclassify domestic prisoners as political prisoners is already often done, sometimes irresponsibly. Joy James presents an important qualification with her admonition that prisoner rights activists recognize that not all prisoners, especially those who continue to participate in exploitative practices, can claim to be "political prisoners" (2003, 11–14). This circumscription duly noted, Alan Eladio Gómez (2006a; 2006b; Chapter 3, in this volume) has shown how prisoner rights movements in the 1960s and 1970s—even those that began as highly localized protests of prison conditions by "common" prisoners—eventually evolved into dialectical materialist and internationalist struggles that not only aligned themselves with internationalist revolutions but also became part of them, both inside and outside the walls of the U.S. prison system.

Gómez reveals that the U.S. detention facility at Guantánamo Bay was not the first prison designed to facilitate the total physical and psychological breakdown of domestic and international political prisoners. It was the Marion Control Unit in Illinois that began torturous behavior modification experiments at the behest of Bertram Brown, chairman of the National Institute of Mental Health. Brown gave direct encouragement to wardens to "undertake a little experiment of what you can do with Muslims"—especially the political activists forcibly relocated to Marion—and then report back for later adaptation to the general prisoner population (Gómez 2006, 63). After the implementation of brainwashing techniques—forcible administration of psychotropic drugs, isolation and sensory deprivation, arbitrary beatings and sanctions, use of rumors and prisoner snitches as well as selective reward system involving pornography—prisoner organizing coalesced around the immediate need to challenge and ultimately stop this organized use of torture. This activism over prisoner conditions segued into the actualization of broader goals being articulated during the era that saw the confluence of third world wars of national liberation and ethnic and racial minority civil rights as well as more mature anticolonial struggles. After all, the Black Power Movement, American Indian Movement, and the ideologically disparate events collectively called the "Chicano Movement" were in full swing at the time. But the most important aspect of this era, Gómez notes, is the simultaneous appeal to both domestic (U.S. Congress and various civil rights organizations like the American Civil Liberties Union [ACLU], Center for Constitutional Rights [CCR], National Association for the Advancement of Colored People [NAACP]) and international bodies, specifically the United Nations. Through aggressive letter campaigns, prisoners won major concessions from the U.S. Bureau of Prisons by exposing how the Marion prison did not meet the United Nations' (UN) "Standard minimum rules for the treatment of prisoners" (Gómez 2006a, 71). Gómez discusses similar successes by prisoners at the Leavenworth federal prison, where prisoners also incorporated simultaneous appeals to domestic organizations like the Black Panthers and the Medical Association for Human Rights "that focused on improving medical conditions for prisoners" (Gómez 2006b, 13).

The value of Gomez's archaeology of this important era in the history of the U.S. carceral, and populist challenges to it, does not solely arise from the prisoners' internationalist politics, but from their *international* strategy. It is important to note that the distinction between "internationalist" and "internationalizing" is deliberate, yet strategic; the call for internationalization of U.S. prisoner rights movements today may not enable prison workers to get beyond the simplistic, and ultimately reformist, civil rights discourses towards a truly revolutionary agenda. (This remains a necessary goal, of course.) But there is an immediate pragmatic dimension that is not inconsistent with this ultimate goal. The appeal to international discourses such as human rights paradigms and, more importantly, the mobilization of international opinion, can again buttress, if not altogether transform, prison activism by providing one more tool that will retain a substantial international currency precisely because of the widely exposed excesses of the war on terror. As the aforementioned public debates on the U.S. war on terror reveal, even capitalists realize that the United States has a human rights problem.

"The Mobilization of Shame": U.S. Prison Work and the Human Rights Paradigm

As Gómez's research reveals, Chicana/o and broader U.S. prisoner appeals to international bodies and human rights standards are not new. After the post-World War II era when the bulk of the relevant human rights and prisoner treatment documents were revised, adopted, or created, Chicana/o prisoners and prisoner rights activists directly and indirectly appealed to international standards for the treatment of prisoners and for the reclassification of *Pintos and Pintas* as political prisoners held under colonial occupation. As polemical and problematic as such blanket claims of political status and the attendant use of the internal colonial model may have been, these early prisoner campaigns were significant for foregrounding a vocabulary of human rights at a time when institutions for the enforcement of human rights were not yet operationalized.[6]

In the groundbreaking 1976 special issue of the Chicana/o cultural nationalist journal *De Colores*, dedicated to Chicana/o prisoners, editors subtitled the edition "*Los Pintos de América*," thereby relocating *Pintas* and *Pintos* to a hemispheric discursive space that enabled them to internationalize Chicano incarceration. The cover design by sociolinguist Fernando Peñaloza is a red, white, and blue watercolor of a perpendicular U.S. flag with the stripes turning into prison bars, behind which stands a Chicano, who exhibits a minimalist pained expression on his face as he reaches through the bars to gaze back at the viewer. The statement by the editor, Anselmo Arellano, further elaborates on the discourse, posing the domestic sphere as a site of containment for the already internationalized Chicana/os, who in fact are also Americanos or Panamericans, "Although the central theme of this issue applies to Pintos behind steel bars, it symbolically refers to all Raza who are held captive by the tentacles of monopolistic corporations and other repressive institutions throughout the Americas—North, Central and South" (4). The term *Pintos* is thus embedded with a simultaneous critique of U.S. imperialism and global capitalism in the Americas. For Chicanos, the domestic and local are simultaneously international and global and vice versa.

In addition to an introduction by Ricardo Sánchez that pairs such disparate historical prisoners as Socrates, Jesus, George Jackson, and Fred Gómez Carrasco, as well as poetry, *testimonios*, and sociological data on Chicana and Chicano prisoners, the special issue of *Los Pintos de América* also carries a prisoner profile of *Pinto* Eddie Sánchez that adumbrates a potential new era for *Pinta/o* human rights work today. Sánchez's story is the epitome of tragedy but it is not unique: he had been institutionalized since the age of three, when his parents were incarcerated for drug use; placed in a juvenile detention center at age ten after being classified as an "incorrigible"; and then subsequently incarcerated in an adult penitentiary at age sixteen after being reclassified as a "sophisticated youth"—all without ever having been charged with any crime! At seventeen, he was sent to Vacaville Prison, the medical facility of the California Department of Corrections. Even though he repeatedly had been certified as sane by prison psychologists, Vacaville Prison administrators ordered a lobotomy for him as retribution for his prisoner activism. To escape the lobotomy, Sánchez had to write a letter to the Secret Service, threatening to kill the U.S. president, in order to get charged with a federal crime and thus be "saved" by being sent to federal prison. But while he was incarcerated in federal prisons in Springfield, Missouri, Leavenworth, Kansas, and Marion, Illinois, Sánchez was subjected to the behavior modification regimens that Gómez describes. *De Colores* reprinted part of Sánchez's complaints of "inhumane treatment" and legal "torture," including the forcible administration of the drug Anectine:

> The first immediate sensation was a tingling sensation all over my body, like when your foot goes to sleep. The next feeling was a heavy feeling on my chest like somebody had dropped a heavy weight on my chest and all the air rushed out of my body. My eyes closed, but I was not asleep. I could not move any part of my body, and I could not breathe at all. I had heard of the drug before, but knew nothing of what to expect. But I did not think it could be anything like what I was experiencing.
>
> I thought the doctor had messed up and given me the wrong thing, or maybe too much of the right thing. I thought I was dying. I want to say something, to tell him I couldn't breathe. But I could not talk or even move or even open my eyes. Then this doctor starts talking to me. He starts talking about knowing what I'm feeling and that it is not pleasant, but it was going to happen to me every time I demonstrated bad behavior in the way of violence. I just wanted some air, not no speech about my behavior. I thought, Oh God, this creep is going to kill me sitting here talking to me when he should be giving me air. Finally after what seemed hours (but was only two minutes) he starts to revive me with air from an oxygen tank. (13)

Significantly, Sánchez's legal strategy involved multiple approaches that sought to expose: (1) *de facto* criminalization of minority populations; (2) extrajudicial punishment and imprisonment of prisoners; (3) guard use of brutal prison regimens that easily qualify as unconstitutional "cruel and unusual punishment"; and (4) legally sanctioned and medically supervised uses of torture techniques deemed illegal by international standards. While the American Civil Liberties Union used Sánchez's testimony in successful lawsuits against the government to end the START behavior modification program, they were never able to save Sánchez from a lifetime of imprisonment.[7] (At the time of the publication, Sánchez was facing four life sentences plus seventy additional years of imprisonment for repeatedly assaulting abusive guards and prison officials responsible for administering his torture and a known informer at Leavenworth prison that guards and administrators used against Sánchez as part of their coordinated behavior modification program.)

Important for this new era of the U.S. carceral, the *De Colores* profile on Eddie Sánchez did *not* invoke an overt appeal to the journal's cultural nationalist and

Marxist discourse that posited all Chicanos as colonial subjects and political prisoners. Rather, the Sánchez profile simultaneously appealed to his civil and human rights, and though the Committee to Free Eddie Sánchez (1976) did not make an explicit call for intervention from international bodies like the United Nations, it deployed a nascent legal vocabulary of human rights even before it had become part of diplomatic discourse.[8] Concurrent with the dawn of the human rights movement, *De Colores* and the Committee to Free Eddie Sánchez presented Sánchez as the quintessential *Pinto*: a *de facto* political prisoner due to the violation of national (e.g., the 1787 Eighth Amendment to the U.S. Constitution outlawing "cruel and unusual punishment") and international standards of prisoner treatment (e.g., 1948 *Universal Declaration of Human Rights*, 1957 *Standard Minimum Rules for the Treatment of Prisoners*, and 1969 International Convention on the Elimination of All Forms of Racial Discrimination), all of which prohibit torture and discrimination. Many other Chicano prisoner rights campaigns made similar discursive appeals that linked prison conditions to a political persecution that was broadened to include torture and the violation of human rights, even for those whose incarceration followed normal domestic legal processes.[9] Guilt was not denied, or even relativized.

Rather, the focus was on brutal prison conditions and torture as a form of political persecution. Many other campaigns were part of multiracial prisoner rights cases, including the rebellions that Gómez has illuminated. On the surface, these prisoner campaigns may appear to be standard grassroots declamations of prejudicial policing, prosecution, and government harassment. But in addition to exposing the long history of the racially biased U.S. justice system, their true value today arises from their implicit and overt invocation of international discourses on human rights that transformed virtually all prisoners in the pre-reform (i.e., pre-1980s) U.S. prison system into internationalized domestic prisoners rather than into political prisoners *per se*.[10] These U.S. prisoners were performing what UN and grassroots human rights activists were simultaneously theorizing pursuant to the establishment of international norms and bodies to define and protect human rights!

The category of political prisoner in this era anticipated and, in a significant way, exceeded the possibilities of the new classification model developed in the "Special International Tribunal on the Human Rights Violations of Political Prisoners/POWs in the USA" held in New York in December 1990. The tribunal's classification sought to expand the use of the term political prisoner by arguing that a political prisoner was: (1) someone imprisoned for overtly political activities; or (2) someone, including prisoners initially convicted of common crimes, who was subsequently subjected to differential treatment while in prison due to political activism.[11] In *Pinto and Pinta* activism from the 1960s and 1970s era of prison rebellions, there was an appeal to the humanity of all prisoners that simultaneously used—but did not overstate or overinvest—the claim to national minority or colonial status of *Pintos and Pintas*. This was not an effacement of their racialized identities, especially given that many prisoners—like Black liberation fighters and their allies (e.g., Ruchell Magee and Marilyn Buck), Puerto Rican *independentistas*, and Chicano nationalists (e.g., Alvaro Hernández Luna)—continue to remain in prison precisely because of their cultural nationalist and anticolonial activities. In an era when U.S. presidents, the U.S. military, and law enforcement agencies have claimed and freely used the term "enemy combatant" to refer to people even suspected of believing in, much less participating in, armed actions against the U.S. government, troops, or civilian population, activists must be wary of donning the cultural nationalist or internationalist mantle in prisoner solidarity cases. To call a prisoner a "revolutionary" could effectively damn them to perpetual incarceration or execution under the *PATRIOT Act* (I and II) and related statutes that deprive them of even a minimal recourse to fair public trials. In an era when armed resistors are always already in danger of being reclassified as "enemy combatants"—witness the immediate end of the campaign to pardon Assata Shakur after the September 11, 2001 attacks—we may be able to more successfully use the international language of human rights in tandem with ongoing prison work based on civil rights claims. (Again, party work will and must continue on its own terms, pursuant to the ultimate goal.)

While this redeployment of a vocabulary to internationalize domestic prisoners is an old strategy, it is important to emphasize that it has potential new uses now that human rights institutions are becoming more mature, strong, and bold enough to challenge even the United States of America (e.g., Amnesty International's 2005 indictment of the U.S. prison at Guantánamo Bay as the "gulag of our times"). Indeed, this simultaneous appeal to civil and international human rights has actually had preliminary but important successes in delaying the execution of Mumia Abu Jamal, even though it has not resulted in a retrial, a pardon, or his release. This multipronged national and international campaign approach, in fact, was the operative model in the groundbreaking *"Critical Resistance"* conferences in 1998 (Berkeley), 2001 (New York), and 2003 (New Orleans), that explored and advocated multiple strategies for intervening into all aspects and levels of the U.S. prison industrial complex. Prison workers really do not have a choice. U.S. prisons and broader domestic political conditions under the war on terror have become so repressive that the critique of U.S. human rights abuses is not mere political sloganeering but a reflection of the real material conditions. Accordingly, the subjective conditions must also be changed.

The *"Critical Resistance"* conferences and follow-up organizing that continues to this day can be seen as both the culmination of, and challenge to, the human rights movement outlined in Paul Gordon Lauren's *The Evolution of Human Rights: Visions Seen* (2003). He traces the centuries-long efforts to establish and implement human rights protocols beginning with antiquity, extending through the eras of slavery, world wars, the Holocaust and related Nuremburg war crimes trials, to the establishment of the United Nations and contemporary attempts to apply the litany of standards delineated in dozens of United Nations conventions, covenants, declarations, treaties, and protocols. Significantly, Lauren (2003) and Donnelly (2003) note that the human rights movement was consolidated in a collaborative effort between grassroots activists, nongovernmental organizations (NGOs), academics, and informal groups and organizations involved in specific human rights campaigns throughout the world. This pragmatic approach distinguishes the human rights movement from the related state terror movement in political science, which is still primarily a descriptive academic enterprise by social scientists. According to Lauren, human rights theorists and workers always have had the goal of intervening in human rights abuse cases through very practical applications of theory (2003, 233).

Any attempt to deploy human rights discourse in U.S. prison work, however, must be cognizant of the trifurcation of human rights theory and activism into isolationist, anticommunist, and Marxist trajectories. With the consolidation of the Universal Declaration of Human Rights in 1948, many countries, including the United States, immediately sought loopholes to subvert the strictures. Their main avenue for subverting enforcement in their own countries has been the national sovereignty clause enshrined in the United Nations Charter in Article 2, which some countries claim protects them from international interventions into their domestic affairs, even in cases where human rights abuses are alleged. Other nations have further perverted the stated intent of promoting the rights of minorities in the Declaration of Human Rights and the UN Charter to claim cultural exceptions. This conflict has emerged in every continent but has been more fully explored under the rubric of the "Asian Values Debate." The main trajectories revolve around claims that international statutes, such as the Universal Declaration of Human Rights, represent an "arrogant universalism" that seeks to impose Western values throughout the world, and equally vociferous retorts that such state resistance to the implementation of a human rights paradigm was based on a "morally vacuous relativism" designed to "justify nondemocratic practices" (Bell, Nathan, and Peleg 2001, 4).

The United States also has been one of the most vociferous nations in efforts to blunt enforcement of international human rights and antitorture statutes within its borders or neocolonial territories. All international treaties, covenants, and declarations must be ratified by two-thirds of the U.S. Congress after they are signed by a United States president in order for them to become applicable domestic law. To date, the United States has signed, but not ratified, the following international statutes:

International Covenant on Economic and Social Rights (1976);
International Covenant on Civil and Political Rights (1976);
International Convention on the Prevention and Punishment of the Crime of Genocide (1951);
International Convention on the Elimination of All Forms of Racial Discrimination (1969);
International Convention on the Elimination of All Forms of Discrimination Against Women (1981); and
International Convention Against Torture and Other Cruel, Inhuman or Degrading Treatment or Punishment (1987).

Furthermore, in May 2002, when President Bush had committed the United States to invading Afghanistan and Iraq, and had already begun the mass arrests and secret detentions of hundreds of Muslim males under provisions in the first USA PATRIOT act, the United States took the extraordinary step of removing its signature from the treaty establishing the International Criminal Court, which had been formed in 1998 to oversee the implementation of international laws enshrined in the above international treaties.[12] The United States, in effect, had become a rogue nation. The United States continues to hypocritically deploy the Geneva Conventions in its unsubstantiated critiques of supposed "human rights violations" in socialist countries and to justify its invasions of Serbia, Somalia, Afghanistan, and Iraq.

These stratagems notwithstanding, human rights standards have become one of the principal operative discourses in the United States and abroad since the implementation of the war on terrorism (e.g., the war was predicated on the presumed existence of weapons of mass destruction that could target civilians). Given that the U.S. war on terrorism has brought increasing international scrutiny and condemnation, even from U.S. allies, the human rights paradigm may offer new opportunities for prison work today.[13]

One of the principal strategic mechanisms in the use of human rights and anti-torture statutes is the "mobilization of shame" (Drinan 2001), the exposure of specific violations through multimedia avenues and juridical mechanisms, that is, both the international courts and the court of public opinion, which sometimes can be even more powerful. Human rights scholars and activists have achieved incredible successes since the Declaration of Human Rights in 1948, and these successes—as well as the failures—have enabled the mapping of an implementation model. Thomas Risse and Kathryn Sikkink (2002) identify the various stages that a human rights campaign is likely to follow, in what they call a "spiral model." They observe five phases in the targeted state's reaction: (1) repression; (2) denial; (3) tactical concessions (cosmetic changes); (4) prescriptive status (i.e., the state's reference to human rights norms to describe its behavior); and (5) rule-consistent behavior. There is a profound dissensus about the current U.S. stage in the post-September 11 human rights campaigns targeting abuses in the war on terror. It could safely be argued that the United States could be in the midst of a combination of all stages but definitely not the last.

The ongoing efforts to enshrine torture techniques, extrajudicial imprisonment, and outright mass surveillance, harassment, and selective repression within the U.S. legal code, correspond to the definition by state terror scholar George Lopez of "national security ideology," that is, "the justification for and maintenance of this patterned and persistent violence by government and against real and presumed adversaries [that] rests in the discrete, identifiable, and self-reinforcing dimensions of a shared mindset of governing elites" (1986, 75). Extending Lopez's examination of Latin American dictatorships from the 1960s to the 1980s, I submit that the protofascist recourse to such an ideology to justify state terror has transformed the United States into the *de facto* "evil empire" it once ascribed to other nations, thereby making a resurgent U.S. human rights movement even more urgently needed.

Toward a *Pinta/o* Human Rights Praxis

How can these past academic and activist interventions into U.S. state terrorism and human rights violations be adapted to domestic prisoner campaigns in the era of the war on terror? First, it must be noted that in this epoch of globalization, the first principle of counterhegemonic organizing revolves around the axiom "act locally, think globally." Accordingly, Thomas Risse and Kathryn Sikkink (2002) argue that "the diffusion of international norms in the human rights area crucially depends on the establishment and the sustainability of networks among domestic and transnational actors who manage to link up with international regimes, to alert Western public opinion and Western governments" (5). They add that these "advocacy networks," needed to coordinate between domestic and international actors seeking to effect a sustainable domestic human rights regime, have three functions:

1. They put norm-violating states on the international agenda in terms of moral consciousness-raising. In doing so, they also remind liberal states of their own identity as promoters of human rights.
2. They empower and legitimate the claims of domestic opposition groups against norm-violating governments and they partially protect the physical integrity of such groups from government repression. Thus, they are crucial in mobilizing domestic opposition, social movements, and NGOs in target countries.
3. They challenge norm-violating governments by creating a transnational structure pressuring such regimes simultaneously "from above" and "from below" (Brysk 1993).

The more these pressures can be sustained, the fewer options are available to political rulers to continue repression (Risse and Sikkink 2002, 5).

While this formulation may appear quite obvious and necessary to many veteran activists, a global and local—or "glocal"—approach still does not inform all prisoner activism today. This is illustrated by the proliferation of legal clinics and institutes, such as the Innocence Project, a nonprofit legal clinic founded in 1992 at the Benjamin N. Cardozo Law School in New York that seeks to uncover buried or missing evidence to prove the innocence of unjustly arrested, convicted, and imprisoned Americans, most of whom are minority males. Like other similar initiatives that have proliferated since the mid-1990s, the Innocence Project uses a campaign approach by marshalling a network of resources and researchers to focus on select cases after their preliminary screening process. Only cases that have clear evidence of police or judicial error or misconduct are taken. While these projects have achieved incredible and well-publicized success that has in turn served to illuminate inherent injustices in the U.S. criminal justice system, they nonetheless rely on appeals to domestic laws that are even more localized by their statutory contexts. No appeals are made to international bodies and the organizations take on only those cases were there is clear police or judicial misconduct or error—that is, the prisoners must be "innocent" of the specific crime for which they were incarcerated.

This does not mean that the "innocence paradigm" is useless to prisoners who do not deny their "guilt" in crimes that led to the incarceration that inevitably transformed them into victims of inhumane treatment and torture, and thus political, or rather, internationalized domestic prisoners. This application of international standards in U.S. prisons is especially relevant in the various "Supermax" prisons that are specifically designed for total surveillance and sensory deprivation. The legal expertise that such projects bring to bear on gross injustices are exactly the skills that need to be utilized, and expanded, toward mastery of international statutes that, I argue, are now in play in all U.S. prisons during the war on terror. But we simply cannot rely on U.S. courts as the principle venues for redress because, as the subversion of *Hamdi v. Rumsfeld* by President Bush and the U.S. Congress reveals, even the U.S. Supreme Court—the highest court in the land—can easily be emasculated by the coordinated efforts of the other two branches of government (with the military by their side), all of which are run by the governing elites that Risse and Sikkink (2002) identify as the agents of the national security rationale for state terror. To further illustrate the point, the Innocence Project would not have helped Eddie Sánchez, who was innocent before going to prison but who, by his own admission, was forced to commit and readily accept guilt in the crime of threatening the president in order to escape a torturous lobotomy ordered for his previous resistance to the brutal regimes of prison.

However, if merged with a domestic version of the Amnesty International prisoner campaigns of the 1980s and 1990s, I believe the "innocence paradigm" might be effectively adapted to the war on terror prisoners, which includes "enemy combatants" and potentially all prisoners in the ever widening net of the U.S. carceral. It must be noted, of course, that Amnesty International "prisoner of conscience" campaigns usually functioned as thinly veiled extensions of Western capitalist hegemony by targeting prisoners in socialist states, with very little attention given to people imprisoned, tortured, and disappeared by western hemisphere dictatorships supported by the United States and other colonial powers. Furthermore, it was not until the late 1980s and early 1990s that Amnesty International began to address the death penalty issue in the United States, and its critiques did not coalesce into charges of gross human rights abuses until the 2005 Amnesty International Annual Report identified the U.S. military prison at Guantánamo Bay as "the gulag of our times." This belated attention to U.S. human rights violations notwithstanding, the Amnesty International "prisoner of conscience" model was highly successful at mobilizing multinational grassroots and institutional (e.g., university and mainstream media) support for select prisoners through its postcard campaigns and attendant teach-ins and cultural programming, which highlighted the given nation's human rights violations. That is, they effectively "mobilized shame" throughout the world to effect local change.

While, to date, Amnesty International has not embarked on a specific U.S. prisoner of conscious campaign—which raises questions about its lingering links to Western imperialist hegemony—its tactics have been utilized in important cases that illuminate the possibilities of this glocal U.S. carceral prisoner approach, specifically the case of imprisoned black nationalist Mumia Abu Jamal. The multimedia, multiorganizational, multinational campaign to free Jamal has involved the mobilization of Hollywood actors, popular musicians, religious orders, grassroots media, French socialists, British antiracists, and a host of community activists who otherwise might never see eye-to-eye on any other issues. This coalescence has supplemented Jamal's own journalistic efforts to save his life, even though it has yet to result in a new trial or a pardon or even a sanction of the United States for state terror and human rights abuses directly linked to this case (e.g., the conflict of interest involving appeals judges, prejudicial trials, and hostile police-community relations involving the Afrocentric MOVE organization, of which Jamal is part).

So with these constraints in mind, what would a *Pinta/o* human rights and U.S. carceral human rights regimen look like? It might involve all of the above—that is, letter writing campaigns, post cards, teach-ins, and so on—which continue to be staples of grassroots organizing. Of course, it also would further deploy technological innovations such as the Internet and text-messaging in an international context. But in this global technologically saturated era, it must not become dependent on class-exclusive technologies that involve computers and expensive electronic equipment but also must include spectacle. Barbara Harlow has discussed how the popular 1990 Special International Tribunal on the Human Rights Violations of Political Prisoners/POWS in the USA, held at Hunter College in New York, included lawyers, musicians, academics, and activists. The tribunal was highly successful in disseminating a broadened definition of "political prisoners," as noted above. Part of the success was the presentation of ideological critiques in populist formats. This was done with even more wide-ranging success during the five-hundred-year anniversary of Christopher Columbus's arrival in the Americas. The Columbus on Trial programming was a series of traveling tribunals that evolved into theatrical, cinematic, poetic and multimedia satire, farce, and even scatological spectacle, all of which was used to deliver biting critiques of colonialism and its contemporary aftermath. The Chicano-Latino comedy troupe Culture Clash even produced a highly popular theatrical production and related video skit, spoofing "discovery" discourses and their racist subtexts. Significantly, the idea behind the admittedly quite belated trial was to empower a people's court to teach the public how to understand and address genocide and, more importantly, to seek redress and prevent a repeat of genocide in the future. Even though these locally produced, very loosely coordinated (and sometimes very uncoordinated) "trials" were not binding anywhere but in the court of public opinion, they both challenged hegemonic discourses and, in many places and among many people, also supplanted them. They became part of the collective consciousness.

Such spectacles of shame and satire are not new in prisoner campaigns. And they are never enough in a world where even nonviolent resistance movements inevitably rely on the violence of their enemies to succeed. We cannot afford to forget that Black South African prisoners were not released en masse until the South African apartheid government was soundly defeated on the battlefield by a multiracial, multinational coalition of Cuban, Angolan, and Namibian troops in the battle of Cuito Canavale in 1988. The point is that the effort to internationalize the domestic U.S. prisoner movement must also involve a variety of alternative strategies and broader goals. A *Pinta/o* human rights regimen is just a start and, perhaps, only a simple stopgap measure. That is, even as I am calling for a hybrid

Pinta/o human rights regimen that already has proven to have some limited successes in previous incarnations, I must be guarded about suggesting a celebratory prescription for a "new" prisoner rights movement. The failure to save the life of former gang member Tookie Williams also serves as a sobering counterpoint to any overzealous prescription for such a glocal approach. Ramsey Muñiz, the former Texas gubernatorial candidate for the Raza Unida Party, is now in his third decade of imprisonment on drug smuggling charges that today would not have yielded even a fraction of the sentence. That is, this internationalization project will not always work. Initially, it will rarely work.

Compounding the difficulties in this call to deploy international statutes in a domestic context are governmental stratagems designs to divest international bodies of their jurisdiction within a given nation. As noted, the United States withdrew from the treaty establishing the jurisdiction of the International Criminal Court shortly after it began its invasion of Iraq and its expansion of the U.S. prison at Guantánamo Bay. The recent Israeli establishment of a team of international lawyers to protect its troops and government officials in the event they are charged with war crimes for their 2006 invasion of Lebanon, or ongoing genocide against Palestinians, suggests that the glocal human rights struggle will be difficult. Indeed, both stratagems were done with the explicit intent of preventing the arrest of U.S. and Israeli military and government officials abroad, as was done to former Chilean dictator Augusto Pinochet, who was arrested while on vacation in Spain in 1998. This danger is particularly real for American officials given the practice of extraordinary rendition whereby citizens of other countries essentially are kidnapped by U.S. troops and shuttled to secret prisons to be tortured. Such a scenario arose in 2007, when the Italian government indicted twenty-six CIA operatives—including one U.S. Air Force colonel—for their role in kidnapping an Egyptian national from Milan in 2003 and flying him to Egypt where he was tortured.[14]

So while legal machinations and mass mobilizations may not be enough, they are necessary preconditions to renewing and remaking a domestic U.S. carceral prisoner rights movement. The key is to internationalize prisoner campaigns while keeping them local. We must show that the new U.S. carceral is in fact inhumane and in regular and deliberate violation of international treaties and norms. As the highly successful "*Critical Resistance*" activists have shown, there are simultaneous targets—from the massive prison building boom to the torture regimens used in the Supermax prisons. Another key is to pair the "political" and "politicized" prisoners with the "common" prisoners, as the conditions for both have steadily merged. The issue at hand is the treatment of human beings, not simply prisoners per se. Again, the aforementioned recent legislation and the ever-widening scope and ever-increasing draconian nature of the war on terror are transforming the entire U.S. carceral, which is making all prisoners within it eligible for protections under international statutes. To be sure, it will be a big battle to seek enforcement of international statutes in the United States and one that will be punctuated by frequent and tragic defeats. The challenge, however, is to internationalize the U.S. prisoner. *Pintos*, *Pintas* and prisoners from the 1960s and 1970s have provided a useful platform for this new era of prison work.

Notes

1. The Geneva Conventions refers to (1) "The Geneva Convention for the Amelioration of the Condition of the Wounded and Sick in Armed Forces in the Field"
   (Geneva 1864); (2) "The Geneva Convention for the Amelioration of the Condition
   of Wounded, Sick and Shipwrecked Members of Armed Forces at Sea" (The Hague,
   1907); (3) The Geneva Convention Relative to the Treatment of Prisoners of War"
   (Geneva, 1929); and (4) "The Geneva Convention Relative to the Protection of Civilian Persons in Time of War" (The Hague, 1949). These resulted in international treaties and were followed by three amendments, subsequently called "Protocols" (1977,
   1977, 2005), governing the treatment of civilians during war.
2. For a discussion of this phenomenon of Latina/o conversions to Islam, see Aidi (2002).
3. In his speech admitting the existence of secret U.S. prisons abroad, Bush noted that
   some prisoners previously held at this location would be sent to Guantánamo Bay in
   preparation for Military Commissions trials and sentencing. He made no mention of
   whether or not the once-secret international prisons would be dismantled.
4. Secretary of Defense Donald Rumsfeld once described Guantanamo Bay Concentration Camp as a "tropical paradise."
5. This number does not include prisoners who became political activists after their
   incarceration (such as Ruchell Magee) or those imprisoned during the war on terror
   (such as Jose Padilla).
6. International human rights covenants and institutions such as the United Nations
   Human Rights Committee did not come into effect until 1976.
7. As Gómez notes, the START program was an acronym for "Special Training and Reha-
   biliation Training." Another such program used an even more Orwellian acronym,
   CARE.
8. Risse and Sikkink note that human rights discourses did not become part of foreign
   policy until the mid-1980s.
9. For information on other prisoner rights campaigns, such as Los Tres de East L.A., see
   Chávez (2002) and García (1995), and Los Siete de San Francisco, see Heins (1972).
10. For an illuminating case study of the pre-reform Texas prison system, see Martin and
    Eckland-Olson (1987).
11. Joy James (2003) has challenged this framework as too inclusive and introduces a
    more detailed taxonomy of different types of political prisoners. For other explica-
    tions of U.S. political prisoners, see Deutsch and Susler (1990).
12. Another motivation for the U.S. withdrawal was the International Criminal Court's
    preparations to levy damages against the U.S. for having mined Nicaraguan harbors
    during the U.S.-funded Contra War against the Sandinista government.
13. Cf. Risse and Sikkink (2002), who provide a history of the human rights movement,
    including its increasing prominence in diplomacy.
14. For details of this case, see Fisher (2007).

References

Aidi, Hisham. 2002. Urban Islam and the war on terror: Amidst media sensationalism over
the capture of American-born jihadis, few are examining why urban youth of color
increasingly gravitate toward Islam. *Colorlines* (Winter). Online Edition, http://www
.colorlines.com

Amnesty International. 2005. *Amnesty International 2005 report: The state of the world's human rights.* London: Amnesty International Publications.

Arellano, Anselmo. "Introduction." In *Los pintos de América. Special issue, De Colores* 3 (1): 4.

Bell, Lynda, Andrew Nathan, and Ilan Peleg. 2001. Introduction: Culture and human Rights. In *Negotiating cultural and human rights,* ed. Lynda Bell, Andrew Nathan, and Ilan Peleg, 3–20. New York: Columbia University Press.

Brysk, Alison. 1993. From above and below: Social movements, the international system, and human rights in Argentina. *Comparative Political Studies* 26 (3): 259–85.

Chávez, Ernesto. 2002. *"Mi Raza Primero!": Nationalism, identity and insurgency in the Chicano Movement in Los Angeles, 1966–1978.* Berkeley: University of California Press.

Committee to Free Eddie Sánchez. 1976. The case of Eddie Sánchez. In *Los pintos de América. Special issue, De Colores* 3 (1): 12–16.

Davis, Angela Y. 2005. *Abolition democracy: prisons, democracy and empire.* New York: Seven Stories.

Deutsch, Michael E., and Jan Susler. 1990. Political prisoners in the United States: The hidden reality. *Social Justice* 18 (3): 92-106.

Donnelly, Jack. 2003. Universal human rights in theory and practice. Ithaca, NY: Cornell University Press.

Drinan, Robert F. 2001. *The mobilization of shame: A world view of human rights.* New Haven: Yale University Press.

Fernandez, Ronald. 1994. *Prisoners of colonialism: The struggle for justice in Puerto Rico.* New York: Common Courage.

Fisher, Ian. 2007. Italy indicts CIA operatives in '03 abduction. *New York Times,* February 17.

Freedman, Dan. 2002. Prison system could be terror breeding ground. *San Antonio Express-News,* June 30.

García, Mario T. 1995. *Memories of Chicano history: The life of Bert Corona.* Berkeley: University of California Press.

Gómez, Alan. 2006a. Resisting living death at Marion Federal Penitentiary, 1972. *Radical History Review* 96 (Fall): 58–86.

———. 2006b. Nuestras vidas Corren casi Paralelas: Aztlán, Independentistas, and the prison rebellions in Leavenworth, 1969–1972. Presented at the *Behind Bars: Latinos and Prisons,* Chicago, Illinois.

Hamdi v. Rumsfeld. 2004. 542 U.S. 507.

Heins, Marjorie. 1972. *Strictly ghetto property: The Story of Los Siete de la Raza.* Berkeley, CA: Ramparts.

Hersh, Seymour. 2004. The gray zone: How a secret Pentagon program came to Abu Ghraib. *New Yorker,* May 24.

James, Joy, ed. 2003. *Imprisoned intellectuals: America's political prisoners write on life, liberation, and rebellion.* Lanham, MD: Rowman & Littlefield.

Lauren, Paul Gordon. 2003. *The evolution of human rights: Visions seen.* Philadelphia: University of Pennsylvania Press.

Lopez, George A. 1986. National security ideology as an impetus to state violence and state terror. In *Government violence and repression: An agenda for research,* ed. Michael Stohl and George A. Lopez, 73–95. New York: Greenwood.

Martin, Steve J., and Sheldon Eckland-Olson. 1987. *Texas prisons: The walls came tumbling down.* Austin: Texas Monthly Press.

Risse, Thomas, Stephen C. Ropp, and Kathryn Sikkink. 2002. "The socialization of international human rights norms into domestic practices: Introduction." In *The power of human rights: International norms and domestic dhange*, ed. Thomas Risse, Stephen C. Ropp, and Kathryn Sikkink, 1–38. Cambridge: Cambridge University Press.

United Nations. 1929/1949. Geneva Conventions 1, 2, 3 & 4. Excerpted in *25+ Human rights documents*. New York: Center for the Study of Human Rights, Columbia University.

United States Congress. 1994. Violent Crime Control and Enforcement Act (Omnibus Crime Bill).

———. 2001. USA Patriot Act (I)

———. 2006. USA Patriot Act II

———. 2006. Military Commissions Act.

Contributors

Erik Camayd-Freixas is Professor of Latin American Literature, Director of the Translation & Interpretation Program, and Director of the Research Initiative on Immigration Reform at Florida International University. He has published and lectured widely on language, literature, and cultural studies. He has interpreted internationally for eight different heads of state, including President Obama and Pope Benedict XVI. Dr. Camayd-**Freixas** was one of sixteen interpreters who served the full two weeks at the Postville, Iowa, hearings after Immigration and Customs Enforcement conducted the largest single-site immigration raid in U.S. history at AgriProcessors, Inc.

Juan Cartagena is a constitutional and civil rights attorney who is presently General Counsel at the Community Service Society, where he litigates cases on behalf of poor communities in the areas of voting rights, housing, employment, and health. A graduate of Dartmouth College and Columbia University School of Law, Mr. Cartagena is a former Municipal Court Judge in Hoboken, New Jersey, and currently lectures on constitutional and civil rights issues at Rutgers University in New Brunswick. A writer on constitutional and civil rights laws, Mr. Cartagena is particularly recognized for his work on the political representation of Puerto Rican and Latino communities.

Mercedes Victoria Castillo works with the *Colectivo Contra las Redadas*, a community group based in Los Angeles with affiliated groups throughout California and the United States. The collective has a hotline where checkpoints and raids are reported and addressed by community members. A graduate of UC Davis Martin Luther King Junior School of Law, she organized legal observer trainings in Northern California in response to the 2006 immigrant rights walkouts and marches. She served as National Vice President of the National Lawyers Guild (2006–8) and is the former Chair of the National Latina/Latino Law Students Association (2004–6).

Juanita Díaz-Cotto is Professor of Sociology, Women's Studies, and Latin American and Caribbean Area Studies (LACAS) and LACAS Director at SUNY-Binghamton. She is the author of *Chicana lives and criminal justice: Voices from el barrio* (2006) *and Gender, ethnicity, and the state: Latina and Latino prison politics* (1996). Under the pseudonym of Juanita Ramos, she is editor of *Compañeras: Latina lesbians* (An Anthology), *Lesbianas latinoamericanas* (3rd ed., 2004) and guest editor of *Sinister Wisdom, volume 74, Latina lesbians* (2008).

Marcia Esparza is Assistant Professor of Latina/o and Latin American Studies at John Jay College of Criminal Justice. From 1997 through 2000, she worked for the United Nations' Guatemalan Truth Commission. Dr. Esparza is the Founding Director of the Historical Memory Project, a resource center documenting state violence and genocide in the Americas. Her edited volume, *State violence and genocide in Latin America: The cold war years* (Routledge, 2009), focuses on uncovering the historical memory of mass violence and genocide in the Americas. Her current research is on state violence against women, particularly women in prison. She is on the Fulbright roster as a Senior Specialist.

Laura E. Garcia is a Spanish interpreter for the Cook County Public Defenders office in Chicago. She is coeditor of *Teatro Chicana: A collective memoir and selected plays* (2008) and editor of the newspaper *Tribuno del Pueblo*, a bilingual publication that gives voice to the poor and to those fighting unjust laws. She lives in Chicago.

Alan Eladio Gómez is a historian and Assistant Professor in the School of Justice & Social Inquiry and a Faculty Affiliate in the Department of Transborder Chicana/o and Latina/o Studies at Arizona State University. He has published articles and interviews in *Radical History Review* and *Latino Studies*, and is currently working on a book about prison rebellions, masculinity, and the politics of U.S. third world radicalism. Dr. Gómez previously taught at Ithaca College and Cornell University.

David Manuel Hernández is Assistant Professor in the César E. Chávez Department of Chicana and Chicano Studies at the University of California, Los Angeles. He is completing a manuscript on immigrant detention, tentatively entitled "Undue process: Immigrant detention, due process, and lesser citizenship." Dr Hernández's research and teaching interests are interdisciplinary and include international migration and Chicana/o and Latina/o politics and social movements.

Rafael Cancel Miranda is a Puerto Rican Nationalist who has fought for the independence of Puerto Rico since his early teens. On March 1, 1954, he and three other Nationalists, including one woman, traveled to Washington, D.C., and assaulted the House of Representatives. They were captured and sentenced to between fifty and sixty years in prison. In September 1979, after an outpouring of international support, President Jimmy Carter released them. Rafael was born in Mayaguez, Puerto Rico.

José Luis Morín is Interim Dean of Undergraduate Studies and Professor in the Latin American and Latina/o Studies Department at John Jay College of Criminal Justice. His areas of specialization include domestic and international criminal justice, civil rights and international human rights, race and ethnicity in the United States, Latina/o studies, and U.S.-Latin America relations. A second edition of his book *Latino/a rights and justice in the United States: Perspectives and approaches* will be released in 2009, with a forward by Professor Richard Delgado.

Suzanne Oboler is Professor of Latin American and Latino/a Studies at John Jay College of Criminal Justice. She is founding editor of the journal *Latino Studies* and coeditor-in-chief of *The Oxford encyclopedia of Latinos and Latinas in the United States.* Among her publications are *Ethnic labels, Latino lives: Identity and representation in the United States,* the edited anthology *Latino/as and citizenship,* and *neither enemies nor friends: Latinos, Blacks, Afro-Latino* (co-edited with Anani Dzidzienyo). She is currently co-editing, with Deena J. Gonzalez, the *Oxford Encyclopedia of Latino/as, Politics and the Law* (2 volumes).

B. V. Olguín is Associate Professor of Literature and Creative Writing at the University of Texas at San Antonio. He is a published poet and translator and is a researcher in Latin American and U.S. Latina/o studies. His book *La Pinta: History, culture and ideology in Chicana/o prisoner discourse* is forthcoming from the University of Texas Press. He is currently working on a book on Chicana/o war narratives.

Victor M. Rios is Assistant Professor of Sociology at the University of California, Santa Barbara. He is a former gang member and juvenile ward. He conducts research on youth culture, the criminalization of youth, and youth social movements with this experience in perspective. Victor is currently writing a book on the criminalization of inner-city youth.

raúlrsalinas (March 17, 1934 - February 13, 2008), Xicanindio elder, poet, and human rights activist, was the executive director of Red Salmon Arts and founder of Resistencia Bookstore—a literary venue and community center for aspiring writers in Austin, Texas. Raúl conducted intensive creative writing clinics locally and throughout the country with disenfranchised youth. For five decades, he worked extensively with the American Indian Movement and the International Indian Treaty Council as well as with numerous national and international organizations. Raúl authored four books of poetry and three spoken-word CDs. In 2006, Dr. Louis Mendoza edited *Raulrsalinas and the jail machine: My weapon is my pen,* a collection of his letters, essays, and newspaper articles. He was a beloved mentor to many artists, writers, and scholar-activists who sought to make a difference beyond the academy.

Laurie Schaffner is Associate Professor in the Sociology Department and the Department of Criminology, Law, and Justice at the University of Illinois at Chicago. Her research focuses on gender, youth, sexuality, and the law. She is the author of *Girls in trouble with the law* (Rutgers University Press, 2006). She was a 2007–08 Fulbright-Garcia Robles scholar at the Universidad de Guadalajara, Jalisco, Mexico.

Víctor Alejandro Sorell is University Distinguished Professor of the Social History of Art and Associate Dean of the College of Arts & Sciences at Chicago State University. He was on the executive committee of the exhibition project, Chicano Art: Resistance and Affirmation, 1965–1985, and a founding member of el Movimiento Artístico Chicano in Chicago. Among his recent publications are *Carlos Cortéz Koyokuikatl: Soapbox artist and poet* (2001), an interpretive exhibition catalog, and a forthcoming coedited anthology, *Born of resistance: Cara a Cara encounters with Chicana/o visual culture.* His current research includes cultural criminological practices of tattooing and pictorial renderings on handkerchiefs by incarcerated Latino/as.

Gabriel Torres-Rivera is Director of the Reentry Initiative at the Community Service Society. Since 2000, he has worked at CSS, heading its nonpartisan voter registration campaign and directing the effort to register disadvantaged people in New York, focusing on the formerly incarcerated, immigrants, and low-wage earners. Since 2005, he has directed the Reentry Initiative at CSS. Torres-Rivera has also worked with the Center for Constitutional Rights focusing on police brutality in New York and nationally. He has served as a spokesperson for Amnesty International, speaking at nineteen colleges and universities throughout Europe. He holds a Juris Doctor degree from the Law School at Queens College, CUNY.

Dicxon Valderruten is Director of Health Education at the Osborne Association, a nonprofit organization in the field of criminal justice in New York. He has worked on health, prison, and community issues since 1991. He is a member of the Board of Directors of the New York AIDS coalition and lectures and teaches courses on health problems in urban communities at the Borough of Manhattan Community College in New York City.

Index

Abu-Ghraib prison, 41
  torture at, 61n3
academia
  cultural obstacles in, 182–83
  intellectual institutionalization in, 243–44
Adams v. Carlson, 85, 91n45, 221n2
  raúlrsalinas and, 215–16
affirmative action, Wilson's attacks on, 105
AFL-CIO v. Chertoff, 170
African American women
  incarceration rate for, 19, 182–83
African Americans
  carceral continuum and, 19–20
  community muralism and, 193
  criminal justice system and, 72
  criminalization/dehumanization of, 5, 10, 18
  de jure/de facto segregation and, 17, 22
  double consciousness of, 115
  and Fannie Lou Hamer, Rosa Parks, and Coretta Scott King Voting Rights Reauthorization and Amendments Act of 2006, 134
  history of, prison literature and, 134
  incarceration rate for, 12n2, 24, 34n3, 54, 100, 141
  Jim Crow racism and, 72–73
  Latino alliances with, 4, 8, 73, 217, 241
  law enforcement and, 22–23
  in López Rivera's art, 196
  mass imprisonment of, 2, 17–18
  prison industrial complex and, 87
  in prison studies, 251, 253
  prison violence and, 71
  resistance by, 72, 85
  sentencing bias and, 27–28
  Voting Rights Act and, 6
  war on drugs and, 25–26, 54
  war on terror and, 42

Agriprocessors raid. *See* Postville raid; Postville workers
Aguilera, Manuel, 81
AIDS education, prisoner empowerment and, 7
Albizu Campos, Pedro, 75, 194–95, 209n17, 232
Alderson, women's unit of, 72
Aldrete, Abel, 81
Alexander, Myrl, 74
Alford plea, for Postville workers, 165
Allende, Salvador, 217
alliances. *See* prisoner interethnic alliances
American Baptist Churches v. Thornburgh, 58
American Civil Liberties Union, 3, 58, 267
  Ricardo Sánchez and, 269
American Indian Movement, 222n3
  and "Cultural History of the Southwest" class, 79
  Cumpián and, 204
  in interethnic prison alliances, 74, 80
  raúlrsalinas and, 213, 217–18
  visual culture in name of, 200–204
American Indians. *See* American Indian Movement; Native Americans
American Indians, genocide of, 71
American Indian struggles, raúlrsalinas and, 217
Amnesty International
  death penalty campaign of, 275
  on Guantanamo Bay imprisonment, 265
Anglo-Saxonism, racial, 20
Angueira, Katherine, 242
anti-immigration sentiment
  and national security, 55
  See also immigration; immigration law; immigration system
Antiterrorism and Effective Death Penalty Act (AEDPA), 55

Index by Suzanne Sherman Aboulfadl.

antiterrorism legislation, 55. *See also* war
   on terror
Arellano, Anselmo, 268
Arrellanes, Alfredo, 81
art
   as resistance, 8–9
   See also prison art
arts-in-corrections, 192
Ashcroft, John, 40
assimilation
   as civil and cultural death, 84
   as extinction, 83
assimilation (*continued*)
   language and, 114. *See also* language, as
      resistance by Latina adolescents;
      language, as survival tool
   resistance to, 83
asylum adjudications
   inconsistency in, 47
   politicized, 54
   post-9/11 suspension of, 42
Attica prison rebellion, 67, 240
Avila, Modesta, 265
Aztlán (nation), 80, 82–83
Aztlán (newspaper), 70, 78, 89n19, 187, 230
   end of, 84
   goals and impact of, 80–82

backyard colonialism, raúlrsalinas on, 214
Bacon, Francis, 198
Balderrama, Francisco E., 53
Balzac v. Puerto Rico, 21
Bedford Hills Correctional Facility, case
   study of Latina prisoners in, 250–52
behavior modification experiments
   ACLU lawsuit and, 269
   in Marion Prison, 230, 267
Beisswenger, Don, 195, 199–200
Bell, Herman, 230
Beltrán, Haydee, 232
Bender, Steven, 42
Bennett, James V., 73
Bennett, William, 101–2
Bermudez, José, 194
bilingual education, opposition to, 118–19
bilingualism
   advantages of, 120–21, 124
   staff need for, 250–51
   See also language
black Americans. *See* African Americans

black youth, superpredator
   characterizations of, 101
Blair House, armed demonstrations at,
   76. *See also* Cancel Miranda, Rafael;
   Collazo, Don Oscar; Figueroa
   Cordero, Andrés; Flores, Irving;
   Lebrón, Lolita; Torresola, Griselio
Bono v. Saxbe, 85
Boricua. *See* Puerto Rican
   Independentistas; Puerto Rico;
   Puertorriqueños
Borofsky, Jonathan, 192
Bosch, Orlando, 74, 89n14
Brennan, William, 1
Brown, Bertram, 267
Brown, Claude, 240
Brown v. Board of Education, 22
Buck, Marilyn, 270
   reclassification as political prisoners, 266
Bukhari, Safiyah, 196
Bush administration
   homeland security and, 40
   national security doctrine of, 7
Bush, George W., 264, 272

Cabral, Amilcar, 77
California
   English-only initiative in, 118
   felon disfranchisement in, 138–39
   Proposition 21 in. *See* Proposition 21
Campos, Albizu, 194, 195, 232
Cancel Miranda, Mario, 89n19
Cancel Miranda, Rafael, 8, 11, 67, 68,
   74–76, 81, 194
   interview with, 227–33
   on Iraq, 232–33
   poems of, 235–36
   raúlrsalinas and, 227–28
   transfer to Marion, 84
   See also Lebrón, Lolita; political
      prisoners
Cancel Rodríguez, Rafael, 232
Cantú, Mario, 77, 79, 81
   after Leavenworth, 79
   release of, 85
carceral continuum
   African Americans and, 19–20
   concept of, 145
   in U.S. prison system, 20
Cardinal, Roger, 192, 194

Cartagena, Juan, 6
Carter, Jimmy, and release of Puerto Rican
   nationals, 227
case studies, of Chicano/a or Latino/a
   prisoners, 246–52
Castañeda, Antonia, 76, 216
Castillo, Nando, 81
Central America, refugees from, 53–54
Centro de la Raza, El, 73
   raúlrsalinas and, 217
Chacon, Ramon Raúl, 77
   after Leavenworth, 79
   release of, 85
Chávez, César, 193
Chávez, Francisco, 78
checkpoints, driver's license, 151–53
Chicano Pinto Research Project, 248
Chicano prisoners, in Leavenworth, 4–5
Chicano Prisoners, 246–48
Chicano/a or Latino/a prisoners
   case studies of, 246–52
   ethical and methodological research
      considerations, 239–59. *See also*
      research ethics and methodologies
   groups studied, 241–42
   See also Latino/a prisoners
Chicano/a movement, 91n38
Chicano/a prisoners
   arguments for reclassification of, 266
   in international context, 265–66
Chicano-*Independentista* collaboration,
   74–77
Chicanos Organizados Rebeldes de Aztlán,
   68, 70
   by-laws of, 88n4
   formation and objectives of, 82–85
   origin of name, 91n39
children, of detainees, 61n7, 62n10
Chin, Gabriel, 50
citizenship rights
   loss of, 6
   See also felon disfranchisement
civic engagement, mass incarceration and,
   133–48
civil death, 135–36
civil liberties
   legislation curtailing, 261–62
   war on drugs and, 261
civil liberties groups, prisoner rights and,
   267

civil rights movement
   Mexican American, 72
   prison literary output and, 193
Clark, Ramsey, 202
Clear, Todd, 135
Cleaver, Eldridge, 240
Clinton, Bill
   Independentistas pardoned by, 266
Cole, David, 26, 49
Collazo, Don Oscar, 68, 74–76, 75, 231
   Blair House armed demonstration and,
      76
   See also political prisoners
Colson, Charles, 263
community muralism, 193–94
Community Service Society
   reentry and, 143
Cook County, Court Interpreters' Office
   of, 158
Cook County Jail, language issues in,
   155–58
C.O.R.A. *See* Chicanos Organizados
   Rebeldes de Aztlán
corrections institutions
   private, 49
   See also prisons; specific prisons
Cortéz Koyokuikatl, Carlos, 201, 204
counsel, prisoner's right to, 157
Court Interpreters' Office, Cook County,
   158
crime(s)
   deportable and detainable: court
      systems involved in, 61n5
   expanded list of, 50, 54
   fear of, 24
   media and, 18
   nonviolent, percentage of persons
      sentenced for, 24–25
   in Proposition 21, 100
   racialization of, 2
   social scientists' role in, 83–84
   violent, drop in, 30
   youths and, 30
crime policies
   impacts of, 24–26
   and media, 24
   See also war on crime
crime rate, decline in, 24
crime victims, racialized, 24
Crime Victims United of California, 99

criminal aliens, detention of, 54–55
criminal class, Durkheim on function of, 105–6
criminal convictions, joblessness and, 144
criminal justice system
  Latinos in, lack of statistics on, 145n6
  See also juvenile justice system; law enforcement; mass imprisonment; police officers; prison industrial complex; prison system; Proposition 21; sentencing bias/policies
"crimmigration crisis," 42
"crimmigration law," 3
Critical Resistance conferences, 271–72
Cruz, Frances Jalet, 73
Cruz, Fred, 73
Cuban *marielitos*, 53
Cuban migrants, detention of, 57
"Cultural History of the Southwest" class, 75, 90n26
cultural identity, Latino, 76
culture, solidarity and, 5
Cumpián, Camilo, 193
  background and art of, 204, 205f

Davidson, R. Theodore, case study by, 246–48
Davis, Angela, 43, 135, 261, 263
death penalty, AI campaign against, 275
Delgado, Ángel, 193, 204–7, 207f, 210n40, 210n41, 210n42
delinquency
  Chicago School's social disorganization theory of, 114–15
  conversion to serious crime, 102–3
  See also Latina juvenile prisoners
Department of Homeland Security, detention capacity of, 45
deportation campaigns, historical perspective on, 59
deportations, Mexican, 62n14
detainees
  children of, 61n7, 62n10
  See also Postville workers
detention. *See* immigrant detention
detention centers
  privatization of, 49
  riots at, 56–57
  and treatment of detainees, 46–47

Deutsch, Michael, 214, 231
Díaz-Cotto, Juanita, 9, 72
  case study by, 250–52
Dilulio, John, 101–2
Dimas, Marcos, 193
disfranchisement, felon. *See* felon disfranchisement
disproportionate minority representation, 116
dissent
  criminalization of, 86
  pedagogies of, 78–80
  See also prison rebellions; resistance
Dobbs, Lou, 30
Dostoyevsky, Fyodor, 208n2, n13
Dow, Mark, 32
driver's license checkpoints, 151–53
drug abuse, HIV/AIDS and prison connections to, 175–80
drug laws
  mandatory, 86
  See also war on drugs
drug wars, political ploys and, 6
DuBois, W. E. B., 115
Dunn, Timothy, 46, 54
Durkheim, Emile, 105–6
Dzidzienyo, Anani, 12

Earnings Suspense File, and confiscated undocumented worker contributions, 171–72
education
  about HIV/AIDS. *See* Prisoners for AIDS Counseling and Education
  bilingual, 118–19
  demands for changes in, 89n25
  elite system of, 176
  immigrant dislocation and, 124
  prisoner reentry and, 7, 33
  reduced social spending on, 105
  society's neglect of, 10, 143, 179, 244, 250
  voter education, 143–44
  See also prison education programs; self-education
Elvey, Maggie, Proposition 21 and, 99
employment
  civic engagement and, 144
  difficulties after incarceration, 143
  felony/criminal records and, 144

illegal, 172
   unequal opportunity in, 81
   use of false ID for acquiring, 168, 178
   See also Postville workers;
      undocumented workers
empowerment
   health/AIDS education and, 7, 176
   through self-education, 4–5
enemy combatant(s), 59
   dangers posed by classification as, 271
   José Padilla as, 41, 263–64
   legal implications of, 10
   legal protections denied to, 262, 266
   post-9/11 detention of, 56
Escobar, Edward J., 72
Escobar, Elizam, 189, 192, 194, 204, 208n2
   background and art of, 196–99, 198f
   and Clinton's commutation of sentence,
      199
   paños of, 189–90
   political activity of, 209n20, n21
Estrella, Ruben, 81
ethics code
   for court interpreters, 158
   See also research ethics and
      methodologies
Ewing, Walter, 42

familialism, 122
   Chicano, 250
   unity of, and Latina offenders, 115
Fannie Lou Hamer, Rosa Parks, and
   Coretta Scott King Voting Rights
   Reauthorization and Amendments
   Act of 2006, 134
Fanon, Frantz, 77
Farrakhan v. Washington, 138, 140
fear, appeals to, 2
federal courts, undocumented workers
   and, 7
Federal Prisoners for Freedom of
   Expression Committee, 84
felon disfranchisement
   as barrier to rehabilitation, 138
   in California, 138–39
   challenges to, 6
   countries outlawing, 136
   effects on black community, 137
   in Florida, 140–41
   joblessness and, 143–45

Latino prisoner activism and, 137–38
   in New York, 139
   state laws on, 135–36
   in Texas, 139
   voter education about, 143
felony convictions
   trades/professions closed due to, 144
   voting rights and, 133–34, 137
felony status, property damage and, 98
Fernandez, Ronald, 265
Figueroa Cordero, Andrés, 68, 74, 81, 231
Florence State Prison, 73
Flores, Antonio, 81
Flores, Irving, 68, 74–76, 231
Florida, felon disfranchisement in, 140–41
Fong Yue Ting v. United States, 50–51
Franklin, H. Bruce, 193, 208n4
Freedman, Dan, 263
Frente Contra las Redadas, 153
Frente Unido por la Defensa de los Presos
   Politicos Puertorriqueños of New
   York, 84–85
Frost, Robert, 1, 2

Galán, Mario, 194
gang-enhancement sentencing, 97
Garcia, Laura, 7
García, María Cristina, 54, 57
Garland, David, 105
gay, bisexual, and transgender issues,
   prison education about, 177
Gender, Ethnicity, and the State, 250–52
Geneva Conventions, 278n1
   Article 3 of, 263
   infringements of, 10–11
   and loss of prisoner rights, 264–65
   Third, protections of, 266
genocide, of American Indians, 71
"get tough" legislation
   methodology in study of, 98–100
   See also Proposition 21; war on crime;
      war on drugs
ghettoization, 23
Gilmore, Ruth Wilson, 10
Gómez Carrasco, Fred, 266
Gómez Eladio, Alan, 11, 267–68
   on prison self-education, 4–5
   raúlrsalinas interview of, 8
Gonzáles, Rodolfo "Corky," 193, 230
González Claudio, Avelino, 232

"Greaser Act," 21
Greenhaven, 72
Groder, Martin, 215
Guantánamo Bay Prison, 41
  and denial of legal rights and, 56
  U.S. precursors of, 267
Guatemalan asylum-seekers, 58
Guatemalan refugees, 53–54. *See also*
  Postville workers; undocumented
  workers
Guerra, Lolo, 81
guilty plea
  collateral consequences of, 144–45
  in Postville ICE raid, 165
gun-enhancement sentencing, 97
Gutiérrez, Andy, 78
Guttentag, Lucas, 3

habeas corpus protections, *Military
  Commissions Act* and, 264
Hagan, John, 49
Haley, Alex, 240
Hamdi, Yasser, 262
Hamdi v. Rumsfeld, 262–63, 264, 275
Hamer, Fannie Lou, 134
Harjo, Joy, 214
Harlow, Barbara, 276
hate crimes, 3
health education, prisoner empowerment
  and, 7
Hernández, Jesse, 81
Hernández, Orlando, 210n39
Hernández Luna, Alvaro, 266, 270
Hernández v. Texas, 22
Hersh, Seymour, 264
Hillman, Grady, 192
HIV/AIDS
  and education about gay, bisexual, and
    transgender issues, 177
  in ethnic minority communities, 175–80
  incarceration and, 175–80
  mentoring and, 178–79
  Prisoners for AIDS Counseling and
    Education program and, 176–79
HIV/AIDS education, prisoner
  empowerment and, 7, 176–80
Homeboys, 248–50
homeland security. *See* U.S. Department of
  Homeland Security
Huerta, Dolores, 193

human rights
  appeals to, 271
  and mobilization of shame, 268–73
  pinta/o. *See* pinto/a human rights
  prisoner loss of, 264–65
human rights advocacy
  functions of, 274
  "glocal" approach to, 274–75
  spiral model of, 273
human rights movements, prison
  rebellions and, 69
human rights protocols, U.S. rejection of, 11
human rights standards, 9–11, 268, 273
human rights theory, in U.S. prison work,
  265
human rights violations, at Marion Prison,
  84–85

Ianni, Francis A. J., 244
identity, development of, forced
  immigration and, 124
identity theft
  bogus charges of, in Postville ICE raid,
    166–72
  Congressional establishment of, 168–69
*Illegal Immigration Reform and Immigrant
  Responsibility Act* of 1996, 55, 116–17
illegality, statutory notions of, 53
immigrant advocacy, before 9/11, 40–41
immigrant detention, 39–66
  contesting, 56–58
  of criminal aliens, 54–55
  expanded goals of, 49
  and expanded list of deportable and
    detainable crimes, 50
  facilities for, 46
  gross mistreatment in, 46
  as growth industry, 49
  history of, 39–40
  ICE rates for, 32
  *Illegal Immigration Reform and
    Immigrant Responsibility Act* of
    1996 and, 55
  lack of standards for, 46–47
  lack of statistics on, 47–48
  Latino/a, 43–45; contextualizing, 59–61;
    genealogy of, 52–55
  length of, 48–49
  medical, 52
  of non-Latino/a groups, 59

"Operation Wetback" and, 53
practices of, 45–49
racialized features of, 39
of refugees, 53–54
subtext to, 49–51
See also Postville raid; Postville workers
immigrant rights, organizations
    supporting, 58
immigrants
    criminalization of, and war on terror, 7
    hysteria about, 3
    incarceration rates for, 30–31
    prisons and, 30–32
    racialization and demonization of, 3
    undocumented, 62n11; misconceptions
        about, 44
    war on, exceptionalism and, 40–43
immigration
    forced, identity development and, 124
    violent response to, 4
Immigration and Nationality Act, 45
Immigration and Naturalization Service
    numbers of noncitizen deportations by,
        126n3
    See also U.S. Immigration and Customs
        Enforcement (ICE)
immigration law
    absence in law curriculum, 3
    and criminal law, 54, 56
    after 9/11, 32
    after 1996, 60
    sociopolitical context of, 43
immigration system
    criminalization of, 3
    lack of legal protections in, 50–51
    Latino(a) incarceration and, 3
imperialism, U.S., Leavenworth rebellions
    and, 74–77
incapacitation
    defined, 100
    of inner-city youth, 107
incarceration
    HIV/AIDS and, 175–80
    See also prison industrial complex;
        prison system; prisoners; prisons;
        specific prisons
incarceration rates
    African American, 12n2, 24, 34n3, 54,
        100, 141
    ethnic/racial breakdown of, 134–35

ethnic/racial inequities in, 239–40
growth since 1972, 86
Latino, top states, 138–41
in promotion of crime rate, 135
Inda, Jonathan, 55
Indians. *See* American Indian Movement;
    Native Americans
Innocence Project, 274–75
institutionalization, post-release impacts
    of, 254. *See also* prisoner reentry
Insular Cases, 21
*Intelligence Reform and Terrorism
    Prevention Act*, 49
International Criminal Court, U.S.
    withdrawal from, 273, 277, 278n12
interpreters
    in Cook County Jail, 155–58
    ethics code for, 158
    police officers as, 156
    after Postville raid, 159–73
Irwin, John, 239
isolation practices, legal challenges to, 85
I Wor Kuen, 217, 222n3

Jackson, George, 72, 81, 214, 229, 240
    murder of, 67
Jacobs, James B., 239
Jamal, Mumia Abu, 271, 275–76
    reclassification as political prisoner, 266
James, Joy, 266–67
Japanese Americans, incarceration of,
    61n7
Jericho movement, 265
Jim Crow, 19–20
joblessness
    felon disfranchisement and, 143–45
    See also employment
jobless rate, for black/Latino men, 143
Johnson, Kevin, 40, 60
judicial protections, limitations on, 60
justice, race and, 100–101
juvenile crime agenda, political and media
    factors in, 101
juvenile justice system
    facilities for, 118
    Latinas in, 115–17
    1990s changes in, 98
    and perceptions of Latino(a)s, 5
    superpredator concept and, 101–2
    See also Proposition 21

juvenile offenders
    Latina. *See* Latina juvenile prisoners
    language and cultural resistance among,
        113–31. *See also* bilingualism;
        language, as resistance
    racialization of, 107
juvenile offenses
    classification of, before Proposition 21,
        99–100
    "entangled" references to, 99–100
    nonviolent percentage of, 103
    sentencing for, after Proposition 21, 102–3
    See also Proposition 21

Kahlo, Frida, 197
Kahn, Robert, 46
Khan, Irene, 265
Kimmel, Adele, 46
King, Coretta Scott, 134
King, Rodney, 23
King, Ryan, 54

language
    and Latina resistance and solidarity, 118–23
    Leavenworth rebellion and, 75
    of research reporting, 244
    as resistance by Latina adolescents,
        89n18, 113–31, 126
    solidarity and, 5
    as survival tool, 124–25
    as window into different realities, 201
    See also bilingualism
language barriers, conventional
    scholarship on, 114–15
language issues, in Cook County Jail,
    155–58
Latin America, U.S. relations with, 5–6
Latin Americans, negative depictions of,
    20–21
Latina adolescents
    language and cultural resistance among,
        113–31
    resettlement difficulties of, *versus* male
        difficulties, 125
    in U.S. and in court involvement,
        115–17
Latina juvenile prisoners, 5
    backgrounds of, 117–18
    and culturally insensitive facilities,
        124–25

    disproportionate minority
        representation of, 116–17
    lack of research on, 114
    marginalization of, 114
    parental death and, 123
    research among, 117–18
    resistance and solidarity of, 118–23
    and transition from victimization, 125–26
Latinas
    stereotyping of, 182
    war on drugs and, 26
Latinas United for Justice, 181–83
Latina prisoners
    barriers to raising awareness of, 184
    at Bedford Hills Correctional Facility,
        case study of, 250–52
    Latinas United for Justice outreach to,
        181–83
    research on, 7
    statistics on, 26
"Latina Women in Prison" seminar, 181
Latino/a culture, sleeping arrangements
    and, 123
Latino/a identity
    C.O.R.A. and, 83
    creation of, 80
Latino/a joblessness, invisibility of, 133
Latino/a politics, emergence of, 70
Latino/a prisoners
    alternative classifications of, 265
    ethical and methodological research
        considerations, 239–59. *See also*
        research ethics and methodologies
    at Green Haven Correctional Facility,
        case study of, 250–52
    incarceration rates for, 17. *See also*
        incarceration rates
    invisibility of, 1
    lack of research on, 9
    population upsurge, 18–23
    research on informal networks of, 241
    survival strategies of, 7
    versus whites, 19
Latino/a youth
    and crime, 30
    and juvenile gangs, 30
    and Proposition 21. *See* Proposition 21
    superpredator characterizations of, 101
    See also juvenile justice system; juvenile
        offenders; juvenile offenses

Latino/a-African American alliances, 4, 8, 73, 217, 241
Latino/as
  criminalization of, 18, 21, 41; media and, 29
  de facto segregation of, 17
  de jure segregation of, 17, 22
  demonization of, 11
  doctoral degrees for, 184n3
  drug use by, 25
  immigrant status or relationships of, 44
  incarceration rate for, 2–3, 12n2. *See also* incarceration rates
  negative media images of, 2
  parental authority and, 125
  as percentage of U.S. population, 115–16
  post-9/11 targeting of, 42
  racialized status of, 22
  as threat to social order, 5, 6–7
  U.S.-born: percentage of, 4; *versus* foreign-born, 31
  and violent offense charges, 30
law enforcement
  immigrant detention as tool for, 45
  racism of, 22
  and treatment of people of color, 28–29
  See also police officers; Proposition 21
leadership role models, 254
League of United Citizens to Help Addicts, 248
Leavenworth
  Chicano prisoners in, 4–5
  conditions at, 74
  history of, 74
  pedagogies of dissent and, 78–80
  Puerto Rican *Independentistas in*, 4–5
Leavenworth prison rebellions, 67–96, 88n5
  context/background of, 71
  exchanges with outside activists, 79
  See also prison rebellions
Lebrón, Lolita, 76, 193–94, 231
legal counsel, lack of immigrants' right to, 47
liberation movements, prison rebellions and, 240
Lindh, John Walker, 262
literature, prison, 192
lockdowns, legal challenges to, 85
López, George, 273

López, Haney, 28
López, Oscar, 232
López Rivera, Oscar, 192, 194
  background and art of, 194–96, 195f
  Clinton's commutation of sentence of, 199
López Tijerina, Reies, 200
Los Angeles Police Department
  and Latino/a rights, 6–7
  terror tactics of, 72
Lucero, Judy, 266

MacDonald, Heather, 60
Madriz, Esther, 182
Magee, Ruchell, 270, 278n5
Magón, Enrique, 77
  reclassification as political prisoner, 266
Magón, Ricardo Flores, 77, 89n20
  reclassification as political prisoner, 266
Malcolm X, 240
Manifest Destiny, 20
Mares, Alberto, 81, 88n5
  release of, 85
marielitos, 53
Marín, José D., 81
Marion Prison, behavior modification/torture in, 84, 215, 230, 267
Marshall, Thurgood, 138
Martínez, Roberto, 41
mass imprisonment
  community impacts of, 135
  defined, 19
  impacts of, 9
  Latino civic engagement and, 133–48
  as Latino issue, 134–35
  of Latino/as and African Americans, 17–18
  proposals for reversing, 33
  racially nonuniform rates of, 18–19
  war on drugs/crime control agendas and, 100
Mauer, Marc, 54
McNeil Island Federal Penitentiary, 72, 74
media
  crime policies and, 24
  and criminalization of Latino/as, 2, 29
  and drop in violent crime, 30
  juvenile crime agenda and, 101
  in promoting fear of crime, 18
medical detention, 52, 62n13

Mendez v. Westminster School District of Orange County, 22
Mendoza, Louis, 213, 215
mentoring
  egalitarian approach to, 181–83
  in PACE program, 178–79
  prisoner reentry and, 7–8
mentors
  role of, 7
  women, need for, 7–8
Mexican American civil rights movement, 72
Mexican American Legal Defense and Education Fund, immigration legislation and, 32
Mexican American Self Help group, 72–73
Mexican Americans, as percentage of U.S. population, 115–16
Mexican Mafia, 104
Mexicans, discrimination against, 22
Military Commissions Act, 261–62, 264
Miller, Teresa A., 39
Miranda, Anthony, 29
Miranda, Ernesto, 156
Miranda, Marie "Keta," 246
Miranda rights, 156–57
  education about, 158
Miranda v. Arizona, 156
Mirandé, Alfredo, 21, 248
Molina, Natalia, 52
Montoya, Daniel, 81
Moore, Joan W., case study by, 248–50
moral poverty, 101–2
Morales, Marciano, 78
Morris, William Wayne, 88n10
Movimiento Chicano/a, El, 193
Muñiz, Ramsey, 277

Nation of Islam, and challenges to prison racial discrimination, 240
National Association of Judicial Interpreters and Translators, 158
national security
  anti-immigration sentiment and, 55
  supposed threats to, 60
national security ideology, 273
Native Americans
  criminalization of, 255n4
  in Cumpián's art, 204
  dehumanization of, 10
  genocide of, 71

"Greaser" Act and, 21
Guatemalans as, 160, 164
in interethnic alliances in prison rebellions, 68–69, 73–75, 85, 89n19
jails under jurisdiction of, 17
Jim Crow racism and, 72
Justice Department statistics on, 34n1
raúlrsalinas and, 213–17
Voting Rights Act challenges by, 138, 140
war on drugs and, 25
See also Peltier, Leonard
Neruda, Pablo, 81
New Jersey State Conference NAACP v. Harvey, 138
New York
  felon disfranchisement in, 139
  prisoner residency policies in, 141–43
  women prisoners of color in, 183
Ngo, Viet Mike, 256n9
Nicaraguan refugees, 53–54
Nimr, Heba, 58
9/11
  civil liberties effects of, 10
  immigration law and, 32, 60
  Latino immigrant detention and, 39–40
  U.S. social transformations after, 261
Nixon, Richard M., war on crime and, 261

Office of Detention and Removal, 48
Oller, Francisco, 197
Omnibus Crime Bill (1994), 261
"Operation Wetback," 22
  detention and, 53
Oquendo, Angel, 21
oral documentation
  in case studies, 252–53
  collaborative research and, 242–43
  forms of, 242
oral histories, need for, in research, 254–55
Ornelas, Rudy, 189, 208n1, n3
"other," criminalization of, 4
Outlaw, The, 240

PACE. *See* Prisoners for AIDS Counseling and Education
Padilla, José, 29, 59, 232, 263, 278n5
  as international prisoner, 264
  as so-called enemy combatant, 41, 263–64
Palloni, Alberto, 49
Parks, Rosa, 134

parole boards, challenges to, 73
PATRIOT Acts, 261, 271
pedagogies of dissent, 78–80
Peltier, Leonard, 8, 11, 193, 210, 230
    raúlrsalinas's poems about, 223–25
    self-portrait of, 202, 203f
    writings of, 201–2
Peña, Leonard, 192–93, 206
    art of, 191
People's Law Office, lawsuits of, 84–85
Pérez, Richie, 143
Pettaway, James, 192
Picasso, 197, 199
Pinochet, Augusto, 277
pinto/a
    defined, 190
    political significance of term, 268
    See also Latino/a prisoners
pinto/a human rights, 261–80
    components of, 276–77
    and mobilization of shame, 268–73
    strategy for, 273–77
plantation economy, evolution into prison
        economy, 193–94
police brutality, resistance to, 72
police officers
    of color, 29
    as interpreters, 156
    treatment of people of color, 28–29
    See also law enforcement
political activists, prison repression of, 240
political prisoners
    expanded use of term, 270–71
    U.S.: Clinton's pardon of, 266;
        controversy over, 265–68; strategies
        for, 275
    See also Cancel Miranda, Rafael; Labrón,
        Lolita; López Rivera, Oscar; Peltier,
        Leonard; raúlrsalinas
Political Prisoners' Liberation Front, 84
Ponce Massacre, 71
Posada Carriles, Luis, 89n14
Postville raid
    arrests in, 7
    and ban on immigration lawyers, 165
    "fast-tracking" strategy in, 165, 169, 173
    interpreting after, 159–73; ethical
        dilemmas and, 162; impartiality
        and, 166–67
    judge's response to, 166

Postville workers
    backgrounds of, 162–64
    identity theft charges against, 166–72
    interviews with, 163
    plea agreements for, 164–66
    sentencing of, 166
poverty
    female incarceration and, 182
    as focus in Aztlán, 81
    as incentive for joining military, 233
    linkage with crime, 24, 106
    of Mexican Americans in Los Angeles,
        21
    moral, 101–2
    racial differences transcended by, 81
    U.S. neglect of, 10
    See also war on poverty
power relationships, researcher-subject,
        245
Preston, William, 51
Prinzhorn, Hans, 191–92
prison art
    American Indian Movement and,
        200–204
    anomalous status of, 194–200
    during Napoleonic Wars, 208n15
prison education programs
    about criminal justice system, 4–5
    on gay, bisexual, and transgender issues,
        177
    on HIV/AIDS, 176–80
    raúlrsalinas and, 214–15, 217
    and reduction of recidivism, 179, 180n2
    transformative effects of, 177–79
prison gangs
    research on, 241
    at San Quentin, 247–49
prison guards, challenges to brutality of,
        73
prison industrial complex, 40, 43
    expansion of, 87
    slave/convict songs and literature in,
        193–94
prison literature, 192
    African American history and, 134
prison movement, raúlrsalinas's
        involvement in, 217
prison rebellion years
    context of, 69
    frontier colonial violence and, 70–72

prison rebellions
empowerment through, 216
examples of, 72
global context of, 69, 85–86, 87, 240
increase in, 68
interethnic coalitions in, 72, 87
at Leavenworth. *See* Leavenworth prison rebellions
repression of activists in, 240
research on, 241
prison system
carceral continuum in, 19–20, 145
ethnic makeup of, 19–20, 43. *See also* incarcerations rates
expansion of, 19–20
immigrants in, 30–32
issues in, 2–6
numbers incarcerated in, 17
population of, *versus* other countries, 19
transnational framework for, 9
prisoner activism
for human rights, 268
against prison mistreatment, 267
tactics of, 69
prisoner classification, battle over, 265–68
prisoner groups
formal and informal, in Díaz-Cotto's study, 251–52
at Green Haven and Attica, 255n6
positive influences of, 254
prisoner interethnic alliances, 4–5, 7
Cancel Miranda and, 76–77
as challenge to racial control, 87
examples of, 72–73
national and international parallels with, 79, 83, 85
prisoner reentry
Community Service Society and, 143
employment and, 143–45
mentors for women in, 7–8
support networks and, 10
Travis's work on, 12n3, 33
prisoner rights movement
internationalist methodologies for, 266–67
internationalization of, 11
mass confinement and, 9
renewal of, 277

prisoners
coalition-building strategies of, 249–51, 255
countries granting right to vote, 136–37
and death behind bars, 156
and right to counsel, 157
U.S.: internationalization of, 277; numbers of, 10; percentage black, 10
voter residency policies and, 141–43
Prisoners for AIDS Counseling and Education, 176–79
and education on gay, bisexual, and transgender issues, 177
mentoring and, 178–79
transformative effects of, 177–79
prisoners of conscience, U.S., 275–76
prisons
Bennett's approach to, 73
invisibility of, 1
and need for bilingual staff, 250–51
political uses of, 2
private, 49
U.S.: in foreign countries, 264, 278n3; Latino(a) population of, 2
Proposition 21
and changes in juvenile sentencing, 102–3
and conflation of serious crime with delinquency, 102
and criminalization of youth of color, 103–6
felony status and property damage, 98
latent references to race in, 104
and race, 100
and social incapacitation of inner-city youth, 107
and white solidarity, 104–5
See also juvenile justice system; Latina adolescent prisoners
Proposition 227 (English-only Initiative), 118
psychotropic drugs, forcible administration of, 267
Puerto Rican *Independentistas*, 68, 70, 270
Clinton's pardon of, 266
collaboration with Chicanos, 74–77
history of, 71
in Leavenworth, 4–5

reclassification as political prisoners, 266
See also Cancel Miranda, Rafael; Collazo, Don Oscar; Figueroa Cordero, Andrés; Flores, Irving; Lebrón, Lolita; Torresola, Griselio
Puerto Rico
  human rights abuse in, 71–72
  independence of, visual culture in name of, 194–200
  language issue in, 75
  second-class citizenship in, 21, 71
  UN status controversy, 76
  U.S. colonization of, 20, 265
Puertorriqueños, art of, 194–200

racial halo effect, 29
racial profiling
  after 9/11, 39–40, 42
  law enforcement and, 22–23
  in political analysis of prison activists, 87
  proposals for curtailing, 33
  sentencing and, 33
  war on drugs and, 25–26
  Zoot Suit riots and, 22
racism
  Jim Crow, 72–73
  juvenile offenders and, 107
  Proposition 21 and, 100
  social scientists and, 83–84
  symbolic, 100
  in women's reformatories/prisons, 255n3
raids, 151–53. *See also* Postville raid; Postville workers
Ramírez, Abrán, 137
Ratner, Michael, 58
raúlrsalinas, 5, 67, 89n20, 90n27, 266
  Aztlán and, 81
  and Cancel Miranda, 227–28
  on conditions at Leavenworth, 74
  death of, 233
  influences on, 214
  interview with, 213–33
  after Leavenworth, 79
  letters from, 76, 90n30
  medicine poems of, 213–14
  on pedagogies of dissent, 78
  Peltier poems of, 8, 223–25

political organizing by, 213–14, 215–16, 217
post-prison work of, 214
on prison as form of colonialism, 68
on prisoner rights violations, 10
on Puerto Rican struggle, 74–75
release of, 85
transfer to Marion, 84
at University of Washington, 215–16
work with AIM and Peltier Defense Committee, 202
Reagan, Ronald, war on drugs and, 261. *See also* war on drugs
recidivism
  economic stability as deterrence to, 144
  reduction of, through prison education programs, 179
Reentry Roundtable, 143–44
reform efforts, prisoner, 5
refugees
  detention of, 53–54
  See also undocumented workers
research
  collaborative, 242–46, 255; for *Homeboys* study, 249; oral documentation and, 242–43; pros and cons of, 243
  future, suggestions for, 254–55
  groups studied, 241–42
  on informal prison networks, 241
  issues studied, 240–41
  oral documentation and collaborative methods in, 242–46
  on prison gangs, 241
  prisoner documentation as, 241–42
  theory generation and, 244
research ethics and methodologies, 239–59
  and choice of subjects, 244
  in documentation of *pintas(os)'* experiences, 246–52
  language and, 244
  power imbalances and, 244–45
  race and ethnicity and, 239–41
researchers
  biases of, 240
  credibility of, 245–46
  "insider," 245, 251
  motivations of, 244–45, 253
  "outsider," 249
research questions, 246

resistance
  art as, 8–9
  challenges to, 58
  to immigrant detention, 56–58
  interethnic approach to, 80
  language as, 89n18; Latina adolescents
    and, 113–31, 118–23
  by Latina adolescents, 118–23
  at Passaic County Jail, 57
  to police brutality, 72
  Puerto Rican, 71
  See also dissent; prison rebellions
restorative justice, transition to culture of
  control, 24, 100
Reuss-Ianni, Elizabeth, 244
Reyes, Juan, 81
Richardson v. Ramirez, 137–38
Risse, Thomas, 273, 274
Rivera, Diego, 197, 199
Rivera, Gabriel Torres, 8, 11
Rockefeller, Nelson, 68
Rodin, Auguste, 191
Rodriguez, Dylan, 68, 256n9
Rodríguez, Raymond, 53
role models, leadership, 254
Rosado, Doña Isabel, 195
Rosaldo, Renato, 41
Rosario, Hector, 194
Ross, Luana, 255n4
Rubio, Joe, 83–84
Ruiz, David, 73
Ruiz, Francisco, 78
Ruiz v. Estelle, 73, 88n10
Rumbaut, Rubén, 42
Rumsfeld, Donald, 278n4

Salinas, Raúl. *See* raúlrsalinas
Salvadoran asylum-seekers, 58
Salvadoran refugees, 53–54
San Quentin
  case studies of Chicano prisoners in,
    246–50
  Chicano self-help groups in, 249–50
San Quentin Six, 72
Sánchez, Eddie, 275
  legal strategy of, 268–70
  as political prisoner, 270
Sánchez, Jesus, 81
Sánchez, Ricardo, 266, 268
sanctuary movement, 57

Santiago Baca, Jimmy, 193, 265–66
"school to prison pipeline," 98
Schuck, Peter, 46
Segoviano, Milton, 79
self-education
  effect on prisoner reentry, 7, 33
  at Leavenworth, 78–80
  prison rebellions and, 89n25
  prisoner reentry and, 7, 33
self-help groups, Chicano, in San Quentin,
  249–50
Senate Bill 2611, 44
sensory deprivation/overload, legal
  challenges to, 85
sentencing bias/policies, 27–29
  ethnic/racial factors in, 27–28
Sentencing Reform Act of 1984, 86
  ineffectiveness of, 28
September 11, 2001. *See* 9/11
sexual abuse, of detained immigrants, 47
Shakur, Assata, 271
Siegel, Mara, 231
Sikkink, Kathryn, 273, 274
Silliman, Scott L., 56
slavery, plantation, transition into prison
  slavery, 193
slavery institutions, 19–20
Social Security Administration, Earnings
  Suspense File of, 170–71
Social Security payments, by illegal
  workers, 170
Soledad Brothers, 72
Soledad State Prison, Jackson's murder
  at, 67
solidarity
  cross-racial and -national, 8
  Latina, 118–23; language and culture
    and, 113–31
Sommers, Joseph, 216
South Carolina Slave Code, 20
Southwest, decolonizing history of, 81–82
Spanish language
  learning/maintaining, 75
  See also language
"Special International Tribunal on the
  Human Rights Violations of Political
  Prisoners/POWs in the USA," 270, 276
Spencer, Eloise, 239
states' rights, felon disfranchisement and,
  135–36

stereotyping
  gender and cultural, 182
  See also Latino/as, criminalization of
Stumpf, Juliet, 42
Sullivan, Charlie, 73
Sullivan, Pauline, 73
Supermax prisons, 275
  purpose of, 84
superpredator thesis, 107
support networks
  reentry and, 10
symbolic racism, 100

Tancredo, Tom, 4
Tangeman, Anthony, 48
Taylor, Margaret, 42–43, 46
testimonios, 242–43
Texas, felon disfranchisement in, 139
Thomas, Piri, 240
Thompson, Stacey, 181, 183
Three Prisons Act of 1891, 74
"three-strikes" legislation, 27
Tombs, 72
Torres, Carlos Alberto, 192, 194, 206, 232
  background and art of, 199–200, 201f
Torresola, Griselio, Blair House
  demonstration and, 76
Torres Rivera, Gabriel, 143, 144, 231
Torres, Tomás, 81
Torrez, Mamie R., 189, 208n1
torture
  at Abu-Ghraib, 61n3
  legal challenges to, 85
  at Marion Prison, 84, 215, 230, 267
  in U.S. prisons, 221
Treaty of Guadalupe Hidalgo, 21
"truth in sentencing" laws, 27

undocumented workers
  and federal courts, 7
  SSA's Earnings Suspense File and,
    170–71
  unemployment rate, omissions from, 143
  See also Postville raid; Postville workers
U.S. Constitution
  Fifth Amendment to, 157
  Sixth Amendment to, 157; Postville ICE
    raid and, 165
  Eighth Amendment to, 85; Sánchez and,
    270

Fourteenth Amendment to, felon
    disfranchisement and, 137
  infringements of, 10–11
U.S. Department of Homeland Security,
    agencies transferred to, 61n8
U.S. Immigration and Customs
    Enforcement (ICE), 46
  expansion of, 169–70
  "illegal aliens" removed by in 2006, 117
  immigrant detention rates and, 32
  Postville raid and, 159–73. *See also*
    Postville raid; Postville workers
U.S.-Mexican War, 20
United Nations
  human rights movement and, 271
  prisoner appeals to, 84, 267
  Sánchez and, 270
  U.S. subversion of covenants of, 272
United States
  antiblack violence in, 71
  international statutes not ratified by,
    272
  nineteenth and twentieth century
    expansionism of, 71
  political prisoner controversy in,
    265–68
  relations with Latin America, 5–6
  withdrawal from International Criminal
    Court, 273, 277, 278n12
United States v. Brignoni-Ponce, 34n12,
    61n4
Universal Declaration of Human Rights,
    U.S. subversion of, 272

veterans of color, racism and, 73–74
Viaje Atras, 189–90, 190f
Vieques, U.S. Navy occupation of, 195–96
Vigliano, Oscar Jorge, 78
Violent Youth Predator Act, 101
visual art. *See* art; prison art
  in prison, 189–212
  redemptive power of, 189, 192
voter education, felon disfranchisement
    and, 143–44
voter registration drives, felon
    disfranchisement and, 143–44
voting rights
  felony convictions and, 133–34, 137
  loss of, 6
  prisoner, 136–37

Voting Rights Act
  felon disfranchisement and, 138, 140
  Latino political power and, 134
  significance of, 6

Wacquant, Loïc, 19–20, 23, 145
Wagner, Peter, 141
war on crime
  convergence with war on terror, 10, 264
  Nixon administration and, 261
war on drugs
  civil liberties and, 261
  "criminal aliens" and, 54
  effects of, 25
  mass incarceration and, 100
  prison population growth and, 25
  and racial profiling, 25–26
  Reagan and, 261
war on terror
  detention practices during, 56
  enemy combatant classification and, 262
  immigrant criminalization and, 7
  immigrant detention and, 60
  Padilla and, 263
  racial discrimination and, 42
Washington, Oscar, 230
waterboarding, 264
"welfare mothers," Wilson's attacks on, 105
white solidarity, Proposition 21 and,
  104–5, 106
Williams, Tookie, 277
Wilson, Pete
  "adult time for adult crime" theme of, 102
  "get tough" legislation and, 98

Mexican Mafia and, 104
Proposition 21 and, 99, 102–5, 107
Winship, Blanton, 231
women prisoners
  incarceration rates for, ethnic disparities
    in, 19
  increased numbers of, 5
  researchers' neglect of, 240
  See also Latina juvenile prisoners; Latina
    prisoners
women prisoners of color, in New York
  State, 183
Wong Wing v. United States, 51
Wretched of the Earth, 77
Wright, Erik Olin, 88n7
Wright, Ronald, 42–43, 46

Ybarra-Frausto, Tomás, 217
Young, Jock, 106
youth
  disconnected, 143–44
  inner-city, social incapacitation of,
    107
  See also juvenile justice system; juvenile
    offenders; Latina juvenile
    prisoners
youth crime, racial politics of, 97–111
youth gangs, fear of, 30
youth of color, Proposition 21's
  criminalization of, 103–6

Zapata, Emiliano, 199
Zentella, Ana Celia, 182
Zoot Suit Riots, 22